CW01246208

Quintus Curtius his History of the Wars of Alexander. To Which is Prefix'd Freinshemius's Supplement. The Second Edition. ... Translated by John Digby, ... of 2

Printed for Bernard Lintot   P. Fourdrinier sc

QUINTUS CURTIUS
HIS
HISTORY
OF THE
WARS of *Alexander*.

To which is Prefix'd

Freinshemius's Supplement.

The SECOND EDITION

In which are added,

A Map and several Copper Plates.
An Account of the Plates
The Judgment of learned Men concerning the Age Condition, Style and History of *Quintus Curtius*
The Genealogy of *Alexander*, and the Epitome of his Life, as also the Division of the *Macedonian* Empire amongst his Followers after his Death, and the Tables of that Division according to *Curtius*, *Arrian*, *Diodorus Siculus*, *Orosius*, &c

Translated by JOHN DIGBY, *Esq*;

In TWO VOLUMES.

LONDON Printed for *Bernard Lintot*, at the *Cross-Keys* between the *Temple Gates* in *Fleet street*. 1726

Quintus Curtius

HIS

HISTORY

OF THE

Wars of *Alexander*.

To which is Prefix'd

Freinshemius's Supplement.

Translated by JOHN DIGBY, *Esq*

VOLUME the FIRST

The SECOND EDITION

LONDON:

Printed for *Bernard Lintot*, at the Cross between the *Temple Gates* in *Fleet-street*.

MDCCXXV

To the Reverend

Dr. *FRIEND,*

MASTER of

Westminster SCHOOL,

This New Translation of

QUINTUS CURTIUS,

Is most humbly Dedicated

By his

Most Obedient Servant,

to Command,

J. DIGBY.

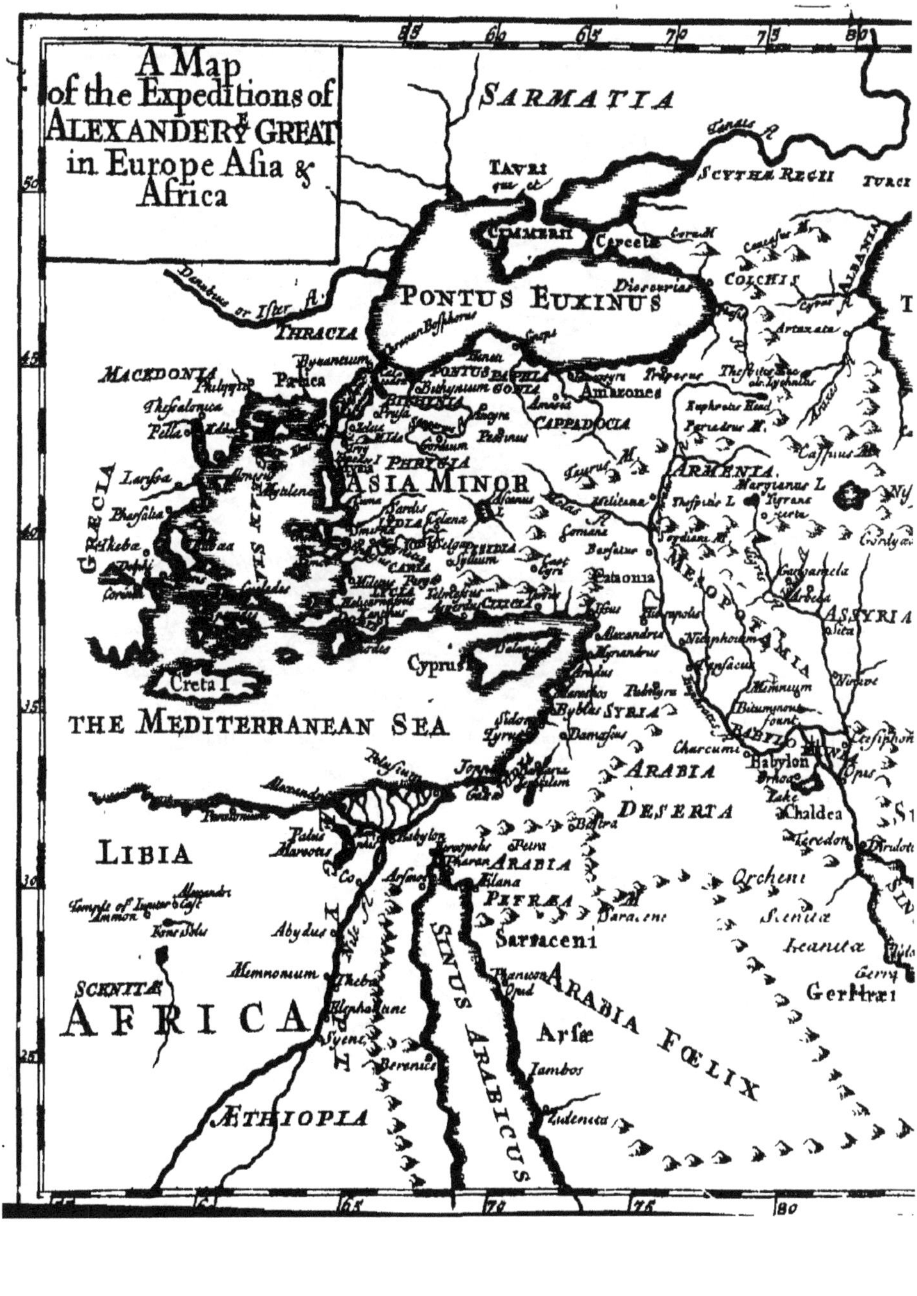
A Map
of the Expeditions of
ALEXANDER the GREAT
in Europe Asia &
Africa
SARMATIA
PONTUS EUXINUS
ASIA MINOR
THE MEDITERRANEAN SEA
Creta I
Cyprus
LIBIA
AFRICA
ÆTHIOPIA
SINUS ARABICUS
ARABIA FŒLIX
ARABIA
DESERTA
ARMENIA
ASSYRIA
CAPPADOCIA
PHRYGIA
MACEDONIA
THRACIA
GRECIA
Babylon
Chaldea
Sarraceni
Amazones
Damascus
Memnonium
Abydus

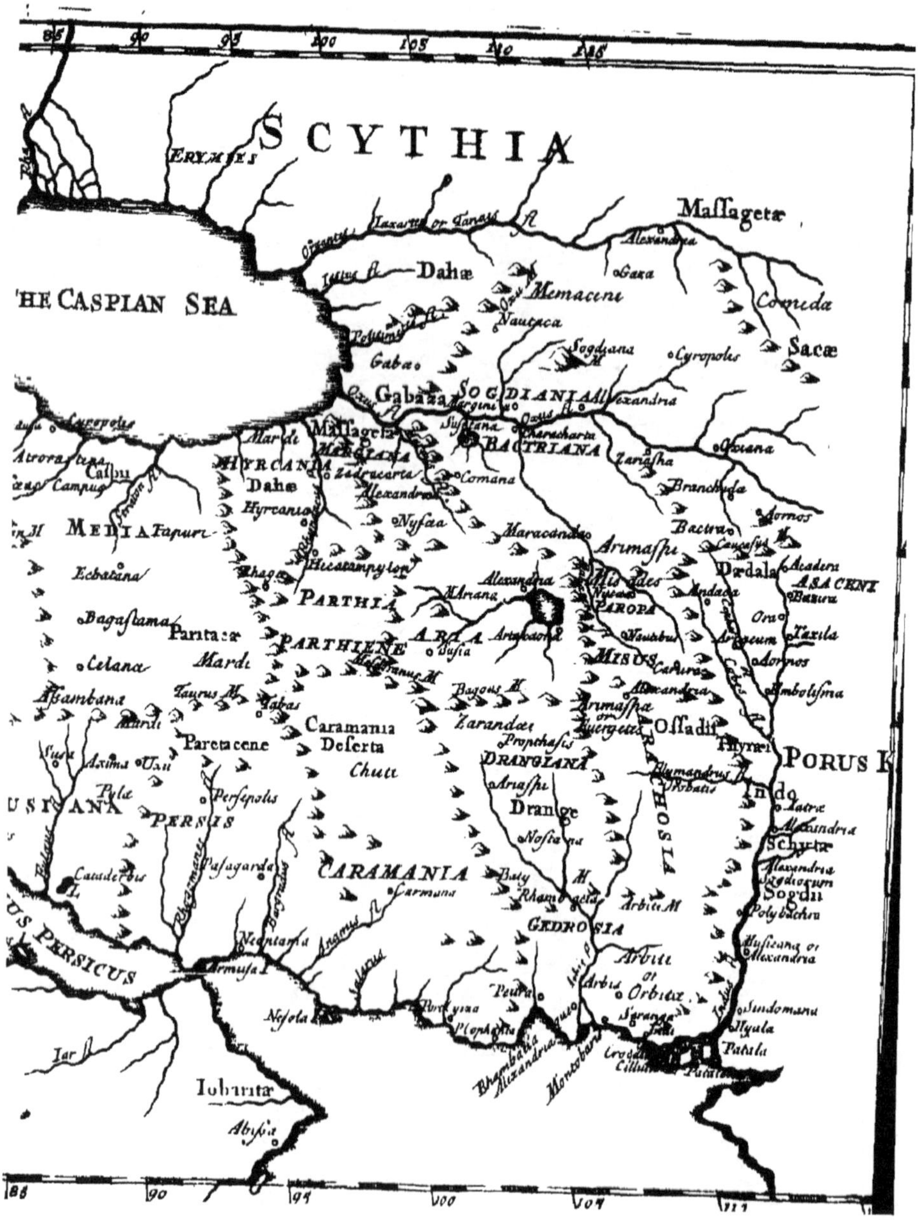

NUMISMATA ALEXANDRI MAGNI

B.... for the ... of Al....

THE
SUPPLEMENT
OF
John Freinshemius,

To *Quintus Curtius*'s HISTORY of the Life and Actions of *Alexander* the Great.

THE Life and Actions of *Alexander*, who wrested the Empire from the *Persians*, and transferr'd it to *Greece*, have been written by many Greek Historians, whereof most were Spectators, and some Companions and Ministers of his Atchievements. And others, He himself, out of a strong Passion that his Fame should survive after his decease, appointed to transmit an account of his Exploits to Posterity. But besides, that the real Facts
were

were truly great in themselves, the love of Fables, which was natural to that Nation, made them deliver Accounts that bore more the air of Romance, than the face of Truth. However, they who deserve most Credit, were *Aristobulus*, and *Ptolemy*, who reign'd after *Alexander*. For after the Death of that Prince, there was no farther occasion either for Fear, or Flattery, which are commonly the Causes of corrupting the Truth of History. And indeed, who can suspect that *Ptolemy* should be guilty of sullying the lustre of Royalty by Lyes and Fables. Moreover, since both of them were not only present at a great many Affairs that concern'd *Alexander*, but even were principal Actors in them, 'tis evident they were the best able to give the most exact and truest Relations of them. For which reason, as often as they agree in their Accounts, we have given them the Preference to all others; and when they disagree, we make choice of such Particulars out of the different Materials that are left us, as, after a strict Examination, seem to approach the nearest to the Truth of Fact. And, after the Age of *Alexander*, I have observ'd, That the *Greeks* who had any regard for Truth, and particularly *Diodorus Siculus* of late, have follow'd the same Method. For such of the *Romans* as applied themselves to the composing of History, were contented with writing of the Affairs of their own Country, and neglected those of other Nations, because in giving an account of the Actions of a victorious People, their Subject abounded with materials in themselves noble, and fit for the Majesty of History, and which they thought to be of more use to the Members of their own Commonwealth than any other they could relate. And as I esteem the Endeavours of those Authors to be praise-worthy, so, I hope, I shall not be blam'd, if I attempt to give my Countrymen an

Idea

ΦΙΛΙΠΠΟΥ

PHILIPPI
MACEDONIS

Idea of that King, who, in the Course of his short Life, conquer'd more Countries than any other Prince ever effected. From whence we may conclude, That humane Affairs are not guided by Chance or Hazard, but that commonly Fortune conforms her self to the Conduct of Men, and that no Felicity can be lasting, which is destitute of Virtue. I find then that *Alexander* was plentifully endow'd and furnish'd with all the Advantages of Fortune and a great Genius, that could be desir'd in a Prince, who was destin'd one day to arrive at such an extraordinary Height of Power and Greatness. The Kings of *Macedon* deriv'd their Pedigree from *Hercules*; and *Olympias*, *Alexander*'s Mother, reckon'd the Origin of her Family from *Achilles*. From his very Infancy he wanted neither Allurements nor Examples to excite him in the pursuit of Glory, nor Masters to teach him Virtue, nor Exercise to accustom him to it. For his Father, *Philip*, did by his continual Wars raise the Reputation of the *Macedonians*, who 'till then were accounted despicable, and by his Conquest of *Greece*, made them formidable every where. In fine, he not only laid the Foundations of the great Things which were done after his Death, but even a little before his decease, having resolv'd to carry the War into *Persia*, he had levied Men, gathered Provisions, raised Money, and, in short, had an Army ready for that Expedition, and had already opened a Passage into *Asia*, by the means of *Parmenio*. But in this very Juncture he was taken away, as if it had been on purpose to leave to his Son so great Forces to carry on the War, and reap the full Glory of it, when it was finish'd, which seems to have been the Contrivance of Fortune, who always yielded entire obedience to *Alexander* alone. This Prince was so much in the Admiration of all Men, not only after he had done so great things, but even at his first

A 4 setting

setting out, that it was a Question whether it were not more reasonable to ascribe the divine original of so great a Man immediately to *Jupiter* himself, rather than mediately to the same God by *Eacides* and *Hercules*. When he went himself to visit the Temple of *Ammon* in *Lybia*, no less would content him than to be call'd his Son, as we shall shew in the Sequel. Moreover it was the Opinion of many, *That* Alexander *was the Offspring of that Serpent which had been seen to enter into his Mother's Bed Chamber, and into which* Jupiter *had transform'd himself That the Dreams of the Priests, and Responses of the Oracles advanc'd the Credit of his divine Pedigree, and that when* Philip *sent to* Delphi *to consult about it, he was admonish'd by the Oracle*, to pay the greatest Reverence to *Ammon*. On the other hand, there are those who affirm, *That all this is mere Fiction, and that there was reason to suspect* Alexander's *Mother was guilty of Adultery: For that* Nectanebus, *King of* Egypt, *who was driven from his Kingdom, did not go to* Ethiopia, *as was commonly believ'd, but went to* Macedonia, *in hopes of receiving Succours from* Philip *against the Power of the* Persians *That he deceiv'd* Olympias *by the force of Magical Enchantments, and defil'd his Landlord's Bed That from that time* Philip *had a jealousie of her, and that it afterwards appear'd this was the chief cause of their Divorce. That the very Day that* Philip *brought* Cleopatra *into his House,* Attalus, *his Wife's Uncle, took the liberty to reproach* Alexander *with the Baseness of his Birth, while the King himself disown'd him for his Son In fine, That the constant Rumor of* Olympias's *Adultery was entertain'd not only in that part of the World, but even among the Nations which he conquer'd. That the Fiction of the Serpent was deriv'd from ancient Fables, on purpose to conceal the Ignominy of that Princess. That the* Messenians *had formerly given out the same*

Story

Story concerning Aristomenes, *and the* Syconians *concerning* Aristodamas. In reality the same Report was spread abroad among our Ancestors concerning *Scipio*, who was the first that ruin'd *Carthage*; and the Birth of *Augustus* was in like manner thought to have had something divine in it. For as to *Romulus*, the Founder of *Rome*, there is no occasion to say any thing of him, since there is no Nation so contemptible, but derives its Origin either from some God, or the Off spring of a God. After all, the Flight of *Nectanebus* does not agree with those times, for *Alexander* was six years of Age, when that Prince was vanquish'd by *Ochus*, and lost his Kingdom and Inheritance; nor is the Tale the less likely to be false, because it is reported of *Jupiter*. It is likewise affirm'd, That *Olympias*, having nothing to fear after her Husband's Death, laugh'd at the Vanity of her Son, who would needs have it believ'd that he was sprung from *Jupiter*, and begg'd him in a Letter, *not to expose her to* Juno's Indignation, *seeing she had been guilty of nothing that deserv'd that Punishment.* However before that time, she is thought to have been the Person that took the most pains to gain Credit to this Fable, and is said to have admonish'd *Alexander* upon his Expedition into *Asia, to be mindful of his Original, and do nothing that was unworthy of so great a Father.*

But it is generally agreed, that between the Conception and Birth of that Prince, it was signified both by Prodigies and divers Presages, how considerable a Person should be born. *Philip* saw in his Sleep the Womb of *Olympias* sealed with a Ring, on which the Picture of a Lyon was engrav'd, the Memory whereof was preserv'd by the City of *Alexandria* in *Egypt*, which was for a long time called *Leontopolis*. *Aristander*, the ablest Diviner of that time, who afterwards accompanied *Alexander*, and was his chief Priest, interpreted that Dream, and said it signify'd the Magnanimity and Courage of the Infant. The same Night that *Olympias* was brought to Bed, the Temple of *Diana* in *Ephesus*, the most famous of all *Asia*, was burnt to Ashes. This was done by a profligate Villain, who being apprehended and put to the Torture, confess'd he had no other view in doing it, but to preserve his Memory by some great and memorable Act of Impiety. Wherefore the *Magi*, who were then at *Ephesus*, not reckoning so great a Misfortune from the loss of the Temple alone, but looking upon it as a presage of a greater Destruction, fill'd the whole City with mournful Exclamations, *That there was a Torch kindled somewhere, which, on the like account, and from the same motive, should one day consume all the East*. It hapned at the same time that *Philip* subdued *Potidæa*, a Colony of the *Athenians*, had news of his being Conqueror at the Olympick Games, whither he had sent Chariots, and receiv'd Dispatches of greater moment by a Courier from *Parmenio*, whom he had sent into *Illyrium*, *That the* Macedonians *had obtain'd a Signal Victory over the* Barbarians. While he was rejoycing at so good, and so universal a Success, he receiv'd the News of *Olympias*'s being brought to Bed, and the Diviners confidently affirm'd, *That he who was born in the midst of so many Victories and Triumphs, should be an invincible Prince*. It is reported, that *Philip* being amazed at such a Crowd of Successes, and dreading the Envy of the Gods, begg'd of the Goddess *Nemesis*, *to be contented with revenging those obsequious Services of Fortune by some moderate Calamity*. It is likewise recorded, *That in the City of* Pella, *two Eagles sat in the Threshold of the House where the Queen was brought to Bed, a whole Day, and that this was a Presage that he should be Master of the two Empires of* Asia *and* Europe: which

was

EFFIGIES ARISTOTELIS

was easie to interpret, after the things were come to pass. I find it mention'd also in some Authors, *That when that Prince was born, there was an Earthquake, and that great Thundring was heard, and Lightning seen in the Heavens.* The most accurate Historians tell us he was born in the beginning of the 106th Olympiad, when *Elpines* was Pretor in *Athens*, on the sixth day of *June*, which Month the *Macedonians* at that time called *Lous*. At this time, the Roman People who had subsisted almost four hundred Years, were engag'd in Wars with their Neighbours, and by their continual Victories, and daily encrease of Dominion, were now shewing the Prelude of that Power which was by degrees to subdue the whole World.

Philip being blessed with a Son, of whom so many happy Omens made him conceive the highest Hopes, turn'd all his thoughts towards his Education For being a wise Man, and a Lover of his Country, he easily perceiv'd that all his Endeavours would be to no purpose, if he should leave an ignorant and slothful Prince behind him, to govern *Macedonia*, while things were in an unsettled state every where; and that his Glory could not be long-liv'd, if the great things he had begun, should be lost and ruin'd by the Weakness or Negligence of a Successor. Among his Letters, that discreet and elegant one which he wrote to *Aristotle*, who was then at *Athens* with *Plato*, is yet extant, and is conceiv'd in words much to this purpose

PHILIP *to* Aristotle *wisheth Health.*

I *Am to acquaint you, that a Son is born to me, nor do I thank the Gods so much for his Birth, as for his being born in your time. I hope that when he shall have been educated and instructed by you, he shall be worthy of us,*

and

and fit to succeed to so great a Kingdom. For I think it much better to be without Children, than to beget them for a Punishment, and educate them to the Shame and Dishonour of their Ancestors.

Nor was *Philip* mistaken, for having been long under the Direction of *Aristotle*, the effect was, that the Instructions he receiv'd from that great Master laid a Foundation for, and enabled him to perform all the great Exploits which he executed from that time. But these were the Occurrences of future years. In the mean time *Leucidas, Olympias*'s Kinsman, and *Lysimachus* of *Acarnon*, were appointed to be his Governors and Tutors Besides these, he had one *Philip* a Physician, of the same Country, to take care of his Health, and a Nurse equally happy in the temperature of her Body, and the disposition of her Mind, whose Name was *Hellanica*, the Daughter of *Drop's*, of one of the best Families in all *Macedon* This care that was taken to bring him up, had so good an effect, that when he was but a Child, he gave promising hopes of his becoming that great King which he afterwards shew'd himself to be For there appear'd a very extraordinary vigor and activity in his tender Limbs, and in all the marks of an heroick Genius he very far out-strip'd his Age. He was by nature of a beautiful and comely Make, and despised Dress, saying, *That an axious Care about adorning of the Body, was proper for Women, who had no other Gifts that could set them off to so much Advantage. That if he could but be Master of Virtue, he should be handsome and fine enough.* When he grew up, there appear'd a perfect Symmetry in his Members, his Joints were strong and firm, and being but of a middle Stature, he was really stronger than he appeared to be. His Skin was white, only his Cheeks and his Breast were dy'd with an agreeable red,

his

his Hair was yellow, and went into a gentle Curl, his Nose was aquiline, and his Eyes of different colours, for his left Eye is said to have been blue, and his right very black. There was a certain secret virtue in them, insomuch that no body could look on his Countenance without Veneration and Fear. He could run with wonderful Swiftness, which he often practis'd, even when he was King, as esteeming it of great use in Expeditions, and he was often seen to run for a Prize with the swiftest Persons about him. He bore Fatigue with a Patience and Firmness that even passes Belief, and by this one virtue he oftentimes sav'd both himself and his Armies in the greatest Extremities. By frequent Exercises, and a very warm Constitution, he did so purge off any bad Humours which commonly lodge under the Skin, that not only his Breath, but also what he perspir'd through the Pores of his Body were sweet, and his very Cloaths had a fragrant smell, and this was the Cause, as some think, why he was so much inclin'd to Wine and Passion. Pictures and Statues of him are yet to be seen, which were the Performances of the best Artists. For lest the Comeliness of his Face should suffer any thing from the unskilfulness of vulgar Sculptors or Painters, he strictly forbid any to draw his Picture without his order, and threatned to punish any one that should disobey it. In consequence whereof, tho' there was abundance of good Workmen, yet *Apelles* was the only Person who had his consent to draw his Picture, *Pyrgoteles* grav'd him on precious Stones, and *Lysippus* and *Polycletus* represented him in Medals. His Governor *Leonidas* is said to have walk'd too fast, which *Alexander* learnt of him, and never was able to help it afterwards by all his Endeavours. I am not ignorant that very much is owing to Education, but I am inclin'd to impute this rather to the Temper of that

young

young Prince, than to his accustoming himself to it; for it was impossible for one of his Ardour and Impetuosity of Spirit, not to have the motions of his Body answerable to it. And this Hastiness of his was so far from being accounted an Imperfection by his Successors, that they studiously affected it, and imitated him therein, as they did in his wry Neck, which lean'd to his left Shoulder, in his piercing Look and high Voice, being incapable to copy the Virtues of his Mind. In reality, there were many of them whose long Lives had scarce any thing in them that deserv'd to be compar'd to his Childhood. Nor did he ever say or act any thing that was mean or base, but all his Words and Actions were equal to, or even surpass'd his Fortune. For tho' he was most ambitious of Praise, yet he did not affect to draw it indifferently from every thing, but would have it arise from things that were most Praise-worthy; being sensible that the Praise which arises from mean Actions is inglorious and dishonourable, and that that Victory which is gain'd over the bravest Enemy, is so much the more noble and illustrious. Therefore when some Persons told him, *That seeing he was an excellent Runner, he ought to list himself among those who were to contend for the Prize at the Olympick Games, after the example of a King of his Name; and that thereby he should acquire a great Fame all over* Greece. He answer'd, *I would certainly do so, if I was to run against Kings.* As often as *Philip* obtain'd any signal Victory, or reduc'd any rich and strong Place, he could not conceal his Grief, amidst the rejoicing of others: and he was heard to complain amongst Boys of his own Age, *That his Father would leave nothing for him and them to do, when they came to be Men.* For he look'd upon every Accession of Power and Riches to be a Diminution to his Glory, and had a stronger Passion for Honour than

for

for Wealth. He was naturally dispos'd to sleep little, and encreas'd his Watchfulness by Art. If any thing happen'd to him that requir'd serious Thought, he put his Arm out of the Bed, holding a silver Ball in his Hand, which by its fall into a Bason might make a noise, and so disperse that Heaviness which was inclining him to slumber. From his very Infancy he lov'd to worship the Gods splendidly, and one day as they were sacrificing, he flung so much Incense into the Fire, that *Leonidas*, who was a severe and parcimonious Man, not being able to bear that Profusion, cried out, *You may burn Incense in this manner, when you conquer the Countries where it grows.* Remembring this Saying afterwards, when he settled the Affairs of *Arabia*, which produces Incense, he sent *Leonidas* a vast Quantity of this Perfume, ordering him withal, *to be more liberal for the future, in paying Honour to the Gods, since he was now convinc'd that they did plentifully repay the Gifts that had been chearfully made them.*

He gave early Marks of a sublime and enterprizing Genius *Artaxerxes*, sirnam'd *Ochus*, was at that time King of *Persia. Artabarus* and *Menajus*, both Governors of Provinces, and *Memnon* of *Rhodes*, a famous General, revolted and made War upon him, but being vanquish'd by the King's Forces, they left *Asia* and fled to *Philip. Alexander*, who was not then seven Years of Age, was wonderfully delighted with them, and often ask'd them Questions which had nothing either childish, or mean in them, concerning the Affairs of *Persia*, such as, *How the royal Dignity and Power were supported? What sort of Arms were used among the* Persians, *and whether they were valiant? Whether their Horses run well? How many Days Journey* Macedonia *was distant from* Susa? *What kind of Life the King led, what were his Exercises and Diversions, and what was his Opinion concerning*

Virtue?

Virtue? Afterwards, when at the Intreaty of *Mentor*, *Memnon*'s Brother, whose Sister was married to *Artabarus*, *Ochus* had pardon'd the Exiles, and demanded them of *Philip*, *Alexander* so struck the Ambassadors of that King with the Admiration of his extraordinary Genius, at so tender an Age, that one of them broke out into these Words *This Boy is indeed a great King, but our's a rich one*. But tho' he seem'd to owe all this to the Bounty of Nature, yet he ow'd it no less to his Education. For his Father being appriz'd, how much Advantage he himself had reap'd in the Company of *Epammondas*, and that he had done much greater things by his Eloquence, than by his Power, was very careful that his Son should be well tinctur'd with the liberal Arts from his very Infancy. Wherefore by extraordinary Rewards, he retain'd *Aristotle*, a Philosopher of great Reputation, to deliver to him even the first elements of Letters. Nor was that most learned Man averse from that Task, as knowing of how much Importance it was, that a Prince who was to wear a Crown, should be rightly instructed in the Beginning, and how ridiculous a thing it was to contemn small things, without which there was no attaining to greater.

He had afterwards several Masters, each of which excell'd in his way, by which means he not only furnish'd his Mind with noble Ideas, but likewise by all kind of Exercises, brought his Body to such a Temper, that it could perform all military Exercises, and bear all manner of Fatigue. Nor was he then idle, when he seem'd to be doing nothing. For he did not so much relax his Mind by Tennis and Dancing, as prepare his Limbs for more important Exercises.

After he had attain'd to riper Years and Parts, and was become more fit for serious Studies, he was continually in *Aristotle*'s Company, whom his Father had

recall'd

recall'd from *Mytelene*, till such time as he succeeded to the Kingdom after his Father's Death, and undertook an Expedition into *Asia*. During that time, he made himself Master of every thing that was to be learn'd from so great an Instructor. He apply'd himself to the Study of Nature, with so much the more Application, as he conceiv'd more extraordinary hopes of being one day the Emperor of the whole Earth, and he carry'd on and encouraged this Study, with a truly Royal Mind and Cost. He commanded all those who liv'd by Hunting, Fowling or Fishing, over *Asia* and *Greece*, and every one that had attain'd to any Skill that way, to obey *Aristotle*, that so he might be the better able to treat clearly and certainly of the nature of Animals. 'Tis certain, he allow'd that Philosopher eight hundred Talents, in order to defray the Charges of that Undertaking. And so much was he enamour'd with that Study, that he laid out Money, and bestow'd pains upon it, of which he was never like to see the Effects. An hundred Years after his Death, Deers were taken with golden Chains about their Necks, which he had put on, to the end Posterity might judge what Credit was to be given to the Stories about the great Age of those Creatures. That he understood the more sublime Sciences, which are commonly call'd *Acroamaticks*, is evident from his Letter to *Aristotle*, wherein he complains, *That he had prophan'd their Dignity, by divulging their Principles.* Upon which, *Aristotle* excus'd himself, by answering, *That those Books were publish'd in such a manner, as that they might be reckon'd not published, for that no body would be able to understand the meaning of them, but such as had already been instructed in the Principles which they contain'd.* When *Alexander* demanded his Books of Rhetorick, he strictly forbid him to let them come to the Hands of any other. For he was no less desirous to excel

excel others in Arts and Sciences, than in Power and Greatness, nor could he endure that Men of the lowest Rank, should share that Glory with him. Besides, it appears from his Letters, that he studied Physick under one *Aristotle*, who was the Son of a Physician, of the Race of *Æsculapius*. But he studied that Part of Philosophy so well, which teaches a Man to command both himself and others, that he is thought to have undertaken the Subversion of that vast Weight and Power of the *Persian* Empire, rather by his Magnanimity, Prudence, Temperance, and Fortitude, than by his Arms and Riches He frankly own'd, *That he ow'd more to* Aristotle *than to* Philip; *for that he was indebted to the one for his Life, to the other, for that Life's being formed upon the Principles of Honour and Virtue* Nevertheless, it has been believed by some, not without ground, That his Mind, which was so fired with Ambition, was yet more enflamed by the too great Value which *Aristotle* set upon Honour and Glory, which he plac'd in the Rank of things that may be called Goods, so that he not only multiply'd Wars upon Wars, in order to extend his Dominions, but would needs be look'd upon as a God.

But to continue the thread of our Story *Aristotle* not only receiv'd great Honours and Rewards in the Reign of *Alexander*, but even in *Philip*'s Life-time he had already received a vast Recompence for *Alexander*'s Education, having obtained the Freedom of his own Country The *Olynthians* had been *Philip*'s bitterest Enemies, for bordering upon *Macedonia*, and being hitherto equal to him in Power, they could not bear, that under a warlike and cunning King, the Kingdom should receive Accessions of Strength and Riches, which were one day like to bring Destruction and Servitude upon his Neighbours. For which Cause, as the Minds of both Parties were enflam'd more than ordinarily, so the Contention was more stubborn, and the Victory prosecuted with greater Severity. *Philip* took and plunder'd the City, and laid it level with the Ground, he sold the Inhabitants, and exercised the same Severity upon all the other Towns in those Parts. *Stagira*, where *Aristotle* was born, suffer'd the same Misfortune, but that Philosopher rebuilt it with the Permission, and at the Expence of *Philip*, and when it was restor'd to its former State, he gave Laws to it, which were observ'd in it from that time. Thus the Wisdom of one Citizen rais'd that City which had been burn'd and raz'd, which the powerful Efforts of so many brave Men could not hinder from being destroyed, when it was standing and in a flourishing State. But in what mighty Esteem *Aristotle* was with *Philip*, may be guess'd from hence. That he often admonish'd his Son to apply himself closely to the Study of Wisdom under so excellent a Master, lest he should afterwards be guilty of many things, which might be the Occasion both of his Shame and Repentance. Nor did *Alexander* ever after fail to shew the highest Respect for his Master, even amidst his most important Affairs. He had frequent Correspondence with him by Letters, and not only ask'd his Opinion about the *Arcana* of the Sciences, but also sought Remedies from him for correcting his Manners. *Aristotle* wrote to him, *That the best way, in his Opinion, to make both himself and his Subjects happy, was to remember, that so great Power was not given him to injure Mankind, but to do them good. That he would do well to set Bounds to his Passion,* which he knew he was very subject to. *That it was below him to fly out in a Passion at his Inferiors, and that he had not his Equal any where to be angry with.* But at last, when Pride had got the Ascendant over him, he began to despise

spise him, especially when he thought he was become his Enemy, upon the account of the Death of *Calisthenes*, and after, he fancy'd that *Aristotle* vex'd him with Disputes, contrary to the Precepts of Wisdom, and out of Revenge, on pretence of despising human Grandeur and Ambition.

It is certain, that a little before his Death, when *Cassander* was endeavouring to vindicate his Father from the Crimes with which he had been charged, he is said to have broke out into these Words· *That he was come instructed with the Artifices of* Aristotle's *Subtilty, to evade the just Complaints of others by fallacious Quibbles;* and then threaten'd *to do both of them a Mischief, if he found what had been complain'd of to be true*. and this he pronounc'd with such an angry and stern Countenance, that long after his Death, *Cassander*, who then govern'd *Greece*, happening to see a Picture of *Alexander* at *Delphi*, was seiz'd with Horror and Trembling all over his Body, when he remembered the Danger he had been in. This gave Occasion to speak very disadvantageously of *Aristotle*; because it was the common Rumour, that it was by his Contrivance that the Poison which was the Cause of *Alexander's* Death, was carry'd to *Babylon* in a Horse's Hoof. He was a great Lover of Musick, and practised it with Attention in his younger Years; till such time as his Father ask'd him in a scornful manner, *Whether he was not asham'd to play so elegantly*; whereupon he began to neglect it, as an Art that did not become his Majesty At that time being desir'd by his Musick master to touch a certain String according to Art, *What matters it*, said he, *if I should touch this one,* pointing to another. To which the Master answered, *'tis no matter for one who is to be a King, but it concerns one who would be a good Player upon Instruments.* He was afterwards delighted
with

Vol 1 Page 20

HOMERICI VVLTVS

P. F. Sc.

with ſtrong and manly Muſick, and had an Averſion
to ſoft and effeminate Airs, as things by which Mens
Manners were corrupted. Upon which account he was
very much taken with *Timotheus*, who was very famous in that Profeſſion; for this Man, accommodating
his Art to *Alexander*'s Humour, did ſo raviſh him upon
ſome Occaſions, by *Phrygian* Airs, that he ſeem'd all in
a Tranſport, and actuated as it were by ſome divine
Inſpiration, and haſten'd to his Arms as if the Enemy
had been juſt at hand. He likewiſe ſtudy'd Eloquence
under *Anaximenes Lampſacenus*, which was afterwards
the Cauſe of ſaving the City of *Lampſacum*, when
Alexander had a mind to deſtroy it for eſpouſing the
Intereſts of the *Perſians*. For beholding *Anaximenes*
coming without the Walls, and apprehending that he
was coming to beg him to ſave his Country, he ſwore
by the *Grecian* Gods, *That he wou'd not grant what he
was coming to ask*. Upon the over-hearing of which,
the Petitioner, who had his Wits about him, ask'd him
to *deſtroy* Lampſacum. *Alexander* being tied by his
Oath, but more charm'd by his old Maſter's Cunning,
granted a Pardon to the People of *Lampſacum*. He
deſpis'd *Comedians*, as People that dealt in Matters that
had no Congruity with his Deſigns, and who were
born for no other End but to debauch Mens Morals.
Nor did he value Gladiators or Fencers, tho' they were
in great Eſteem all over *Greece*, perhaps becauſe he
look'd upon them as idle Fellows, who pamper'd their
Bodies, and gave themſelves up to ſhew Tricks upon a
Stage, inſtead of employing their Strength and Activity
in the Service of their Country. But he was a great
Encourager of all other Arts, and even of ſuch as had
never come the leaſt in the way of his own Studies.
For which reaſon, all that eſteem'd themſelves excellent
in any Art, came flocking to him from all Parts of the
World,

World, and either presented him with some Piece of their Ingenuity, or some Specimen of their Art, for which they commonly receiv'd immense Sums from a most liberal and munificent King, whose Fortune was equal to the Largeness of his Soul. He likewise sent rich Presents to such as were remarkable either for great Learning or Virtue, in the remotest Parts; which was the Reason why there appear'd at that time so many learned Men, and excellent Artificers, insomuch that scarce any Age ever abounded more with useful and fine Arts. For nothing is more certain, than that the Manners and Studies of Subjects are formed according to the Example of the Prince, and that all the Decays that happen to States, are to the Honour or Disgrace of those who govern.

Of all the Monuments of Antiquity, he had the greatest Esteem for *Homer*, who he thought was the only Person that had perfectly describ'd that Wisdom by which Empires subsist, and had such a Passion for him, that he was called *Homer's Lover*. He was wont to carry his Books always along with him, and even when he went to Bed, he put them and his Sword under his Pillow, calling them *his military* Viaticum, *and the Elements of warlike Virtue*. He esteem'd *Achilles* to have been happy in finding so great a Man to celebrate his Virtues.

Having found a most curious Cabinet both for Matter and Workmanship, amongst the Plunder of *Damascus*, and his Friends having ask'd him, *What Use it was most proper for?* he answer'd, *We will dedicate it to* Homer, *since 'tis but reasonable that the most precious Monument of human Wit, should be preserv'd in the finest Piece of Workmanship*. From hence the most correct Edition of that Poet, which *Alexander* was at much Pains to get, was call'd the *Edition of the Box of Perfumes*,

fumes, becaufe in that Cabinet the *Perſians* had us'd to keep Odours and Perfumes. One Day as a certain Meſſenger of good News run towards him, in all haſte ſtretching out his Right-hand, with the higheſt Marks of Joy in his Countenance, *What News can you tell me*, ſays he, *that's worthy of ſo much Joy, unleſs that Homer is alive again?* He was then arriv'd to ſuch a Degree of Happineſs, that he thought there wanted nothing to compleat his Glory, but one capable to trumpet his Praiſe By frequent reading of him, he had got him almoſt all by Heart, ſo that no Perſon could quote him more readily or familiarly, or judge of him more juſtly. But of all his Verſes, he was beſt pleas'd with that wherein *Agamemnon* is prais'd both as a good General and a valiant Soldier, and look'd upon it as his chief Incentive to Virtue, and the Guide of his Manners

Thus being Maſter of thoſe Arts and Accompliſhments, he notably maintain'd the Grandeur and Dignity of his Fortune, and kept himſelf free from Haughtineſs and Libertiniſm, by which moſt Princes are acted His Ornament and Dreſs did hardly diſtinguiſh him from a private Perſon, for he was of Opinion, that a Prince ought to ſurpaſs his Subjects rather in the Culture of Virtue, than in the Finery of his Cloaths. He was chearful, civil, and affable, but ſo as not to appear little He was a Lover of Wine, but went not the length of Drunkenneſs, for in his leiſure Hours, he preferred Converſation to Drinking He had ſuch a Contempt for Pleaſures, that his Mother was afraid he was unfit for begetting Children He held it as an inviolable Law, That he ought never to defile another's Bed He followed theſe Maxims of Life and Manners a long while, and acted the Part of a great and worthy King, till ſuch time as he was ſhaken by a certain *Impetus*, and changed by a ſtrong current of Fortune, ſo as to

depart

depart from his former Moderation by degrees. He shew'd an extraordinary Courage and Dexterity, to the great Astonishment of his Father and others, in managing the Horse *Bucephalus*, which Name was given him from his being mark'd with the Figure of an Ox's Head. *Thessaly* was very much fam'd at that time for fine Horses, and great Numbers of them were bred in that Country, but none of them was to be compar'd to *Bucephalus* either for Mettle or Beautifulness, for which reason *Philonicus* a *Pharsalian*, thinking him worthy of the greatest Prince in those Parts, brought him to *Philip*, and propos'd to sell him for sixteen Talents. But when they came to try his Speed and Management, by riding him out into the Fields, there was none of the King's Friends or Attendants that durst venture to manage him, for he rose upon them, and frighten'd all that essay'd to mount him, by his Fierceness. So that he was now look'd upon as unmanageable and useless, upon the account of his Wildness; at which *Alexander* sighing said, *What a fine Horse those People lose through their Ignorance and Cowardice!* After having repeated these Words over and over, his Father chid him, *for finding fault with Horsemen that were both older and more skilful than himself, as if he could manage that Horse better than they.* To which he answer'd, *I will manage him better than they, Father, if you will give me leave.* Upon this, his Father ask'd him, *What he wou'd forfeit if he could not execute what he had undertaken.* *I will forfeit the Price of the Horse*, reply'd he. At this every body smil'd, and agreed, *That if he won, the Father should pay for the Horse, but if he lost, he should lay down the Money himself.* Then *Alexander* taking the Horse by the Bridle, turn'd him directly to the Sun, that so he might not see his Shadow; for he had observ'd, that this frighten'd him, and made him

more

more untractable. Finding his Fury was not much bated notwithstanding this, he ſtroak'd his Mane, laid his Armour aſide gently, and jump'd upon him at once, though he was foaming with Rage. Then *Bucephalus*, that was not us'd to obey, begun to fling with his Heels, and throw about his Head, and very obſtinately refuſe to be guided by the Bridle, then he eſſay'd to get looſe, and run away full ſpeed. He was then in a ſpacious Plain that was fit for riding in. Wherefore *Alexander* giving him the Rein, and ſetting his Spurs to his Sides, he run with incredible Speed, and with all the Vigor and Fury imaginable. And after he had travers'd a vaſt ſpace of Ground, till he was weary, and willing to ſtop, he ſpur'd him on till ſuch time as his Mettle was exhauſted, and he became tame, after which, he brought him back very gentle and tractable. When *Alexander* alighted, his Father embrac'd him with Tears of Joy, and kiſſing him, ſaid, *He muſt ſeek out a larger Empire for himſelf, for that the Kingdom of* Macedon *was too ſmall for ſo vaſt a Spirit.* Afterwards *Bucephalus* continu'd the ſame Fierceneſs towards others, while he obey'd *Alexander* alone with a wonderful Submiſſion; and after he had been his Companion in many Labours and Dangers, he was at laſt kill'd in a Battle againſt *Porus*. The moſt excellent Artificers thought this was a worthy Subject to celebrate their Skill upon. And there are two marble Statues of *Alexander* taming his Horſe, which were a Tryal of Skill between *Praxiteles* and *Phidias*. And tho' it is not certain that they are the Statues of *Alexander*, yet ſome Authors of very good Note have believ'd them to be ſo.

By theſe and ſuch like Tryals of his Genius and Courage, he came to ſo high an Eſteem with *Philip*, that when he laid Siege to the City of *Byzantium*, he

Vol. I   B   thought

thought his Son fit to be trusted with the entire Management of the Affairs of all *Macedonia*, tho' he was then but sixteen Years of Age. Some of the *Medari* (who were a People of *Thrace*, and subject to *Macedonia*) perceiving this, thought they had now found a fit Opportunity for a Revolt, which they had long meditated, and so made no scruple of discovering their Designs. But the young Prince, glad of this Occasion of shewing his Courage and Conduct, march'd against them in all haste, with the Captains that his Father had left behind him, and having overcome the Rebels, and banish'd them from the City, he gave it to be inhabited by Strangers of several Nations, which they call'd *Alexandropolis*, after the Name of their Founder. Tho' this Success was the Cause of great Joy to *Philip*, yet fearing lest the young Prince might undertake, to his own Destruction, things beyond his Power, if he was left to his own Conduct, he sent for him, to the end that under his Tutorage he might learn to moderate his Heat with Prudence, and made use of his strenuous and ready Service, which was ever full of Spirit and Alacrity, in subduing the Cities of the *Chersonesus*. But finding that the Siege of the City of *Byzantium* drew into length, both because the Place was strong, and the Inhabitants fought bravely in Defence of their Liberty, and besides, being inform'd that both the *Greeks* and *Barbarians*, who were jealous of the Growth of *Philip*'s Power, were coming from all Parts to their Assistance, he despair'd of being Master of that City, and was only solicitous how to break up from the Siege with the greatest Safety for his Men, and his Honour. *Atheas* was at that time King of the *Gotæ*, a People of *Scythia*, who being press'd by the *Istrians*, demanded Succours of *Philip* promising at the same time to make him his Heir, if by his Assistance he could retrieve his desperate Affairs. But when he found that the Enemy's General was dead, and himself deliver'd from the Apprehension of War, he sent back the *Macedonians* without fulfilling his Promise, telling them, *That he neither wanted their Assistance, nor the Adoption of* Philip, *That he had Troops enough of his own to defend him against his Enemies, and that he had a Son to succeed him in his Kingdom.* Philip being nettled at this foul Dealing, and bent upon Revenge, rais'd the Siege of *Byzantium*, and march'd his Troops into *Scythia*, where he engag'd the *Barbarians*, whom he overcame by his wise Conduct, notwithstanding their Superiority in Number. All the Booty of that Victory consisted of vast Flocks of Cattle and Horses, and female Captives and Children, nor was there any other Prey taken, for the *Getæ* were not desirous of Riches, but contenting themselves with daily Sustenance, reckon'd Poverty amongst the Conveniencies of Life. When *Philip* return'd from *Scythia*, and march'd through the Country of the *Triballi* with a vast Equipage and much Baggage, that People taking Possession of all the Roads, denied him Passage, unless he would give them a Share of his Booty. There were *Greek* auxiliary Troops in *Philip*'s Army, who took it ill too, that they had not a Share in the Fruits of that Victory, since they had been Sharers in the Danger.

This occasion'd a Mutiny in the Army, which issued in a very hot Dispute, in which many of both sides lay dead on the spot, and the King himself was wounded in the Thigh, and his Horse was kill'd with the same Wound, such was the force of the Dart, and so great the strength of him that threw it. Here *Alexander* was the first Person that ran in to the Relief of his Father

Father, who was lying upon the Ground, and covering him with his Shield, kill'd some that were rushing upon him, and turn'd others into flight. Thus was the Father sav'd by the Piety and Duty of his Son, while those who were just ready to dispatch him ran away, as believing he was already dead, so that he seem'd to owe his Life to the desperate condition of his wound, and escaped Death, by the supposition of his having already suffer'd it.

Mean while, in this Hurry and Confusion, the Booty was lost. Philip was lame by this wound, and when at first he seem'd to regret that imperfection of his Limbs, his Son comforted him by this Saying, that deserves to be remembered by all succeeding Ages, *That he ought not to be angry at a wound, which put him in mind of his Valour at every step he took.*

Philip had by this time acquired Fame and Power enough; he had receiv'd abundance of Wounds, and gone through Dangers enough, if his Mind that was blinded with Ambition could have suffer'd him to live in quiet. He made the *Macedonians*, who had formerly been Tributaries to the *Illyrians*, Masters not only of all their Neighbours, but also of very distant Nations. He had subdu'd the *Triballi*, reduc'd *Thrace* under his obedience, and commanded many of the *Greek* States, and influenc'd others, either by Fear, or by Bribes. *Daochus, Cineas, Thracidaus, Eudicus,* and *Scino* of *Larissa*, had conquer'd the *Thessalians* for him; *Ceridas, Hieronymus* and *Eucalpidao*, the *Arcadians*, *Myrtis, Telecamus* and *Muascas*, the *Argives*, *Euixtheus, Cleotimus* and *Aristachmus*, the *Eleans*, *Neon* and *Thrasylochus*, the Sons of *Philiades*, had subdu'd the *Messenians*, *Aristratus* and *Damarallus*, the *Syconians*, *Noedorus, Helixus* and *Perilaus*, the *Megarensians*, and *Hipparchus, Clitarchus,* and *Sosistratus*,

the

the *Euobeans*. Now all these great Men, were Chiefs of their City. Besides, *Euthycrates* and *Losthenes* deliver'd up *Olynthum* to him.

In short, *Sparta* was the only Commonwealth that nobly preserv'd her Liberty, and was free from Treachery. But as *Philip* aspired at the Conquest of all *Greece*, he easily perceiv'd that the Power of the *Athenians* was the greatest Bar to his Enterprizes. Nor was that Commonwealth without Traitors: but the People, who could do what they had a mind to, oppos'd the growing Power of the *Macedonians*, by the persuasion of *Demosthenes*; having understood by frequent Contentions (as it often falls out among powerful Neighbours) how daring and cunning *Philip* was, and how little he regarded either Reputation or Faith, when Dominion was in the dispute. The King was mightily enrag'd against the *Athenians*, because it was to them that his late Miscarriage at *Byzantium* was owing, for they not only sent to their Assistance a Fleet of a Hundred and twenty Sail, but likewise prevail'd upon the People of *Chio* and *Rhodes* to do the same thing. Wherefore, while the Wound which he had receiv'd in the Country of the *Triballi* was a curing, he made all manner of Preparations secretly, in order to fall upon the *Athenians*, when they least suspected his design. He kept an Army on foot, on pretence that the *Illyrians*, who were naturally fierce, and unacquainted with Servitude, had already attempted to shake off the Yoke that had been lately put upon them.

Alexander was sent against those *Barbarians*, whom having defeated and put to flight, he gave the World such hopes of his Fortune and Virtue, and conceiv'd the same of himself, that he now thought he was able to govern Affairs by himself, without his Father's direction.

direction. These things were done in the space of two years. Now *Philip* having all things ready for his Enterprize, and thinking it was high time to put in execution what he had for some time design'd, took hold of as good an occasion as he could have wish'd, to lead his Army into *Greece*, which he did before the Spring of the year, and sent for the Troops of his Allies out of the *Peloponnesus*. He had been created General of the *Greeks* by a Decree of the *Amphyctiones*, to chastise the Insolence of the *Locrians*, who inhabited the City of *Amphyssa*. For in Contempt of the Authority of the *Amphyctiones*, they continued to possess the Territory of *Cyrrha*, which was dedicated to *Apollo*, and had wounded their General, and cut to pieces several of their Men. *Philip* was at that time in Alliance with the *Athenians*, but they lookt upon that but as a small Security, if the King could make any Advantage of breaking his Faith. Wherefore they sent Ambassadors to him, to desire him *to observe the Treaty, or at least to commit no Hostility 'till the Spring was well advanc'd. That in the mean while the* Athenians *would consult about measures to accommodate the Differences that were between them.* They likewise sent an Embassy to *Thebes, to represent to the* Thebans *the common Danger, and to exhort them to concur with them in the Defence of all* Greece.

But *Philip* preserv'd the Friendship between the *Thebans* and *Macedonians*, through the mediation of his Partizans and Friends, the chief of which were *Trinolacco*, *Theogiton*, and *Anoemetas*, who had great influence over their Countrymen. In fine, persuading himself, that he should easily gain his point, if he had to do only with the *Athenians*, and having overcome the *Locrians* and their Confederates at *Amphyssa*, he march'd his Army with all speed into the *Phocides*,

made

made himself Master of *Elatea*, which equally commanded the Borders of the *Thebans* and the *Athenians*, put a Garrison into it, and fortified it, as if he had design'd to make it the seat of the War. When this News was brought to *Athens* in the Night, the whole City was fill'd with such a Consternation, that early next Morning, when the People were assembled as usual, by the publick Criers, no body stood up to ask, *Whether any one there present had any thing to say, that tended to the Safety of their Country?* At last *Demosthenes*, after having discoursed of such things as were suitable to the occasion, persuaded the people, *That they ought without delay to draw out their Army and their Fleet, and send Ambassadors to all the* Grecian *States, but especially to the* Thebans. A Decree being made agreeable to this Proposition, *Chares* and *Lysicles* were appointed Generals of the Forces, and *Demosthenes* was order'd to go Ambassador to the *Thebans*. These Proceedings could not escape the Vigilance of *Philip*, who knew very well he should have a heavy War upon his hands, if those People should join in Confederacy. For the *Athenians* were at that time both rich and powerful; nor was either the Power or the Reputation of the *Thebans* to be contemned. Nor was the Memory of the famous Battle of *Leuctra* yet out of Men's Minds, by which Victory they wrested the Dominion of *Greece* out of the Hands of the *Lacedemonians*.

Wherefore that he might both confirm his Confederates, and baffle the Contrivances of the opposite Faction, he sent thither two *Macedonians*, *Amyntas* and *Clearchus*, and with them one *Pitho* a *Byzantine*, on whose Eloquence he depended. This *Byzantine* is said to have spoke in the Assembly of the *Bœotians* in the following manner.

"If you had no Alliance with *Philip*, and the *Athenian* Army were in Possession of *Elatea*, while he lay idle in *Macedonia*, yet I have no room to doubt but you would even then be desirous of his Friendship and Alliance. For indeed, who would not prefer so potent a King, who has done so many brave things, to a Republick whose Reputation and Fame are superior to its Strength? But now, since that Prince, who, as it were, possesses the very Gates of your City, with his victorious Troops, is your Friend and Ally, and since you have receiv'd many Affronts and Injuries from the *Athenians* both formerly and of late, it would be an Insolence to persuade you to an Alliance with them, and to contemn the Friendship of so great a King. But those People, who are the proudest and haughtiest of Mortals, fancy that they alone are wise and prudent, and that all the rest of Mankind, but especially the *Bœotians* (for 'tis chiefly you that they insult) are foolish and unpolish'd, and understand neither what is profitable nor honest. Thus they fancy they shall be able to persuade you to what you can never do without the extreamest folly, and that is, to chuse Friends and Enemies rather according to their Humours than for your own Benefit; confiding in a Flourish of Words, in which consists all their Strength. But no Man in his Senses ever prefer'd Words before Facts, especially in War, wherein the Hands are of Service, but the Exercise of the Tongue is impertinent. Whatever stress they may lay upon their Eloquence, the Fortune and Virtue of *Philip*, which are supported by both his own and his auxiliary Forces, will always be superior. In earnest, 'tis hard to say, whether the Folly or the Impudence of their Demands be greatest. *Thebans*, say

"they,

"they, *expose your selves to the Thunder that hovers*
"*over* Athens, *make War upon a King who is your*
"*Friend and Ally, at the Hazard of your own Ruin,*
"*that we may continue in Safety. Stake down your*
"*Lives before him, to prevent* Philip *from revenging*
"*the Injuries of the* Athenians. Are these the De-
"mands of Men who are in their Senses, or think
"others have the use of theirs? They who but very
"lately omitted no Occasion of oppressing you, they
"who pursued you with Reproaches, Outrages and
"Arms, as much as in them lay, and look'd upon your
"Dangers and Misfortunes as their Happiness, these
"same People have the Confidence to propose to you,
"to chuse to perish with them, rather than be victo-
"rious with *Philip*. But this Prince, who was once
"your Guest and Pupil, who was brought up with
"that famous General *Epaminondas*, whose Life and
"Morals bear the fairest Character, has from his
"Youth imbib'd an Affection for your City, and the
"OEconomy and Manners of its Inhabitants. He re-
"venged the Injuries done to you and to *Apollo* in
"the *Phocian* War, when the *Athenians*, out of Hatred
"to you, sent Succours to one of your Countrymen
"who was guilty of Sacrilege, and when he was
"again invited by the unanimous Decree of the *Am-*
"*phyctiones*, he reveng'd the Contempt of the same
"Deity upon the *Locrians*. And so careful was he of
"your Interests, that he would not depart, till such
"time as he had deliver'd you from the Jealousy of
"that rival City, which has always been your Enemy.
"If you are inclined to execute this Design by your
"common Councils and Forces, he will not be a-
"gainst your coming in for a share of the Booty,
"rather than a share of the War. But if you had
"rather be Neuter, only grant him a Passage, for he

B 5   alone

"alone is able to revenge all your common Injuries
"Even in that case you shall reap equal Fruits of Vi-
"ctory The Flocks, Herds and Slaves that shall be
"won from the Enemy, shall most of them fall to
"your Share, as being the nearest Neighbours, and
"thus shall you make up the Loss you sustain'd in
"the *Phocean* War I leave you yourselves to judge
"whether this will not be more advantageous for you,
"than to have your Dwellings burnt, your Towns
"storm'd, set on fire, and plunder'd, and all your Af-
"fairs put in Disorder and Confusion, just as the *A-*
"*thenians* wish them In truth, Sincerity that is un-
"justly suspected, turns to Rage, and the greatest
"Good will, when it is slighted, concludes in the bit-
"terest Revenge I do not say this, as if I was up-
"braiding you for Ingratitude, which I have not the
"least apprehension of, nor to strike terror into you,
"which I trust there will be no occasion for, but
"that the memory of *Philip*'s good Offices towards
"you, and of yours towards him, may convince you,
"that those Alliances only are firm and perpetual,
"which it is the Interest of both Parties to observe
"If he has merited more of you than you have done
"of him, it will be your Duty, to shew the same
"good Dispositions, and use the same Endeavours not
"to fall short of him in this respect He thinks that
"the greatest Recompence for all his Labours is his
"having supported *Greece* by his Succours, for the
"Safety and Honour of which he has waged conti-
"nual War with the *Barbarians* Would to the Gods
"the Madness of the *Athenians* had permitted him to
"follow his own Courses! you would have heard by
"this time, that his Arms, which he is now con-
"strain'd to move about *Greece*, to repress the Distur-
"bances raised by seditious and ill designing Persons,

were

"were triumphing in *Asia.* He might certainly have
"been in Friendship with the *Athenians,* unless he had
"thought it below him, and of bad Example, to be-
"come a Vassal to this *Demosthenes,* and some others,
"who drive the ignorant Multitude whither they please
"by the Breath of their Orations, as the Winds drive
"the Waves of the Sea. Doubtless, had they any regard
"for Honour or Honesty, they would do their Duty
"without being brib'd to it. But they who are accu-
"stom'd to sell their Honour, make no Distinction be-
"tween things that are useful, and things that are dan-
"gerous, between Justice and Injustice, if they find their
"advantage in Wickedness as well as in Goodness, they
"are wrought upon by Interest, and not by the Love
"of Virtue or their Country, nor Respect for Gods
"or Men. In vain will you expect any thing from
"those Men that is either virtuous or reputable. They
"who have the Interest of their Country so little at
"Heart, will never be concern'd for your Interests.
"they will involve you in the same Calamities from
"which you have been lately deliver'd by the Cou-
"rage and Faith of the *Macedonians.* Calamities so
"much the greater, by how much *Philip* must be a
"more formidable Enemy than *Philomelus* or *Onomar-
"chus* were. For in a precarious Command, the En-
"deavours of a good and able General will be no less
"travers'd by his own Countrymen, than by the Ene-
"my. Whereas none dares to oppose or disobey the
"King's Command. His Will alone is the Rule by
"which they are governed, and of what Importance
"this is in Affairs of War, you all know. Nor is that
"Security of the *Macedonians* confin'd to one Person.
"Tho' Fate should dispose of *Philip,* we have an *Ale-
"xander* to rise up in his stead, who has even at so
"green an Age given such Proofs of his Courage
"and

"and Genius, that it is almoſt evident he will be equal
"to the moſt renowned Generals. On the contrary,
"the Power of Peace and War reſiding in all the
"People promiſcuouſly among the *Athenians*, the
"boldeſt Pretender aſſumes it to himſelf, as a thing
"that belongs to the firſt Seizer. There all things are
"managed rather by Starts of Paſſion, than by Coun-
"ſel and Deliberation Men of ill Deſigns perſuade,
"and the Ignorant decree. War is undertaken with
"more Heat than it is carried on, and Treaties are
"broke with the ſame Eaſe that they were made For
"they have a Treaty with *Philip*, which how ſacredly
"they keep, appears from their Actions and Beha-
"viour Nor do they think it enough that they break
"Faith themſelves, unleſs they ſpread that Contagion
"wider But your Steadineſs, O *Thebans*, by which
"you are no leſs famous and great, than by your
"brave and ſucceſsful Exploits, leaves no room to
"doubt, but you will prefer the Friendſhip of a King
"which you have had repeated Proofs of, to that of
"a City which has always been your Enemy, and en-
"vious of your Glory Nor will *Hercules*, the Aver-
"ter of Evil, whom your City adores as their own
"inmate Tutelary Deity with a peculiar Veneration,
"ever ſuffer you to engage in an unjuſt, and impious
"War, againſt one who is deſcended from his Blood
"As to his other Allies, you may learn from them-
"ſelves, what Value they have for the King's Friend-
"ſhip."

Theſe were the Words of Pitho Then the Deputies of
the Allies were heard, who prais'd the King's Affection to
them; and then remonſtrated

"That he who was the Protector of *Greece*, ought
"rather to be follow'd, than the *Athenians*, who were
"the Diſturbers of it.

But

But when *Demosthenes* had liberty to speak, "I was not ignorant, *said he*, that those Mercenaries of *Philip* would neither spare their Praises upon him, nor their Reproaches upon us. For they who have laid aside all Shame, are little solicitous either what they say or do, so they gain their Point. But, O *Thebans*, if I understand your Temper, they will find themselves mightily disappointed in their Expectations, and carry back an Answer to *Philip* that is worthy of your Virtue, and of the Discipline of the *Greeks*. In the mean while, pray take good heed to what lies upon us to do at this time. For that your whole Fortune depends upon this Day's Deliberation, I shall shew, by irrefragable Arguments, and not by the Charms or Magick of Words, by which they are afraid you may be imposed upon. They may lay aside their Fear, since they have no Occasion to be so solicitous about you, for we shall not in the least endeavour to appear more eloquent than they. A bad Cause, indeed, has sometimes been mightily indebted to the Power of Eloquence, but when it is the Business of him that speaks, to shew the naked Truth, if he is wise, he will never take up his time in a Flourish of Words. As to *Philip*, we are very little concern'd about his Character, let him, for us, resemble the Picture they have drawn of him, let him be handsome, eloquent, or a good Companion at an Entertainment, for some People have praised him even for these Qualifications, and thus confess'd him deficient in real and solid Glory. But I cannot help wondering, that his Ambassador should reproach us in your Presence, with those things, which if they are Crimes, do without dispute equally affect the *Thebans* and the *Athenians*. They have been endeavouring to expose the Inconveniences

"vemences of a popular Form of Government, which
"tho' both you and we are sensible of, yet do we
"prefer it to Regal Tyranny. They have talk'd to
"you at such a rate, as if they had a mind to obtain
"Favour by tickling the Ears of a popular Circle, or a
"publick Assembly of *Macedonians*, and not as if they
"came to a free City, to execute the Office of Am-
"bassadors. We very well know the irreconcileable
"Hatred that Kings and their Slaves have to free Ci-
"ties and People, and they have done very foolishly
"to discover this. But we are to take so much the
"greater Care, *Thebans*, to defend our Laws and Pri-
"vileges. It were to be wish'd, above all things,
"that those who are call'd to the Administration
"of Affairs in Commonwealths, were engaged only
"in this glorious Contention, who should consult the
"Interests of their Commonwealth best, or who
"should best execute the Resolutions that are taken.
"Then none would prefer his own Advantage to the
"common Good, none would receive Bribes, and
"none would betray his Country to *Philip*, after the
"Example of those Deputies. But, *Thebans*, entire
"and perfect Felicity was never the Lot of any Man
"or any State. He is the happiest Person whose Cir-
"cumstances are freest from Misfortunes. It is past
"dispute, that we have bad Citizens, nor have you
"been without them in former Times, *Thebans*, nor
"are you even at this time. If this were not so,
"*Philip* would not threaten our Liberty at this Day
"from *Elatea*, but should be obliged to contend with
"us for the Kingdom of *Macedonia*. However, we
"have good Citizens too, and these more numerous
"and more powerful than the bad ones. Do you
"want a Proof of this? We are free. We are not
"*Philip*'s Slaves, as you thought to have made your

"By-

" *Byzantines, Python*; but as for you *Daochus*, and
" you *Thrasidæus*, you sold your *Thessalians* to the
" King. In effect, *Thebans*, you behold *Thessaly* lan-
" guishing under the Servitude of *Philip* at this day,
" and if I mistake not, you deplore their hard Con-
" dition as well as we. No thanks to *Python* that
" *Byzantium* did not suffer the same Fate with *Olyn-
" thus*, but its Deliverance is owing to us. For that
" religious and venerable Protector of *Greece*, had re-
" solved to oppress that *Greek* City, which was in our
" Alliance and Confederacy, and in no Apprehension
" of being attack'd. Behold, wherein consists the
" Prudence of this great Prince! With him Artifice
" and Cunning is good Policy, Perjury is an Art of
" Science, and Perfidy a Virtue.

" If this be not the Case, pray let him tell what
" other way he arrived at that formidable Power he
" he is now possess'd of? If it was not by surpri-
" sing the *Greeks* with Frauds, Stratagems, and Trea-
" chery, if it was not by conquering the *Barbarians*
" rather with Gold than with the Sword, or in fine,
" whether he ever stuck at his Faith to any Mortal, or
" breaking it when it was engag'd. And yet these Deputies
" give him the glorious Title of Protector of *Greece*,
" and call us the Disturbers of it! But what will they
" be asham'd of, who had rather charge us with their
" own faults, than not discover to you those they are
" evidently guilty of? If any one was guilty of Trea-
" chery, you would make it your business to defend,
" protect, and shelter him from the Punishment of
" the Laws, now that you accuse others, you con-
" demn your selves. If you did this without any Aim
" or Design, then pray where was your Sense or Pru-
" dence? But if you did it wittingly and willingly,
" then where was your Honesty? It is a sufficient

" Vin-

"vemences of a popular Form of *Government*, which
"tho' both you and we are sensible of, yet do we
"prefer it to Regal Tyranny. They have talk'd to
"you at such a rate, as if they had a mind to obtain
"Favour by tickling the Ears of a popular Circle, or a
"publick Assembly of *Macedonians*, and not as if they
"came to a free City, to execute the Office of Am-
"bassadors. We very well know the irreconcileable
"Hatred that Kings and their Slaves have to free Ci-
"ties and People, and they have done very foolishly
"to discover this. But we are to take so much the
"greater Care, *Thebans*, to defend our Laws and Pri-
"vileges. It were to be wish'd, above all things,
"that those who are call'd to the Administration
"of Affairs in Commonwealths, were engaged only
"in this glorious Contention, who should consult the
"Interests of their Commonwealth best, or who
"should best execute the Resolutions that are taken.
"Then none would prefer his own Advantage to the
"common Good, none would receive Bribes, and
"none would betray his Country to *Philip*, after the
"Example of those Deputies. But, *Thebans*, entire
"and perfect Felicity was never the Lot of any Man
"or any State. He is the happiest Person whose Cir-
"cumstances are freest from Misfortunes. It is past
"dispute, that we have bad Citizens, nor have you
"been without them in former Times, *Thebans*, nor
"are you even at this time. If this were not so,
"*Philip* would not threaten our Liberty at this Day
"from *Elatea*, but should be obliged to contend with
"us for the Kingdom of *Macedonia*. However, we
"have good Citizens too, and these more numerous
"and more powerful than the bad ones. Do you
"want a Proof of this? We are free. We are not
"*Philip*'s Slaves, as you thought to have made your

"By-

"Byzantines, Python; but as for you *Daochus*, and
"you *Thrasidaus*, you sold your *Thessalians* to the
"King. In effect, *Thebans*, you behold *Thessaly* lan-
"guishing under the Servitude of *Philip* at this day,
"and if I mistake not, you deplore their hard Con-
"dition as well as we. No thanks to *Python* that
"*Byzantium* did not suffer the same Fate with *Olyn-*
"*thus*, but its Deliverance is owing to us. For that
"religious and venerable Protector of *Greece*, had re-
'solved to oppress that *Greek* City, which was in our
"Alliance and Confederacy, and in no Apprehension
"of being attack'd. Behold, wherein consists the
"Prudence of this great Prince! With him Artifice
"and Cunning is good Policy, Perjury is an Art of
"Science, and Perfidy a Virtue.

"If this be not the Case, pray let him tell what
"other way he arrived at that formidable Power he
"he is now possess'd of? If it was not by surpri-
"sing the *Greeks* with Frauds, Stratagems, and Trea-
"chery, if it was not by conquering the *Barbarians*
"rather with Gold than with the Sword, or in fine,
"whether he ever stuck at his Faith to any Mortal, or
"breaking it when it was engag'd. And yet these Deputies
"give him the glorious Title of Protector of *Greece*,
"and call us the Disturbers of it! But what will they
"be asham'd of, who had rather charge us with their
"own faults, than not discover to you those they are
"evidently guilty of? If any one was guilty of Trea-
"chery, you would make it your business to defend,
"protect, and shelter him from the Punishment of
"the Laws, now that you accuse others, you con-
"demn your selves. If you did this without any Aim
"or Design, then pray where was your Sense or Pru-
"dence? But if you did it wittingly and willingly,
"then where was your Honesty? It is a sufficient

"Vin-

"'Vindication of my Innocence, and of theirs who
" are embark'd in the same Cause with me, that you
" your selves own we have receiv'd nothing from
" *Philip*, for had we ask'd any thing of him, we
" should not have gone away empty-handed from so
" liberal a King as you give out yours is. Would not
" he who thought it worth his while to corrupt you,
" have also given us Bribes, if we had ask'd them?
" But you have just now admonish'd the *Thebans* not
" to follow the Council of those who have not the
" Interests of their Country at heart. From this Mi-
" nute I cease to oppose them, *Thebans*, if they are
" really of that Mind. I come over to their Senti-
" ments, and I exhort, pray, and beseech you with
" all the Earnestness possible, and conjure you by your
" own Safety, and that of all *Greece*, to embrace their
" Proposition. If you come in to this, you will not
" suffer your selves to be sold for Droves of Cattle,
" nor suffer your Possessions to be made your Prisons,
" nor shall be Slaves under the *Pæonians* and *Triballi*,
" like the rest of *Philip*'s Slaves. For they would have
" you to look upon Flocks and Slaves, which are the
" glorious Reward of Servitude, and contemn your
" Wives, your Children, your Parents, your Liberty,
" your Reputation, your Faith, and in fine, every
" thing that is sacred and venerable among the *Greeks*,
" as not worthy your Care. Thus certainly, *Thebans*,
" you have lost and forfeited all these, unless you u-
" nite with us in resisting the Fraud and Violence of
" *Philip*. But if you should imagine your selves safe
" in the Care and Endeavours of others, I am afraid
" you will find your selves egregiously mistaken. For
" if *Philip* should accomplish his Designs (which I can-
" not think of without Horror and Detestation) who
" can doubt but that all *Greece*, as well as you, will
" lose

"lose their Liberty? And who, but they who have
"a mind to perish, would lay any stress upon the
"Faith of such a Prince? But if Victory should de-
"clare for us, pray consider what you ought to ex-
"pect from Men whom you deserted and abandon'd,
"when both their Safety and their Glory were at
"stake? For whatever way your Opinion may sway
"you, you may depend upon it, that the *Athenians*
"are resolv'd to venture all, and that they will never
"lose their liberty but with their Lives. Nor do we
"distrust our Strength, to which if you will join
"yours, we shall, when united, be superior to the
"Enemy, to which either of us singly might perhaps
"be equal. The *Athenians* are not ignorant of his
"Power, which they foresaw while it was rising and
"encreasing, and had all the *Greek* States been of one
"and the same Mind, we might easily have set bounds
"to it. For we waged War with him a long time,
"not for *Amphipolis* or *Halonesus*, as many believ'd,
"but for the Safety and Liberty of *Greece*; till being
"abandon'd by all, and attack'd by some, we were
"forc'd to make a necessary rather than an honou-
"rable Peace. But now, I trust, *Minerva*, the Guar-
"dian Goddess of our City, and the *Pythian Apollo*,
"who is the native God of our Country, and all the
"rest of the *Grecian* Gods, have at last open'd their
"Eyes, and raised the Courage of all their Worshippers
"in defence of our ancient Liberty, which has been
"transmitted to us by our Fore-fathers. Sure *Hercules*
"could not hear the Words of the Ambassadors with-
"out Indignation, when they derived *Philip*'s Pedigree
"from that God. For can that God own him who
"is a Contemner of all Religions? Can a *Greek* ac-
"knowledge a *Macedonian* for his Descendant? Can
"one that hates, punishes, and extirpates Tyranny,
"own

"own a Tyrant? For in this appeared the illustrious
"and memorable Deeds of *Hercules*, more than in any
"thing else. *Philip*, on the contrary, exercises unjust
"Dominion over *Greece*, and has set Domestick Tyrants
"over several Cities thereof, such as *Philistides* over *Ore-*
"*um, Hipparchus* over *Eretica*, and *Taurosthenes* over *Chal-*
"*cides*. For this reason the *Euboeans, Achaeans, Corin-*
"*thians, Megarensians, Leucadians,* and *Corcyraans* have
"declared for us. Others wait the Event, which has
"hitherto been the only Support of the Power of
"*Macedonia*, and which will fall of itself, whenever it
"begins in the least to decline. As to the *Thessalians*,
"by whom *Philip* is now so well furnished with Horse,
"they never stood firm to one side long. The *Illy-*
"*rians* and other *Barbarians* bordering upon *Macedo-*
"*nia*, who are naturally fierce and savage, and mighti-
"ly enraged at their new Servitude, will immediately
"declare for us, and ease us of the Burthen of the
"War, if *Philip* should meet with bad Success at first.
"Only concur heartily with us in so glorious a De-
"sign, and in the mean while lay aside those Conten-
"tions, which a very slight Cause often produces a-
"mong neighbouring States. Publick Joy will turn
"private Grudges into mutual Benevolence, when
"Success crowns our Endeavours, or when we have
"leisure to give vent to our unreasonable Passions,
"they may be resum'd perhaps to the Dishonour and
"Damage of us both, but without destroying us en-
"tirely. I would not have you to be afraid of the Ar-
"tifices of *Philip*, only shut your Ears against his Pro-
"mises, and keep your Hands clean of Bribes. If you
"have your Liberty most at Heart, Cunning and Gifts
"will have no Effect upon you. As the Discords of
"the *Greeks* have rais'd his Power, so their Union will
"overthrow it. Besides as he is rash and headstrong,

"he

"he may be easily catch'd, and if this happens, there
"is no Danger to be fear'd from others, For he
"seeks Glory and Dominion, while those who are
"subject to him desire nothing more than Quiet
"But perhaps you dread *Alexander*, because his
"Partizans contemn you at such a rate, that
"they think you may be frighten'd at the Name of a
"Boy

You would have thought that this Speech of *Demosthenes* had perfectly chang'd the *Thebans* into other Men all of a sudden. They who had heard the Ambassadors of *Philip*, but a little before with Attention, and even Pleasure, were now so far of another mind, that they declar'd, they would look upon *Philip* as an Enemy, unless he quickly departed from their Borders, and those of their Allies, that they would drive from their City all that were in the *Macedonian* Interest, and receive into it the Troops of the *Athenians* But *Philip*, who was more vex'd than frighten'd at the *Thebans* abandoning him so unexpectedly, continu'd to carry on his Enterprize. After two slight Engagements, in both of which the *Athenians* had the better, the two Armies encamped with all their Forces near *Cheronæa* a City of *Bœotia* The *Greeks* were animated by the Deeds of their Ancestors, and their Concern for Liberty, and *Philip* trusted to his excellent Troops, that had been victorious in so many Battles: Nor did he put small confidence in his own Conduct, because he excelled in the Art of War, besides that, the most renowned Generals of the *Greeks* were dead The *Thebans* were ruled at that time by *Theagenes*, a Man who had but little Experience in War, and was not Proof against Money, and *Philip* infinitely surpassed the *Athenian* Generals both in Experience and Courage But the united Forces of two powerful States, whose Authority

thority was followed by the *Corinthians* and others, made him apprehend, that the Fortune of a small part of one Day might cost him both his Life and his Dominions. The Leading Men among the *Thebans* seem'd inclin'd to listen to Proposals of Peace, but the Ardor of the *Athenians* prevail'd so far, as to make them consent to hazard all the Hopes and Power of *Greece* in one Battle. On the other side, *Alexander*, whose Fire and Spirit could not be restrained, conjured his Father, not to let so favourable an Opportunity of getting Glory slip out of his Hands, and having obtain'd leave to venture a Battle, he was the first that began the Attack upon the Enemy. The Fight was carried on with Obstinacy, and Success was doubtful for a long time, till at last the young Prince, to whom his Father had given the Command of one of the Wings of the select Troops, having with great Vigour and Resolution attack'd the sacred Cohort of the *Thebans*, which consisted of their best Troops, oblig'd them to give Ground, and so open'd a Way to Victory. For the *Athenians* being disheartned by the Misfortune of their Allies, and weaken'd with the Heat and their Wounds, were not able to make Head against the *Macedonians* any longer. Besides, *Philip* being rais'd by Emulation and Shame, lest he should come short of his Son, who was but a Youth, fell upon them with such Fury, that they were no longer able to stand their Ground. Thus one Battle determin'd concerning the Liberty of *Greece*. Of the *Athenians* above a thousand were kill'd, and above two thousand taken Prisoners, a great many of the Allies also were either kill'd in the Action, or forc'd to surrender themselves to the Power of the Conqueror. After which, *Alexander* was sent to *Athens*, to assure the *Athenians*, that *Philip* both forgave 'em, and sent

'em

'em Peace, and likewise restor'd to them their Prisoners without Ransom, neither did he hinder them from burying their Dead. For as the King being wholly intent on the *Persian* War, endeavour'd to secure himself of the Fidelity and Affection of the *Greeks*, by his Clemency and Moderation, yet he took from the *Athenians* the Sovereignty of the Sea, and the Islands. He dealt more severely with the *Thebans*, by whose Defection, he remember'd his Affairs were brought into the greatest Danger, and because he thought, that as they were his antient Allies, and had receiv'd Favours from him, they had no reason to join with the *Athenians* against him; therefore, upon the surrender of their Town, he put into it a Garrison of *Macedonians*, and having put to Death those he most hated and suspected, and banish'd others, he conferr'd the Magistracy and Judicature on those of his own Faction, whom he had recall'd from their Exile. He reduc'd the other People who had taken up Arms against him, with the same Torrent of Victory, insomuch that there was not in all *Greece* any, except the *Spartans* and the *Arcades*, that remain'd exempt from his Power, forcing some by his Arms, and others by disadvantageous Alliances, to comply with his Authority. Having therefore appointed a General Assembly of all *Greece*, at *Corinth*, he made a Speech to 'em about carrying the War into *Persia*, telling 'em, *It was necessary to go and meet the* Barbarians, *whose Pride had already laid a Scheme for Universal Empire, that they must resolve to be Slaves for ever, or in time oppose their Power. For the Case was not, whether the* Greeks *would have War or Peace, but, whether they had rather carry the War into the Enemy's Country, or receive it in their own. That they ought not only to revenge former Injuries, but also remove the*

present

present Shame, by *delivering the* Greek *Cities, situate in* Asia, *from the* Persian *Slavery. That this might be easily effected, if settling the Affairs of* Greece, *they were at liberty to turn all their Forces to the War beyond the Sea. That Peace at Home would thereby be secur'd, having remov'd and employ'd in a remote and foreign War those restless and audacious Spirits, whose Idleness was usually the Grounds of Sedition, and Civil Commotions. That they ought therefore to make choice of a General, and settle the Number of Troops with which they design'd to carry on this War.*

Most People were sensible of the vastness of the Demand, but they judg'd it unseasonable to assert by Words, that Liberty they had lost in Arms. Wherefore, without any farther Deliberation, *Philip* is with loud Acclamations declar'd General of *Greece*, and order'd to march into *Asia*, for the Safety and Delivery of the whole World. An Account is therefore taken of the Wealth of every one, and it is enter'd into Books, what Soldiers, Corn and Money each should supply. I find they engag'd for Two hundred thousand Foot, and Fifteen thousand Horse, in which Number, neither the *Macedonians*, nor the *Barbarians* that were Subjects to 'em, were compris'd.

But as there is no Felicity in Human Affairs, without a mixture of Adversity, the Prosperity abroad was succeeded by domestick Troubles. *Olympias*, as we hinted before, by her Moroseness and haughty Temper, every Day more and more alienated the Mind of her Royal Husband. Some alledge that, for the Cause of her Divorce, but I find, that even whilst he cohabited with her, he admitted *Cleopatra* into a Matrimonial Familiarity. Indeed, it is not reasonable to think that *Alexander* would have been present at the Wedding of his Mother-in-Law, which was so dishonourable

honourable to his own Mother whom he lov'd so dearly, and whose Disgrace reflected on himself, for there was a Suspicion of her being removed for Infidelity However, he was there, and a Quarrel arising at the Entertainment, he carry'd off his Mother For *Attalus* the Bride's Uncle, being elevated with Wine, and not being able to conceal his Hopes, telling the *Macedonians*, *That they ought to offer up their Prayers to the Gods, to implore a Lawful Successor to* Philip *by this new Wife*, *Alexander*, who was otherwise prone to Anger, being provok'd by so gross an Affront, reply'd, *What do'st thou then make of us, Wretch as thou art? Am I Bastard?* and at the same time flung the Glass which he had in his Hand, in his Face *Attalus* flinging another at him. A Quarrel arising, *Philip*, who was not at the same Table, being offended at the Interruption of the Mirth of the Day, drew his Sword, and had kill'd his Son, if his Anger, and the Wine, and a Lameness contracted from a former Wound, had not hinder'd him, by causing him to fall down, which gave his Friends (who were surpriz'd at the suddenness of the thing) time to interpose, and convey *Alexander* away

Nor was it a matter of less difficulty to prevail with him to save himself He thought he was injur'd many ways, and though they put him in mind of the terms of Father, and King, and of the Law of Nature, and Nations, yet he could not forbear insulting *Philip*, representing to the *Macedonians*, *what a fine Leader they were like to have for the* Asian *Expedition, since he could not go from one Table to another without falling*. After which, being in fear for his Mother, he took her along with him, and left her in *Epirus*, where her Brother reign'd, and went himself to the King of *Illyrium*. Being afterwards return'd to *Macedonia*, through the Mediatorship of *Demaratus* the *Corinthian*, this perverse Woman could not forbear prompting her Son (who was of himself solicitous enough for Power) *to make himself what Friends he could by a winning Carriage, and by Money, and to fortifie himself against his Father's Anger, by contracting an Alliance with the Men in Authority.* It is true, *Philip* himself had formerly counsell'd him to gain the affection of Men, by his affability and courteous behaviour, but he no wise approv'd of his doing it by Presents, nay he even reprimanded him by Letter, *for daring to hope for the Benevolence of those Men whom he had corrupted by Gifts, telling him he was mistaken, who thought that became a King, it being rather the business of a Servant, or mean Officer.*

But as he would frequently brag, that all things were penetrable by Money, and that he made use of it himself as often as of his Arms, he did not seem to write that, so much with an intention to instruct him in what was proper, as out of Fear, lest the Youth, his Son, should make use of his own Artifices against him. He also chid him for courting the Daughter of *Pexodorus*, that his Father intended for *Aridæus*, calling him degenerate, and unworthy the Fortune his Birth and Education gave him hopes of; who could covet for a Father-in Law, a barbarous *Carian*, the Subject of a Barbarian King. Yet he himself had never slighted any Condition to confirm his Power, but could marry *Illyrian* and *Getic* Women, the roughest and unpolitest of all *Barbarians*, tho' he had at the same time a great many Children by other Wives and Concubines, which seeming to make *Alexander* somewhat uneasie, he took up his Son with a gentle reproof, and exhorted him, *That since he was to have a great many Rivals for the Kingdom,*

dom, he would take care to make himself more worthy and deserving than the rest, that he might not seem to be oblig'd to Philip *his Father for the Crown, but to his own Merit.*

But as for this and the like Causes, they frequently disagreed, and that Friendship and Benevolence being once broken, it was not easie to cement new Affections again into a real Fidelity, so they fell to the last Extremities. The violent Temper of *Olympias* was the chief spring of this Mischief, whose haughty and imperious Mind, prompted the contumacious stubborness of the Sex, with a masculine and unwarrantable Thirst of Revenge. She had us'd her endeavours to make her Brother *Alexander* declare War against *Philip* But the wise King, that he might not be necessitated to that at so unseasonable a time; tho' his Power was superior, contriv'd to strengthen their Friendship by a new Alliance, giving *Cleopatra*, *Alexander*'s Sister, to the *Epirote* for Wife All the petty Princes of the neighbouring Nations, and the Embassadors of the *Greek* States, met at *Aga* to celebrate this Marriage. *Philip* made choice of this Place, not without some kind of Omen, of what afterwards happen'd, for the *Macedonian* Kings us'd to be bury'd there.

It is likewise reported that the *Delphick* Oracle, when he consulted it, on the account of the *Persian* War, foretold his Death, which being ambiguous, as Oracles generally are, he flatter'd himself that it signify'd the Destruction of the *Barbarians* There were several other Presages, that no body then took notice of, 'till the Event made 'em plain Among the King's Guards, there was one nam'd *Pausanias*, whom the King, to comfort him for the Affront he had receiv'd from *Attalus*, had promoted to that Honour. For *Attalus*

C

talus had expos'd him, being loaded with Wine, to the scandalous insults of the Guests. *Pausanias* having apply'd himself to the King for Revenge, in lieu thereof receiv'd this Honour. *Philip* was so far from being able to resolve on the Punishment of a Man of that known fortitude in War, and whom he had united to himself lately by a near Alliance, that he gave him the Command of part of his Troops with *Parmenio* and *Amyntas*, and sent him into *Asia*, designing to make use of him in the *Persian* Expedition, and therefore desir'd *Pausanias* that he would for his sake, and the publick good, put up the Affront, endeavouring by fair words, and a better Sallary, to appease and pacifie him. But the young Man, having a greater regard to the Injury, than the Favours he receiv'd, turn'd the aversion he had for the Author of the Affront, on him that refus'd to vindicate it.

It was thought he had consulted with those who were Enemies to *Attalus*'s Family, and were at variance with *Philip*, but no body doubted of it, when it came to be known, that *Olympias* had plac'd a Crown of Gold on the Head of the Parricide, as he hung upon the Cross. There were several other base Actions committed, by which the whole Contrivance and Cause of the Villany came to light. By break of day the Theatre was crowded with the multitude that came thither to behold the publick Shews, which it was said, would very much exceed in Expence and Magnificence those of the preceding days. Among other things, in which wealthy Kings, and such as are not capable of the greatness of their Fortune, are us'd to sport and squander away their Riches, there were the Effigies of twelve Deities so exquisitely wrought, that the Art of the Workmen seem'd to vie with the Excellency of the Materials. There was a thirteenth

that

that represented *Philip*, in nothing inferior to the rest. This Contempt of his mortal Condition was quickly reveng'd; and he, whom Success had render'd so insolent as to equal himself to the immortal Gods, was prevented by Fate, from enjoying an Honour that no way belong'd to him. For *Pausanias* having watch'd him as he was going into the Theatre alone (he having sent before those that attended him, and order'd his Guards to stay behind, designing to shew, that he was so generally belov'd, as to have no occasion for 'em) the Murtherer assaulted him on the sudden, and plung'd a Sword of the *Barbarian* make, which he conceal'd under his Cloaths, into his Body, while he suspected no such Attempt.

Such was the End of the greatest King of his time. He had mightily improv'd the State of *Macedon*, making it, of a poor and inconsiderable, both a great and flourishing Kingdom. He had conquer'd the neighbouring *Barbarians*, enslav'd all *Greece*, and was preparing to reduce the *Persian* Empire. The *Greek* Auxiliaries were gathered together, he had already sent several Generals before him into *Asia*, was on the very point of executing his Designs (promising to himself great and durable Advantages from the Victory) when he unexpectedly lost his Life.

Thus we see how the greatest things are frail and uncertain, a small Accident being able to disappoint the boldest Hopes of Mortals.

Olympias being inform'd of the King's Death, forc'd *Cleopatra*, *Attalus*'s Neice, to hang her self; and a few days before *Philip*'s Death, she had barbarously murther'd the Child she had by him, roasting it in a brazen Vessel. Not content with this, she made all her Relations and Dependents feel the Rage with which she was transported, and very cruelly laid hold of this Opportunity to gratifie her implacable female Revenge.

While these things were doing, *Alexander*, like a benevolent Planet, seasonably appear'd to compose and calm so furious a Tempest. The *Greeks*, whom *Philip* had oppress'd, began already to conceive some hopes of their Liberty, the Neighbouring *Barbarians* began to be troublesome, and the Affairs of *Macedon* it self were in some Confusion. *Attalus*, who was at the Head of no contemptible Army, by a dextrous and insinuating use of his Power, had procur'd to himself a great Esteem among the Soldiery, and besides his being related to the principal Men of *Macedon*, had engag'd to marry the Sister of *Philotas*. And there was no relying on him, who had been both hated and offended by *Alexander* and his Mother. *Amyntas*, who was Son to *Perdiccas*, *Philip*'s Brother, and whom *Philip* had chosen for his Son-in-Law, giving him *Cyna* in Marriage, aspir'd to the Succession of his Father's Kingdom, by the Murther of *Alexander*. A great part of the People, out of an Aversion to the Tyranny of *Olympias*, and others out of a desire of Novelty, were variously inclin'd to the one or the other, and some again did not scruple to say, the Crown (that *Amyntas* first, and *Philip* afterwards, had by Force and Fraud usurp'd from the lawful Heir) ought to be restor'd to *Alexander* the Son of *Ceropus*.

The Army likewise being compos'd of different Nations, disagreed both in their Councils and Discourses, according to the Inclination and Hopes of each Party. On the other side, *Alexander* was new in his Government, and *Philip*'s sudden Death had not given him time to make any Provision against these unexpected Motions, and although he appear'd very

prom sin;

promising and hopeful, yet they despis'd his Youth. They could not imagine that a young Prince of twenty years of Age, could take upon him so great a Weight, or if he did, they could not believe he would be able to support it. Moreover the Nerve of great Actions, Money, was wanting, and the *Persians* abounding with that, had dispatch'd Emissaries all over *Greece* to corrupt the People. And that nothing might be wanting to these Evils, the *Tuscan* Pirates infested and plunder'd the maritime Places of *Macedonia*. *Alexander* having therefore assembl'd his Friends, and the present State of Affairs being lay'd before them, some were of opinion, *That omitting all concern for* Greece, *he should endeavour by soft and gentle usage to keep the Barbarians in their Duty, the intestine Motions being once compos'd and quieted, he might with more ease apply himself to the settling those at a greater distance.*

But the young Prince's Magnanimity was such, as made him look upon these cautious Counsels as cowardly, and therefore disdain'd 'em. He told 'em, *he should be for ever expos'd to the Contempt of all the World, if in the beginning of his Reign he suffer'd himself to be despis'd, that the opinion he rais'd of himself at his entring upon the Government, would influence the whole course of his Life, That the Death of* Philip *was no less unexpected to the Rebels, than to himself, that therefore while they were yet in a Hurry and Confusion, and unresolv'd what Measures to take, they might easily be suppress'd, whereas the Delay of the* Macedonians *would be an Encouragement to the Authors of the Sedition, and those that were still wavering would have time to joyn the Malecontents, by which means the Danger would become greater, and the Success more doubtful, against a prepar'd and confirm'd Enemy. But now it was not so much the business of Strength, as who should be most expeditious, and prevent the other That if he shew'd himself to be afraid of 'em while single, and as yet disunited, what would become of him, when after such Signs of Tim'dity, they should with their united Forces fall all at once upon him?* Having therefore made a Speech to the People to the same purpose, he added, *That he would take care, that both his Subjects and Enemies should acknowledge, that by his Father's Death, the Name and Person only of the King was chang'd, as for Conduct and Courage, they should find the want of neither That notwithstanding some ill-minded People had taken this Opportunity to make a Disturbance, they should in a little time be punish'd according to their Deserts, if the Macedonians would but lend him the same Bravery and Arms, they had with so much Glory to themselves, and advantageous Fruits of Victory, assisted his Father with for so many Years And that they might do this with the greater Chearfulness and Alacrity, he discharg'd 'em of all Duties, except that of the War*

Fortune approv'd of the King's Counsel, and he executing each particular, with no less Vigour than he had spoke, every thing succeeded according to his Wish, for he prevented *Amyntas*, having discover'd his treasonable Practices, and he took off *Attalus* by the means of *Hecataus* and *Parmenio* Of all those that were said to have conspir'd against *Philip*, he only pardon'd *Lyncistes*, and that because he had attended him at his first entrance on the Sovereignty, and was the first that saluted him as King He put all the rest to death, being of Opinion that he provided for his own Safety, by revenging *Philip* after so severe a manner, and that thereby he should stifle the Report, that represented him as privy to his Father's Death

Their frequent falling out, had giv'n some credit to that Rumour, and *Pausanias* having made his Complaint

plaint to him, he is said to have encouraged his wicked Design, by a Verse out of a Tragedy, in which *Medea* not only threatens her Rival with Destruction, but likewise him that gave her in Marriage, and him that took her. However, he afterwards in his Answer to *Darius*'s Letter endeavour'd to cast the Odium of that Action on the *Persians*, saying, that *Philip*'s Murtherers had been corrupted with their Gold. But that he might more effectually take away all suspicion of his having been concern'd in so foul an Action, he was thinking a little before his Death, to build a magnificent Temple in honour of *Philip*. But that as well as many other things that were found in his Memorials, was neglected by his Successors.

Judging therefore that his retaining the Sovereignty of *Greece*, that *Philip* had acquir'd, would be of great Moment to facilitate the Execution of his Designs, he march'd his Army with the utmost Expedition, and broke into *Thessaly* when no body had the least Suspicion of his Motions. Some of the *Thessalians* began to raise their Spirits, and having possess'd themselves of the Streights at *Tempe*, they block'd up the way that leads thither from *Macedonia*. These Countries are separated by the celebrated Mountains *Olympus* and *Ossa*, through whose Valleys the River *Peneus* runs, and renders them delightful even to Admiration, for which it is honour'd with publick Sacrifices. It has on each side its current shady Groves, where the little Birds seem to join in a Consort from the neighbouring Trees, with the noisy Fall of the Waters. There is a narrow way that extends itself five Miles in length, being hardly broad enough for a Beast that is loaded, so that ten Men are able to defend it against any number whatever. But he made his way through those Rocks that were thought altogether impracticable, cutting the sides of Mount *Ossa* into Steps after the manner of winding Stairs; and so terrify'd the People by his wonderful Haste and Expedition, that without the least Opposition, they decreed him the same Tributes and Revenues, together with the Sovereignty of the Nation, and on the same Conditions *Philip* had enjoy'd them. He granted an Immunity of all Duties to *Pthia*, in consideration of its being the Birth-place of *Achilles*, from whom his Family deriv'd it self, and said, he made choice of that Hero for his Companion and Fellow-Soldier, in the War he was undertaking against the *Persians*.

From *Thessaly* he march'd to *Thermopylæ*, where the publick Diet of *Greece* was held. They call it the *Pylicium*. There, in the publick Assembly of States, he was created Captain General of the *Greeks* in the room of his Father, by the Appointment of the *Amphictyones*, he confirm'd the Liberty of the *Ambraciotæ*, which they had recover'd a few days before, by driving out the *Macedonian* Garrison, assuring them that he should of his own Motion have restor'd it to them, if they had not prevented his Intention. From thence he advanc'd to *Thebes* with his Army, and having overcome the Obstinacy and Stubborness of the *Bœotians* and *Athenians*, who very much oppos'd his Designs, he order'd all the *Greek* Deputies to meet him at *Corinth*. There the Decree of the *Amphictyones* was confirm'd, and he was by the common consent of all, commission'd to be Captain General of *Greece*, in the place of *Philip* his Father, and the Aids and Supplies were appointed for the *Persian* War. It happen'd that *Diogenes* liv'd in the same City, who having embrac'd a voluntary Poverty, according to the Institution of the *Cynicks*, preferr'd the Liberty and Freedom of his Mind to Riches and Cares. He was sunning himself in the

the *Craneum*, which is in the Suburbs of *Corinth*, where there is a Grove of Cypress Trees. *Alexander* being de-
...us to see him, went thither, and having granted
...a the Liberty to ask him what Favour he would, he bid the King *go a little aside, and not intercept the Sun from him.* The *Macedonian* much surprized at this unexpected Reply, could not but admire the Man, whom in that height of Prosperity he had it not in his Power to oblige, and said, *He should chuse to be* Diogenes, *if he were not* Alexander. For that Greatness of Soul which made him look down (as it were from an Eminence) on all those things, for whose sake the rest of Mankind gladly cast themselves away, did not altogether deceive the Mind of the penetrating Youth; yet being blinded with insatiable Desires, he could not plainly discover, that it was much better to want those Riches which were superfluous, than to have those that were necessary.

From *Peloponesus* he went to *Delphi* to consult *Apollo* concerning the Event of the War he had in hand. But the Virgin Priestess who pronounc'd the Destinies, or fatal Decrees, having declar'd it to be unlawful to consult the Deity for some days, he went to her himself, and taking hold of her, dragg'd her to the Temple. As she was going along, reflecting within her self, that the Custom of the Country was overcome by the King's Obstinacy. She cry'd out, *Thou art invincible, my Son.* At which Words he stopp'd her, saying, *He accepted the Omen, and that there was no Occasion for any farther Oracle.* These things being quickly dispatch'd, he return'd to his Kingdom, and with the utmost Assiduity, apply'd himself to the punishing those who had done any thing in Contempt of the *Macedonian* Majesty. Having by this time, got all things in readiness, he left *Amphypolis* in the Beginning of the Spring, and march'd against the free People of *Thrace*, and after ten Encampments, arriv'd at Mount *Hæmus*. A great Body of *Thracians* had possess'd themselves of the Top of the Mountain, with a Design to hinder the King's Passage. They had plac'd their Chariots round their Camp in the nature of an Entrenchment, intending to drive 'em against the Enemy, if they were attack'd. But *Alexander* having discover'd the Cunning of the *Barbarians*, gave Orders to his Soldiers, That upon the Chariots coming furiously against 'em, they should open to the Right and Left, and so let 'em pass by without doing any Mischief, or if they had not time for that, they should fling themselves upon the ground, covering themselves with their Bucklers, in the form of a *Tortoise*. Thus the Enemy's Stratagem became ineffectual, for a great part of the Chariots passed through the Lanes contriv'd for 'em, and those that fell among the Men, driving over the Bucklers, by the Violence of their Course, bounded over them, without having Weight enough to crush those that were under 'em, so that this Storm past over without doing any Mischief. The *Macedonians* being deliver'd from this Terror, with joyful Acclamations gave the Onset. The Archers advancing from the Right Wing, gall'd the most forward of the *Barbarians*, with their frequent Flights of Arrows. So that the *Phalanx* or *Macedonian* Foot, having gain'd the Top of the Mountain without Danger, had no sooner got firm footing but the Victory ceas'd to be doubtful, they driving and dispersing the Enemy, who was either naked or but slightly arm'd. But on the other side, that very thing that had expos'd the *Barbarians* during the Engagement, help'd them very much in their Flight, for not being loaded with

Arms,

Arms, they eafily made their Efcape, being well acquainted with the Country. Thus about fifteen Hundred of 'em being kill'd, the reft fav'd themfelves. A great number of Women and Children were taken, and confidering the Condition of the Country, the Conqueror had a confiderable Booty

Having after this manner open'd himfelf a Paffage through Mount *Hæmus*, he penetrated into the very heart of the Country of *Thrace* Among thofe People there is a Wood, confecrated to *Bacchus*, which they have a long time held in great Veneration. Here, as *Alexander* was facrificing after the Cuftom of the *Barbarians*, there arofe fuch a flame from the Wine he pour'd on the Altar, as fpread above the Roof of the Temple, and feem'd afpiring to the very Heavens. From hence, all that were prefent inferr'd, that the King's Glory was to have no other bounds Upon the Neck of this, another accident happen'd, that confirm'd the Truth of this Conjecture In the Country of the *Odryfæ*, who are a People of *Thrace*, there is a Mountain call'd *Libethrus*, and a City of the fame Name, famous for being the Place where *Orpheus* was born The King was inform'd, by thofe that pretended to have been Eye-witneffes to the thing, that his facred Statue that was made of Cyprefs wood, had fweat moft plentifully. Every body being follicitous for the Event, *Ariftander* remov'd their Fear, affuring them, that it referr'd to *Alexander*'s Exploits, which fhould make the Poets and the Mufes Sons toil and fweat, in their Compofitions which fung of thofe Exploits

The *Triballi* are a brave People that inhabit the Country that lies beyond Mount *Hæmus* *Alexander* marching againft them, *Syrmus* their King (being inform'd before hand of the *Macedonian* Expedition) had fled

fled to *Peuce*, an Island form'd by the *Ister*, there he defended himself, with the rest of what was weak, either by reason of Sex or Age, the River serving him as a Fortification: *Alexander* having but few Ships, and the Bank of the River was high and steep, and being thereby of difficult Ascent, it was easily defended by a vigilant and brave Enemy. The *Macedonians* were therefore forc'd to retire without doing any thing, and be contented with the Advantages they had gain'd some days before, for in their way hither, they had attack'd another Army of the *Triballi*, and with the loss of hardly fifty Men, had kill'd three thousand of the Enemy.

Having in vain attempted to force King *Syrmus*, he turn'd the Fury of his Arms against the *Getæ*, who had, on the other side of the River, drawn up in Order of Battle four thousand Horse, and ten thousand Foot. He enter'd upon this dangerous undertaking, not so much on the account of its Usefulness, with reference to the War, as out of a desire of Fame; that he might be able to boast, that (notwithstanding the Opposition of the fiercest Nations) he had forc'd his Passage over the largest River in *Europe*. Having therefore shipp'd off as many of the Cavalry as he could conveniently, he convey'd part of his Infantry over in little Boats, (of which there was a great number) and the rest upon Skins, contriv'd for that purpose. The *Getæ*, being struck with Terror, at the sudden and unexpected Attack of the *Macedonians*, (for the Night, and the Corn that grew very thick on the Bank of the River, had favour'd their Passage) hardly bore the first Charge of the Cavalry. But *Nicanor* was no sooner come up with the *Phalanx*, or *Macedonian* Foot, than they, with the greatest Precipitancy and Confusion, took to their Heels, making the best of

their

their Way to a Town four Miles distant from the River, and upon *Alexander*'s pursuing them closely, they carry'd off their Wives and their Children, and whatever else they could load their Horses with, and abandon'd the rest to the Conqueror.

Alexander committed this Booty to the Care of *Meleager* and *Philip*, and having demolish'd the Town, and erected Altars to *Jupiter* and *Hercules*, and to the *Ister*, on the Bank thereof, for his prosperous Passage over that River, he retir'd the same Day with his Army, having obtained a Victory without Bloodshed. Hereupon, Ambassadors came to him from the neighbouring People, as also from King *Syrmus*, with Presents of such Things as were in esteem among them. The *Germans* too, that inhabit all that Tract of Ground that lies between the Head of the *Ister* and the *Adriatick*-Gulph, sent their Ambassadors to him; for the *Ister* has its rise in *Germany*, and in the Language of the Country, is call'd the *Danube*. He admiring at the Largeness of their Bodies, and Sprightliness of their Mind, ask'd them, *What of all things they most dreaded and fear'd?* thinking with himself that they were apprehensive of his Power, and that he should extort such a Confession from 'em. But they, instead thereof, reply'd, *That they were not much afraid of any thing, unless it were, lest the Heavens should fall upon 'em; tho' at the same time, they had a value for the Friendship of brave Men* Being surpriz'd at so unexpected an Answer, he remain'd silent for some time, and then broke out in this Expression, *That the* Germans *were a haughty and arrogant People* However, as they desir'd, he contracted an Alliance with them, and granted Peace to *Syrmus* and the rest, and thinking he had gain'd Honour enough by that Expedition, he turn'd his Mind to the *Persian* War, from
which

which he propos'd to himself greater Advantages, with less Hazard and Danger. It is said, his Uncle afterwards upbraided him with that Notion, when he found the Difficulties he had to struggle with in the *Italian* War, for, complaining of the Inequality of their Lot, he said, *He had to do with Men, whereas the* Macedonian *made War against Women*.

Alexander therefore taking along with him the little Princes of *Thrace*, and all those who by reason of their Wealth or Courage were likely to cause any Innovation in his absence, under the pretence of doing them Honour, by chusing them for his Companions in the *Persian* War, he by this means took away the Heads of the Faction, who would not dare to attempt any thing without their Leaders.

As he was returning to *Macedonia* by the *Agriana* and *Paonians*, News was brought him of the Commotions in *Illyricum*. A certain Collier, whose Name was *Bardylis*, had advanc'd himself to the Dignity of King over several People in those Parts, and was become a troublesome Enemy to *Macedonia* it self, till *Philip* overcame him in a great Battle, however, he having made a shift to renew the War, *Philip* gave him a total Overthrow, and made him become his Vassal. This *Bardylis* was now dead, having liv'd to be fourscore and ten Years of Age. His Son *Clitus* thinking it a proper time to recover his Liberty, while *Alexander*'s Arms were employed against the powerful Nations beyond the *Ister*, he prevail'd with the People to revolt, making an Alliance with *Glaucias* King of those People of *Illyricum*, they call *Taulantii*. The *Autariatæ* were likewise to fall upon the *Macedonians* as they were on their March. But *Langarus* King of the *Agrians* adher'd firmly to *Alexander*'s Interest, and beg'd *he would commit the Care of*

that

that People to him, assuring him he would find them so much Employment at home, that they should no longer think of disturbing the Macedonians, *but how to defend their own.* The King having mightily commended the young Prince, and honour'd him with magnificent and noble Presents, dismiss'd him, promising him his Sister *Cyna* in Marriage, whom his Father had had by an *Illyrian* Woman, and had marry'd to *Amyntas*. The *Agrianian* was as good as his Word, but falling sick, he was prevented by Death from receiving the Reward that was promis'd him for his Services. The *Autariatæ* being thus reduc'd, *Alexander* arriv'd at *Pelium* (a Town in *Dessutetia,* situate on the River *Eordaicum*) without any Engagement. 'Tis true, they made a shew as if they desir'd to come to Action, marching out of their Fortresses with great Fury, but yet they retir'd before the Fight could begin, notwithstanding they had possess'd themselves of all the advantageous Posts which were full of Difficulty, by reason of the Woods and narrow Ways. Here the *Macedonians* beheld a dismal Spectacle, three Boys, three Girls, and three black Rams lying together in a confus'd Slaughter, the *Barbarians* having out of a cruel Superstition sacrific'd 'em to their Gods, to inspire them with Courage in the Engagement: But the incens'd Deity reveng'd the Impiety on their guilty Souls, by giving them Cowardice, instead of Courage.

The King having driven them within their own Fortifications, had resolv'd to block them up in them, by an outward Wall he intended to raise, when the next Day *Glaucias* arriv'd with a great Body of the *Taulantii:* so that laying aside all Hopes of taking the Town, he began to think of making a safe Retreat. In the mean time, *Philotas* being sent out to forage with

with the Cattle that bore the Baggage, under Convoy of Horse, *Alexander* was informed his Men were in Danger, for *Glaucias* had possess'd himself of all the Hills and Eminences round the Plain, watching all Opportunities to come to an Engagement. *Alexander* therefore leaving part of the Army in the Camp, to prevent any Sallies from the Town, march'd in all Diligence with the rest of the Troops to their Assistance, by which Means having terrify'd the *Illyrians*, he brought the Foragers safe back to the Camp. However, his March was like to be attended with many Dangers and Difficulties, for on one hand, the River, and on the other, the steep and craggy Hills so straiten'd the Way, that in several Places four Men arm'd could hardly march a-breast; and *Clitus* and *Glaucias* had posted on the Tops of the Hills, several Companies of Archers and Slingers, and a considerable Detachment of heavy-arm'd Soldiers. This made *Alexander* place two hundred Horse before the Right, and as many before the Left of the *Phalanx*, commanding them *to hold up their Spears, and on the Signal given, to present 'em to the Enemy, as if they were going to charge 'em, turning themselves sometimes to the Right, and sometimes to the Left*. By this Stratagem he kept the Enemy in suspence; and having divided his *Phalanx*, that had hastily advanc'd, and afterward reunited it again into one Corps, he at last drew it up in the Form of a Wedge, and fell furiously on the *Illyrian* Forces, who being amaz'd at the Readiness and Skill of the *Macedonians*, fled hastily towards the Town. There remain'd but few on the Top of the Mountain that the *Macedonian* Troops had already pass'd, so that having dislodg'd 'em, he with two thousand Men took Possession of the Post of the *Agrianian* Archers, intending to cover and facilitate

the

the Passage of the *Phalanx* over the River: The Enemy having observ'd this, march'd with their whole Army towards the Mountains, that those that were compleatly arm'd, having gain'd the other side of the River, they might attack the Rear, where the King himself was in Person. But the King receiv'd them with an undaunted Courage, and the *Phalanx* huzzaing at the same time, as if they design'd to repass the River to succour their Fellow-Soldiers, struck a Terror into the Enemy. The King judging how things would happen, had order'd his Troops to draw up in order of Battle, as soon as they were landed on the other side, and to extend their Left (which was nearest the River, and the Enemy) as far as they could, that they might make the greater Appearance. By which Stratagem the *Taulantii*, imagining the whole Army was ready to fall upon them, retir'd a little. *Alexander* therefore taking this Opportunity, march'd in all haste to the River, where being arriv'd, he pass'd it over with the first Body, and as the Enemy harrass'd very much those that brought up the Rear, he so dispos'd his Machines on the Bank, and play'd so furiously on the Enemy from them, that he forc'd 'em to give back. They that were already enter'd the River, plying them at the same time with their Darts and Arrows. By this means he march'd off quietly, without the Loss of one Man. Three Days after, he was inform'd, that the Enemy imagining he was fled through Fear, and looking on themselves to be out of all Danger, straggled up and down without Order, having neither Breast-work nor Trench before their Camp, nor so much as Guards or Centinels. Taking therefore with him the Arche and *Agrianians*, and that Body of *Macedonians* th Perdiccas and *Canos* commanded, he repass'd the Riv in the Night, and march'd towards them with the utmost Diligence, commanding the rest of the Army to follow him. But being apprehensive he should let slip the Opportunity, if he waited till that came up, he sent before him the light-arm'd Soldiers, then falling himself with the rest upon the Enemy, that was half asleep, and without Arms, he made a great Slaughter of 'em, took a good number Prisoners, and put the rest to flight, pursuing them as far as the Mountains of the *Taulantii*. *Clitus*, in so great a Consternation, first went to *Pelium*, but afterwards, either distrusting the Fortifications of the Place, or the Courage of his Men, setting fire to the Town, he went and liv'd in Exile among the *Taulantii*.

About this time a Rumour was spread all over *Greece* that *Alexander* was kill'd by the *Triballi*, which fill'd the Enemies of the *Macedonian* Interest with great hopes of some Revolution. And indeed it may be reckon'd none of the least Misfortunes in human Affairs, that how inconsiderable soever the Authority is, we are apt to believe those things we wish for, with as much Confidence and Assurance, as if an impertinent and ill-grounded Opinion was able to bear down even Truth it self.

Nay, there was one went so far, as to affirm, that he saw the King surrounded; and that they might the less doubt of the Truth hereof, he assur'd them, he had himself receiv'd a Wound in that Action. This being easily credited, and spread up and down, was the occasion of the greatest Calamities to the *Thebans*. For some of them that *Philip* had banish'd, being animated and encourag'd by it, did, under the Conduct of *Phænix* and *Prothytes*, basely murther the Officers of the *Macedonians*, that kept Garrison in the *Cadmea*, as they were walk'd out of that Citadel,

del, not having the least suspicion of any Treachery; and the Citizens flocking together on the specious and plausible account of delivering their Country from Oppression, besieg'd the Garrison, surrounding it with a double Rampart and Ditch, to prevent their receiving either Provisions or Succour.

This done, they sent Embassadors in a suppliant manner to all the *Greek* Towns, to entreat them that they would not refuse their Assistance to those who were so generously endeavouring to recover the Liberty they had been so unworthily depriv'd of *Demosthenes* too, out of an antient Pique to the *Macedonians*, mov'd the *Athenians* to send speedy Succours to 'em They were not however sent, because they were so surpriz'd at the unexpected Arrival of *Alexander*, that they thought it advisable to see first which way Fortune was inclin'd *Demosthenes* nevertheless sent the *Thebans* what private Assistance he could, supplying them with a great quantity of Arms at his own Expence, by the help whereof, they who had by *Philip* been depriv'd of their own, straiten'd the Garrison of *Cadmea* very much.

There was also a strong Body of *Peloponesians* got together at the *Isthmus*, to whom *Antipater* (who was Governor of *Macedonia* in the King's Absence) having dispatch'd Messengers, requiring them not to joyn with *Alexander*'s profess'd Enemies in violation of the General Decree of all *Greece*, they, notwithstanding, gave Audience to the *Theban* Embassadors The generality of the Soldiers seem'd to be mov'd with Compassion, but *Astylus* their Leader, who was an *Arcadian* by Extraction, spun out the time in Delays, not so much out of any apprehension he had, from the Difficulty of the Undertaking, as out of an avaricious Temper, hoping, that their pressing Necessities

sities requiring a speedy Succour, he should obtain from them a larger Sallary. He demanded ten Talents, but the *Thebans* not being able to make them up, those of the *Macedonian* Party offer'd him that Sum to be quiet. Thus the *Thebans* were frustrated of their hopes of any Assistance from the *Arcadians*. However, *Demosthenes* with a sum of Money prevented some other Troops of *Peloponesus* from taking up Arms against the *Thebans*, for he is said to have receiv'd three hundred Talents from the *Persians* in order to embarass *Alexander*'s Affairs as much as he could. *Alexander* receiving Advice hereof, he march'd his Army with all possible Expedition along *Bordæa* and *Elymiotis*, and the Rocks *Stymphæa* and *Pargæa*, and the seventh day after he set out from *Pelium*, he arriv'd at *Pellene* a Town in *Thessaly*. In six days more he reach'd *Bœotia*, marching to *Orchestus*, which is about six Miles distant from *Thebes*. In the mean time the *Thebans* acted with greater Courage than Prudence, as being entirely ignorant of the Enemies Transactions. They did not believe the *Macedonian* Army had yet pass'd the *Pylæ*, and as for the King's coming in Person, they were so far from giving Credit to it, that they did not scruple to assert it was another *Alexander*, the Son of *Æropus*, that now headed the Army,

The King having pitch'd his Camp near the Temple of *Iolus*, before the Gate *Prætida*, was resolv'd to give 'em leisure to repent. But they instead thereof made a Sally, and fell upon the Out Guards of the *Macedonians*, killing some, and driving the rest from their Post, and were got pretty near the Camp, when the King order'd the light-arm'd Troops to drive them back. The next day the King advanc'd his Army to the Gates that lead towards *Attica*, that he might be

ready

ready at hand to succour those that were shut up in the Cittadel, still expecting their last Resolution; and giving them to understand he was yet dispos'd to pardon them, if they did but repent of their Error. But they that were inclin'd to Peace, were over-rul'd by the Power of the Exiles, and the Interest of those who had recall'd 'em, for they being sensible there was no hopes of Safety for them, if the *Macedonians* became Masters of the Town, chose rather to be bury'd in the Ruins of their Country, than to purchase its Safety with their own Destruction.

They had also prevail'd with some of the Princes of *Bœotia* to come into their Measures. But to what degree of Folly and Madness they were arriv'd, will from hence appear, that when *Alexander* requir'd they would deliver up to him, the Authors of the Rebellion, assuring them, that two Heads should expiate the Crime of the whole City, they were so bold as to demand on their part, that *Alxander* would surrender to them *Philotas* and *Antipater*, two of the greatest Favourites the King had, and at the same time caus'd a Herald to make Proclamation, *That if any were willing to joyn with the great King* (meaning the King of *Persia*) *and the* Thebans *against the Tyrant, for the Recovery of their Liberty, they might repair to* Thebes, *as to a place of Safety*.

All this notwithstanding, *Alexander* did not give orders for the storming of the Town, but as *Ptolomeus* relates (though there are some that give another Account) *Perdiccas* (who commanded that part of the Army that fac'd the Works the Enemy had cast up, in order to block up the *Cadmean* Fort) fell furiously upon them without expecting the Signal, so that having forc'd the Works, he came to a close Engagement with them. *Amyntas* (who lay next to him) charg'd them

at

at the same time with the Troops under his Command being encourag'd by his Example, all which *Alexander* observing, and fearing the ill Success of his Men, approach'd with the main Body of the Army, and having commanded the light-arm'd Troops to succour their Companions, he remain'd with the rest before the Trenches

The Fight was obstinate, and *Perdiccas* (being desperately wounded, as he was labouring to force the inward Retrenchment) was carry'd off from the place of Action, a great many of the *Cretan* Archers, with their Leader *Eurybotas*, were destroy'd The *Thebans* press'd hard upon the *Macedonians* (who in their Fright gave way) and pursu'd 'em as they retir'd to *Alexander* Whereupon the King having drawn up the *Phalanx* in order of Battle, fell upon the Enemy, whose Troops were in Confusion and Disorder, and routed 'em

It was here that Fortune shifting the Scene, the *Thebans* were put into such a Consternation, that they had not presence of Mind enough to shut the Gates after them, through which they enter'd the Town The Garrison of the *Cadmea* sallying out at the same time, into the Streets that lay next the Citadel, produc'd such a happy Effect, that the noblest City in all *Greece* was taken the very same day it was attack'd There was no instance of Cruelty omitted in the Destruction of this unhappy Place, Men and Women were promiscuously slaughter'd, nor did Weakness and Childhood find Compassion

This inhuman Barbarity was chiefly owing to the *Phocenses*, *Plataenses*, the *Orchomeni* and the *Thespienses*, to whom the Prosperity and Wealth of *Thebes* had been, by reason of its Vicinity, very per-

nicious

nicious and prejudicial. As for the *Macedonians*, they kept themselves within the bounds of the Laws of War.

Orders were now giv'n to abstain from any farther Slaughter, there having perish'd already six thousand Men, the rest were made Prisoners, of whom thirty thousand Free Persons were sold. *Clitarchus* says, that the whole Booty amounted to four hundred and forty Talents, others will have it, that the very Captives were sold for that Sum. The *Thessali* were indebted to the *Thebans* in a hundred Talents, which Sum *Alexander* forgave them, as being his Allies. Some few, who were known to have been against the War, escap'd Captivity, as also the Priests, and those with whom the King and his Father had us'd to reside when in that Town, among the rest, *Timoclea* receiv'd as a Reward of her noble and manly Behaviour, not only her Liberty, but likewise the Honour of having her Fame celebrated to Posterity.

A certain *Thracian*, who was a Captain of Horse in *Alexander*'s Service, having offer'd Violence to this Woman, in a threatning manner ask'd her where she had hid her most valuable Effects? She being more afflicted at the loss of her Honour, than concern'd for her Riches, turn'd the Covetousness of the Barbarian into an Opportunity of Revenge, and pointing to a Well, she pretended she had secur'd therein her Jewels, and other things of Value, he presently went thither, and as he was with a greedy Curiosity looking down the Well, she tripp'd up his Heels, and push'd him into it, and flinging Stones upon him, kill'd him, he labouring in vain to get out of it, it being very deep and narrow. His Men seiz'd her, and brought her before *Alexander*, that she might be duly punish'd, for having kill'd their Officer. The King

King having ask'd her who she was, and what she was brought before him for? she, with an undaunted Countenance, reply'd, *That she was the Sister of that* Theagnis *who commanded the* Thebans, *and lost his Life for the Liberty of* Greece. *I have reveng'd the Affront that was offer'd me, by killing the Ravisher of my Honour. If you command me to suffer Death by way of Attonement, know, that to a virtuous Woman, there is nothing so despicable as Life, after her Chastity has been violated; let me then perish as soon as you please, I shall still die late enough, since I am so unhappy as to have outliv'd my Reputation and Country.* Alexander having with Attention heard her, declar'd the *Thracian* deservedly kill'd, and that he neither approv'd nor allow'd of Rapes to be committed on Gentlewomen, and those that were free-born. Having therefore spoke much in her Commendation, he gave her her Liberty, and on her Account, to all her Kindred, with the Privilege of departing to what Place she pleas'd. He also pardon'd *Pindar*'s Posterity, out of Respect to that Poet, who had made mention in his Poems, of *Alexander* the present King's Great-grand-father, and gave Orders that his House should not be burnt. For he not only lov'd the Virtue of his own Days, but also had a Veneration for the Memory of great Men, heaping Favours on their Posterity. For afterwards having, in the last Action against *Darius*, overcome that Prince, he sent part of the Booty to the *Crotoniates*, in consideration, that in *Xerxes*'s War, when all the rest of the *Greek* Colonies despair'd of *Greece*, they had sent one Galley to *Salamis*, under the Command of *Phayllus*. He likewise bestow'd several Honours and Gifts on the *Plataeans*, because their Ancestors had given their Territory to those *Greeks* that fought against *Mardonius*.

The Destruction of *Thebes* was preceded by several strange and wonderful Appearances. About three Months before *Alexander*'s coming before *Thebes*, was observ'd in the Temple of *Ceres*, call'd *Thesmophoros*, a black Cobweb, which had appear'd white about the time of the *Leuctrian* Fight, by which *Thebes* attain'd to its highest point of Glory and Prosperity; and a little before the Arrival of the *Macedonians*, the Statues in the *Forum* were seen to sweat, and dismal Cries were heard from the Lake near *Onchestus*, which, together with the fountain *Dirce*'s issuing great streams of Blood, instead of Water, might have terrify'd these obstinate People, if their Pride had not predestin'd them to their Ruin: For looking back on the Glory of their Ancestors, whose Manners they had altogether forsaken, they promis'd themselves the same good Fortune and Success, without having the same Virtue and Merit, and so hasten'd on their Destiny; for they were so foolishly rash, as with little more than an Army of ten thousand, to make head against thirty thousand Foot, and three thousand Horse, all Veteran Troops.

Alexander having made himself Master of the Place, call'd a Council of his Allies and Friends, and referr'd it to them, to consider what use should be made of it. There were amongst 'em *Phoceans*, and a great many *Bœotians*, whose ancient Discords with the *Thebans* had been very detrimental to 'em. These could not think themselves either sufficiently reveng'd, or their Safety duly provided for, if *Thebes* should be left standing, wherefore their Authority prevail'd, that the Walls and Edifices should be demolish'd; and the Territory belonging to it should be divided among the Conquerors, at the Pleasure of the King. Thus one Day took from the very middle of *Greece* this noble City, that could boast of not only having produc'd

D great

great Men, but even Gods, after it had for almost eight hundred Years from the Oracle of the Crows, been inhabited by the same People.

The *Bœotians* having been formerly driven out of their Country by the *Thracians* and *Pelasgians*, they were told by the Oracle, *That after four Ages they should recover their paternal Habitations, that in the mean time they should settle themselves where they should behold white Crows.* Being therefore come to *Arne*, a Town in *Thessaly*, and seeing some Crows that the Children had whiten'd over with Parget, they settl'd there. The Town was demolish'd at the sound of the Flute, in the same manner as *Lysander* had threescore Years before demolish'd *Athens*. However, *Alexander* gave Orders to abstain from the Temples and other sacred Buildings, being solicitous, lest through want of Care, they might also be damnify'd, being inclin'd to it (besides his own natural Veneration for the Gods) by the sad Example that had been made of some Soldiers, who attempted to pillage the Temple of the *Cabiri* that stood before the Town, who, while they were employ'd in this prophane and impious Work, were consum'd by a sudden Storm of Thunder and Lightning. The Images and the Statues of the Gods, as well as those of Men renown'd for their Virtue, were also left untouch'd in the publick Places where they stood, and it is recorded, that in the Consternation and Fright People were in, upon the taking and plundering the City, some had hid their Gold in the Folds and Plaits of the Garments of those Statues, and found it safe, when *Cassander*, *Antipater*'s Son, twenty Years after rebuilt the Town, which he is thought to have done, not so much out of Compassion to the Exiles as out of Hatred to *Alexander*, thinking to lessen his Glory by that Action. But notwithstanding he restor'd it.

the former Compass of its Walls, yet he could not restore its ancient Manners and Prosperity, so that it never could recover its primitive Strength, but being frequently afflicted with Calamities, it has with Difficulty preserv'd to our Days the Appearance of a small inconsiderable Town. It is said that *Alexander* afterwards repented what he had done, when he reflected, that by the Destruction of *Thebes*, he had put out one of the Eyes of *Greece*. It is also said, he look'd upon the Death of *Clitus*, and the Obstinacy of the *Macedonians*, who cowardly refus'd to penetrate any farther into the *Indies*, as a vindictive Judgment of *Bacchus* upon him, for having ruin'd and destroy'd the Place of his Birth, nay, some did not scruple to say, that the King's Death that proceeded from an Excess of Wine, was also a Punishment inflicted on him by the Resentments of that Deity.

These things being finish'd, he sent to *Athens*, to let the People know, *that he requir'd they would deliver up to him those Orators, that were perpetually stirring them up against the* Macedonians, *and that if they were unwilling to part with them, they must expect the same Reward of their Contumacy, as they might view in a late Instance of the Miseries of the* Thebans. Upon this, *Phocion*, (who was in great Esteem with the People, on the account of the Integrity of his Life) representing, *that it was not advisable to irritate and provoke the Mind of the young victorious King*, and that he exhorted those whom the Danger particularly threaten'd *that in imitation of the Daughters of* Leus *and* Hyacinthus, *they would not scruple to lay down their Lives for the Good of their Country*. *Demosthenes*, who was by name demanded, now rose up, and inform'd them, That the *Athenians* were *mistaken, if they imagin'd, that by the surrender of a few, they should pro-*

cure Safety to themselves; that on the contrary, the Macedonians *cunningly requir'd those Persons from 'em, whose Vigilance and Virtue they most suspected and hated, and that having remov'd the Patrons and Protectors of the publick Liberty, they would afterward fall upon the defenceless and destitute City, as Wolves do upon the Sheep, when their Guardian Dogs are remov'd.*

Demosthenes had shewn himself a bitter Enemy of the *Macedonians*, and therefore very reasonably concluded, there was not the least room left him to hope for Mercy. For *Philip* being kill'd, he mov'd the *Athenians* to build a Chappel in Honour of *Pausanias*, that publick Thanksgivings might be made in the Temples of the Gods, and that all the other usual Marks of great Joy might be express'd, calling *Alexander* sometimes a Child, and sometimes the *Margite*, a word of contempt, that meant his prodigious Folly and Madness. And being corrupted by the *Persian* Gold, he had been the Incendiary and Promoter of almost all the Wars the *Greeks* had made with *Alexander*, and *Philip* his Father.

He had beside excited *Attalus* (who was *Alexander*'s bitterest Enemy) to declare open War against the King, promising him the Assistance of the *Athenians*. And the *Athenians* had not offended a little, having cast down *Philip*'s Statues, and converting the Materials to the most scandalous uses, committing besides all the other Indignities the ignorant Rabble (who have no concern for the future) are apt to be guilty of, when instigated by the Direction and Management of a few. But of all their Transgressions, none offended the King so much, as the Humanity and Compassion they express'd for the *Thebans*, whom they had contrary to his Edict receiv'd, when they made their escape from the Ruins of their Country; shewing so great a Concern for their Misfortunes, as to put off the Solemnity of the Mysteries they were wont to celebrate with the greatest Devotion every Year in honour of *Bacchus*, merely on the account of this publick Calamity. But out of his strong Inclination to the *Persian* War, he chose rather to forgive the *Greeks* their Injuries, than to punish them.

Wherefore *Demades* (who had been in great favour with *Philip*) having presented to him the humble Intercessions of the City, he granted to the *Athenians*, that they should keep *Demosthenes*, *Lycurgus*, and the others he had requir'd of 'em, provided they did but banish *Charidemus*. Hereupon *Charidemus* went over to the *Persians*, and did them great Service, 'till giving his Tongue too great a Liberty, he was kill'd by *Darius*'s Order. Many other considerable Persons, out of Hatred to the King, left the City, and repair'd to his Enemies, and gave the *Macedonians* a great deal of trouble. After so great a tide of Success, there was no Power left in *Greece*, that reflecting on the *Theban* Victory (whose heavy arm'd Soldiers were formerly in great esteem) or on the taking of *Leucadia*, could repose any confidence, either in their own Strength, or that of any Fortifications, for he reduc'd the *Leucadians* (who were elated and arrogant, on the account of the strong situation of their Town, and the great quantity of Stores and Provisions they had laid in for a long Siege) by Famine, first making himself master of all the Forts and Castles round it, and giving to those he found therein, Liberty to go into *Leucadia*, by which means the People daily increasing in multitude, soon emptied their Magazines. Ambassadors, were therefore sent him from

from *Peloponnesus*, to congratulate him on his having, according to his desire, finish'd the War against the *Barbarians*, and chastis'd the Insolence and Temerity of some of the *Greeks*.

The *Arcadians*, who had been in motion, preparing to assist the *Thebans*, gave him to understand they had pass'd Sentence of Death on those Leaders who had been the cause of their extravagant Proceedings. The *Eleı* acquainted him likewise that they recall'd those they had banish'd, out of this consideration only, that *Alexander* had a Kindness for them. And the *Ætoli* excus'd themselves, that in so general a Disturbance of *Greece*, they had not been free from some evil Practices. The *Megareans* caus'd the King and those about him to laugh, by the new kind of Honour they pretended to confer upon him, telling him, *That in consideration of his good disposition and favours to the* Greeks, *the* Megareans *had by a Decree of the People, made him free of their City*. But being afterwards inform'd, that to that very day they had not bestow'd that Honour on any except *Hercules*, he graciously accepted of it. To the others he made answer, *That he had nothing more at heart than the Quiet and Safety of* Greece, *and that provided they refrain'd making any disturbance for the time to come, he readily forgave them what was past*. However, he very much distrusted the *Spartans*, and therefore restor'd the Sons of *Philias* to *Messene*, from whence they had been driven, he gave also to *Charon* the Government of *Pelene*, a Town belonging to the *Achæans*, and put *Sicyon* and other Towns of *Peloponnesus* into the hands of his Friends and Dependents, that they might have an Eye uppon the Counsels and Deportment of the *Lacedæmonians*.

A

A few Months suffic'd him for the performance of so many great and weighty things, in which he put an end to so difficult and doubtful a War, with more ease than another could in that time have been prepar'd for it. He acknowledg'd he ow'd his Conquest to Expedition and Celerity, telling one that ask'd him by what means he chiefly subdu'd *Greece?* *That it was by delaying nothing.*

The Second Book of *John Freinshemius*'s Supplement TO Quintus Curtius.

CHAP. I.

DARIUS was King of *Persia* at that Time, having been rais'd to that Dignity by the Interest of *Bagoas* the Eunuch, a little before the Death of *Philip*. King *Ochus* and his Son *Arses* being dead, and all that Line utterly extinct, *Bagoas* thought it advisable to make a friendly Present of that Empire, which he could not keep himself, judging he should for ever be sure of the Favour of him he should so highly oblige. At the same time *Darius* was not look'd upon by the People to be unworthy of that high Station, he not being altogether a Stranger to the Royal Family. For *Ostanes*, *Ochus*'s Uncle, had for his Son *Arsanes*, who was Father

ther to *Codomannus*, this being *Darius*'s Name, while a private Person. But after he was seated in *Cyrus*'s Throne, according to the Custom of the *Persians*, he laid aside his former Name, and took that of *Darius*. He had also distinguish'd himself in the Army, having kill'd his Adversary upon a Challenge, during the War *Ochus* was engag'd in against the *Cadusii*, and thereby establish'd a great opinion of his Bravery and Courage. He was the tenth from *Cyrus* (who founded that Empire) who recover'd *Persia*. For *Ochus* succeeded *Artaxerxes* his Father, who had succeeded *Darius*. To this, *Artaxerxes* the Son of *Xexes* left the Kingdom. *Xerxes* succeeded his Father *Darius*, who was the Son of *Hystaspes*, and who (when *Cyrus*'s Line was extinct by the Death of *Cambyses*) in the famous Conspiracy of seven *Persians*, wrested the Empire from the *Magi*. Under these Kings the *Persian* Affairs flourish'd in an un-exampled state of Prosperity, for the space of two hundred and almost thirty Years, having had a noble and brave beginning, while the Nation, no way addicted to Pleasure and Voluptuousness, fought gallantly for Liberty, Glory, and Riches. In process of time, when they had reap'd the advantageous Fruits of their Virtue, they at length neglected the thing it self, and ow'd their Safety not so much to their own Strength and Bravery, as to the Reputation of the Power their Ancestors had acquir'd, and their Riches, with which however they were not much less successful against the *Greeks* than with their Arms.

At last then, when they found their Gold ineffectually oppofed to the Power of *Alexander*, and that upon the Removal of all other Foreign Means of Assistance, they were now to depend upon themselves, so debauched were their Minds, their Spirits so broken and soften'd to so low a degree of Effeminacy, that they could not support themselves under the first shock of their declining Fortune. *For Poverty sharpens Industry; whereas Luxury and Idleness are the Effects of Affluence and Plenty.* Being, however, inform'd of the Death of *Philip*, (whose Success and Preparations alarm'd and terrify'd 'em) they were freed from their Fears, and despis'd *Alexander*'s Youth, who they imagin'd would be well enough satisfy'd, if he might walk up and down unmolested at *Pella*. But receiving every Day fresh Intelligences of his Wars and Victories, they began very much to dread the Youth they before contemn'd, and accordingly, with great Care and Diligence, prepar'd themselves for a vigorous and long War. And having in their former Wars found by Experience, that the *Asiatick* Troops were not a Match for the *Europeans*, they sent proper Persons into *Greece*, to hire into their Service Fifty thousand Men, the Flower of the Youth of that Country. *Memnon* the *Rhodian* was appointed to command these Forces, he having on several Occasions given the *Persians* Proof of his Fidelity and Bravery. He was order'd to make himself Master of *Cyzicum*, marching therefore in great diligence through that part of *Phrygia* that joins to the *Trojan* Territory, he came to Mount *Ida*, which declares the Nature of its Situation by its Name, for the Ancients us'd to call all Places which were planted thick with Trees, *Ida's* This Mountain rises higher than any of the rest that are near the *Hellespont*. In the middle of it there is a Cave much celebrated in Fables, out of a religious Horror, for it is said, the *Trojan* here pass'd his judgment on the Beauty of the Goddesses, when having been expos'd by his Father's Command, he was educated to Manhood upon this Mountain. It is said also to

have

have been the Birth-place of the *Idæan Dactyles*, who by the Inſtruction of *Cybele*, or the Great Mother, found out the various Uſes of Iron, it being no leſs uſeful and beneficial to us, when our Occaſions require it, or our Labours, than pernicious, when it is the cruel Inſtrument of our Anger and Rage. There is another thing worthy Admiration, reported of it, *viz.* That when the Winds, at the riſe of the *Dog-ſtar*, ruffle and diſturb the lower Parts, the Air in the top of Mount *Ida* is calm and quiet. As alſo, that while there is yet a great part of the Night hovering over the Earth, the Sun is there to be ſeen, not in the Figure of a Globe or Round, but extended in a large Breadth, and embracing both ſides of the Mountain, as it were with diſtinct Bodies of Fire, till by degrees it unites again, and becomes one, and that at the approach of the Light, it does not take up a greater ſpace than that of an Acre of Ground, and contracting itſelf a little after into its uſual Compaſs, it performs its appointed Courſe. As for my part, I am of Opinion, that this falſe Miracle appears to our Eyes, when the imperfect Image of the Riſing Sun ſpreads itſelf through the Air that is condens'd by the Nocturnal Cold, and no way ſhaken or divided by the Wind, 'till the Sun thawing and diſſipating it by degrees, gives the Eye a free Paſſage to the Orb of this Planet. For then the Air is pure and ſerene, and the Rays of the Sun are eaſily tranſmitted through it, whereas when it is condens'd, it obſtructs and ſtops them, and as if they fell upon a Looking-glaſs, it diſperſes 'em with an encreaſe of Splendor and Brightneſs.

The Territory of *Cyzicum* extends itſelf from the foot of Mount *Ida* to *Propontis*. The Town is ſituate in an Iſland of a moderate compaſs, being join'd join'd to the Continent by two Bridges But *Alexander* undertook the Work some time after, and was upon the Sea when *Memnon* undertook his Expedition. *Memnon* having, by his unexpected Attempt, in vain terrify'd the *Cyzikians*, (the Inhabitants making a vigorous Resistance, and defending themselves gallantly) was forc'd to retire, having first plunder'd the Country round about it, and carry'd off a considerable Booty All this while the *Macedonian* Generals were not idle, for *Parmenio* took *Grynium* a Town in *Æolia*, and made Slaves of the Inhabitants. After which, passing the River *Caicus*, he lay down before *Pitane*, a rich and wealthy Place, having two convenient Ports, whereby it could receive Relief from *Europe*, but, upon the seasonable arrival of *Memnon*, he was forc'd to raise the Siege Calas, with a small number of *Macedonians*, and some hir'd Troops, carry'd the War into the Country of *Troy*, and came to an Engagement with the *Persians*, but finding he was not a Match for their Multitude, he retir'd to *Rhœtium*.

CHAP. II.

IN the mean time, *Alexander* having settled the Affairs of *Greece*, and being return'd to *Macedon*, was deliberating with his Friends about those Things he ought to provide against, and about those he ought to execute, before he enter'd upon so great a War. *Antipater* and *Parmenio*, who were the chief amongst 'em, both for their Age and Quality, earnestly begg'd of him, *that he would not in one Person expose the Welfare*

Welfare and *Prosperity of the whole Empire to the treacherous Uncertainties of Fortune, but would first marry, and get Children, and having by that means provided for the Safety of his Country, afterwards apply himself to the enlarging his Dominions.* The reason of which Advice was, that there was at this time only *Alexander* left of *Philip*'s Blood, that was worthy of the Empire, *Olympias* having destroy'd all *Cleopatra*'s Issue: And *Aridæus*, on the account of the mean Extraction of his Mother, and the Disturbance of his Mind, was look'd upon as one that would not become the *Macedonian* Sceptre. However, *Alexander* being of a restless Temper, could think of nothing but War, and the Glory that results from Victory, wherefore he reply'd in this manner. *Like Men of Probity, and good Patriots, you are not without Cause solicitous about the thing that may either benefit or damnifie your Country. No body can deny but it is a hard and difficult Task we are undertaking; which if we rashly attempt, and the Event should not answer Expectation, a late Repentance could make no Amends. For it is our Business, before we hoist our Sails, to consult, whether it be adviseable to undertake the Voyage, or keep quiet at Home. But when we have once committed ourselves to the Winds and the Waves, we are altogether at their Mercy. I therefore do not take it ill, that you differ from my Opinion; on the contrary, I commend your Sincerity, and desire you will shew the same Integrity with reference to those Matters that shall hereafter become the Subjects of our Debates. They, who are really their King's Friends, if there be any worthy that Title, in their Advice, do not so much consider how to procure his Favour, as how to promote their Interest and their Glory. He that advises any otherwise than he would act himself, is so far from instructing him that consults him, that*

he

he imposes upon him, and deserves him. Now that I may lay my own Opinion open to you, I am satisfy'd, that nothing is less conducive to the Interest of my Affairs, than Delay. After having curb'd all the Barbarians in the Neighbourhood of Macedon, and quieted the Commotions of Greece, shall we suffer a brave and victorious Army to waste away in Ease and Idleness, or lead it into the wealthy Provinces of Asia, which they have already taken Possession of in Hopes, desiring the Spoils of the Persians, as a Reward of those Labours they have gone through in their long Service under my Father, and for these three Years past under our Command? Darius is but lately come to the Crown, and by his putting Bagoas to Death, by whose means he obtain'd it, has giv'n his People a Suspicion of his being both cruel and ungrateful, which Vices are apt to cause an Aversion in the best Subjects against their Rulers, and to render 'em less ready to Obey, if not altogether Refractory. Shall we sit still then till he has confirm'd his Authority, and having settl'd his Affairs at home, of his own accord, translates the War into Macedon? There are great Advantages to be reap'd from Celerity and Dispatch, which, if we lye still, will accrue to the Enemy.

The first Inclination of the Mind, is of great Moment in things of this nature, now that is always ready for them that lay hold of it. For no Body by delay, courts the Reputation of being strongest and bravest. But he is esteem'd the strongest and bravest, that declares and carries abroad the War, and not he that receives it at home. Besides, how much shall we hazard our Reputation, if we deceive the Hopes of them, who, notwithstanding our Youth, have thought us worthy of that Honour that our Father, who was a Great Captain, and had given so many Proofs of his Bravery and Conduct, did not yet receive till a little before his Death? Nor did

the

the Council of Greece decree us the Sovereign Command, that we should live idly in Macedon, minding nothing but our Pleasures, without the least Concern for former Injuries and those that have of late been offer'd to the Grecian Name: But that we should revenge and punish these Insolencies, which the Extravagance of their Pride has induced them to offer with such an Air of Boldness and Arrogance What shall I say of those Greek Nations, that being scattered up and down Asia, are oppress'd by the insupportable Slavery of the licentious Barbarians? It were needless to represent to you with what Prayers and Arguments Delius the Ephesian pleaded their Cause, since it is still fresh in your Memories. This is however certain, that the very Moment they behold our Standards, they will immediately repair to us, and readily embrace the greatest of Dangers, for the sake of their Deliverers and Protectors, against their unjust, cruel, and inhuman Masters But why, as if we had forgot our selves and our Enemies, should we look about for Assistance and Succour against a People, which to be slow in conquering, would redound more to our Shame than Glory? In our Father's Time, a small Body of Lacedæmonians having march'd into Asia, were in vain oppos'd by vast Armies of the Enemy, who suffer'd Phrygia, Lydia, and Paphlagonia, to be harrass'd and plunder'd, or if they offer'd to hinder or oppose it, they were beaten and slain, even to the tiring their Enemies with their Slaughter, till Agesilaus being call'd away with the Troops under his Command, on the account of some Commotions in Greece, gave 'em (when they were in the greatest Confusion, and altogether uncertain what measures to take) sufficient Time to recover themselves from their Fright. A few Years before him, scarce ten thousand Grecians, without Leaders, and without Provisions, open'd themselves a Passage with their Sword,

through

through so many Nations of Enemies, even to the Heart of the Persian Empire, though they were pursu'd at the same Time by the King's whole Army, with which he had lately disputed the Crown with his Brother Cyrus, and conquer'd him, and yet whenever they came to an Engagement, this victorious Army was always beaten by the Greeks, and put to flight Shall we then, after we have overcome Greece in so many Victories, and brought it under our Obedience, having either kill'd the bravest amongst 'em, or got 'em in our Camp, Shall we, I say, be afraid of Asia, when a few of those whom we have beaten, have given it so many shameful Defeats?

After this, he said a great deal more to the same Purpose, by which he so mov'd the Minds of his Hearers, that they all came into his Opinion, nay, *Parmenio* himself, who stickl'd most to have the War delay'd, was now for having it enter'd upon with all speed, and even made pressing Speeches to *Alexander* on that account. Wherefore making it his whole Business to get every thing in readiness for his March, he offer'd a solemn Sacrifice to *Jupiter* the *Olympian*, at *Dium* a Town in *Macedon*. This Sacrifice was originally instituted by *Archelaus*, who reign'd after *Perdiccas*, the Son of *Alexander*. He also had Stage-Plays in Honour of the Muses, which lasted nine Days, according to the Number of those Goddesses After this, he gave a magnificent Entertainment, in a Tent that held a hundred Beds, there he feasted with his Friends, his Generals, and the Deputies of the Towns; he order'd likewise, that Part of the Victims should be distributed among the Soldiers with other Provisions, that this Day, which was dedicated to Mirth, might be celebrated with all Entertainments, and lucky Omens of the future War

CHAP.

CHAP. III.

IN the beginning of the Spring, having gather'd his Forces together, he pass'd into *Asia*, the Strength of his Army consisted more in its Courage and Bravery, than in its Number of Men. *Parmenio* led thirty thousand Foot, of which there were thirteen thousand *Macedonians*, the rest were Troops sent by the Confederates. These were follow'd by five thousand others, made up of *Illyrians*, *Thracians*, and the *Triballi*, to which were added a thousand *Agrianian* Archers. *Philotas* had the Command of the *Macedonian* Horse that consisted of one thousand eight hundred. *Calas* headed the like Number of *Thessalians*. The rest of *Greece* sent only six hundred Horse, which he gave the Command of to *Erigyus*. *Cassander* commanded the Van, which consisted of nine hundred *Thracians* and *Pæonians*. With this Army, having only thirty Days Provision, he ventur'd to make Head against an infinite Number of *Barbarians*, relying on the Strength and Bravery of his Men, who being grown old in a continu'd Series of Victories, were by their Courage and skilful Use of their Arms, more than a Match for any Number of Enemies whatever. He entrusted the Government of *Macedonia* and *Greece* with *Antipater*, leaving him twelve thousand Foot and fifteen hundred Horse, giving him withal this Charge, to make constant Levies to recruit his Army, and supply the Consumption of War, and the necessary Decays of Mortality. This was the only thing he had reserv'd to himself, when he divided the rest amongst

his

his Friends. For before he took shipping, he had distributed among 'em all that he could, without impairing the Majesty of Regal Dignity. *Perdiccas* refus'd the Lands that were offer'd him, and desir'd the King to tell him, what he would have left for himself? To which the King answer'd, *Hopes. Why then*, reply'd he, *we shall partake of them, since we fight under your Conduct and Fortune*. There were a few that imitated him, the rest accepted his Gifts. *Alexander* being again asked, *Where his Treasures were now?* answer'd, *in the Hands of his Friends*. And indeed, as he had flung himself upon Fortune, and staked his All upon the Hazard of her Dice, he did not seem to have misplac'd his Riches. For as by conquering he stood fair for greater, so if he were overcome, he could expect no less than to lose those he had; in the mean time, he was sure of being serv'd with greater Cheerfulness and Alacrity. And as for the present Necessities, they did not suffer much by the Grants he had made of his Lands, Manors, and Revenues, whose Time of Payment was still remote. As for the Money, it was set apart for the Use of the War, and was with so much the greater Care husbanded in the Dispensation, by how much it was less in Quantity. For when *Philip* was kill'd, there was hardly threescore Talents of coin'd Money in the Exchequer, and a few Silver and Golden Vessels. Whereas the Debts at that Time, amounted to five hundred Talents. And notwithstanding he had very much augmented the *Macedonian* Power and Interest, and so far improv'd the Golden Mines near *Crenides* (which he call'd *Philippos*) that he drew from thence the yearly Income of a thousand Talents, yet by reason of his continual Wars, and the large Presents he made, the Treasury was quite exhausted. He had besides, laid out vast Sums in repairing and

adorning

adorning *Macedonia*, which he found in a very poor and low Condition. A great many could remember, that at his coming to the Crown, he was but in indifferent Circumstances, insomuch that he us'd to lay under his Pillow, every Night when he went to Bed, a Gold Cup which he had, that weigh'd about fifty Drachma's. And yet this Man's Son ventur'd to attack the King of *Persia*, who had five thousand Talents of Gold for his Pillow, and three thousand Talents of Silver for his Footstool, plac'd under the Head and Feet of his Bed, in proper Repositories, altho' he had added to his Father's Debts eight hundred Talents, which he had taken up upon Loan, of which there hardly remain'd the tenth Part. He is said to have set out, *Timotheus* playing on the Flute, and the Army expressing the greatest Cheerfulness imaginable, as having already engross'd in their Thoughts, all the Wealth and Riches of the *Barbarians* they were going to fight against. After this manner he was carry'd to the *Strymon*, through a Lake call'd *Circinites*, (from a neighbouring Mountain) where he had a Fleet. He came first to *Amphipolis*, from whence he proceeded to the Mouth of the *Strymon*, which having pass'd, he march'd by the side of the Mountain *Pangæus*, and struck into the Way that leads to *Abdera* and *Maronea*. He on purpose march'd along the Shore, that he might be ready to assist his Fleet that sail'd by him, in case the *Persians* should attack it, for they were at that Time also Masters at Sea, and he had but a moderate Fleet. Whereas the Enemy had Ships from *Cyprus* and *Phenicia*, and Mariners harden'd to Sea-affairs, and very experienc'd Rowers. For the *Macedonians* having but lately attempted the Sovereignty of the Sea, did not abound with Ships, and the Allies furnish'd 'em but sparingly, and as it were against

their

their Will. Even the *Athenians*, when they were requir'd to send in their Gallies, sent but twenty Their Orators persuading 'em that it was dangerous, lest upon its Arrival, it should be employ'd against those who had sent it

From hence he march'd to the River *Hebrus* which having pass'd without much Difficulty, he came into *Patica*, a Country in *Thrace*, from thence passing over the River *Melas*, on the twentieth Day from his setting out, he arriv'd at *Sestus*, a Town situate in the Extremity of the Continent, and looking into the *Hellespont*, where the Sea contracting it self into several Windings, divides *Asia* from *Europe*, for *Macedon* is join'd to *Thrace*, which extending itself to the Eastward in two Points, would reach *Asia* if it were not separated from it by the Sea, on the right hand the *Hellespont* hinders it, and farther on the *Bosphorus*, sirnam'd the *Thracian*, divides *Byzantium* from *Chalcedon*. *Propontis* that is contracted between these Streights, enlarges its Channel near the Countries of *Bithynia* and *Pontus*. Below *Bithynia* lies *Mysia*, and then *Phrygia*, and *Lydia* that joins to that, are more remote from the Sea, the more inward Provinces that are very spacious and large, and celebrated for their Fertility and Riches, are inhabited by several Nations. The Coasts that face *Thrace* and *Greece* are possess'd by the *Hellespontins*, and farther on by the *Trojans*, famous for their Misfortunes and Calamities Beneath these *Æolis* and *Ionia*, in a long Extent of Shore, stretch themselves out on the Borders of *Lydia* In the next Place is *Caria* that joins to the Country of *Doris*, and is in a great measure encompass'd with the Sea, and the Inland Parts of which are of a large Extent Near these Territories are the noble Islands, the *Æolic Lesbus*, the *Ionian Chius* and *Samus*, and the

Doric

Doric Rhodus, and several others whose Names are celebrated in the Writings of the *Greeks*. For formerly the *Greeks* had Colonies in these Places, which were still remaining, but when they became subject to the King of *Persia*, and his Governors, they lost their antient Liberty, and became Slaves. *Alexander* being arriv'd at *Sestus*, order'd the greatest Part of his Army to repair to *Abydus*, seated on the opposite Shore, under the Conduct of *Parmenio*, with whom he left for this purpose, a hundred and threescore Gallies, besides several Ships of Burthen while he with the rest went to *Eleunte*, which is dedicated to *Protesilaus*, whose Grave is there, with a Tomb erected to his Memory. The Tomb is encompass'd with a great many Elms, which are of a wonderful Nature, for the Leaves that put out in the Morning, on those Branches that look towards *Huim*, fall immediately, while the others retain a lasting Verdure. It is thought that they hereby express the untimely Fate of the Hero, who being in the Flower of his Age, when he accompany'd the *Greeks* in their *Asian* Expedition, fell the first Victim of the *Trojan* War. *Alexander* therefore paying him the Rites of the Dead, implor'd that he might be attended with better Fortune when he landed on the Enemies Shore. From hence he went to *Sigeum* taking with him fifty Gallies, and beheld that Haven that was become remarkable by the *Greeks* putting in there with their Fleet in the *Trojan* War. When he was in the middle of the *Hellespont* (for he himself was Pilot of his own Ship) he sacrific'd a Bull to *Neptune* and the *Nereias*, flinging the golden Vessel (out of which he had made the Libation) into the Sea, as a Present to the Deities of the Sea. The Fleet being come into the Harbour, the King casting a Dart upon the Shore, leap'd out of the Ship, and was

the

the first who landed, protesting at the same time, *that with the Assistance of the Gods, he propos'd by a just War to make himself Master of* Asia. He afterwards erected Altars in the Place where he made his Descent, to *Jupiter*, *Minerva* and *Hercules*. he also order'd Altars to be built in that Place of *Europe* from whence he set out.

CHAP. IV.

FROM hence he proceeded on to the Plains, where he was shew'd the Seat of the antient *Troy*. Here, while he was examining curiously the Monuments of the Works of the Heroes, one of the Inhabitants promis'd him *Paris*'s Harp. To whom he made Answer, *That he did not set any Value on the mean Instrument of effeminate Pleasures. But give me, if you can, that of* Achilles, *on which he us'd to celebrate the Praises of the Heroes, with the same Hand, with which he surpass'd their Atchievements.* For he was a great Admirer of *Achilles*, valuing himself for being descended from him; he therefore with his Friends run naked round his Tomb, and anointed it with Oil, and adorn'd it with a Crown. *Hephæstion* likewise put a Crown upon that of *Patroclus*, hinting thereby that he held the same Rank in *Alexander*'s Favour, that the other did in *Achilles*'s. Among the various Discourses they had concerning *Achilles*, the King said, he look'd upon him to have been doubly happy, for having had, while living, a true and faithful Friend, and when dead, a good Poet to celebrate his Actions. He also sacrific'd to the other Heroes whose Tombs are to be seen in those

Countries.

Countries He offer'd Sacrifices likewise to *Priamus*, on *Hereius*'s Altar, either to appease his Ghost, as having being kill'd by *Achilles*'s Son, or else on the account of the Relation he thought there was between him and the *Trojans*, since *Neoptolemus* married *Andromache*, *Hector*'s Widow. He with great Devotion sacrific'd to *Minerva*, for whom he had a particular Veneration; and hanging up his Arms in the Temple, he took down others that were said to have been there, ever since the time of the *Trojan* War. These he caus'd to be bore before him, as if they were lent him by the favour of the Deity, to conquer and subdue *Asia*; and it is said he actually had them on, when he fought the *Persian* Generals near the *Granicum*. Otherwise he took great Delight in fine Arms, being in nothing so nice as in them. I find him to have made use of a Buckler that was very bright, and that his Head-piece was finely set off with a Tuft of Feathers, that fell down on each side, and were remarkable for their extreme Whiteness and Largeness. It is true his Headpiece was of Iron, but then it was so neatly polish'd that it look'd like Silver, and was the Work of *Theophilus*. His Collar was also of Iron, but it was curiously adorn'd with precious Stones that cast a glorious Lustre. His Sword was remarkable both for its Edge and Temper; and it was the more valuable for this, that notwithstanding its Strength, it was light and easily handled. Over this Armour he would sometimes wear a military Sur-tout of that kind that was then call'd the *Sicilian* Fashion. Some of these Arms he had not till afterwards; as for instance, the Breastplate, which we mentioned, was found amongst the Spoils after the Battel near *Issus*; the Sword was presented him by the King of the *Cities*, a People of *Cyprus*. The *Rhodians* made him a Present of his Belt, which

which was wrought with incomparable Art, by *Helicon* that famous Artificer. We are not asham'd to relate these Particulars which have deservedly found Place in the Works of ancient Authors, besides the Sayings and Actions of great Kings, how minute and light soever they may be, are reflected on, with both Profit and Pleasure. It is most certain that the Arms of *Alexander* were held in great esteem by following Ages, nay Time it self, that general Destroyer, seem'd to shew a respect to them, for one of the *Roman* Generals, after the Conquest of the *Pontick* Kingdoms, wore his Cloak at the Solemnity of his Triumph, another having put on his Breast-plate, run up and down the Bridge he had made over the Sea, in Imitation of *Darius* and *Xerxes*. *Alexander* march'd from the Temple of *Minerva* to *Arisbe*, where the *Macedonians*, that *Parmenio* commanded, were encamp'd.

The next day he pass'd by the Towns *Percote* and *Lampasceus*, and came to the River *Practius*, which rising out of the *Idæan* Mountains, runs through the Territories of *Lampascus* and *Abydus*, and then winding a little to the Northward, empties itself into *Propontis*. From thence passing by *Hermotus*, he march'd to *Colone*, a Town situate in the middle of the *Lampsacenian* Territory. Having taken all these into his Protection, upon their Submission to him (for he had pardon'd the *Lamsacemans*) he sent *Penegorus* to take Possession of the Town of the *Priapeus*, which the Inhabitants surrender'd to him. Then he order'd *Amyntas*, who was the Son of *Arrabeus*, to take four Troops, (whereof one consisted of *Apolloniates*, and was commanded by *Socrates*) and go upon the Scout in order to get Intelligence of the Enemy, who was not now far off, and was making all the Preparations possible for the War. Among them *Memnon*, for Skill in military matters, far exceeded the rest. He endeavour'd to persuade them, *To destroy every thing all round about them that could be of any use to the Enemy, and then retire farther into the Country, to cause the Cavalry to trample down and waste all the Grass, to burn all the Villages and Towns, leaving nothing behind 'em but the bare, naked Land.* That the Macedonians had hardly a Month's Provision, and they would afterwards be necessitated to live upon Plunder, now if that means of subsisting were remov'd, they would in a little time be forc'd to retire, so that all Asia wou'd be safe at a cheap rate. It was true, that there was something very dismal in his Advice, But on all occasions, where Dangers were impending, wise Men made it their Business to get off with as little Damage as they could. Thus the Physicians, if one part of the Body be seiz'd with a Distemper, which is likely to spread into other parts, they lop it off, and so with the Loss of a Limb, secure the Health of the rest of the Body. That the Persians would not do this without a Precedent. For Darius had formerly destroy'd all these Countries, lest the Scythians in their Passage through them, should find Accommodation. If they came to a Battle, all would be at stake, and if the Persians were beat, all that Country would fall into Alexander's hands; whereas, if they got the better, they would be still but where they then were. That indeed there was no small Danger from the Macedonian Phalanx, that the Persian Foot, tho' much more numerous, would not be able to resist it. Besides, the King's being present would not contribute a little to the gaining of the Victory, since the Soldiers fighting in the Presence of their General, would be spurr'd on with Hope, Shame, and Glory at the same time, all which advantages the Macedonians had, while Darius was absent from them. Besides, no body doubted but that it was much better to make War in a foreign

E   *Country*

Country than in ones own, that they would be sure of that Advantage, if they follow'd his Advice and invaded Macedon.

But this Speech did not please any of the other Generals. They said, *Perhaps this might seem proper to* Memnon *the* Rhodian, *who would find a Benefit by protracting the War, since he would thereby enjoy his Honours and Salaries so much the longer, but it would be a foul Disgrace to the* Persians *to betray the People that were committed to their Trust and Care, and that they could not answer it to the King, whose Instructions to them laid down a very different Scheme for the Prosecution of the War.* For *Darius* being inform'd of *Alexander*'s Motion, had sent Letters to his Governors and Lieutenants, commanding them, *First to put that rash Youth of* Philip*'s in mind of his Years and Condition, by whipping him, and then to send him to him cloath'd in Purple and bound, to sink his Ships with their Crew, and carry all his Soldiers to the remotest Parts of the* Red-Sea.

So secure was he of Futurity, through his excessive Pride and the Ignorance of his Destiny, he divested himself of all Sense of human Weakness, pretending to be related to the Gods, rather because he did not seem much inferior to 'em in Power, than on the score of the ancient Fable that deriv'd the Pedigree and Name of the Kings of *Persia* from *Perseus* the Son of *Jupiter*. He had a little before writ to the *Athenians* in the same haughty style, adding, *That since they had preferr'd the Friendship of the* Macedonian *to his, they must not for the future ask him for any more Gold, for though they should beg it of him, he would send them none.*

CHAP

CHAP. V.

BUT *Alexander* being advanc'd as far as that Portion of Land that the King of *Persia* had bestow'd on *Memnon*, gave special Orders not to offer any Injury either to the Persons of his Tenants, or the Product of the Lands, by which Proceeding he prudently contriv'd to cause at least a Suspicion of the only Man he did not despise among all the Enemy's Generals, if he should not be able to bring him over to his Interest. Hereupon some wondering at the King's Moderation and Goodness, did not scruple to say, that he being the most cunning and bitter Enemy the *Macedonians* had, he ought to be put to Death as soon as they could get him in their Hands, and in the mean time they ought to do him all the Damage they could. To which the King reply'd, *That on the contrary, they ought to win him by good Offices, and to make him a Friend of an Enemy, and that then, he would exert the same Courage and Conduct on their Side.*

They were now come into the *Adrastean* Plains, through which the River *Granicus* runs with a swift Current. There, some of those that were sent before with *Hegelochus* to get Intelligence, bring him an Account, that the *Persians* waited for him, in order of Battel, on the other side of the River. He therefore halted for some time, to consult about the passing the River, and call all his Generals together. The major part were of Opinion, that it was altogether rash and impracticable to stem the Current of that deep River,

River, in the Presence of so many thousand Horse and Foot, that were drawn up on the other side, and the Bank itself being very steep and of difficult Access. There were not wanting some, that suggested, that it was then the Month call'd *Desius*, (which answers to that of *June*) which was always very unfortunate to the *Macedonians*. Hereupon *Alexander*, tho' he was not uneasy on the account of the Danger, yet he did not despise the Superstition, being sensible of the powerful Effects even of vain and ill-grounded Religion, in weak Minds. He therefore ordain'd that they should repeat the Name of the preceding Month, and instead of *Desius*, have another *Artemisius*. And the more effectually to settle the Minds of them that were alarm'd, he caus'd *Aristander* (who was to sacrifice for a prosperous Passage) to be secretly admonish'd, to write with an artificial Ink, on that hand that was to receive the Intrails, (inverting the Characters, that the Liver being impos'd thereon might by its Heat attract the same, and express 'em properly) *That the Gods granted the Victory to* Alexander. This Miracle being divulg'd, fill'd every Body with such mighty Hopes of the future, that they unanimously declar'd, in loud Acclamations, *That after such Tokens of the Favour of Heaven, there was no room left to doubt of any thing.* Thus being by a Wile brought into a Confidence of Success, they as it were ran away with the Victory, because their Thoughts were convinc'd it was their own.

The King thinking it advisable to make use of this bold Disposition of their Minds, immediately led them over, notwithstanding *Parmenio* very much entreated him to stay till the next day, (for the best part of the day was already spent) passing a Jest at the same time upon *Parmenio* for his Concern, telling him,

That

That the Hellespont *would have Cause to blush, if after he had surmounted the Difficulties of passing that, they should boggle at the passing of a Brook.* The King with thirteen Troops of Horse had hardly pass'd through the Violence of the Streams, but before he could either get firm Footing on the Shore, or make good the Ranks that had been disorder'd in the Passage, he was on all Sides press'd by the *Persian* Cavalry. For upon their disapproving *Memnon*'s Advice, and their resolving to fight, (*Arsites*, who was Governor of *Phrygia*, having openly declar'd, he would not suffer the least Hut to be burnt within his Jurisdiction, and the rest having enter'd into his Sentiments) they had posted themselves along the River *Granicus*, to the number of one hundred thousand Foot, and twenty thousand Horse, making use of the River as of a Fortification, and designing as it were, to bar that Door of *Asia* against *Alexander*. Being therefore inform'd of his Arrival, they so drew up their Cavalry (in which consisted the main Strength of their Army) that the Right Wing of the *Macedonians*, which was commanded by the King himself, (for the Left he had committed to *Parmenio*'s Care) was opposed by *Memnon* and his Sons, together with *Arsanes* the Persian, *Arsites* was also here with the Auxiliary *Paphlagonian* Horse *Spithridates*, who was the King's Son-in-Law, commanded the Body of Reserve he was accompanied by his Brother *Rhæsaces*, who was Governor of *Lybia* and *Ionia*, and by the *Hyrcanian* Horse. In the Right of the Foot were two thousand *Medes* and as many *Bactrians* under the Command of *Rheomithres*. The main Body was commanded by *Pharnaces* the Queen's Brother, *Arbupales*, and *Mithrobarzanes* Governor of *Cappadocia*, these were join'd by *Niphates* and *Petanes*, as also

by

by *Arsaces* and *Atrzyes*, who had brought along with 'em Troops of several Nations, these being superior in number, and having the Advantage of the Ground, press'd vehemently upon the Enemy, and the Fight was very sharp the King was here particularly in Danger, who being remarkable by his Arms, by his Bravery and by the Orders he gave up and down, was chiefly attack'd by a great many.

In the Heat of the Action a Dart that was levell'd at the King, stuck fast in the Folds of the lower part of his Armour, but did not wound him; however he was in real Danger from *Rhæsaces* and *Spithridates*, two of the boldest of all the *Persian* Generals, who attack'd him at the same Time For having broke his Lance upon *Spithridates* his Breast-plate, as he was going to make use of his Sword, *Spithridates*'s Brother riding up to him, struck so great a Blow with his Cymeter on his Helmet, that he cut it through, and lightly touch'd the King's Hair, part of the Helmet falling down by the force of the Stroke, he was just going to give him another, on that part of his Head that lay bare, when *Clitus* observing the King's manifest Danger, flew to his Assistance and prevented him, by cutting off the Sword Arm of the *Barbarian*, *Alexander* slew *Spithridates* at the same time.

Notwithstanding this the *Persians* made a gallant Resistance; till at last, being disheartend'd by the Loss of their Generals (of whom the major Part were already kill'd) and the Approach of the *Macedonian Phalanx*, that by this time had pass'd the River, they betook themselves to a precipitous Flight. After which the Foot made but a small Resistance; for imagining that their Horse was more than sufficient to overcome the Enemy, their Mind was more intent

on

on the Plunder than on Danger. till by the sudden and unexpected Event, they became a Sacrifice to the *Macedonians*, for it was now no longer a Fight, but a perfect Butchery The Mercenaries however, who were commanded by *Omares*, having possess'd themselves of an Eminence, made a vigorous Defence. For he had admitted of none that would surrender upon Terms. In this Conflict therefore there fell more *Macedonians* than in the Engagement of the Horse Nay, the King himself (who fought amongst the forwardest) was here so near Danger, that the Horse he rid upon was run thro' the Body, with a Sword. This Accident so enflam'd his Anger, that having surrounded them, both with his Cavalry and *Phalanx*, he made an entire Slaughter of 'em, except two thousand that surrender'd at Discretion. There were in all kill'd of the Enemy, twenty thousand Foot, and two thousand Horse, and very near the like Number taken Prisoners. The Generals *Memnon*, *Arsaces*, *Reomithres*, and *Antixyes*, sav'd themselves by flight, the others dy'd honourably of their Wounds. *Arsites* being got into *Phrygia*, laid violent Hands on himself, under a Conflict of Shame and Repentance, that he should not undeservedly be looked upon as the Cause of this Defeat *Alexander* lost in this Battle but few in Number, but they were the boldest and best of his Men. Of the Foot only thirty were kill'd, and seventy of the Horse. That all might therefore be sensible, that they were sure of a Reward from him in their Fortune, he enrich'd the Survivors with the Spoils of the *Persians*, and magnificently interr'd the Bodies of the Dead, with their Arms, and other Ornaments; granting at the same time to their Parents and Children, an Exemption of all Offices. The wounded were also parti-

E 4 cularly

cularly taken care of, for the King going about their Tents, visited them one by one, and express'd thereby his Concern even for the meanest Soldier, comforting them in their Misfortune, either by his Bounty, Commendations, or Promises. This condescending Carriage so endear'd him to them, that they were ready on all Occasions to encounter the greatest Dangers for his sake, with the utmost Constancy and Fidelity, none being unwilling to lay down their Lives for him, who neither suffer'd them to live in Want, nor to die without Marks of Honour. But he in a special manner distinguish'd the five and twenty of the Band of his Friends, who fighting in a disadvantageous Ground, were at the first Onset oppress'd by a Multitude of the *Persians* For he commanded *Lysippus* (who alone on the account of his wonderful Art, had the Privilege to cast his Statue in Brass) to represent every one of them in a Statue on Horseback, which were set up in *Dion* a Town of *Macedonia*, and were afterwards upon the Fall of that Empire, translated to *Rome*, by *Metellus* The chiefest Glory of this Victory was due to the King himself, who drew up the Army with all the Skill imaginable, and having observ'd the Nature of the Ground, he led them thro' the River in an oblique Order, that they might not be attack'd by the *Persians*, immediately on their getting out of the Water; then, when they were put in Disorder, and somewhat terrify'd, he animated them by his Exhortations, and prevail'd with them at least to make one vigorous Attack more, this was not all, for he fought gallantly in his own Person, killing several with his Lance, others with his Sword, insomuch that those that he encounter'd with himself, were the first that fled. His Conduct likewise, though it had an Appearance of Temerity and Rashness,

ness, yet it was grounded upon Reason, for as his Army was to engage with a new Enemy, much superior to it in Number, he had a Mind to arm it also with Despair, that observing their Retreat to be cut off by the River, they might place all their Hopes of Safety in the Victory. The *Thessalians*, in whom the main Strength of his Cavalry consisted, signaliz'd themselves on this Occasion, nor were the rest wanting in their Duty, especially the Horse, for it was the Horse that chiefly did the work, the Enemies Foot making but little Resistance, and soon giving way. Moreover, he gave Orders that the most considerable of the *Persians* should be decently buried, as also the mercenary *Greeks* that serv'd the Enemy. But those of 'em that were taken alive, he caus'd to be distributed among the Prisons in *Macedonia*, because that contrary to the general Decree of all *Greece*, they had serv'd the *Barbarians* against their own Country. However, he dismiss'd the *Thebans*, in Consideration that their Town being raz'd, and their Lands taken from 'em, they seem'd to be necessitated to what they did; besides, the many Calamities they had sustained, had in a manner glutted even Revenge, and made room for Pity. After this, he chose three hundred Bucklers out of the Spoils of the Enemy, and sent 'em to *Athens* to be hung up in the Temple of *Minerva*, with this pompous Inscription, Alexander *the Son of* Philip, *and the rest of the* Greeks, *excepting the* Lacedæmonians, *dedicate these Spoils taken from the* Barbarians *who inhabit* Asia. He did this with this View, that by making the *Greeks* partake of the Glory and Praise of the Victory, they might the more readily comply for the future with the other Necessities of the War, at the same time he upbraided the *Lacedæmonians* contumacious Temper,

E 5 who

who acting by a separate Interest, had cut themselves off from the main Body of the *Greeks*, and by that Deportment had depriv'd themselves of their Share in so great an Honour. Neither was he unmindful of his Mother, for whom he had always a true filial Duty and Veneration, for he sent her the Plate, the Purple, and the other valuable Spoils of that nature, reserving only a few for his own Use.

CHAP. VI.

AFTER this Battle, *Alexander* repair'd again to *Troy*, and return'd Thanks to the Goddess, who had upon his undertaking so dangerous a War, furnish'd him with Arms, and encourag'd him with prosperous Presages of the Event. For when he went thither first, immediately after his passing the *Hellespont* (as we before took notice) he saw an Equestrian Statue lying on the ground, just opposite to the Temple of *Minerva*, which represented *Ariobarsanes*, who had formerly been Governor of *Phrygia* Upon the sight hereof, *Aristander* promis'd *Alexander* a glorious Victory in some Horse Engagement, more especially if the Action happen'd not far from *Phrygia*, and also that he should with his own Hand slay the General of the Enemy. Accordingly the Event made good the Prediction, for *Spithridates* being kill'd by the King's Sword, fulfill'd the Prophecy. He therefore not only made rich Presents to the Temple, but gave the Title of City to *Troy*, that before hardly exceeded in Compass a moderate Village, and that it might with Credit bear that Honour, he appointed proper

Persons

Persons to restore and enlarge it, bestowing on it at the same time, all manner of Immunities. And because he observ'd that the Temple of the Goddess was too small, for the great Concourse of People that resorted thither out of a religious Motive, and that it was decay'd, he had resolv'd hereafter to build a magnificent one in the room thereof. But these, as well as a great many other noble Designs, were prevented by his Fate, his Successors neglecting to put them in Execution. By this Victory, the King laid open to himself all that part of *Asia* that is on this side Mount *Taurus* and the *Euphrates*, the Inhabitants being astonish'd at the unexpected Overthrow. For having not only lost their Troops, but their Generals too in the Battle, they had now no Hopes left, but in the King's Clemency, in the obtaining of which, they endeavoured to prevent one another, by a speedy Surrender of themselves to his Mercy. *Arsites* had, by laying violent Hands on himself, render'd *Phrygia* defenceless, *Alexander* therefore constituted *Callas* (who was General of the *Thessalians*) Governor of that Country. There came several Embassies likewise from the mountainous Parts, to surrender themselves and all they had to *Alexander*, who having taken them into his Protection, sent them home. He also forgave the *Zeliti*, because he knew they had been compell'd by the *Persians*, to serve against him. He impos'd the same Tribute on them all, that they had us'd to pay to *Darius*, observing the same Method with reference to all the other Provinces of *Asia* he afterwards reduc'd. *Alexander* was sensible, that all foreign Government is odious and subject to Envy, notwithstanding it be administered with more Lenity and Mildness than the Domestick, but if the former Burdens of the Subject, are increas'd by the Addition

of

of new ones, it is then look'd upon as altogether intollerable, wherefore when a certain Person told him, that he might draw much greater Tributes and Revenues from so large an Empire, he answer'd, *That he hated even a Gardener, that pull'd those Plants up by the Roots, which he ought only to crop.*

Being inform'd, that *Dascylium* was possess'd by a Garrison of *Persians*, he sent *Parmenio* thither, whom the Inhabitants readily received, the *Persians* having quitted it, as soon as they heard of the Approach of the *Macedonians*. In the mean time, he went himself to *Sardis*, which is the *Metropolis* of all the Places which the Kings of *Persia* had put under the Jurisdiction of the Governours of the maritime Country. He was within threescore and ten Furlongs of the Town, when *Mithrenes* (to whom *Darius* had committed the Care of the Citadel of *Sardis*) with the Chief of the *Sardinian* Nobility, came and surrender'd to him the Citadel, with the Money that was deposited there. Having graciously receiv'd 'em, he advanc'd to the River *Hermus*, that is about twenty Furlong distant from the Town, having there pitch'd his Camp, he sent *Amyntas*, *Andromene*'s Son, to take Possession of the Citadel. It is situated on the Top of a very high Hill, and every way of difficult Access, so that it might have been maintain'd against any Force whatever, even without the Help of its Wall, that had also a tripple Rampart. Having therefore applauded his Success upon the Surrender of so important a Place, which by reason of its Strength, might have held out a long Siege, and so retarded the Execution of his other great Designs, he resolved to build a Temple there, in Honour of *Jupiter Olympius*, and as he was diligently looking about, to find out what Place would be most proper for such a Structure,

there

there arose on a sudden a furious Storm, which pour'd down a great Quantity of Rain on Part of the Citadel, where formerly the Palace of the *Lydian* Kings had stood. Believing therefore that the Gods thereby pointed out what Place they had destin'd for that purpose, he order'd the Temple to be built there. Then he made *Pausanias*, who was one of the Band of his Friends, Governor of the Citadel, assigning to him the Auxiliaries of the *Argives*. The other Troops of his Allies he allotted to *Calas* and *Alexander* the Son of *Æropæus*, giving them *Memnon*'s Government. He appointed, at the same time, *Nicias* to collect the Tributes and Imposts. *Assander*, *Philotas* his Son, had the Government of *Lydia*, with the same Bounds and Limitations *Spithridates* had held it before. He granted to the *Lydians* the Privilege of living according to their own Laws. And because he understood the *Sardinians* were very much devoted to *Diana*, whom they call *Coloene*, he gave her Temple the Privilege of an Asylum. He did great Honours to *Mithrenes*, that by his Example others might be encourag'd to revolt, and in process of Time, he bestowed on him the Government of *Armenia*. In this Citadel, he found an Account of what Money had been distributed by *Darius*'s Generals, to bring about a War upon *Macedon*, from the *Greeks*. It appear'd also, that *Demosthenes* had received vast Sums for this purpose, some of whose Letters were there to be seen. But by reason he had made a Peace, and concluded all Matters with the *Athenians*, he did not think it proper to complain publickly of these Proceedings; however he thought it necessary, to be the more careful to keep the *Athenians* in their Duty, and to prevent their being prevail'd upon by this Man's wonderful Eloquence, since their Defection would go near to

draw

draw along with it that of all *Greece*. He had no Body in greater Esteem than *Phocion*, whose Integrity and Innocency, together with his constant Adherence to Virtue, render'd Poverty it self honourable. He valu'd him at first for the use he made of him, but being afterwards on several Occasions convinc'd of his Magnanimity, he honoured him out of Admiration of his Virtue, insomuch that, when (after *Darius*'s Overthrow) he was grown so haughty, as to think it beneath him to honour any one he writ to with the common Form of Salutation, he reserv'd that mighty Favour for *Antipater* and *Phocion* only. It is certain the King sent him a hundred Talents at a time, and gave him the Choice of four no inconsiderable Towns in *Asia*, viz. *Cius*, *Elæa*, *Mylassa*, and *Gergetho*, some put *Parata* instead of the last, but he refused all those Offers, yet left he should seem to slight the Friendship of so great a King, he desir'd that *Echeratides* the Sophist, *Athenodorus* the *Imbrian*, with *Demaratus*, and *Spartan*, *Rhodians*, who were Prisoners in the Castle of *Sardis*, might be set at Liberty. But these Transactions run into a later Date.

After this, he march'd to *Ephesus*, which the Garrison had quitted (being inform'd of the Defeat of the *Persians*) going off in two *Ephesian* Gallies, among the rest, was *Amyntas*, *Antiochus*'s Son, who had fled from *Macedonia*, without any other Provocation, than that he was afraid of the King, whom he mortally hated, making a Judgment of his Disposition from his own. *Alexander* enter'd into *Ephesus* the fourth Day after he left *Sardis*. Here he recall'd those that were banish'd in the time of the *Oligarchy*, and restor'd the Government to the People. The People having now obtain'd their long-wish'd-for *Liberty*,

berty, defir'd that thofe who had call'd in *Memnon*, and thofe who had plunder'd the Temple of *Diana*, and had caft down *Philip*'s Statue that ftood there, or had dug up *Herophythus*'s Monument that was plac'd in the *Forum*, as to the Deliverer of the City, might all fuffer the Punifhment they deferved. Of thefe therefore *Pelagon*, with his Brother *Syrphaces*, and his Coufin, were dragg'd out of the Temple, into which they had fled for Protection, and ftond to Death. All things tended to Blood and Confufion, when *Alexander* putting a Stop to the outrageous Licenfe of the Rabble, forbad making any farther Enquiry into thofe Matters, or molefting any one on that account. Thus the chiefeft and beft Citizens were fav'd, who would otherwife on the fcore of their Dignity or Riches, under the Pretext of real or fictitious Crimes, have been expos'd to the Hatred and Avarice of the enrag'd Multitude While thefe Things were doing, the *Magnefians* and *Trallians* fent Ambaffadors to him to notify their Submiffion to his Will and Pleafure; he therefore fent *Parmenio* thither with five thoufand Foot and two hundred Horfe, he fent *Alcimalus* with the fame Number, to the *Æolick* and *Ionian* Cities, within the *Perfian* Jurifdiction, giving Orders to both to abolifh the *Oligarchy's*, and to eftablifh every where a popular State; for he had found by Experience, that the People were well inclin'd to him, which had been the Caufe of the *Barbarians* reftraining 'em by the Government of Tyrants.

While *Alexander* ftay'd at *Ephefus*, he frequently went to *Apelles*'s Shop to divert himfelf after the Fatigues of Bufinefs, who was the only Perfon he would allow to draw his Picture, and was fo high in his Favour, that he beftow'd on him the beft belov'd belov'd of his Concubines, because he found *Apelles* was deeply in love with her. Her Name was *Pancasta*, she was born at *Larissa*, a considerable Town in *Thessaly*. And the King lov'd her tenderly, as well for her exquisite Beauty, as because she was the first he took a Fancy for in his youthful Days. This Action was very suitable to *Alexander*'s Greatness of Soul. But I do not give Credit to the Report, that *Apelles* by a shrewd Repartee, silenc'd *Alexander*, who let his Tongue run very fast, but unskilfully, concerning many Things in his Art; for this is not agreeable to the Veneration that is due to the Majesty of so mighty a King, nor to the Modesty of the Painter, who neither wanted Parts, or the Address of a Man of Letters. Besides, as *Alexander* from his tender Years, had been conversant with the liberal Sciences, it is to be suppos'd he could make a proper Judgment, even in those Arts, he was not thoroughly vers'd in. What others say, seems more probable, that it was one of the *Ephesian Diana*'s Priests, generally call'd *Megabizi*, that was so reprov'd by *Apelles*, who told him, *That while he held his Tongue, his Ornaments of Gold and Purple render'd him venerable to the Ignorant, but when he pretended to speak concerning things he knew nothing of, he became ridiculous even to the Boys that grind the Colours.* It was in this City that *Herostratus* burnt the so much celebrated Temple, as we before observ'd.

The *Ephesians* were now very intent on the rebuilding that curious Structure, sparing no Expence in the Work. *Alexander* therefore, to assist their Zeal, ordain'd, that the Subsidies which they us'd to pay before to the *Persians*, should, for the future, be paid to *Diana*, and confirm'd to it the Privilege of an *Asylum*, which he understood had formerly been preserv'd to it, both by *Bacchus* and *Hercules*, and enlarg'd its Bounds, allowing them to reach every way to the extent of a Furlong. Some time after, when he had settled all things in *Asia*, he writ to the *Ephesians*, *That he would reimburse all the Charges they had been at in the restoring that Edifice, and moreover, would supply whatever should hereafter be wanting, provided his Name were inscrib'd on the new building.* But the *Ephesians* excus'd themselves from granting that, and because it was of dangerous Consequence to refuse *Alexander* any thing he requir'd, their Ambassador had recourse to Flattery, which he knew had a mighty Influence over him, and told him, *That it was an Affront to his high Dignity, to consecrate any thing to the Gods, since he was himself a God, that being an Honour paid by Men to the Deity, as to a superior Nature.* So great was the Contention for Glory betwixt this mighty *Monarch* and one single *City*. However, the *Ephesians* gain'd their Point, chusing rather to go without so vast a Sum, than to yield to the *King*, the *Inscription* of the new *Temple*. Now how great their Expences were in this Work, may be guess'd from the price of one single *Picture* they hung up in it, which cost 'em twenty Talents of Gold. It represented *Alexander* with a Thunder-bolt in his hand. *Apelles* had drawn this Piece after so inimitable a manner, that he made use of but four Colours, which heighten'd the Admiration of all who had any Taste or Judgment in that Art.

CHAP.

CHAP. VII.

ABOUT this time the *Smyrnaeans* had the Seat where they had formerly flourish'd, restor'd to 'em, after they had for the space of four hundred Years liv'd scatter'd up and down in Villages, upon the *Lydians* having destroy'd the ancient *Smyrna*. The King rebuilt it about twenty Furlongs distant from the Place where the Town had stood, being admonish'd in a Dream to do so. *Alexander* us'd (when his Affairs of Moment would permit) to divert himself in hunting, one time particularly having fatigu'd himself with that Exercise, he fell asleep on a Mountain call'd *Pagus*, while he was taking his Rest, he fancied he heard the *Nemesis* (who had a Temple hard by) command him to build a City in that very Place, and people it with the *Smyrnaeans*. This Dream was afterwards confirm'd by the *Oracle* of *Apollo Clarius*, which promis'd the *Smyrneans*, that their Removal would redound to their Advantage, hereupon the Foundations of the new Town are laid by the *King's* Orders, but *Antigonus* had the Glory of finishing it. *Alexander* having some time after committed to him the Government of *Lydia*, *Phrygia*, and the neighbouring Countries.

The *Clazomenii* inhabit that part of the Gulph of *Smyrna* that is narrowest, and joins to the Continent, the Lands that run into the Sea, for the space of sixty Furlongs, making a kind of *Peninsula*. *Taos* stands on that side of the *Isthmus* which is opposite to the *Clazomenii*, and *Erythra* is situate in the utmost Point of the *Peninsula*,

ninsula, which was even then famous for its Prophetesses. Hard by this Town is the high Mountain *Mimas*, over-against the Isle of *Chio*, and looks into the Sea; then falling with a gentle Declivity, not far from the Straits of the *Clazomenu*, it terminates in Plains. *Alexander* having view'd the nature of the Place, resolv'd to cut through that narrow neck of Land, and divide it from the Continent, that so he might encompass *Erythræ* and *Mimas* with the Sea, and unite the upper and lower Gulph. It is observ'd, that this was the only thing in which he was disappointed, Fortune labouring, as it were, to accomplish all his other Undertakings. This Disappointment caus'd a sort of religious Reflection, *as if it were not lawful for Mortals to change the face of Nature,* since others who had made the same Attempt had likewise been frustrated before, however, he join'd *Clazomena* to the Continent by a Bank of two Furlongs, the *Clazomenu* having heretofore made an Island of it, out of fear of the *Persians*, but these Works were committed to the Care of the Governors. As for himself, having been very magnificent in his Sacrifices at *Ephesus*, he made a general Exercise of all the Troops that were with him, in honour of the *Goddess*, and march'd the next Day to *Miletum*, taking with him all the Foot, the *Thracian* Horse, and four Troops of those he call'd his Friends, the Royal being one of them. For *Hegistratus*, who commanded the Garrison, had given him hopes in a Letter, that he was ready to surrender to him; but understanding afterwards that the *Persian* Fleet was at hand, he alter'd his Mind, and was for preserving the place to *Darius*, for he wanted neither Arms nor Provisions, nor any other Necessaries requisite to endure a long Siege, besides, his Garrison was numerous, *Memnon* having reinforc'd it, (when

he

he fled thither after the Battle) with a confiderable Body of Troops he had with him. *Alexander* therefore coming fuddenly upon 'em with his incens'd Army, he, at his very firft Arrival, poffefs'd himfelf of the outward Town, as they call it; for the Townfmen and Soldiers (that the Strength of the Place might not be too much fcatter'd) had retir'd into the inner Town, refolving there to wait for the Succour of their Friends, who, as they were inform'd, were not far off. But thefe Hopes were fruftrated by the feafonable Arrival of the *Macedonian* Fleet, under the Command of *Nicanor*, who had taken Poffeffion of the Ifland *Lade*, that lies above *Miletum*, and, upon Information that the Enemy's Fleet lay at Anchor under the Mountain *Mycale*, failing into the *Milefian* Harbour, he cut off all hopes of Succour from the *Perfians* to the befieg'd. Neither did the *Barbarians* offer to oppofe him, notwithftanding they were fo much fuperior to him in number of Ships, for they had near four hundred Sail, whereas *Nicanor* had not above one hundred and fixty.

While thefe things were doing, *Glaucippus*, the moft confiderable Man of the Town, was fent to *Alexander*, to defire that the Town and Harbour might be in common to the *Perfians* and *Macedonians*, but he return'd with this melancholy Anfwer, *That he did not come into* Afia *to receive what others would beftow on him, but that every body fhould be contented with what he fpar'd them, that they ought to know it was their Duty to refign all their Fortunes to their Superior, or be ready the next Morning to decide the Matter by the Sword.* But the Townfmen repell'd the firft Shock of the Enemy with a great deal of Gallantry, killing amonft the reft, the two Sons of *Hellenica*, who was

Alexander's Nurse, and Sister to *Clitus*, who had with so much Bravery sav'd the King's Life. Hereupon the *Macedonians* being inrag'd with Grief and Anger, and having planted their Machines, they soon made a considerable Breach in the Wall, and were just ready to storm the Town, when the Besieged perceiving the Enemies Gallies in the Port, were seiz'd with a fresh Terror, and some of them betook themselves to the opposite little Island for Safety upon their Bucklers, others got into little Boats, and endeavour'd to imitate 'em, but were taken by the Enemies Ships at the very Mouth of the Harbour. *Alexander* having thus made himself Master of the Town, dispatch'd Ships after those who had gain'd the Island, providing them with Ladders, whereby the Soldiers might overcome the difficult ascent of the Coast, as if they were scaling the Walls of a City. But observing the *Greeks* that were in the Enemies Pay, (who did not in all exceed three hundred Men) ready to undergo the last Extremities, he took Compassion of 'em on account of their Bravery, and seeing 'em so constant to those that hir'd 'em, as to venture perishing for their Fidelity, he pardon'd 'em, and took 'em into his Service.

As for those *Barbarians* he found in the Town, he made 'em all Slaves, granting at the same time to the surviving *Milesians*, their *Liberty*, in Consideration of the ancient *Glory* of their *City*. For *Miletus* was once so rich and powerful as to have no less than twenty *Colonies* in the neighbouring Seas, moreover, it was celebrated on the score of several of its *Gallant Citizens*, who had in the sacred *Combats* often won the *Prize*, and thereby advanc'd the Glory of their Country. For these kind of Victories were (according to the Practice even of the *Greeks*) esteem'd the
greatest

greatest Ornaments of Vertue. This made *Alexander*, when he beheld the great number of Statues that were erected on this account, ridicule the Custom with a biting Reproach; for he ask'd 'em, *where were the strong Arms of those Men, when they receiv'd the* Persian *Yoke?* For, as he was a gallant Man, and judg'd of all things that were subservient to War, he thought it a shameful thing to waste that Strength that ought to be employ'd only in Battles of Moment, in the fruitless Diversion of the Rabble, out of a vain and unprofitable Ostentation. In the mean time the Soldiers who had enter'd the Town by mere Force, pillag'd every thing before 'em, and were come to the Temple of *Ceres*, and as some of 'em broke into it, with a Design to plunder it, a sudden Fire that came from the inner Parts, struck the sacrilegious Wretches blind. Here *Alexander* found some Monuments of his Progenitors, and particularly a Fountain, whose Waters, tasted at the Spring-head, were salt, and yet were fresh when they ran into Streams. The *Milesians* call it *Achilles*'s Fountain, and it is rumor'd, that that Hero bath'd himself near it, after he had vanquish'd *Strambelus*, *Telamon*'s Son, who was bringing Succour to the *Lesbians*. The *Milesians* had with 'em also the Oracle of *Apollo Didymeus*, much celebrated for its Riches and Fame. *Seleucus* (who was very powerful after *Alexander*) then consulted it, about his Return to *Macedon*, and receiv'd for Answer, *That bidding adieu to* Europe, *he should embrace* Asia.

There was another thing that awaken'd the *King*'s Attention, whose curious Genius was greedy of Knowledge, and was wonderfully delighted with Novelty, he was told, that a Youth of *Jaffus*, that is not far distant from *Miletum*, was belov'd by a *Dolphin*, and that the Fish knew his Voice so well, that whenever

he

he call'd upon it, and would be carry'd on its Back, it readily receiv'd him, whereupon the *King* inferring, that he was in *Neptune*'s favour, made him his *High Priest.*

CHAP. VIII.

*A*Lexander after this manner made himself Master of *Miletum,* and as the numerous Fleet of *Barbarians* kept still hovering thereabouts, and out of Confidence in their Multitude, and Superiority of Skill in maritime Affairs provok'd the Enemy to Battle, frequently presenting it self before the Port where the King's Ships rid, he sent *Philotas* with the Horse, and three Regiments of Foot to Mount *Mycale,* near which the *Persian* Fleet lay at Anchor, giving him Orders to repel the *Enemy,* if they offer'd to land, either to take in fresh Water or Wood, or any other Necessaries. This reduc'd the *Barbarians* to the greatest Straits, and kept them, as it were, confin'd in their Port, without being suffer'd to land, or accommodate themselves with those Necessaries they wanted. Hereupon they call'd a Council, and steer'd towards *Samos,* where having taken in Provision, they came back again to *Miletum,* and presented themselves before the Harbour in order of Battle. In the mean time five of the *Persian* Ships perceiving several of the Enemy's Fleet in a certain Port between the little *Island* we before mention'd, and the Road where the *Macedonian* Fleet lay, made all the sail they could thither, imagining they shou'd find 'em in a manner unmann'd, and consequently an easie Prize, for they conjectur'd,

that

that the major part of their Men were taken up in many other different Employments But the *King* immediately putting those that were present on board ten Gallies, commanded them *to go and meet the Enemy*. Who being terrify'd both by the number of Ships, and the unexpectedness of the thing (finding themselves attack'd by those they thought to have surpriz'd) made off as fast as they could, however, one of their Ships that was mann'd with *Jaſſians* was taken, the rest being swift Sailors regain'd their *Fleet* Thus the *Barbarians* were forc'd to leave *Miletum* without effecting any of the things they intended. *Alexander* considering now that his Fleet was inferior to that of the Enemy, and wou'd be of no great use to him for the future, and besides that it was a great Charge to him, resolv'd to dismiss it, retaining only a few Ships with him to transport the Machines and Engines necessary in Sieges, but *Parmenio* was of a different Opinion, and advis'd the *King* to hazard a Sea engagement, *since if the* Macedonians *were victorious, many Advantages wou'd arrive therefrom, and if they were beaten, they would lose nothing, since the* Persians *were even now Masters at Sea, and it would be no very difficult Task for those that were strongest at Land to defend their Coasts.* That his Advice might the sooner prevail, he offer'd *to execute it himself, and to share the Danger with the rest of that Fleet the King should assign him for this Purpose.* Moreover, his Opinion was back'd by lucky Presages, for some Days before an Eagle was seen to rest on the Shore behind the King's Fleet However, *Alexander* reply'd, *That his Opinion was ill grounded, when he flatter'd himself that so small a Fleet was able to encounter with so great a Multitude of Enemies, and that it was not adviseable to oppose skilful Rowers and expert Sailors, to raw and unexperienc'd Men in both*

Waves

Capacities, *that tho' he did not distrust the Bravery of his Subjects, yet in Sea-fights he was sensible, that was but of little Moment towards the obtaining the Victory. That those Actions were liable to many Dangers from the Waves and the Winds, both which were, by the Experience of the Pilots and Rowers, either declin'd or turn'd to an Advantage, That a great deal depended even on the very building of the Ships, That the* Macedonians *would in vain use their bravest Endeavours, since it would be in the Power of the* Barbarians, *either to baffle 'em, or, if an Accident happen'd, totally to destroy 'em, which was a thing of the last Consequence as Affairs stood, since all* Asia *would be animated and encourag'd, if in the beginning of the War he should receive so great an Overthrow, That the generality of Men were naturally of such Tempers as to expect the Event of things to be answerable to the pre-conceiv'd Hopes or Fears from the first Successes, and that we may not doubt of the Truth hereof, with respect to* Asia, *who will insure me that the* Greeks *themselves will remain in their Duty, if they find our Felicity and Success once forsake us, which, to speak the Truth, is all they admire and venerate in us? I must confess I look upon it to relate to my Fortune, that an Eagle was seen behind my Fleet, and I take it as an Omen of Prosperity But then the Augury seems plainly to indicate, that we shall overcome the Enemy's Fleet by Land, for the Eagle that presages the Victory, did not rest upon our Ships, but on the Shore, and so does not more expresly point at the Event than at the Place of Action This is certain, that if as we have begun, we continue to possess our selves of the Maritime Towns, the* Persian *Fleet will waste of it self, for it will neither have Recruits, Provisions, nor Harbours, and if these are remov'd, the greater their Strength is at Sea, they sooner they'll be undone By this means we shall*

F   *make*

make good the Prophecy that was engrav'd on the copper Plate that was (as we are inform'd) cast up by a Fountain in Lycia, and signify'd that the Persian Empire was hastening to its Period. Having therefore discharg'd his Fleet, he left Pontus and its adjacent Countries to his Governors to subdue, and pursuing his intended Designs he advanc'd towards Caria, for he was told, *a great Number of the Enemy had resorted thither* Indeed Halicarnassus, which was strong by its Situation, and was besides provided with two Citadels, gave some hopes that the Macedonian, who like a Torrent bore down all before him, might be stopt there, as by a strong Bank. There was great hopes also in Memnon, who was, with the utmost diligence, making all the necessary Preparations for maintaining a long Siege, for he had lately been made Admiral by Darius, and Governor of all the Maritim Coasts, and as he was a Man of great *Subtilty*, and an Observer of the Turns and favourable Occasions of Times, so he was very sensible that he exceeded all the *Persian* Generals in the War, notwithstanding which, he was not rewarded according to his Merit, for this Reason only, that as he was a *Greek* by Extraction, and had formerly been well receiv'd in the *Macedonian* Court, there was some room to suspect him of Treachery, he therefore sent his *Wife* and *Children* to Darius, as if he were solicitous for their Safety, but in truth by those Pledges to convince the *King* of his Fidelity However, Alexander having enter'd *Caria*, had, in a little time, made himself Master of all the places between Miletum and Halicarnessus, most of 'em being inhabited by *Greek* Colonies, to whom it was his Custom to restore their *Liberty*, and the *Privilege* of living after their own *Laws*, assuring them *he came into Asia to deliver them from Oppression* Not long after he insinuated

nuated himself into the Favour of the *Barbarians*, by his courteous Behaviour to *Ada*, a Woman of Royal Blood, who being inform'd of his March into those Parts, repair'd to him and implor'd his *Protection*, desiring him to re-establish her in her Kingdom; for *Hecatomnus*, King of *Caria*, had three Sons and two Daughters, of whom *Mausolus* marry'd *Artemisia*, and *Ada*, the youngest Daughter, had marry'd his Brother *Hidricus*. *Mausolus* being dead, was succeeded by his Sister and Wife, according to the Custom of the Country, which allows those that are born of the same Parents to be join'd both in Marriage and Dominion, but *Artemisia* dying with Grief for her deceas'd Husband, *Hidricus* enjoy'd the Crown, and dying without Issue, left the same to *Ada*, but *Pexodarus*, who was the only one left of *Hecatomnus*'s Sons, drove her out of the Kingdom, and altho' he also was dead, she remain'd still depriv'd of her Right, because *Pexodarus* had marry'd his Daughter to *Orontobates*, a Nobleman of *Persia*, that he might by his Wealth and Interest be protected in his new Usurpation, so that his Father-in-Law being dead, he held the Kingdom in Right of his Wife. *Ada* having therefore made her Condition known to *Alexander*, and surrendring to him at the same time the strong Castle of *Alinda*, obtain'd from him the Approbation of her calling him Son, and a promise of his speedy Assistance to restore her to her Dignity. In the mean time the Rumour of this Queen's courteous Reception being spread all over that Country, procur'd *Alexander* the Affection of a great many Towns; for most of 'em were in the hands of *Ada*'s Relations or Friends, insomuch that they sent Ambassadors to him with Presents of Crowns of Gold, and solemn Assurances, *That they put themselves under his Protection and Power, and that they would readily obey his Command.*

While these Things were doing, *Ada* was wholly taken up with providing the most exquisite Meats for Taste, and dress'd after the most curious Manner, and Sweetness of all Kinds, and sent 'em with the Cooks and Confectioners to the *King*, as a Present, thinking to shew her Gratitude for the Favours she had receiv'd from him, if she entertain'd him after his Fatigues and Toils, with the Delicacies of the *Asian* Luxury. But being too wise not to know, that *Intemperance* is of pernicious Consequence to the Man that is employ'd in serious and weighty Matters, he very civilly return'd her Thanks, but told her at the same time, *She had been needlesly solicitous for him, who had himself better Cooks, with which his Tutor* Leonidas *had formerly provided him, viz. a Walk early in the Morning to get him a Stomach to his Dinner, and a frugal Dinner to prepare him for Supper.*

CHAP. IX.

BY this time almost all *Caria* had submitted to *Alexander*, except *Halicarnassus*, the Capital City thereof, in which there was a strong Garrison, wherefore concluding the Siege would be tedious, he order'd *Provisions, and all the necessary Machines, for battering the Place, to be brought from on board his Fleet,* and went and encamp'd with the Foot at the distance of five Furlongs from the Town. But while his Men were battering the Walls of the Place, near the Gate that leads to *Mylassa*, the Besieged made an unexpected Sally, however, the *Macedonians* behav'd themselves

with

with a great deal of Bravery, and drove 'em back to the Town with little Loss. Some few Days after, *Alexander* having had Hopes given him that the Town *Myndus* would, upon *his* appearing before it, be deliver'd up to *him*, he took along with him part of the Army, and march'd thither in the dead time of the Night. But no Body offering to stir, he commanded the heavy-arm'd Soldiers to undermine the Wall, for he had brought neither Ladders nor Machines along with him, by reason he did not go thither with an intention to make a formal Siege. These Men flung down one of the Towers, and yet for all that made no Breach they could enter at, for the Tower fell after such a manner that the Ruins defended the same Ground that the Tower did while standing, and the Inhabitants made a vigorous Resistance, and were reinforc'd by Succours from *Halicarnassus*, which *Memnon* (hearing of the Danger they were in) had sent them. Thus the *Macedonian*'s Attempt was frustrated. *Alexander* being now return'd to the Siege of *Halicarnassus*, resolv'd first of all to fill up a Ditch about thirty Cubits broad, and fifteen in depth, that the Enemy had made for the better Security of the Place, he therefore prepar'd three *Tortoises*, under the Protection of which the Soldiers might with *safety* bring the Earth, and what other Materials were necessary for that Purpose, and having fill'd the Ditch, he order'd *the Towers and other Machines us'd in the battering of Walls, to be properly apply'd*. By these means having made a sufficient Breach in the Wall, he endeavour'd to force his Way into the Town through it, but the *Enemy* being strong in Number, was constantly succeeded by fresh Men in the room of those that were tir'd, and being besides encourag'd by the Presence of their Generals, omitted

no-

nothing that was necessary for a vigorous Defence. The Day being wasted in a drawn Fight, and *Memnon* imagining the Enemy might be tir'd with the fatigue of the Action, and so would be more negligent in keeping their Guards, made a strong Sally out of the Town, and set Fire to their Works, hereupon the *Macedonians* advancing to oppose them, while these labour'd to extinguish the Flames, and the others to encrease 'em The *Macedonians*, tho' much superior to their Enemy in Strength and Courage, and their familiarity with Danger, yet were mightily press'd by the Number and Contrivance of the *Persians*, and as the Fight was not far from the Walls, they were very much gall'd from thence by their Engines and Machines, so that the *Macedonians* receiv'd many Wounds, which they had no opportunity of Revenging The Shouts were great on both Sides, each encouraging their own Men, and threatning their Enemy, besides, the Groans of the wounded and dying, together with the darkness of the Night, fill'd every thing with Horror and Confusion, which was still encreas'd by the Clamour of the rest of the Multitude, who while their Companions were fighting, were intent on the repairing the Damage the Walls had sustained from the Shock of the Engines and Machines. At last the *Macedonians* pushing bravely on, drove the Enemy within the Walls, having kill'd about one hundred and seventy of 'em, and among the rest *Neoptolemus*, who with his Brother *Amyntas* had fled to the *Persians* Of the *Macedonians* there did not fall in that Action above sixteen, but there were near three hundred wounded, which may be ascrib'd to the Night, in the darkness of which they could not decline the Blows, nor avoid the random Darts. A few Days after,

ter, an Accident, inconsiderable in it self, prov'd the occasion of a notable Contention, which begun between two of *Perdiccas* his Veterans; they were Comrades, and had been drinking together, and among the rest of their Discourse, they happen'd to enlarge on the Gallant Actions they had each perform'd, till at last they quarrell'd about the Preference, upon which one of 'em broke out in this Expression, *Why do we sully so glorious a Contention with empty and useless Words? The Master is not who has the best Tongue, but the strongest Arm, and here is a fine Opportunity to decide the same. If you are the Man you pretend to be, follow me.* They were both heated with Wine and Emulation, and therefore of their own accord took their Arms, and advanc'd to that part of the Wall that stands near that side of the Citadel that faces *Mylasse*

Their rash Enterprize being observ'd by those of the Town, caus'd some of the Enemy to go out against 'em, they undauntedly stood their Ground, and came to an Engagement, and receiv'd those who came nearest 'em Sword in Hand, flinging their Darts after those who retreated But their bold Attempt had not remain'd long unpunish'd from so many, who had, besides their Number, the Advantage of a rising Ground, if a few of their Fellow-Soldiers at first observing the Danger they were in, had not come to their Assistance, and afterwards, as occasion requir'd, more and more the Besieged doing the same to succour their Men This made the Success various, according as each Party was superior either in Strength or Number, till *Alexander* himself coming up with those that were about him, struck a Terror into the Enemy, and drove 'em within their Fortifications, and was very near entring the Town at the same time with 'em For the

the Besieged being wholly intent on what pass'd before the Town, the defence of the Walls was carelesly minded, and two Towers were already beat down with the adjoining part of the Wall, by the repeated Violence of the Battering Rams, and the third was so shaken that it could not stand long against the Mines. But by reason of the suddenness of the Action, and that the whole Army was not drawn out, this Opportunity, however favourable, was lost. *Alexander* hereupon desir'd a suspension of Arms, and leave to bury his dead, notwithstanding that, according to the *Greek* Notion, it was yielding the Victory to the Enemy, yet he chose rather to do it than leave the Bodies of his Men unburied. But *Ephialtes* and *Thrasibulus*, *Athenians* (who were then in the *Persian* Service, and who had a greater regard to their Aversion to the *Macedonians* than to *Humanity*) openly declar'd, *That such an Indulgence ought not to be granted to such inveterate Enemies*; however, this did not hinder *Memnon* from representing, *That it was altogether unbecoming the Practice of the* Greeks, *to refuse an Enemy the privilege of burying their Slain, that Arms and Force were to be us'd against Enemies that made Head against us, and that it was an unworthy thing to insult those whose Fate had put it out of their Power to do us either Good or Harm.* It is most certain, that *Memnon*, besides his other Virtues, was remarkable for his *Moderation*, for he did not think it at all honourable, out of a virulent Prejudice, to slander an Enemy, and load him with Invectives, on the contrary, he strove to overcome him by Bravery and Conduct. This made him, when he heard one of the Mercenaries speak with Disrespect and Petulancy of *Alexander*, strike him with his Pike, and tell him, *he did not hire him to rail at* Alexander, *but to fight against him*.

CHAP

CHAP. X.

IN the mean time the Besieged took all the Care they could for their Security, and rais'd a Brick Wall within that which was beat down, and instead of carrying it on in a strait Line, they made it bend inwardly after the Resemblance of the new Moon. This Task was soon finish'd by the help of a great many Hands. The next Day *Alexander* began to batter this Wall, that he might with less difficulty beat it down while the Work was yet fresh. The Besieged took the Opportunity of the *Macedonians* being thus employ'd, to make a vigorous Sally from the Town, and set Fire to some of the Hurdles with which the Works were cover'd, and to part one of the Timber Towers. But *Philotas* and *Hellanicus*, who had that Day the Guard of the Machines, hinder'd the Fire from spreading, and *Alexander* appearing seasonably, struck such a Terror into the Minds of the Enemy, that flinging away their Torches, and some their Arms, they fled back to the Town with great Precipitation. The Advantage they had here from the Situation of the Place, enabled them to repel the Force of the Enemy with ease, and the Wall (as we before took Notice) was built so, that what part soever the *Macedonians* attack'd, they were not only oppos'd in Front, but were also sure to be flank'd from each side thereof.

While these Things were doing, the *Persian* Generals finding themselves straiten'd every Day more and more, and being well assur'd that the *Macedo-*

nian would not go off till he had made himself Master of the Town, held a Council on what was necessary to be done in the present Juncture of Affairs and *Ephialtes*, a Person equally remarkable for the Strength of his Body, and the Courage of his Mind, made a Speech on the many Inconveniencies of a tiresome Siege, and argu'd against *expecting till they were altogether weaken'd, and unable to resist, and of course fall a Prey, with the Town, to the Enemy,* and advis'd 'em, *that while they had yet some Strength, to engage the Enemy chearfully, with the choicest of the hir'd Troops That this his Counsel, by how much it was more bold in Appearance, was by so much the more easie to Execute, for the Enemy expecting nothing less than this, might be easily surpriz'd, being altogether unprepar'd against such an Accident.* Nor did *Memnon* (who otherwise us'd to prefer the cautious and wary Counsel, to the specious and plausible in Appearance) oppose him; for he consider'd, that altho' no great Alterations should happen, yet as there was no hopes of any Succour at hand, the Issue of the Siege would be fatal, he therefore did not think it improper, in so great an Extremity, to try what so brave a Man could do, since he seem'd, as it were, inspir'd to execute the boldest Undertakings.

Ephialtes therefore having made choice of two thousand, out of the whole Body of hir'd Troops, commanded *them to get a thousand Torches, and by break of Day to be ready with their Arms to receive his Orders* Alexander, as soon as Day appear'd, had advanc'd the Machines again to the Brick Wall, and the *Macedonians* were intent on their Business, but *Ephialtes* sallying out of the Town on a sudden, order'd one half of his Men with their Torches to set Fire to their Works, and he follow'd in Person with

the

the other half to oppose those who should offer to hinder them in the Execution of their Design. But *Alexander* being inform'd of what was doing, quickly drew up his Army, and having strengthen'd the Succours with chosen Men, he dispatch'd some *to put out the Fire*, while he himself attack'd those that were with *Ephialtes*, and *Ephialtes*, on his part, as he was of a prodigious Strength, kill'd all those that engag'd him Hand to Hand, animating his Men by his Voice and Looks, but most by his Example. The Besiegers were not a little annoy'd also from the Walls, for the Besieged had erected a Tower thereon of a hundred Cubits in height, from which (having conveniently planted their Engines) they gall'd the Enemy with Javelins and Stones. While these things were doing, *Memnon* likewise with another Body of Troops, made another Sally, from a different part of the Town, whence it was least expected this caus'd so great a Confusion in the Camp, that the *King* himself was at a stand what Measures to take. However, by his Magnanimity and seasonable Orders, he obviated all the Danger, and Fortune came to his Assistance in a very proper time, for they who had set Fire to the Machines, were repuls'd with great Loss, by the *Macedonians* that kept Guard there, and the Reinforcement he had sent 'em, and *Ptolemy*, the Son of *Philip* who was Captain of the King's Guards, having with him the Regiments of *Addæus* and *Timander*, besides his own, receiv'd *Memnon* so warmly, that the *Macedonians* on that side had much the better of it, notwithstanding they lost in the Action *Ptolemy*, *Addæus* and *Clearchus*, Captain of the Archers, and about forty private Men. The Enemy retir'd with so much Precipitation and Disorder, that in the hurry they broke down the narrow Bridge they had laid over the Ditch, and push'd those headlong down that were upon it, of whom some were trod to Death by their own Men, and others perish'd by the *Macedonians* Darts from the higher Ground. A great many that had escap'd this *Calamity* were destroy'd at the very Gate of the Town, for the Inhabitants (being in the utmost Confusion, and apprehending that the *Macedonians* would enter at the same time with their own Men) over hastily shut the Gate, delivering up their Friends to the fury of the Enemy. In the mean time *Ephialtes*, who was no less formidable by his Hopes than his Despair, gallantly maintain'd the Fight against the King's Troops, and had made the Victory doubtful, if the Veteran *Macedonians* had not seasonably come to the Assistance of their distress'd Companions. These Veterans, tho' in the Camp, were exempt from all Duty, except in case of Necessity, notwithstanding they enjoy'd at the same time their Salaries, and other *Præmiums*, and indeed they had deserv'd this Honour by their brave Behaviour under former Kings, and even under *Alexander*, as having pass'd their whole Life in military Exercises. These Men therefore observing their Companions terrify'd, and declining the Engagement, and looking about, as it were for a Place to retire to, flew to their Relief under the Command of *Atharias*, and having renew'd the Fight that began to grow languid, they forc'd the young Soldiers, by reproaching them with their shameful Behaviour, to resume their Courage; then making a furious Attack all at once, and out of Emulation striving who should do the *Enemy* most Mischief, in a moment Fortune turn'd to their side, *Ephialtes*, with the bravest of his Party, was slain, and the rest

were

were drove into the Town, a great many *Macedonians* enter'd it at the same time with 'em, and the Town was near being taken by Storm, when the King gave Orders to sound a Retreat, either out of a desire to save the Place, or else because the Day being in a manner spent, he apprehended Danger from the Night, and the Ambuscades that might be laid for him, in the unknown parts of the City. This Fight consum'd the chief Strength of the Besieged, wherefore *Memnon* having deliberated with *Orontobates* (who was Governor of the Town) and the other Generals, on what was proper to be done, caus'd the wooden Tower, and the Arsenals where their Arms were kept, to be set on Fire in the dead time of the Night, as also those Houses that were near the Wall, which soon taking Fire, and the Flames from the Tower and Arsenal (being blown by the Wind) increasing, it made a dreadful Conflagration. The bravest part of the Inhabitants and Soldiers retir'd into a Castle built within an Island, others got into *Salmacis*, another Castle, so call'd from a Fountain that is there, of great Fame, and the Generals sent the rest of the Multitude, and all their most valuable Things, into the Island of *Cos* *Alexander* being inform'd by Deserters, and his own Observation, of what pass'd in the Town, altho' it was Midnight he commanded the *Macedonians to enter the Place, and put all to the Sword they should find promoting the Fire, but to forbear injuring those who kept themselves within their Houses* The next Morning he took a View of the Fortresses the *Persians* and hir'd Troops had possess'd themselves of finding they would require a long Siege to reduce 'em, and that having made himself Master of the Capital City of the Country, it was not worth his while to trifle away his time about 'em, he raz'd the Town, and commanded

Ptolemy,

Ptolemy, to whose Care he had committed the Country of *Caria* (leaving with him three thousand Foreigners, and two hundred Horse, for that Purpose) to observe those Castles, which were encompass'd both with a Wall and Ditch. Not long after *Ptolemy*, having joyn'd his Forces with those of *Asander*, Governor of *Lydia*, defeated *Orontobates*, and the *Macedonians* being enrag'd, and not able to endure so tedious a delay, apply'd themselves strenuously to the Siege of the Castles, and reduc'd them.

But the *King*, whose Thoughts had already laid the Scheme of taking into his Conquests *Phrygia*, and the adjoining Provinces, sent *Parmenio* with the Bands he honour'd with the Title of his Friends, the auxiliary Horse, and the *Thessalians* commanded by *Alexander Lyncestes*, to *Sardis*, with Orders from thence, *to make an Irruption into* Phrygia, *and get from the Enemy Provisions and Forage for the Army that was coming after,* allotting him *Waggons* for that use. Afterwards understanding that several of the *Macedonians* (who had marry'd a little before the Expedition) impatiently desir'd the Company of their Wives. He gave *Ptolemy*, *Seleucus*'s Son, the Command of 'em, and order'd him *to conduct 'em home*, that they might pass the Winter with their Wives. *Cœnos* and *Meleager*, two of his Captains, went along with them on the same account. This endear'd the King mightily to the Soldiers, and made 'em more chearfully undergo the remote Service; for they perceived he had a Consideration for 'em, and reasonably hop'd they should now and then obtain leave to see their Friends. At the same time, he commanded the Officers *to be very diligent in raising Recruits during their Residence in* Macedonia, *and at the Beginning of the Spring, to bring him as many Horse and Foot as they could, besides those they now conducted home.*

home. Here he obſerv'd, that his *Army* was infected with the Manners and Cuſtoms of the *Aſiaticks*, and that there was in the Camp a great number of *Catamites*, he order'd therefore a ſtrict Search to be made for 'em, and ſent 'em into a little Iſland in the *Ceramick* Gulph. The place partook of their Infamy, and to perpetuate the Memory thereof, the Town was called *Cinædopolis*.

CHAP. XI.

THESE Affairs being thus tranſacted, *Alexander* continu'd in his firſt Reſolution of reducing all the maritime Coaſt, and by that means render the Enemy's Fleet uſeleſs to 'em, and therefore having made himſelf Maſter of the *Hyparnians* by the Treachery of the hir'd Troops (who ſurrender'd the Caſtle to him) he march'd towards *Lycia*. Here taking into his Protection the *Telmiſſenſes*, and having paſs'd the River *Xanthus*, the Town that bears that Name, with *Pinara* and *Parara*, conſiderable Places in that Country, and about thirty more, ſubmitted to him ; ſo that having ſettled things well enough for the preſent, he proceeded on to *Mylias*, which is a Part of the greater *Phrygia*, but the *Kings* of *Perſia* had thought fit to join it to *Lycia*. While he was here receiving the Fealty of the Inhabitants, Ambaſſadors came to him from the *Phaſelitæ*, deſiring his Friendſhip, and preſented him with a Crown of Gold, as a Token of their kind Reception of him , a great many Towns of the lower *Lycia*, did the ſame. The *King* therefore having ſent proper Perſons to take Poſſeſſion of the Towns of the

Pha-

Phaselita, and the *Lycu*, in a few days march'd himself to *Phaselis*. This City was then endeavouring to reduce a strong Fort, that the *Pisidæ* had rais'd within their Territories, from whence they did the Inhabitants a great deal of Mischief. But upon *Alexander*'s Arrival, this Fort was soon taken. He remain'd with the *Phaselitæ* some Days to refresh himself and his Army, the Season of the Year inviting him to do so; for it being then the middle of Winter, the Badness of the Roads would have made his Marches uneasie. Here having indulg'd a Glass, and being in a merry Humour, and beholding the *Statue* that the People had erected to *Theodectes*, he went to it, and dancing about it, flung several Garlands of Flowers upon it, for he had contracted a Familiarity with him, and receiv'd him into his Favour, when they were both at the same time Pupils to *Aristotle*. However, this *jovial* Humour was soon interrupted by the shocking Message he receiv'd from *Parmenio*. This General had taken up a *Persian* call'd *Asisinas*, whom *Darius* had indeed sent publickly to *Atysies* Governor of *Phrygia*, but with these private Instructions. *That he should watch an Opportunity to speak in private to* Alexander Lincestes, *and promise him the Kingdom of* Macedon, *and a thousand Talents of Gold, if he perform'd what was agreed between 'em*; for *Lyncestes* had formerly gone over to the *Persians* with *Amyntas*, and had took upon him the treasonable Office of killing the *King*.

He hated *Alexander* on several Accounts, but particularly for having put to Death *Heromenes* and *Arrabæus* his Brothers, for being privy to the Murther of his *Father*. And notwithstanding he himself was pardon'd, and loaded with Honours, so as to be doubly indebted to the *King*, yet his natural *Cruelty* was such, and his Ambition of Power so great, that he thought

nothing

nothing a Crime that was inftrumental to his obtaining a *Crown*. The thing being examin'd in Council, the *King*'s Friends reprefented to him, *his exceffive good Nature, which had made him not only pardon a Man detected in the foulest of Crimes, but heap Honours upon him, even to the giving him the Command of the choicest Part of the Horfe.* Who, could he hope, would be faithful to him hereafter, if Parricides not only went unpunifh'd, but were received into the greateft Favour, and had the chiefeft Dignities and moft confiderable Employments confer'd upon 'em? That it was neceffary to redrefs in time, the Error he had been led into by his too great Clemency, left if Lynceftes fhould be fenfible that he was difcover'd, he fhould ftir up the inconftant Temper of the Theffalians *to a Revolt*. That the Danger was not of a nature to be contemned, fince there could not be a greater imagin'd. Befides, that it would be no lefs than flighting the Deity's Care it felf, who was pleafed after fo remarkable a manner, to admonifh him of the treacherous Defigns againft him. For the *King*, during the late Siege of *Halicarnaffus*, being laid down in the Afternoon, to refresh himfelf after his Fatigues and Labours, a *Swallow*, which is Bird remarkable for Omens, flutter'd round about his Head as he was afleep, making a confiderable Noife, and fometimes fettling on this fide, fometimes on that fide of the Bed, chattering louder than is ufual. But as the King was much tir'd, it did not altogether waken him; however, as it was troublefome to him, he brufh'd it away with his Hand. Notwithftanding which, the Bird was fo far from being frighten'd, that it even fettled upon his Head, and did not leave off chirping, till having thoroughly waken'd him, he fcar'd it quite away.

This

This Accident was, by *Aristander*, interpreted after this manner He said the King was in Danger from one of his Friends, but the Treason would not remain undiscover'd, the Nature of the Bird seeming to foretel as much, for it is more familiar with Man than any other, and at the same time is a great Chatterer Having duly consider'd these things, and finding *Asisines*'s Discovery to agree with the Diviner's Answer, and moreover having been carefully warn'd by his Mother, *to have a particular Eye upon this Man*, he thought all farther Delay might be of ill Consequence, and therefore sent Instructions to *Parmenio*, what he should do upon this Occasion For as we took notice before, *Alexander Lyncestes* was gone along with him into *Phrygia* Now lest by some Accident or other, the King's Design should be unseasonably betray'd, he would not trust 't in writing, but sent it by word of mouth, by a trusty and honourable Person *Amphoterus*, Brother to *Crater*, was pitch'd upon, who putting on a *Phrygian* Habit, instead of the *Macedonian*, and taking along with him some of the *Pergenses* for his Guides, he came in Disguise to *Parmenio* Hereupon, *Alexander Lyncestes* is seiz'd, and notwithstanding his Punishment was for a long time put off, in consideration of his own and his Family's Quality and Interest, yet three Years after, when *Philotas*'s Accomplices were executed, he was put to death likewise, sharing in their Punishment, for having participated in their Crime Besides the Detection of this Plot against his Life, the *King* moving from *Phaselis*, had soon another Token of the Deity's Favour and Protection He had sent Part of his Army to the Town of the *Pargenses*, and follow'd himself with the rest thereof, along the Coast, where the Mountain *Climax* looks into the *Pamphylian* Sea, and leaves but a narrow Way to Travellers, even when the Sea is calm; but when this is tempestuous, the other is drown'd by the overflowing Waters; which frequently happens in Winter, if not always. But *Alexander*, who dreaded nothing more than Delay, led his Army through the rough, as well as smooth, with equal Ardour and Expedition. The South Wind having blown for some Days, had cover'd the Ways with Water. There fell at the same time great and frequent Rains, as is usual when those Winds blow. However, upon *Alexander*'s Approach, the North Wind rose on the sudden, and dispers'd the Clouds, and driving the Waters back into the Sea, open'd a Passage to the *Macedonians*. Notwithstanding which, he was forc'd to wade thro' several unknown Fords, which took his Men sometimes up to the Middle. At the same time that I allow *Alexander*'s great Assurance in Dangers, to proceed from the undoubted Greatness of his Soul, yet I cannot but think it receiv'd some Increase from the many *Presages* and *Omens* in his Favour, since he thereby conjectur'd he was destin'd to perform great and noble Exploits.

While he was yet in *Macedonia*, there appear'd to him a Person of a Figure more venerable than one of human Extraction, advising him to follow him into *Asia*, to overthrow the *Persian* Empire. When the *King* came into *Phœnicia*, he was put in mind of his Dream, by the High-Priest of the *Jews*, whose Dress reviv'd in his Memory that of the Object he had beheld in his Vision. For while *Alexander* was employ'd in the Siege of *Tyre*, he had commanded the neighbouring *Kings* and People to submit to him, and raise him Soldiers. But the *Jews*, who were Masters of the famous City of *Jerusalem*, excusing themselves, as being in Alliance with *Darius*, rejected the *King*'s Friendship.

ship. He therefore being incens'd thereat, march'd into *Judæa*, with a Design to punish the *Contumacy* of that People. But the Inhabitants of *Jerusalem*, to appease the *King*'s Anger, went out of the Town to meet him, with their Wives and Children, in a suppliant manner. The *Priests* led the Procession, being cloath'd with fine Linnen, the People follow'd cloath'd also in white, and *Jaddus* the *High-Priest* in in his Pontifical Habit, was at the head of the Multitude. The *King* admiring the Beauty of this pompous Procession, alighting from his Horse, advanc'd alone, and having first ador'd the Name of God that was engrav'd on a gold Plate in the *High-Priest*'s Mitre, he afterwards saluted the *High-Priest* himself. The unexpectedness of the thing, struck all the Spectators with Amazement. And the *Jews*, who not only saw themselves freed from their imminent Danger, but also taken into Favour, contrary to their expectation, surrounded the King, praising and congratulating him, and offering up their Prayers for his Prosperity. On the contrary, the little *Kings* of *Syria*, who were bitter Enemies of the *Jews*, and had follow'd *Alexander* in hopes to gratifie their Eyes with the Punishment of their inveterate Foes, were so astonish'd, that they in a manner doubted, whether what they beheld was a Reality, or whether their Senses were impos'd upon by a Dream, nay, the *Macedonians* themselves were not less surpriz'd at the unusual Spectacle, insomuch that *Parmenio* approaching the King, took the Liberty to ask him, *Why he shew'd so much Respect to foreign Ceremonies, since to receive it from so vile a Nation, were unworthy so great a King?* Hereupon *Alexander* told him his Dream.

After which, he enter'd into the Town, and in their most beautiful Temple offer'd Sacrifices to God according

ing to the receiv'd Custom of the Place, bestowing on it many noble Presents. Here he saw also their sacred *Books*, which contain'd several ancient Prophecies, among which, there was this, that *Tyre* should yield to the *Macedonians*, and that the *Persians* should be overcome by a *Greek* He looking upon *himself* to be the Person meant therein, granted the *Jews the liberty of living both at home and abroad, according to their own Customs and Laws*. And because their Land lies *untill'd every seventh Year*, he ordain'd that they *should be freed from that Proportion of their Taxes* He was mightily taken also with the Nature of the Country, which (besides the other Fruits which it produces in as plentiful a manner as any other) alone affords the Balm-Tree. *Alexander* made *Andromachus* Governor of these Provinces, whom the *Samaritans* (the *Jews* mortal Enemies) barbarously murder'd a little time after But these things were transacted after the Reduction of *Tyre* and *Gaza*, tho' we lay hold of this Occasion to relate 'em before-hand.

CHAP. XII.

ALEXANDER having pass'd the narrow Way that lies along the *Pamphylian* Sea, upon his March from *Perga*, was met on the Road by Ambassadors from the *Aspendii*, desiring they might not be compell'd to receive a Garrison, promising in consideration of that Exemption, fifty Talents towards the Soldiers Pay, and as many Horses as they us'd to maintain by the way of Tribute for the King of *Persia* From thence the *King* advanc'd to the *Sideta*, who

who are seated near the River *Melas*, they are of the Race of the *Cumæans* of *Æolia*, but are barbarous in their Speech, having lost their *Greek*, not by length of *Time*, as it often happens, but they say, that their *Ancestors* at their first coming into those Parts, on the sudden forgot their native *Language*, and spoke one till then unknown.

Having taken Possession of *Sida*, which is the *Metropolis* of *Pamphylia*, he was marching towards *Syllium*, a Town strong by its Situation, and provided with a numerous Garrison of Foreigners and neighbouring *Barbarians*. In consideration whereof, and because he was inform'd that the *Aspendii* had revolted, he alter'd his Course, and march'd to *Aspendus*. The Inhabitants were so mightily surpriz'd at the sudden Arrival of the *Macedonians*, that forsaking their Houses, they retir'd into the *Cittadel*. So that *Alexander* taking Possession of the empty Town, encamp'd under the Castle, and as he had with him very able Engineers, he by the Sight of his Preparations to attack 'em, oblig'd 'em to sue for Peace on their first Terms. Nothing could happen more to *Alexander*'s Wish (who had greater Designs in view) than that he was not stopt in his Career by a long Siege, for the Place was no way contemptible. However, that the Revolters might not go altogether unpunish'd, he required *the most considerable of the Citizens to be deliver'd to him as Hostages, and as the Tax of Money that had been first impos'd, was not yet paid, he now impos'd upon 'em double that Sum*. He also added, *That they should obey the Governour he set over 'em*, and pay a yearly Tribute to the *Macedonians*, and as for *the Territory, from whence they had driven some of their Neighbours by Force, they were to be determin'd in that Point by the Law*.

Having

Having perform'd thefe things, he took the Road that leads to the Town of the *Pergenfefis*, and from thence march'd into *Phrygia* But in his March that way, he was oblig'd to pafs through a very ftrait and narrow Lane, form'd by two Mountains that almoft join to one another, near *Telmiſſus* a Town belonging to the *Piſida* The Entrances into this Lane are fo ftrait, that they may be compar'd to Gates Here the *Barbarians* had pofted themfelves, refolving to difpute *Alexander*'s Paſſage But he prefently caus'd his Army to encamp at the very Entrance, concluding (what afterwards happen'd) that the *Telmiſſenſes*, feeing the Tents pitch'd, would imagine the Danger to be delay'd, and fo would not long remain in thofe Straits, but leaving a competent Number of Men to guard 'em, would retire into the Town *Alexander* therefore laying hold of this Opportunity, order'd the *Archers* and *Slingers* to advance, as alfo thofe of the heavy-arm'd Troops that were leaft encumber'd, and having beat thofe that guarded the Pafs, he went and encamp'd before the Town Here Ambaſſadors came to him from the *Selgenſes*, who (out of their inveterate Hatred to the *Telmiſſenſes*, a'tho' of the fame Nation) offer'd their Friendſhip and Affiftance to the *King* He having receiv'd 'em very gracioufly, that he might not wafte his Time in the Siege of one Place, he went and encamp'd before *Sagalaſſus*, which is a ftrong Place, and was well provided with the Flower of their Forces for its Defence, for tho' all the *Piſida* are warlike and brave, yet the *Sagalaſſenſes* are efteem'd the ftouteft of 'em all Thefe being reinforc'd with Troops from the *Telmeſenſes*, their Allies, and having more Confidence in their own Courage, than in their Walls, had drawn up their Army on a neighbouring Hill, and by reafon of the

Advantage

Advantage they had of the Ground, they repuls'd the light-arm'd Forces *Alexander* had sent against 'em However, the *Agrians* made an obstinate Resistance, and seem'd to be encourag'd by the Approach of the *Macedonian* Phalanx, and the *King*'s Presence, whom they beheld before the Colours. The Soldiers labour'd under great Difficulties while they forc'd their Way up the Hill, but as soon as they had got a little firmer Footing, they easily dispers'd the Multitude of Mountaineers that were but half arm'd. There fell in this Action, of the *Macedonians, Cleander*, who was a Captain, and about twenty private Men Of the *Barbarians*, five hundred were slain, the rest sav'd themselves by flight, and the Knowledge of the Country. The *King* pursu'd them as fast as Troops so encumber'd with Arms, possibly could, and at the same time made himself Master of their Town He carry'd his Arms against the other strong Places of *Pisidia*, of which he reduc'd some by Force, others he receiv'd by Composition. He raz'd *Telmissus*, for the Obstinacy of its Inhabitants, whom he depriv'd of their *Liberty*, and a little after, he united 'em, with some other Cities of *Pisidia*, to the Government of *Celænæ*. *Alexander* having thus quieted these bold People, continu'd his March into *Phrygia*, by the Lake *Ascanius*, whose Waters naturally come to a Concretion, and so save those who live within its Neighbourhood the trouble of going farther for Salt.

While these Things were doing, *Memnon* having got together the scatter'd Remains of his Army, resolv'd to carry the War into *Greece* and *Macedonia*, and by that Diversion, force *Alexander* to leave *Asia* For *Darius* now put all his Hopes in him alone, seeing he had by his Bravery and Conduct kept the Conqueror so long in play at *Halicarnassus*; He therefore
made

made him *Generalissimo* of all his Forces, and sent him a vast Sum of Money. *Memnon* by this Help, having hir'd as many Troops as he could, sail'd up and down the Seas without Opposition, his Fleet consisting of three hundred Ships. He now took into serious Consideration, what could either favour or cross his Designs. And having made himself Master of those Places that were less carefully guarded, (among which was *Lampsacus*) he attack'd the Islands which the *Macedonians* could not succour for want of a Fleet, notwithstanding they were Masters on both sides the Continent.

The great Divisions that reign'd among the People was of mighty Advantage to *Memnon* in his Undertaking. For as some were in *Alexander's* Interest on account of their *Liberty*, which he had restor'd to 'em; there were others, who, having got together great Riches under the *Persians*, preferr'd their own private Power, under their old Masters, to a general Equality in a free *Republick*. This made *Athenagoras* and *Apollonides*, (who were two of the most considerable Men of the Isle of *Chios*) having communicated their Design to *Phisinus* and *Megareus*, and others of their Faction, invite *Memnon* thither. Thus *Chios* was taken by *Treachery*, where having left a sufficient Garrison, the Administration of Affairs was by him put into the Hands of *Apollonides* and his *Associates*.

From thence sailing to *Lesbos* he with small Opposition made himself Master of *Antissa*, *Pyrrha*, and *Eressus*. He establish'd *Aristonicus* in the Regency of *Methymna*, and reduc'd the whole Island, except the famous City of *Mitylene*, which held out a considerable time, and was not taken by *Memnon* himself. For when *he* had rais'd a great many Works about the *Town*, had shut up the Port, and dispos'd his Ships in proper Places, to cut off all Succour from the Place; he was seiz'd with the Plague, and so frustrated all the Hopes of the *Persians*, to their irreparable Damage. But when he found he was near his End, he resign'd his Command to *Pharnabasus* his Sister's Son, whom she had by *Artabasus*, 'till *Darius* being inform'd of his Death, should provide otherwise. *Pharnabasus* therefore dividing the Duties of the Siege with *Autophradates*, the Admiral; so streighten'd the besieg'd, that they surrender'd upon the following Conditions: *That the Garrison should be permitted to march off unmolested. That the* Pillars *on which were engrav'd the Terms of their Allegiance with* Alexander *should be flung down, and swearing Allegiance to* Darius, *they should call home half of those who were banish'd.* But the *Persians* did not observe all the Articles of Capitulation, for having introduc'd Soldiers to the Town, they made *Lycomedes* the *Rhodian*, Governor, assigning the Regency of the Country to *Diogenes*, on the Account of his Zeal for the *Persian* Interest. After this they extorted Money from the richest Inhabitants, notwithstanding which the common Tax of the *Mytilenians* was not at all lessened.

QUINTUS CURTIUS.

BOOK III.

CHAP. I.

IN the mean time *Alexander* sent *Cleander* with a considerable Sum of Money to raise Recruits in *Peloponnesus*, and having settl'd the Affairs of *Lycia* and *Pamphilia*, advanc'd his Army before the Town *Celenæ*, which the River *Marsias* at that time divided in two. This River was much celebrated by the fabulous Relations of the *Greek* Poets. Its Spring rises out of the Top of a Hill, and falls afterwards upon a Rock beneath it, with a mighty Noise, from whence it diffuses itself, and waters the neighbouring Plains, being very clear, as carrying along with it nothing but its own pure Streams. Its Colour therefore resembles that of the calm Sea, and thereby gave birth to the Fiction of the Poets, who pretend, *that the Nymphs being in love with this River, took up their Residence in that Rock.* So long as it runs within the Walls, it retains its own Name, but when it leaves the Town it grows larger, and becomes more rapid in its course, and is then call'd the *Lycus.* Alexander finding the Town deserted by its Inhabitants, enter'd it, and was preparing to attack the Cittadel into which they had fled. He therefore sent a *Herald* to 'em, to let them know, that if they did not surrender the place, *they must expect the utmost Severities.* But they taking the *Herald* into a high Tower, strong both by Nature and Art, bid him *take a view of its height, and acquaint* Alexander, *that the Inhabitants and he had different Notions of its Fortifications: They knew they could not be reduc'd, but however, let the worst come that could, they were ready to lay down their Lives for their Loyalty.* Yet when they saw they were formally besieg'd, and that every thing grew scarcer with 'em from one day to another, *they agreed upon a Truce for two Months, in which time if they receiv'd no Relief from* Darius, *they promis'd to surrender,* and accordingly (no Succour appearing) they submitted to the *King,* on the day prefix'd for that purpose. About this time Ambassadors came to *him* from the *Athenians,* to desire that those of their *City,* who had been made Prisoners at the Battle near the River *Granicus* might be restor'd to 'em. *Alexander* made Answer, *that not only their Citizens, but likewise all the other* Greeks *should be restor'd to their respective Cities, as soon as the* Persian *War was ended.* However, as he long'd to come to an Engagement with *Darius,* who, as he was inform'd, had not yet passed the *Euphrates,* he from all Parts summon'd his Troops, that *he* might be able with his whole Strength, to come to a decisive Action with him. He was then leading his Army

through

NODVS IVGI.

P F Sc

Vol 1 Page 149

P F S

through *Phrygia*, which abounded with Villages, but had not many Towns. Yet there was one still in Request call'd *Gordium*, the ancient seat of *Midas* The River *Sangarius* runs through it, and it is seated between the *Pontick* and the *Cilician* Seas. These Seas almost unite, having but a small Neck of Land to part 'em, each Sea striving to encroach upon the Land, and reducing it into a narrow Straight. But yet tho' it reaches the Continent, and as it is almost surrounded with Water, it seems to represent an Island, insomuch, that were it not for this slender Partition, these Seas would join *Alexander*, having made himself Master of the Town, went into *Jupiter*'s Temple: where they shew'd him *Gordius*'s Chariot, who was father to *Midas*. This *Chariot* in outward Appearance differ'd very little from the common sort But there was one thing in it very remarkable, which was a Cord so mysteriously ty'd into Knots, so artfully interwoven, one within the other, that no body could find out where they began, nor where they ended The Inhabitants giving him to understand, *That the Oracle had declar'd that he that could untie that Knot should conquer* Asia, he was mighty desirous to fulfil the *Prophecy* The *King* was then surrounded with a great many *Phrygians* and *Macedonians*. Those impatiently waited for the Event, and these were full of Concern for the rash Undertaking of their *Prince* For the Series of Knots was so perplex'd, that neither Reason nor Sense could direct him in the Discovery either of its Beginning or End. Hereupon the *King*, being apprehensive that his failing in this Point might be look'd upon as ominous, after a long and fruitless Struggle with the Intricacy of the Knots, broke out into this Expression, *That it was not very material how they were unty'd*, so taking his Sword he cut them all asunder, and by that means either eluded or fulfill'd the *Prophecy*.

Alexander being now resolv'd to find out *Darius* where-ever he was, that he might leave all things in Safety behind him, he gave to *Amphoterus* the Command of his Fleet, on the Coast of the *Hellespont*, and declar'd *Hegelochus* General of the Land-forces, giving them Orders to drive out the *Persian* Garrisons from *Lesbos*, *Chios*, and *Coos*, and order'd them fifty Talents for the said uses. he sent at the same time to *Antipater*, and the other Governours of the *Greek* Cities, six hundred Talents. He requir'd also of the Confederates that they should with their own Ships defend the *Hellespont*. The *King* was not yet inform'd of *Memnon*'s Death, who was then the chiefest of his Care, being well assur'd that he should meet nothing to stop him, unless it was through his means.

Alexander was by this time come to the Town *Ancyra*, where having muster'd his Army, he enter'd *Paphlagonia*, which border'd upon the *Eneti*, from whence some are of Opinion the *Venetians* are descended. All this Country readily submitted to the *King*, and having given him Pledges for their future Loyalty, they obtain'd an Exemption from *Tribute*, it appearing they had not paid any even to the *Persians*. He gave *Calas* the Government of this Country, and march'd himself into *Cappadocia*, taking with him the new Levies that were lately come from *Macedonia*.

CHAP.

CHAP. II.

BUT *Darius* receiving the News of *Memnon*'s Death, was no less griev'd thereat than the Importance of the thing requir'd, and hereupon laying aside all other Hopes, resolv'd to decide the Matter in Person. for he blam'd all his Generals, concluding that most of them had been negligent, but that they were all unfortunate. Having therefore form'd a Camp near *Babylon*, that they might enter upon the War with greater Courage, he drew all his Forces together in Sight of the City; where having intrench'd such a Space of Ground as would conveniently hold ten thousand Men, after *Xerxes*'s Method, he took a List of the Number of his Army From the rising of the Sun till Night, they kept moving into this intrench'd Ground, according to their respective Rolls, and from thence they were distributed in the Plains of *Mesopotamia*.

The Multitude of his Horse and Foot was almost innumerable, and yet in appearance they seem'd to be still more than they really were. Of *Persians* there were one hundred thousand, whereof thirty thousand were Horse. The *Medians* made up ten thousand Horse and fifty thousand Foot. The *Barcanians* consisted of two thousand Horse, arm'd with two-edg'd Bills and light roundish Bucklers, and ten thousand Foot arm'd after the same manner. The *Armenians* had sent forty thousand Foot, and seven thousand Horse The *Hircanians*, who were in great Repute among those Nations, furnish'd six thousand Horse. The *Der-*

bicas had fitted out forty thousand Foot, most of 'em arm'd with Pikes, and the rest with Staves harden'd in the Fire; these were also accompany'd with two thousand Horse of the same Nation. From the *Caspian* Sea there came eight thousand Foot, and two hundred Horse. These had with 'em of the less considerable *Asiaticks* two thousand Foot, and double that Number of Horse. Besides these Troops, there were thirty thousand *Greeks* in their Pay, all chosen young Men. As for the *Bactrians, Sogdians,* and *Indians,* and the other Inhabitants bordering on the *Red Sea,* whose Names were hardly known to him, the Haste he was in would not permit him to wait for their coming. It is plain from hence that he wanted nothing less than Number of Men.

The Sight of this vast Multitude was so grateful to him, and his Nobles, according to their usual Flattery, so swell'd his Hopes, that turning to *Charidemus* an *Athenian,* an experienc'd Soldier, and an Enemy to *Alexander* on the Account of his Banishment (for he had been expell'd *Athens* by his Order) he ask'd him, *Whether he thought him well enough provided to overthrow his Enemy?* But *Charidemus,* unmindful of his Condition, or the *King*'s Pride, made this Answer. *Perhaps, Sir, you may not be pleas'd with the Truth, and yet if I do not tell it now, it will be in vain for me to tell it hereafter. This Army of yours that makes so great an Appearance, this vast Multitude compos'd of so many different Nations, and of all the Eastern Countries, perhaps may be terrible to the neighbouring People. The Purple and Gold with which it is adorn'd, the Splendor and Riches of its Arms is such, that they who have not beheld it with their Eyes, can hardly bring their Thoughts to conceive an Appearance of this nature. But the* Macedonian *Army is dreadful* to behold, and are inur'd to protect their immoveable Wedges, and the united Strength of their Men with their Pikes and Bucklers. Their Phalanx is a firm Body of Foot; the Men stand in close Order, and their Arms are in a manner united, they are so perfectly well exercis'd, that they know how (upon the least Signal giv'n) to follow their Colours and observe their Ranks. The Word of Command is by all obey'd at once. Whether it be to repel the Enemy, to wheel about, or change the Order of Battle, the Officers themselves are not more expert, than the common Soldiers. And that you may not think they value Gold or Silver, they have learn'd this Discipline in the School of Poverty. When they are tir'd, the Ground is their Bed, they satisfie their Hunger with any thing they can get. Now as for the Thessalian Horse, the Acarnanians, and the Ætolians, they are an invincible Body of Men, and shall I believe they are to be repuls'd with Slings, and Pikes harden'd in the Fire? No, Sir, there must be an equal Strength, and you ought to seek for Succour in that Country that produc'd these Men. Send therefore that Gold and that Silver, to hire Troops from whence they came. Darius was naturally of a mild and tractable Disposition, but his high Station now and then tainted it. Being therefore unable to bear the *Truth*, he broke through the Laws of *Hospitality*, and commanded both his Guest and Suppliant and best Adviser, *to be hurried away to Execution*. However even that did not hinder him from speaking his Mind freely, for he told the King, *I have one at hand that will revenge my Death, and he that I advis'd against will chastise you for slighting my Counsel. And you, that by the Regal Prerogative are so suddenly chang'd, shall be an Example to Posterity, that when Men abandon themselves to their Fortune, they even forget*

Nature.

Nature. While he was making this publick Declaration, the Executioners cut his Throat. The *King* was afterwards touch'd with too late a Repentance; and acknowledging *he had spoke the Truth,* order'd him *to be buried.*

CHAP. III.

THymodes, *Mentor's* Son, was a brisk young Man *Darius* commanded him to receive from *Pharnabazus* all the foreign Forces, for he had great Confidence in 'em, and design'd therefore to make use of 'em in the War At the same time he gave to *Pharnabazus* the same Commission that *Memnon* had. Now as *Darius's* Thoughts were wholly taken up with the Views of the present important Affairs, he had also in his Sleep several Dreams, that seem'd to foretel the Event of things; which whether they proceeded from Solicitude and Care, or that his Mind had a real Foreknowledge of what was to happen, is uncertain. He dream'd that the *Macedonian* Camp was all on Fire, and a little after, that *Alexander* was brought to him in the same Garb he was in himself when he was chosen *King*, and that having rid through the City, he on the sudden vanish'd, Horse and all The Judgments of the *Soothsayers* were various, and kept People in suspence for some of 'em said, *His Dream portended good Luck, by reason that the Enemies Camp was on fire, and* Alexander *having laid aside his Regal Robes, had been brought to him in the private Dress of the* Persians Others were of a clear different Opinion, and said, *That the Brightness*

of

of the Macedonian *Camp was a Token of* Alexander's *future Splendour, who they conjectur'd would make himself Master of* Asia, *because he had appear'd in the same Dress* Darius *had when he was saluted King.* The present Anxiety had also revived past Presages, as it usually happens. Darius *in the Beginning of his Reign* had order'd the Persian *Scabbard to be chang'd into that Form that the* Greeks *us'd, hereupon the* Chaldeans *prognosticated that the* Persian *Empire should pass into the Hands of those, whose Arms they had imitated.* However he was wonderfully pleas'd with the *Interpreter's* Exposition, which was spread among the Vulgar, and with the Representation of his *Dream*, and therefore gave Orders for his Army to move towards the *Euphrates*.

It was an ancient Custom among the *Persians* not to break up their Camp till the Sun was rose, and then the Trumpet gave Notice from the *King's* Tent, upon which the Image of the *Sun* was plac'd, enclos'd in a Chrystal Case.

The *Army* march'd in the following Order. The *Fire*, which they hold to be sacred and eternal, was carry'd before on Silver Altars. The *Magi* follow'd next, singing Verses after their Country Manner. These were succeeded by three hundred sixty five Youths, cloath'd in scarlet, answering the Number of the Days of the Year; for the *Persian* Year is divided into so many Days. After these came the Chariot consecrated to *Jupiter*, which was drawn by white Horses, these were follow'd by a *Horse* of an uncommon Height and Bulk, and was call'd *the Horse of the Sun*. The *Drivers* were adorn'd with golden Wands, and white Habits. At a small distance follow'd ten Chariots embellished with a great deal of Gold and Silver finely engrav'd. Next came the Cavalry

Nature. While he was making this publick Declaration, the Executioners cut his Throat. The *King* was afterwards touch'd with too late a Repentance; and acknowledging *he had spoke the Truth,* order'd him *to be buried.*

CHAP. III.

*T*Hymodes, *Mentor*'s Son, was a brisk young Man. *Darius* commanded him to receive from *Pharnabazus* all the foreign Forces, for he had great Confidence in 'em, and design'd therefore to make use of 'em in the War. At the same time he gave to *Pharnabazus* the same Commission that *Memnon* had. Now as *Darius*'s Thoughts were wholly taken up with the Views of the present important Affairs, he had also in his Sleep several Dreams, that seem'd to foretel the Event of things; which whether they proceeded from Solicitude and Care, or that his Mind had a real Foreknowledge of what was to happen, is uncertain. He dream'd that the *Macedonian* Camp was all on Fire, and a little after, that *Alexander* was brought to him in the same Garb he was in himself when he was chosen *King,* and that having rid through the City, he on the sudden vanish'd, Horse and all. The Judgments of the *Soothsayers* were various, and kept People in suspence; for some of 'em said, *His Dream portended good Luck, by reason that the Enemies Camp was on fire, and* Alexander *having laid aside his Regal Robes, had been brought to him in the private Dress of the* Persians. Others were of a clear different Opinion, and said, *That the Brightness*

of

of the Macedonian Camp was a Token of Alexander's future Splendour, who they conjectur'd would make himself Master of Asia, because he had appear'd in the same Dress Darius had when he was saluted King. The present Anxiety had also reviv'd past Presages, as it usually happens. Darius in the Beginning of his Reign had order'd the Persian Scabbard to be chang'd into that Form that the Greeks us'd, hereupon the Chaldeans prognosticated that the Persian Empire should pass into the Hands of those, whose Arms they had imitated. However he was wonderfully pleas'd with the Interpreter's Exposition, which was spread among the Vulgar, and with the Representation of his Dream, and therefore gave Orders for his Army to move towards the Euphrates.

It was an ancient Custom among the Persians not to break up their Camp till the Sun was rose, and then the Trumpet gave Notice from the King's Tent; upon which the Image of the Sun was plac'd, enclos'd in a Chrystal Case.

The Army march'd in the following Order. The Fire, which they hold to be sacred and eternal, was carry'd before on Silver Altars. The Magi follow'd next, singing Verses after their Country Manner These were succeeded by three hundred sixty five Youths, cloath'd in scarlet, answering the Number of the Days of the Year; for the Persian Year is divided into so many Days After these came the Chariot consecrated to Jupiter, which was drawn by white Horses, these were follow'd by a Horse of an uncommon Height and Bulk, and was call'd the Horse of the Sun. The Drivers were adorn'd with golden Wands, and white Habits. At a small distance follow'd ten Chariots embellished with a great deal of Gold and Silver finely engrav'd. Next came the Cavalry of twelve Nations, different in their Manners, and variously arm'd. After these march'd those whom the *Persians* call the *Immortal*, being ten thousand in Number, among all the *Barbarians* none were more richly clad. They had gold Chains about their Necks, and their Clothes were embroider'd with Gold, besides which they had sleev'd Jackets, finely adorn'd with Pearl. At a small distance follow'd those who went by the Denomination of the King's Relations, consisting of fifteen thousand Men. This Band being dress'd almost after the manner of Women, was more conspicuous for its *Luxury* than for its *Arms*. The *Doryphori* came next, who carry'd the King's Apparel, these preceded the King's Chariot, where his Seat was so high that he was easily seen. Each side of the Chariot was curiously set off with the Images of the Gods, wrought in Gold and Silver, the Beam of it glitter'd with precious Stones, and bore two Images of Gold, about a Cubit high, one whereof represented *Ninus*, and the other *Belus*. Between these was plac'd a sacred Eagle of Gold with its Wings expanded. But the Magnificence of the King's Apparel exceeded every thing, his Purple Vest was neatly interwrought with Silver Stripes, and his upper Garwas most artfully embroider'd with Gold, and was besides beautified with the Representation of two Hawks wrought in Gold, who seem'd to peck at one another. His Girdle was after the Womens Mode also of Gold, at which hung his Sword, which had a Scabbard of Pearl. The Royal Ornament for the Head, is by the *Persians* call'd a *Cidaris*, this was encompas'd with a Roll of a sky Colour, with a Mixture of white. The Chariot was follow'd by ten thousand Pikemen, whose Pikes were plated with Silver, having their Spikes tipp'd with Gold. The King had on his right

right and left about two hundred of the noblest of his Relations. This Body was attended by thirty thousand Foot, who were follow'd by four hundred of the King's Horses. After these, within the distance of one Furlong, was *Sysigambis*, *Darius*'s Mother, in one Chariot, and his *Queen* in another. The Troop of Servants that waited on the *Queens*, was on Horseback. Next came fifteen cover'd Waggons, in which were the *King*'s Children with their *Tutors* and *Eunuchs*, which are not accounted contemptible in these Nations. Then follow'd three hundred and sixty of the *King*'s Concubines, all in regal Apparel. The *King*'s Money, which was carry'd by six hundred Mules, and three hundred Camels, attended by a Guard of Archers, went next. After these came the Wives of the *King*'s Relations and Friends, who were follow'd by Crowds of Servants and Slaves. The whole was concluded by the light-arm'd Soldiers with their respective Officers who brought up the Rear. Such was *Darius*'s Army.

But he that beheld *Alexander*'s would find it altogether different, for neither the Men nor the Horses glitter'd with Gold nor rich Apparel, but with their Iron and Brass, yet his Troops were always ready either to halt or to march, being neither burthen'd with Followers, nor overloaded with Baggage, ever attentive, not only to the General's Signal, but even the least nod of his Head. He had room enough to encamp in, and Provision enough for his Army; so that when it was drawn up in order of Battle, he could see a single Soldier was not wanting. Whereas *Darius*, who was *King* of so vast a Multitude, by the straightness of the Place in which he fought, was reduc'd to the small Number he had despis'd in his Enemy.

CHAP.

CHAP. IV.

IN the mean time *Alexander*, having appointed *Abistamenes* Governor of *Cappadocia*, march'd with his Army towards *Cilicia*, and was already come to the Place they call *Cyrus*'s Camp, this part of the Country was so call'd from *Cyrus*'s having encamp'd there, as he was marching into *Lydia* against *Crœsus*. It was about fifty Furlongs distant from the narrow Passage that leads into *Cilicia*, which by the Inhabitants is call'd *Pyla*, being narrow Straits, which Nature seems by Situation to have made as strong as if they had been fortify'd by the Hand of Man. Upon Advice of this, *Arsanes*, who was Governor of *Cilicia*, calling to mind *Memnon*'s Counsel at the beginning of the War (when it would have been of Use) executed the same when it was too late, ravaging *Cilicia* with Fire and Sword, that the Enemy might find it a mere Desart, spoiling every thing that could any way be useful, that he might leave that Country naked and barren, which he could not defend, but it had been much more advisable to have seiz'd the Pass, and to have guarded it with a strong Body of Men, and to have made himself Master of the Mountain that commands the Road, from whence it had been easie, without the least danger, either to have kept off, or to have oppress'd the Enemy However, he having left a few to defend the same, went back himself to lay waste that Country, that he ought to have preserv'd from Depredations. This made those he left there (imagining they were betray'd) not so much

much as wait for the fight of the Enemy, when at the same time a smaller number might have defended that Place, for *Cilicia* is hemm'd in by a Ridge of craggy steep Hills, which beginning at the Sea on one side, and fetching a compass about, joins again to the Sea on the other side. The back of the Mountain that lies farthest from the Sea, has three very narrow Passes, by the one of which you enter *Cilicia*, that part of it that lies towards the Sea is Champain, and has its Plains water'd by several Rivers, of these *Pyramus* and *Cydnus* are the most considerable. The *Cydnus* is not so remarkable for the Largeness of its Stream, as for the Clearness of its Water, for falling gently from its Fountain-head, it is received in a pure Soil, and has no Torrents falling into it to disturb its gentle Current. This is the cause that its Waters are very clear, and at the same time mighty cold, for being shaded by the Trees that grow on its Banks on each side, it preserves its Purity all the way, till it falls into the Sea. Time has impair'd a great many ancient Monuments in this Country, which have been celebrated by the Poets. Here are to be seen the Ruins of the Towns *Lyrnessus* and *Thebes*, as also *Tryphon*'s Cave, and the *Corycian* Grove, which affords Saffron, with the Fame of many other Curiosities, which subsist now only in Report.

Alexander having enter'd these Straits, and consider'd the Nature of the Place, was seiz'd with an Admiration *of his own Felicity*, for he did not scruple to confess, *That he and his Army might have been knock'd on the Head with Stones only, if there had been but Hands to have rowl'd 'em down upon 'em as they pass'd under the Mountain.* The Way was so narrow that four Men could hardly march a-breast; besides, the back of the Hill hung over it, and it was not only

only difficult on the score of its streighness, but also for its being in many Places broken, by the several Rivulets that flow from the bottom of the Hills.

Alexander therefore order'd the light-arm'd *Thracians* to march before, *and examine the narrow ways, for fear the Enemy should lye there in Ambuscade to surprise him.* He also sent a Body of Archers to possess themselves of the top of the Hill, ordering them to march with their Bows ready bent, admonishing 'em that they were not entring upon a March, but upon an Engagement. In this Order he advanc'd to the City of *Tarsus*, which the *Persians* were then setting on Fire, that so rich a Place might not fall into the Hands of the Enemy. But the *King* having sent *Parmenio* before with a Detachment of light Horse, to put a stop to the Fire, sav'd the Place, and understanding that upon approach of his Men the *Barbarians* were fled, enter'd the Town he had preserv'd.

CHAP. V.

THE River *Cydnus* (of which we before made mention) runs thro' this *City*, and it was then the summer Season, at which time the Heat is no where more violent than in this Country of *Cilicia*, and it was the hottest time of the Day. The clearness of the Stream invited the *King* to wash the Sweat and Dust off his Body, which at that time was over heated, therefore he pull'd off his Clothes in sight of the Army, (thinking it would still encrease their Esteem for him, if they perceiv'd he was not over

nice

nice in the Care of his Perſon, but was contented with that Refreſhment that was cheap and always at hand) and went into the River: He was no ſooner in it but a ſudden Horror ſeiz'd all his Limbs, and he turn'd pale, the vital Heat having almoſt forſaken his Body. Hereupon his Servants took him up, and carry'd him into his Tent, he being like one expiring, and equally inſenſible.

The Camp was now in the greateſt Affliction and Concern, nay almoſt in Tears; they *bewail'd the hard Fate of their King (the greateſt and moſt memorable Prince of any Age) that he ſhould be in ſuch a manner ſnatch'd away, in ſo promiſing a courſe of Succeſs, and that too, not in Battle, nor by the Hand of the Enemy, but bathing himſelf in a River* That Darius *was now almoſt in the Neighbourhood, and would be a Conqueror without ſo much as ſeeing his Enemy. That they ſhould be forc'd to march back as Men vanquiſh'd, through thoſe Countries they had ſo lately ſubdu'd, and as either they themſelves or the Enemy had laid every thing waſte in their March, they ſhould periſh even by Famine and Want, in ſuch vaſt Wilderneſſes, altho' no Enemy purſu'd 'em Who would preſume to be their Leader in their Flight? Who would dare to ſucceed* Alexander? *And admitting they made a good Retreat to the* Helleſpont, *who would prepare a Fleet to tranſport 'em?* Then turning their Pity again to the King, they lamented, *that ſuch a Flower of Youth, ſuch a Genius and ſtrength of Mind, their King and their Fellow-Soldier at the ſame time, ſhould be as it were torn from 'em, after ſo ſurprizing a manner.* In the mean time Alexander began to breathe a little more freely, and to open his Eyes, and by degrees recovering his Senſes, to know thoſe about him, and the height of his Diſtemper ſeem'd to abate, if it were but in this, that he was now ſenſible

sible of the greatness of his Sickness. The Indisposition of his Body now affected his Mind, for he was inform'd, *that Darius was but five Days March off of Cilicia.* It griev'd him to think, *that he should be deliver'd as it were bound into the Hands of his Enemy, that so glorious a Victory should be wrested from him, and that he should die after an obscure and ignoble manner in his Tent.* Having therefore called together his Friends and Physicians, he spoke to 'em to this Effect, *You see in what Juncture of my Affairs Fortune has surpriz'd me, methinks I hear the noise of the Enemy's Arms, and I that was the Aggressor am now provok'd to Battle; one would think that when* Darius *writ those haughty Letters to me, that my Fortune had been of his Council, but yet in vain, if I may be permitted to be cur'd my own way. My Occasions do not require slow Medicines, nor timorous Physicians, nay, I had better dye resolutely, than to recover my Health slowly, therefore if there be any Help or Art in my Physicians, let them know, that I do not seek so much a Remedy against Death, as against the impending War.* This violent Temerity fill'd all the Standers-by with Concern, every one therefore began to entreat him, *that he would not encrease his Danger by too precipitous a haste, but that he would commit himself to the Care of his Physicians, that they did not without Cause distrust untry'd Remedies, since the Enemy had with Money tempted those about him to his Destruction* (for Darius had publickly notify'd, that he would give a thousand Talents to whoever should kill Alexander,) *that on this Account they did not believe any Body would dare to make tryal of a Remedy, that by its novelty might give just cause for Suspicion.*

CHAP.

CHAP. VI.

THERE was among the eminent Physicians that had follow'd the *King* from *Macedonia*, one nam'd *Philip*, an *Arcanian* by Nation, a faithful Friend of the *King's*, to whose Care *Alexander* had been committed from his Childhood; he therefore lov'd the *King* with a particular tenderness, looking upon him not only as his *King*, but also as his Pupil. This Man promis'd *Alexander* that he would give him a Dose of Physick that should work its Effects soon, and yet should not fail of curing his Distemper. This Promise pleas'd no body but him at whose Peril it was made, for he lik'd any thing better than delay. The Armies were constantly before his Eyes, and he thought himself sure of the Victory if he could but head his Men. The only thing he dislik'd was, that he was not to take this Medicine (for so the Physician had pre-acquainted him) till three days were elaps'd.

While these things were doing he receives Advice from *Parmenio*, in whom he chiefly confided, not to trust *Philip* with his Health, *for that* Darius *had corrupted him with the Promise of a thousand Talents, and the hopes of his Sister in marriage*. These Letters fill'd him with Anxiety and Care, he weigh'd within himself whatever either Fear or Hope could suggest to him. *Shall I take this Potion? That in case it be Poyson I may be thought to deserve whatever happens? Shall I distrust the Fidelity of my Physician, or shall I resolve to be opprest in my own Tent? However, it is better I should dye by another's Crime than my own Fear.* These things
work'd

work'd his Mind different ways, yet he did not reveal to any Body the Contents of the Letter, but sealing it with his Ring, he laid it under his Pillow. Having pass'd two days in this Agitation of Mind, the third was now at hand, which was the Day prefix'd by his Physician for the taking his Medicine, the which he accordingly brought him. *Alexander* seeing him, rais'd himself upon his Elbow, and holding *Parmenio*'s Letter in his left hand, took the Potion from him and drank it off boldly. and then gave *Philip* the Letter to read, keeping his Eye fix'd upon his Countenance all the time, judging that if he were guilty, there would appear some Symptoms of Guilt in his Looks. *Philip* having read the Letter, shew'd more Indignation than Fear, and flinging down his Cloak and the Letter at the Bed side, he said, *Sir, my Life has always depended on your Majesty, but I look upon it now to do so in a particular manner, since the sacred Breath you draw must determine mine. As for the Treason and Parricide I am charg'd with, your Recovery will sufficiently declare my Innocence, and I beg that when I have sav'd your Life, you'll graciously grant me mine In the mean time suffer the Medicine to work itself into your Veins, and compose your Mind, that your Friends, tho' out of Duty, have unseasonably disturb'd* This Speech not only made the King easy, but chearful, and full of Hopes. He therefore told *Philip*, That if the Gods had given him the choice of an Expedient to know how he was affected towards him, to be sure he would have pitch'd upon some other. But however, he could not have wish'd for any more certain than that which Fortune now offer'd him, for you see that notwithstanding the Letter I receiv'd, I took the Potion you gave me, and I believe you are now no less solicitous for your own Fidelity, than for my Recovery.

Having

Having spoke these Words, he gave him his Hand, but when the Medicine began to exert it self, the Symptoms that ensu'd seem'd to back *Parmenio*'s Advice, for he was so far spent that he with much Difficulty drew his Breath. However, *Philip* omitted nothing that was proper, he apply'd Fomentations to his Body, and when he fainted he restor'd him by the Odour of Meats and Wine, and as soon as he perceiv'd him to grow sensible, he put him in mind sometimes *of his Sister and Mother, and then again of the approaching Victory.*

But when the Physick had wrought itself into his Veins, there began to appear manifest Tokens of his Recovery, for his Mind was first restor'd to its former Vigour, and then his Body regain'd Strength sooner than could have been expected. For in three Days time he shew'd himself to the Army, which was overjoy'd to see him, and almost with equal Eagerness beheld *Philip*, whom they caress'd, returning him Thanks as to a present Divinity. Besides the natural Veneration this Nation has for its *King*, it is not easy to express, how particularly they admir'd and lov'd *Alexander*. For in the first Place, he seem'd to undertake nothing but with the immediate Assistance of the *Deity*, and as *Fortune* sided with him in every thing, his very Rashness always turn'd to his *Glory*. Besides, as his Years did not seem ripe for such great Performances, yet as he acquitted himself worthily thereof, they were so far from lessening 'em, that they even added to their Lustre. Moreover, there are many things which, tho' inconsiderable in themselves, yet are very acceptable to the Soldiery, as his exercising his Body amongst 'em, his extraordinary Apparel that differ'd little from that of a private Man,

and

and his military Vigor, by which Endowments of Nature, or Arts of his Mind, he made himself both belov'd and respected.

CHAP. VII.

AS soon as *Darius* was inform'd of *Alexander's* Indisposition, he march'd with all the Expedition so great a Multitude would admit of, to the *Euphrates*, and having laid a Bridge over the same, his Army pass'd it in five Days, for he desir'd to prevent his Enemy in the Possession of *Cilicia*. But *Alexander* having recover'd his Strength, was now come to the Town call'd *Soli*, which he made himself Master of, and rais'd by Contribution from it, two hundred Talents, putting a Garrison into the Castle. Here he perform'd the Vows he had made for the Recovery of his Health, and celebrated Sports in Honour of *Æsculapius* and *Minerva*, shewing thereby with what Assurance he despis'd the *Barbarians*. While he assisted at these Games, he receiv'd an Express from *Halicarnassus*, which brought him the favourable News of the *Persians* being beat by his Forces, and that the *Mindians* and *Caunians*, with several other People in those Parts, were brought under his Obedience.

The Sports being ended, he decamp'd, and having laid a Bridge over the River *Pyramus*, he came to the City of *Mallos*; from whence he broke up, and came to *Castabala*. Here he was join'd by *Parmenio*, whom he had sent to view the Passage of the Forest through which

which he was to march to the Town *Issus*. *Parmenio* having seiz'd these Passes, and left a sufficient number of Men to guard them, had also taken Possession of *Issus*, which the Inhabitants had abandon'd, from hence he advanc'd farther on, and drove the Enemy from their Holds in the Mountains, and having secur'd the Roads, as we said before, he return'd to the *King*, both the Performer and the Messenger of these Successes. Upon this *Alexander* march'd his Army to *Issus*, where he held a Council to consider, *Whether he should advance any farther, or wait there for the coming up of the new Levies that he suddenly expected from* Macedonia. Parmenio *was of Opinion, that he could not pitch upon a properer Place to give a Battle in, since there the Troops of both Kings, would be reduc'd to an equal Number, by reason the Straits would not admit of a Multitude. That they ought to avoid the Plains and open Fields, where they might be surrounded, and oppress'd by the Inequality of Number. For he did not fear so much their being overcome by the Bravery of the Enemy, as by their own Weariness. Whereas the* Persians *in a more spacious Place, would be constantly reliev'd by fresh Troops.* So wholesome a Counsel was easily approv'd of, and therefore he resolv'd to wait there for the Enemy.

There was at this time in the *Macedonian* Army, a *Persian* named *Sisines*, who had formerly been sent by the Governor of *Ægypt* to King *Philip*. This Man being courteously entertain'd, and honourably promoted in *Macedon*, chose rather to remain there, than return to his own Country; but upon *Alexander*'s Expedition into *Asia*, he accompany'd him, and was of the Number of those the *King* confided in. A *Cretan* Soldier having one Day deliver'd him a Letter seal'd with an unknown Seal, from *Nabarzanes* one of *Darius*'s Lieutenants,

tenants, he exhorted him therein, *to do something worthy his Quality and Merit, assuring him, that the King would not fail to requite him for it.* Sismes being altogether innocent, had often endeavoured to shew *Alexander* this Letter, but finding him always busie, and taken up with his Preparations for the ensuing Action, he waited for a more favourable Opportunity, but this Delay gave a Suspicion of his being ill inclin'd. For the Letter was brought first to *Alexander,* who having read it, seal'd it with an unknown Seal, and order'd it to be deliver'd to *Sismes,* intending thereby to try his Fidelity. But he not attending on the *King* for several Days, was look'd upon to suppress the Letter out of an evil Design, so that he was kill'd by the *Cretans,* no doubt by *Alexander*'s Order.

CHAP. VIII.

BY this time the *Greek* Mercenaries that *Thymodes* had receiv'd from *Pharnabazus,* and in whom *Darius* plac'd his chief Hopes, were arriv'd in his Camp. These would fain have persuaded him *to retire, and gain the Plains of* Mesopotamia. *If he did not approve of this, at least to divide his vast Army, and not suffer the whole Strength of his Kingdoms to depend upon one single Stroke of uncertain Fortune.* This Advice was not so disagreeable to the *King* as to his Nobles. They urg'd, *That there was no relying upon the Fidelity of these Men; that they were brib'd to betray the Army,* which they would have divided for no other Reason but that they might deliver up to Alexander *whatever should be com-*

Book III. *Quintus Curtius.* 169

committed to their Trust. Therefore the safest way were to surround 'em with the whole Army, and cut 'em to pieces at once, for an Example to all Traytors. But as *Darius* was a religious Prince, and of a mild Disposition, he abhorr'd so barbarous a Counsel, as that of butchering those who had put themselves under his Protection, and were actually in his Service. Which of all the foreign Nations, said he, would trust their Lives with him hereafter, if he should stain his Hands with the Blood of so many Soldiers? Besides, no Body ought to suffer Death for giving weak Advice, since there would be no such thing as Counsellors, if their Lives must be in Danger for speaking their Opinion. That they themselves were every Day consulted by him, and he heard their different Sentiments, yet he did not esteem them that gave him the most prudent Counsel, to be more faithful than the rest. Wherefore he made this Answer to the *Greeks*, That he thank'd 'em for the good Disposition they express'd, but as for his going back, he did not think it convenient, since he should thereby deliver up his Kingdom as a Prey to his Enemy. That the Reputation of War depended on Fame, and he that retires, is look'd upon to fly. As to the prolonging the War, it was impossible, by reason the Winter was coming on, and there would be no Means to subsist so vast an Army, in a Country already wasted both by himself and the Enemy. That he could not divide his Forces, without acting contrary to the Practice of his Predecessors, who always brought their whole Strength when they hazarded a Battle. And in Truth, that terrible King, who while he was at a distance, was puff'd up with such a vain Assurance, when he understood that he was near at hand, of rash was become cautious, and lay lurking in the Straits of the Forest, like the cowardly Beasts, who at the least Noise of the Passengers, hide themselves in the Woods. That even now he counterfeited being sick,

Vol. I.   H   *to*

to disappoint his Soldiers. But however, it should now be no longer in his Power to refuse fighting, for if he did, he would seize him in the very Den his faint Heart had made him repair to for Safety.

This Speech had more of Oftentation in it, than of Truth. However *Darius* having fent all his Money, and his moft precious Moveables, under a moderate Guard, to *Damafcus* in *Syria*, march'd with the reft of his Army into *Cilicia*, his Royal Confort and Mother following in the Rear of the Army, according to the Cuftom of the Country. His Daughters alfo and little Son, accompany'd their Father. *Alexander*, as it happen'd, came the fame Night to the Straits that lead to *Syria*, and *Darius* to a Place call'd the *Amanicæ Pylæ*. The *Perfians* made no doubt but the *Macedonians* had abandon'd *Iffus* which they had taken, and were fled. For they had intercepted fome of the wounded and fick, that could not keep up with the Army, and *Darius* at the Inftigation of his Nobles, who were urg'd on by a barbarous Inhumanity, having caus'd their Hands to be cut off and fear'd, order'd them to be led about his Camp, that they might take a View of his Army, and having fatisfy'd their Curiofity, report to their King what they had feen. After this, *Darius* decamp'd, and pafs'd the River *Pinarus*, with a Defign to purfue the routed, as he thought 'em. In the mean time, thofe whofe Hands had been cut off, arrive in *Alexander's* Camp, and inform him, *that Darius was following 'em with the utmoft Diligence*. The King haidly believ'd 'em, and therefore fent Scouts to the Maritime Regions, to know for certain, *whether Darius was there in Perfon, or whether fome of his Grandees did not counterfeit coming with the whole Strength of the Kingdom.* But by that time the Scouts return'd, the vaft Multude appear'd at a diftance, and in a little time, Fire were kindled all over the Camp, which had the Appearance of a general Conflagration, the disorderly Multitude dispersing themselves more loosely for the Conveniency of their Cattle. Hereupon *Alexander* ordered his Army to pitch their Tents, being over-joy'd that he was to come to a decisive Action in those Straits, a thing he had long wish'd for. Nevertheless (as it usually happens, when the Time of Danger draws nigh) his great Assurance began to turn into Solicitude and Care. And he now seem'd to distrust that *Fortune*, by whose Assistance he had been so successful, and did not without some Reason conclude her to be very fickle, from the many Advantages she had bestow'd on himself. He reflected, *That there was now but the space of a single Night between him and the Event of so great a Hazard*. Then again he consider'd, *That the Reward would be still much greater than the Danger, and altho' it was as yet doubtful, whether he should gain the Victory or not, however, this was undeniably certain, that if he perished, he should die honourably and with universal Applause*. He therefore ordered the Soldiers *to go and refresh themselves, and to be in readiness with their Arms at the third Watch*: In the mean time, he went himself to the Top of a high Hill, having with him several Torches and Lights, and there after the manner of his Country, offer'd Sacrifice to the *Gods* of the Place. The Trumpet had now given the third Warning, according to Order, and the Soldiers were ready either to march or to fight; and being commanded *to march with the utmost Diligence*, they came by break of Day to the Straits they design'd to possess themselves of. By this time, they that were sent to get Intelligence, came and acquainted him, that *Darius* was but thirty Furlongs off. He therefore commanded the Army to halt, and having put on his Armour, he drew up his Army in Order of Battle. The affrighted Peasants came now to *Darius*, giving him to understand, that the Enemy was at hand, who could hardly be persuaded that those he thought to pursue as Fugitives, should dare to give him the meeting: Hereupon his People were all seiz'd with a sudden Fear, for they were better prepar'd for a March than for Battle, they therefore take to their Arms in haste, and the very Hurry they were in on that Occasion, increas'd their Terror Some got up to the Top of the Hill, that from thence they might take a View of the Enemy, others were bridling their Horses So that the Discord that reigned in this Army, which was not guided by the Direction of any single Person, fill'd all things with a tumultuary Confusion At first *Darius* had resolv'd with part of his Troops to take Possession of the Top of the Hill, in order to attack the *Enemy* both in Front and Rear, appointing others to do the same on the side of the Sea which cover'd his Right, that so he might press upon 'em from all Parts Moreover he had sent before twenty thousand Foot with a Band of Archers, with Orders to pass the River *Pyramus* (that runs between the two Armies) and charge the *Macedonians* And if they found that impracticable, to retire to the Mountains, and secretly surround their Rear But Fortune, that is superior to all Reason, disappointed his prudent Measures, for some out of fear did not dare to execute their Orders, and others executed them to no Purpose For where the Parts fail, the whole is confounded.

CHAP.

CHAP. IX.

AS for the main Body of his Army, it was drawn up after this manner, *Nabarzanes* was in the Right Wing with his Horse, and about twenty thousand Slingers and Archers, here were also the thirty thousand mercenary *Greeks* commanded by *Thymodes* These were beyond all doubt the main Strength of the Army, a Body equal to the *Macedonian Phalanx* In the Left was *Aristomedes* the *Thessalian*, with twenty thousand of the *Barbarian* Foot, behind 'em were plac'd the most warlike Nations, as a Body of Reserve. The *King* being here in Person, was attended by three thousand chosen Horse, the usual Guard of his Body, and forty thousand Foot, which were follow'd by the *Hyrcanian* and *Median* Cavalry That of the other Nations was dispos'd on the Right and Left, as Occasion requir'd.

The Army thus drawn up, was preceded by six thousand Slingers and Darters There was not the least Space in the *Straights* but was fill'd with Troops, insomuch that one of the Wings extended it self to the Mountains, and the other to the Sea The Queen Consort, with *Darius*'s Mother, and the rest of the Women, were received in the Center of the Army

Now *Alexander* drew up his Army so that the *Phalanx*, which is the chief Strength of the *Macedonians*, was in the Front The Right was commanded by *Nicanor*, the Son of *Parmenio*, next to him were

Cænos, Perdiccas, Meleager, Pto'emy, and *Amyntas,* with their respective Corps. On the Left (that extended it self to the Sea) were *Craterus* and *Parmenio*, but *Craterus* had Orders to obey *Parmenio*. The Horse were plac'd as Wings on each Side, the *Macedonians* with the *Thessalians* on the Right, and the *Peloponnesians* on the Left. In the Front of all was a Body of *Slingers* intermixt with *Archers.* The *Thracians* likewise and the *Cretans,* who were also lightly arm'd, advanc'd before the main Army. The *Agrianians* who were lately arriv'd from *Greece,* were commanded to make Head against those whom *Darius* had sent before to take Possession of the Top of the Mountain. The King had order'd *Parmenio, to extend his Forces as far as he could towards the Sea, that they might lie at a greater distance from the Hills, that the* Barbarians *had taken Possession of.* But *Darius*'s Men neither oppos'd the Troops that march'd against 'em, nor dar'd to surround those who had pass'd 'em, but fled at the very first Sight of the Slingers; which secur'd *Alexander*'s Army from being flank'd from the higher Ground, which was what he was afraid of. They march'd thirty two in a Rank, for the Straightness of the Place would not admit of a greater Number. But as the Passage between the Mountains, by Degrees grew wider and wider, and stretch'd it self out into a larger Space, the Foot had not only Room to extend their Ranks, but the Horse had also Liberty to form their Wings on each side of 'em.

CHAP.

CHAP. X.

THE two Armies were now in sight of each other, but out of the reach of their Darts, when the *Persians* first gave a confus'd but terrible Shout, which the *Macedonians* return'd with Advantage, altho' fewer in Number, by reason of the Repercussion from the neighbouring Hills and Woods, which multiply'd every Sound that reach'd 'em. *Alexander* rid at the Head of his Army, making Signs with his Hand to his Men, not to march too fast, that they might not be out of Breath, and so might be able to charge the Enemy with the greater Fury. Then riding along the Line, he made a different Speech to the several Troops, suitable to their different Dispositions. *He reminded the* Macedonians *of their experienc'd and harden'd Courage, and of their numberless Victories in* Europe, *and that they were come thither voluntarily under his Conduct, to subdue all* Asia, *and to extend their Conquests even to the utmost Bounds of the* East. *That they were the Deliverers of the Opprest, throughout the whole World, and that having carry'd their Victories as far as* Hercules *and* Bacchus *had formerly done, they were to give the Law, not only to the* Persians, *but also to all the Nations of the Universe. That* Bactra *and the* Indies *were to be theirs. That what they had in View at present was but inconsiderable, in comparison of what the Victory promis'd 'em. That the broken Rocks of* Illyria, *or the barren Country of* Thrace, *should no longer be the Reward of their Labour, for now the Spoils of all the* East *were laid before 'em. That there would hardly be Occasion for their Swords; their very Reputation having already made such an Impression upon the fearful Diffidence of the Enemy's Army, that they might drive 'em with only their Bucklers.* He refresh'd their Memory, *with the Victory his Father* Philip *had gain'd over the* Athenians, *with the late Conquest of* Beotia, *and the razing its principal City.* He put them also in mind *of the* Granick River. *Of the many Towns they had either reduc'd by Force, or receiv'd by Submission.* In fine, He reminded 'em of *all their past Conquests.* When he came to the *Greeks*, He told 'em, *that these were the People that had made War upon* Greece, *through the Influence of* Darius *first, and then of* Xerxes, *who requir'd no less than all the Water as well as Land, even to the drinking their very Fountains dry, and consuming all their Provisions. That these were they who had destroy'd and burnt the Temples of their Gods, taken and plunder'd their Towns, in a Word, had broken through all the Laws divine and human.* As for the *Illyrians* and *Thracians*, who were accustom'd to live by Rapine, He bid 'em *behold the Army of their Enemy, how it glitter'd with Gold and Purple, insomuch that they might not be said to carry Arms, so properly as a Booty. That as Men, they had nothing to do but to rifle those weak Women of their Gold, and to make an Exchange of their craggy Mountains, and naked Tracts, which were perpetually cover'd with Ice and Snow, for the fruitful Plains and Fields of* Persia.

CHAP.

CHAP. XI.

BOTH Armies were now within the Cast of their Darts, when the *Persian* Horse gave a furious Charge on the left Wing of the Enemy. For *Darius* was desirous to decide the Matter by the Horse, being sensible that the *Phalanx* was the chief Strength of the *Macedonian*, and *Alexander*'s right Wing was near being surrounded, which he perceiving, order'd two Squadrons to keep Possession of the Top of the Hill, and commanded the rest to assist their Fellows who were engag'd. Then having drawn off the *Thessalian* Horse, he commanded their Officer secretly to fall behind the Army and join *Parmenio*, and vigorously to execute his Orders.

By this time the *Phalanx* was in a manner enclos'd by the *Enemy*, but yet bravely maintain'd its Ground. However as they stood too close to one another, they could not cast their Darts with Freedom, for those that were flung at the same time, meeting in the Air, so intermingl'd that they fell with little or no Force, very few of 'em reaching the Enemy, and the greatest Part falling on the Ground without doing any Execution. Wherefore they gallantly drew their Swords, and engag'd the *Persians* in a close Fight. Here it was that a great deal of Blood was spilt. For the two Armies were so near each other that they parry'd their mutual Thrusts with their Swords, directing their Points in one another's Faces. Here the cowardly or the timorous were not suffer'd to be idle. For joining Foot to Foot, they fought after the manner of single Duellists, and kept the same Spot of Ground, till having slain their Adversary they made themselves Way. And even then a fresh Enemy engag'd him that was already fatigu'd. Besides, the Wounded could not, as is customary, withdraw from the Fight, the Enemy pressing upon 'em in Front, and their own Men in the Rear. *Alexander* not only discharg'd the Duty of a General, but also of a private Soldier, and was ambitious of killing *Darius* with his own Hand. For as he was so loftily seated in his Chariot, that he was easily seen by all, it was a mighty Encouragement to his own Men to defend *him*, and at the same time no less a Provocation to the Enemy to attack *him*. This made *Oxathres* the King's Brother, as soon as he perceiv'd *Alexander*'s Design, bring the Horse that he commanded before *Darius*'s Chariot. He was remarkable for the Splendor of his Arms, as well as for his personal Strength, and had a tender Affection for the *King*, and distinguish'd himself very much in his Defence, killing those who press'd on too rashly, and putting others to flight. But the *Macedonians*, who were also near the *King*, so encourag'd each other, that with *him*, they broke into the Enemies Horse. Here the Slaughter was like a meer Butchery. The noblest Commanders lay wallowing in their Blood round *Darius*'s Chariot, having had the Satisfaction of his being a Witness to their dying gallantly for his Defence. They all fell upon their Faces, in the Places where they fought, having all their Wounds in the fore Part of their Body. Among the rest, were to be seen *Atixyes*, *Rheomithres*, and *Sabaces* the Governor of *Egypt*, who had all commanded great Armies, and round them lay Heaps of Foot and Horse of an inferiour Rank. Of the *Macedonians* there did not fall many, but the bravest and

fol-

Vol 1 Page 178

forwardeſt among 'em; *Alexander* himſelf being ſlightly wounded in the Thigh. The Horſes that drew *Darius*'s Chariot being ſtuck in many Places, and enrag'd with the Pain, began to kick and fling, and were like to caſt him out of his Seat, when fearing leſt he ſhould fall alive into the Hands of his Enemies, he leap'd down, and mounted a Horſe that was ready for that purpoſe, ingloriouſly flinging away the Tokens of his *Dignity*, leſt they ſhould betray *him* in his Flight. *Darius* being fled, the remaining Part of the Army was ſoon diſpers'd through Fear, every one flinging down thoſe Arms he had taken for his Defence, and making the beſt of his Way ſuch being the Nature of Fear, as to dread even that which ſhould protect it

Parmenio order'd a Body of Horſe to purſue them that fled, and it happen'd that all that Wing had taken to their Heels. But in the right Wing the *Perſians* preſs'd hard upon the *Theſſalian* Horſe, and had already broke down one of their Squadrons, but the *Theſſalians* wheeling about and rallying, charg'd the *Perſians* afreſh with ſo much Bravery, that they eaſily routed their diſorder'd Troops, who had broken their Ranks, thinking themſelves ſecure of the *Victory*. The *Perſian* Horſes as well the Riders, being loaded with Armour, could not wheel about but with great Difficulty, and as that is an Act that depends on Celerity, the nimbler *Theſſalians* kill'd a great many of 'em before they could perform their Wheel When *Alexander* was inform'd of his Advantage alſo on this ſide, tho' he did not dare to purſue the *Barbarians* before, yet as ſoon as *he* found *he* had gain'd a compleat Victory, he reſolved to purſue the Enemy. The King had not above a thouſand Horſe with him, and yet he made a prodigious Slaughter of the Enemy.

But

But who examines into the Number of Troops either in a Victory or Flight? They were drove therefore by this handful of Men, like so many Sheep, and the same Fear that made 'em fly, retarded their Flight. But the *Greeks* that were hir'd by *Darius*, and commanded by *Amyntas* (formerly one of *Alexander*'s Lieutenants, tho' now a Malecontent and a Deserter) separating themselves from the rest, retreated in good Order.

The *Barbarians*, in their Confusion, took several Roads, some took the direct Road to *Persia*, some fetching a Compass, repair'd to the Rocks and the close Woods of the Mountains, a small Body of 'em betook themselves to *Darius*'s Camp, but the Enemy had already enter'd the same, where they found all manner of Riches. There was an immense Treasure of Gold and Silver (which seem'd rather to be intended for Pomp and Luxury, than for the Use of the War) which fell a Prey to the Soldiers. And as they increas'd their Plunder, they lighten'd themselves by flinging away what their Avarice made 'em think of less Value in comparison of a richer Booty. They were now come among the Women, who the richer they were clad, were by the Soldiery more outragiously strip'd of their Ornaments. Nay, their very Bodies were not exempt from what Power and Lust could inspire. The whole Camp was fill'd with Cries and Lamentations, according to every one's Fortune, there being no sort of Evil that they did not experience, since the Cruelty and Licentiousness of the *Victor* rag'd through all Ranks and Ages.

Here was at the same time, a particular *Specimen* of the Impotency of *Fortune*, for those very Persons who had dress'd up *Darius*'s Tent with all the Opulency and Luxury imaginable, took Care of the same

for

for *Alexander*, as if he had been their first Master. For this was the only thing the Soldiers had left untouch'd, in compliance with an ancient Custom, that preserv'd always the Tent of the conquer'd Prince, for the Reception of the Victorious. But of all the Captives, the Mother and Wife of *Darius* drew the Eyes and Reflections of all Beholders upon 'em. The first was venerable, not only by her Majesty, but also by her Age; the latter, by her consummate Beauty, which even her present Calamities did not impair. She held in her Lap her young Son, who did not yet exceed six Years of Age, and who was intitl'd by his Birth, to that vast *Fortune* his *Father* had just lost. *Darius*'s two Daughters, that were then marriagable, lean'd on their *Grandmother*'s Bosom, not more afflicted at their own Misfortune, than at hers. Round about her stood a Crowd of noble Ladies, with their Hair and Garments torn, unmindful of their former Splendor, calling upon the *Queens* with the distinguishing *Titles* of *Majesty* and *Sovereign*, which once belong'd to them, tho' they now depended upon another's Pleasure. But the *Queens* themselves forgetting their own Disaster, were inquisitive *in which Wing* Darius *fought, and what was his Success?* For they still deny'd they were Prisoners, if the King were safe. At the same time, as he often chang'd Horses, he was got a great way off. There fell of the *Persians* in this Action, one hundred thousand Foot, and ten thousand Horse. On *Alexander*'s side, there were of the Foot, five hundred and four wounded, and thirty two kill'd, and of the Horse, one hundred and fifty were slain. So inconsiderable was the Loss that procur'd him so glorious a Victory.

CHAP.

CHAP. XII.

THE *King* being very much fatigu'd in his Purfuit after *Darius*, finding that Night approach'd, and that there were no hopes of overtaking him, return'd to the Camp which his Men had a little before taken Poffeffion of. Here he invited thofe of his Friends he was moft familiar with, to an Entertainment; for the Hurt he had receiv'd in his Thigh, being but Skin deep, it did not hinder him from being prefent at the Banquet. But a fudden mournful Clamour, intermixt with a barbarous Outcry from a neighbouring Tent, difturbed their Merriment. Hereupon the Band that kept Guard at the King's Tent, thinking it was the Beginning of a greater Mifchief, immediately took to their Arms. The Caufe of this unexpected Alarm, was owing to the Cries and Lamentations of *Darius*'s Mother, his Wife, and the reft of the noble Ladies, who believing the King was flain, bewail'd him after their Country manner. For one of the captive *Eunuchs*, who chanc'd to ftand before their Tent, faw one of the Soldiers carrying *Darius*'s Cloak, which he had caft away left it fhould betray him in his Flight, and judging thereby that the King was kill'd, had acquainted the Queens with the falfe Suppofition. It is faid, *Alexander* being inform'd of the Ladies Miftake, wept in Compaffion of *Darius*'s Fortune, and the pious Difpofition of the Women. He therefore firft fent *Mithrenes* (who had furrender'd *Sardis*) to 'em (he being well vers'd in the *Perfia* Language)

Language) to comfort 'em in their Affliction, then reflecting that the Sight of this Traitor might aggravate their Grief, he order'd *Leonatus*, one of his Nobles, to assure 'em, *That they were in the wrong to lament* Darius *as dead, since he was actually living*. *Leonatus* taking a few arm'd Soldiers with him, went accordingly to the Tent where the *Royal Captives* were, and notify'd that he was come thither with a Message from the *King*. But they that waited at the Entry of the Tent, as soon as they perceiv'd the Men in Arms, concluding the Fate of their Mistresses was now at hand, run into the Tent, crying out, *That their last Hour was come, and that the King had sent Soldiers to kill 'em*. However, the *Queens* not being able to make any Opposition, and not daring to give Orders for their coming in, made no Answer at all, but silently expected the Pleasure of the *Conqueror*. *Leonatus* therefore having waited a considerable time for some Person to introduce him, when he found no Body dar'd to come to him, leaving his Men without, he enter'd into the Tent alone, that of it self was sufficient to frighten the Ladies, because he rush'd in without having obtain'd Admittance Hereupon *Darius*'s Mother and Wife, flinging themselves at his Feet, implor'd him *to grant them leave to bury* Darius's *Corps after the manner of their Country, before he put them to Death*, telling him, *that after they had perform'd the last Rites to their King, they were ready to submit to their Fate*. But *Leonatus*, to their great Surprize, assur'd 'em, that *Darius* was living, and that for their own Parts, they should not only be in Safety, but be us'd as *Queens*, with all the Splendor of their former Grandeur. Upon this *Darius*'s Mother suffer'd her self to be help'd up. The next Day *Alexander* took Care to bury his Dead, and order'd

the

the same Honour to be shewn to the most considerable among the Persians *that were slain.* And gave leave *to* Sizygambis *to bury as many as she pleas'd, after the manner of the Country* But she was contented to shew that Honour only to some few of her nearest Relations, and even in reference to them, *had a Regard to her present Circumstances,* imagining *that the Pomp that the* Persians *use on that Occasion, might be taken ill by the Conquerors, who are contented to burn their own dead with little or no Ceremony* Alexander having discharg'd this Office to the Dead, notify'd to the Captive *Queens,* that *he* was coming to pay them a Visit, and leaving his Attendants without, enter'd the Tent with *Hephæstion* only, who of all his Friends was most in his Favour, as having been educated with him He was privy to all his Secrets, and alone had the Privilege of speaking freely to him, even to admonish him upon Occasion, which Liberty he was so far from abusing, that whenever he us'd it, he seem'd to do it rather by the King's Permission than of his own Authority, and as he was of like Age with the King, so he had the Advantage of him in the Beauty of his Person. The *Queen* therefore mistaking him for the *King,* paid him Homage after their manner, but some of the *Eunuchs* reminding her of her Error, and shewing her which was the *King,* she flung her self at his Feet, *excusing her Ignorance, as never having seen him before.* But the King lifting her up, said to her, *Mother, you were not mistaken, for he too is* Alexander Now if he had preserv'd the same Moderation to the End of his Life, I should have esteem'd him happier than he seem'd to be when he imitated the Triumph of *Bacchus,* after his Conquest of the several Nations from the *Hellespont* to the *Ocean. He* would then have suppress'd his

Pride

Pride and his *Anger*, which he afterwards found *invincible Evils*. He had not then embru'd his Hands in the Blood of his Friends at Table. He would then have been asham'd to put to Death those renowned Warriors (who had help'd him to conquer so many Nations) without so much as giving them a Hearing. But at that time, the Greatness of his *Fortune* had not got Possession of his Mind, so that he bore its first Beginning with Moderation and Prudence, tho' at last she grew too vast for his Capacity. At first he behav'd himself so as to excel all the *Kings* before him, in *Clemency* and *Continency*; for his Deportment towards the Royal Virgins, was so religiously virtuous, tho' they were perfect Beauties, that he could not have acted with more Reserve, had they been his own Sisters. And as for *Darius*'s Wife, notwithstanding her Beauty was such as to be exceeded by none of her time, he was so far from offering Violence to her, that he took due Care that no Body else should offer at that Usage of his Captive. He commanded *all manner of Respect to be paid to the Royal Ladies*, insomuch that there was nothing wanting to their primitive Magnificence tho' in Captivity, except Confidence in the Conqueror. *Sizygambis* therefore address'd her self to *him* in this manner.

You deserve, Sir, that we should offer up the same Vows for you that we formerly made for Darius, for as far as I can see, you are worthy to surpass him, not only in Felicity, but also in Justice. You are pleas'd to call me Mother and Queen, but I acknowledge my self to be your Servant, for notwithstanding I am able to bear my former Dignity, yet I find I can conform my self to my present Servitude. But it is for your Glory and Honour, that you express the Power you have over us, rather by your Clemency and Goodness, than by your Anger and Severity the same Honour to be shewn to the most considerable among the Persians *that were slain.* And gave leave *to* Sizygambis *to bury as many as she pleas'd, after the manner of the Country* But she was contented to shew that Honour only to some few of her nearest Relations, and even in reference to them, *had a Regard to her present Circumstances,* imagining *that the Pomp that the* Persians *use on that Occasion, might be taken ill by the Conquerors, who are contented to burn their own dead with little or no Ceremony* Alexander having discharg'd this Office to the Dead, notify'd to the Captive *Queens*, that *he* was coming to pay them a Visit, and leaving his Attendants without, enter'd the Tent with *Hephastion* only, who of all his Friends was most in his Favour, as having been educated with him He was privy to all his Secrets, and alone had the Privilege of speaking freely to him, even to admonish him upon Occasion, which Liberty he was so far from abusing, that whenever he us'd it, he seem'd to do it rather by the King's Permission than of his own Authority, and as he was of like Age with the King, so he had the Advantage of him in the Beauty of his Person. The *Queen* therefore mistaking him for the *King*, paid him Homage after their manner, but some of the *Eunuchs* reminding her of her Error, and shewing her which was the *King*, she flung her self at his Feet, *excusing her Ignorance, as never having seen him before.* But the King lifting her up, said to her, *Mother, you were not mistaken, for he too is* Alexander Now if he had preserv'd the same Moderation to the End of his Life, I should have esteem'd him happier than he seem'd to be when he imitated the Triumph of *Bacchus*, after his Conquest of the several Nations from the *Hellespont* to the *Ocean*. *He* would then have suppress'd his

Pride

Pride and his *Anger*, which he afterwards found *invincible Evils.* He had not then embru'd his Hands in the Blood of his Friends at Table. He would then have been asham'd to put to Death those renowned Warriors (who had help'd him to conquer so many Nations) without so much as giving them a Hearing. But at that time, the Greatness of his *Fortune* had not got Possession of his Mind, so that he bore its first Beginning with Moderation and Prudence, tho' at last she grew too vast for his Capacity. At first he behav'd himself so as to excel all the *Kings* before him, in *Clemency* and *Continency*; for his Deportment toward the Royal Virgins, was so religiously virtuous, tho' they were perfect Beauties, that he could not have acted with more Reserve, had they been his own Sisters. And as for *Darius*'s Wife, notwithstanding her Beauty was such as to be exceeded by none of her time, he was so far from offering Violence to her, that he took due Care that no Body else should offer at that Usage of his Captive. He commanded *all manner of Respect to be paid to the Royal Ladies*, insomuch that there was nothing wanting to their primitive Magnificence tho' in Captivity, except Confidence in the Conqueror. *Sizygambis* therefore address'd her self to *him* in this manner.

You deserve, Sir, that we should offer up the same Vows for you that we formerly made for Darius, *for as far as I can see, you are worthy to surpass him, not only in Felicity, but also in Justice. You are pleas'd to call me Mother and Queen, but I acknowledge my self to be your Servant, for notwithstanding I am able to bear my former Dignity, yet I find I can conform my self to my present Servitude. But it is for your Glory and Honour, that you express the Power you have over us, rather by your Clemency and Goodness, than by your Anger and Severity.*

Severity. The King hereupon *bid 'em not be dejected,* and then took *Darius*'s Son in his Arms, who was so far from being frighten'd, tho' it was the first time he had seen him, that he put his Hands about his Neck. The King was so mov'd at the Child's Constancy, that turning to *Hephæstion* he said, *how glad should I be, if Darius had had something of this Child's Disposition.* Then taking his leave of the *Queen,* he went away, and having caus'd three *Altars* to be erected on the Bank of the River *Pinarus,* in Honour of *Jupiter, Hercules,* and *Minerva,* he march'd into *Syria,* sending *Parmenio* before to *Damascus,* where the King's Treasure was kept.

CHAP. XIII.

*P*Armenio understanding that one of *Darius*'s Lieutenants was gone before him, and apprehending that the small Number he had with him might appear contemptible to the Enemy, had resolv'd to send for a Reinforcement, but it happened that a certain *Mardian* fell into the Hands of his Scouts, who bringing him to *Parmenio,* deliver'd to him Letters from the Governor of *Damascus* to *Alexander,* telling him withal, *that he did not doubt but the said Governor intended to deliver up to him all the King's Furniture and Money.* Parmenio having set a Guard upon him, opens the Letter, in which was writ, *That* Alexander *should send with Expedition one of his Generals with a small Body of Men.* Upon this Information, *Parmenio* sent back the *Mardian,* with a small Guard to the Traitor. But he making his Escape, arriv'd at *Damascus* before Day

This made *Parmenio* somewhat uneasie, for he began to suspect some Ambuscade might be laid for him, and therefore was afraid to march without a Guide; however, confiding in the good Fortune of his Prince, he order'd some Peasants to be intercepted to serve him as Guides, and his Men having quickly found some, he reach'd the Town on the fourth Day, when the Governor began to think his Letter had not been credited Wherefore pretending to distrust the Strength of the Place, before the Sun was up, he order'd the King's Money and the most valuable Moveables, to be brought forth, pretending to fly, but in reality to deliver the Booty to the Enemy He was accompany'd out of Town by a great many thousand Men and Women, a deplorable Spectacle to all the Spectators, except him to whose Care they were committed. For that he might be the better rewarded for his Treachery, he intended to deliver to the Enemy a more acceptable Booty than that of Money, *viz.* several Noblemen, with the Wives and Children of *Darius*'s Governors Besides these, there were the Ambassadors of the *Greek* Towns, all which *Darius* had put into his treacherous Tuition, as into a Place of Safety The *Persians* call those who carry Burthens on their Shoulders, *Gangaba.* These Men not being able to endure the Cold (for there had fallen a great deal of Snow, and besides it was a hard Frost) put on the rich Garments of Gold and Purple, with which they were loaded as well as with Money; no body daring to oppose their so doing, the King's hard Fate having render'd him contemptible even to the vilest Wretches. This Multitude seem'd at first to *Parmenio* to be no despicable Army, he therefore having made a short Speech to his Men to animate and encourage 'em, commanded 'em *to clap Spurs to their Horses, and to charge*

charge the Enemy vigorously. But those that carry'd the Burthens, perceiving what was doing, flung down their Loads, and took to their Heels out of Fear. The Soldiers that follow'd 'em, being also intimidated, cast away their Arms, and fled through the Bye-ways they were well acquainted with, the Governor himself counterfeiting Fear likewise, had caus'd a general Confusion. The King's Riches lay scatter'd up and down the Fields, *viz.* That Money that was to pay so vast an Army, with the rich Apparel of so many Noblemen and Women, Golden Vessels, Gold Bridles, Tents adorn'd with Regal Magnificence, Chariots forsaken by their Drivers, loaded with infinite Riches, insomuch that it was a dismal Sight even to the Plunderers themselves, if it was possible for any thing to stop the greedy Desire of Wealth. Here was to be seen all that immense Treasure and rich Furniture (that had been heaping up in so long a Course of Prosperity, that almost exceeded all Belief) expos'd to be pillag'd, some things being torn from the Bushes where they hung, others dug out of the Mire where they lay. There were not Hands enough for this inglorious Work. By this time those that first fled, were overtaken; there were a great many Women among 'em, whereof some led their little Children by the Hand. Here were also three Maiden Ladies, the Daughters of *Ochus*, who had reign'd last before *Darius.* they had fallen from their Paternal Rank and Dignity by the former Change of Affairs, but now Fortune seem'd cruelly to aggravate their Calamity. In this Crowd there was, beside the Wife of *Ochus*, and the Daughter of *Oxatres*, *Darius*'s Brother, with the Wife of *Artabazus* (who was the first Nobleman of *Persia*) and his Son nam'd *Ilionens.* With these were also taken the Wife and Son of *Pharnabazus*, to whom *Darius*
had

had given the chief Command of the Maritime Coast, *Mentor*'s three Daughters, and the Wife and Son of that noble Captain, *Memnon*. In fine, there was hardly any noble Family that did not share in the Misfortune. Here were taken also, several *Lacedemonians* and *Athenians*, who contrary to the League with *Alexander*, had sided with the *Persians* *Aristogiton*, *Dropides*, and *Iphicrates* were considerable People among the *Athenians* both for their Birth and Renown *Pausippus*, *Onomastorides*, with *Monimus* and *Callicratides*, who were likewise considerable Men among the *Lacedemonians* The Sum of coin'd Money that was taken, amounted to two thousand and sixty Talents, the wrought Silver was equal to five hundred Talents in Weight, besides all which, there were thirty thousand Men, and seven thousand Beasts of Burthen taken But the Gods quickly punish'd the Betrayer of so much Wealth, for one he had imparted the Matter to, retaining still a Veneration for *Darius*, even in his Calamity, cut off the *Traitor*'s Head, and carry'd it to the *King*, as a seasonable Comfort to a Prince so foully betray'd, for he not only was reveng'd of his Enemy, but had moreover the Satisfaction to find that all his Subjects had not lost the Respect and Fidelity that was due to the Dignity of Majesty

QUIN-

QUINTUS CURTIUS.

BOOK IV.

CHAP. I.

DARIUS, who but a little while since was at the Head of so powerful an Army, riding in his Chariot more after the manner of a Triumph, than of one that was going to give Battle to his *Enemy*, was now forced to a shameful flight thro' those Places he had lately fill'd with his numerous Troops, but were now, by his Misfortune, become desolate and waste. Some few follow'd their *King*, for the broken *Army* did not all take one Road, and as the *King* chang'd Horses frequently, his Followers not having the same Advantages, could not keep Pace with him. He first came to *Concha*, where he was receiv'd by four thousand *Greeks*, who guarded *him* to the *Euphrates*, for he look'd upon that only to be his now, that he could by his Expedition prevent the Enemy's seizing. In the mean time *Alexander* gave Orders to *Parmenio*, who had taken the Booty at *Damascus*, to place good Guard over it, as also upon the Prisoners, and made him Governour of *Syria*, which they call *Cœle*. But the *Syrians* could not at first brook the new Government, because they had not yet sufficiently felt the Scourge of the War, however, being suppress'd as fast as they revolted, they were glad at last to conform to its Orders.

Aradus, which is an Island, was about this time surrender'd to *Alexander*. *Strato*, who was King of that *Island*, had also the Sovereignty of the Maritim Coast, and a considerable Inland Territory.

Alexander having receiv'd his Submission, and taken him into his Protection, march'd his Army to *Marathon*. Here Letters were brought him from *Darius*, at which he was very much incens'd, they being writ in a very haughty Style. But what vext him most was, that *Darius* then writ himself King, without giving *Alexander* that *Title*, and requir'd, rather than desir'd, *That he would restore to him his Mother, Wife and Children, promising for their Ransom as much Money as all* Macedonia *was worth, and as for the Empire, he would try for it again, if he pleas'd, in a fresh Action*. At the same time he advis'd him, if he was still capable of wholesom Advice, to be contented with his own Dominions, and to retire from that Empire he had no Right to, and from being an Enemy, to become a Friend and Ally, he being ready both to give and receive any Engagements on that Account. To this Letter *Alexander* made answer much after this manner. Alexander King, to Darius, *That Prince whose Name you have taken, having committed great Hostilities on those* Greeks, *who inhabit the Coast of the* Hellespont, *and also*

on

on the Ionian Colonies, who are also Greeks, put to Sea with a powerful Fleet and Army, and invaded Macedonia and Greece. After him Xerxes, who was a Prince of the same Family, attack'd us with an infinite Number of Barbarians, and notwithstanding he was beaten at Sea, yet he left Mardonious in Greece, to pillage the Cities in his absence, and burn the Country. Besides all which, who does not know that my Father Philip was inhumanly murder'd by those you had basely corrupted with your Money? You make no scruple to enter upon unjust Wars, and altho' you do not want Arms, you unworthily set a Price upon the Heads of your Enemies, your self having given a late Instance of that, in offering a thousand Talents to him that would murder me, tho' you had so mighty an Army at command. It is plain therefore, that I am not the Aggressor, but repel Force by Force, and the Gods, who always side with the just Cause, have already made me Master of great part of Asia, and given me a signal Victory over you your self. However, tho' you have no reason to expect any Favour at my hands (since you have not so much as observ'd the Laws of War towards me) yet if you come to me in a suppliant manner, I promise you shall receive your Mother, Wife and Children without any Ransom at all. I know how to conquer, and how to use the conquer'd. If you are afraid to venture your Person with me, I am ready to give you Sureties, for your doing it with Safety. But I would have you remember for the future, when you write to me, that you do not only write to a King, but also to your own King. Thersippus was charg'd with this Letter. After this he descended into *Phœnicia*, where the City of *Biblos* was surrendred to him, from whence he march'd to *Sydon*, a City famous for its Antiquity, and the Splendour of its Founders. *Strato* was *King* there, and had receiv'd

Succours from *Darius*, but becaufe the Town had been furrendred to him, more by the Agreement of the Inhabitants than by *Strato*'s own Confent, *Alexander* judging him unworthy of the Crown, gave leave to *Hephaſtion to beſtow the Crown on him, that the* Sydonians *ſhould think moſt worthy of that Honour* Hephaſtion was lodg'd with two young Noblemen of confiderable Note, among the *Sydonians*, he therefore offer'd them the *Kingdom*, but they refus'd it, telling him that it was contrary to the Laws of the Country, *to admit of any one to that Dignity, that was not of the Royal Family* Hereupon *Hephaſtion*, admiring their Greatnefs of Soul, which made 'em flight what others covet at any price of Danger, encourag'd 'em *to perſiſt in that virtuous difpoſition ſince they were the firſt that underſtood how much greater it was to deſpiſe a Kingdom than to accept of it.* However, he defir'd 'em *to name one of the Royal Race, who might remember he receiv'd that Dignity at their hands*

They feeing a great many made Intereft for the obtaining that diftinguifhing Rank, courting the Favour of *Alexander*'s Friends, in hopes to obtain it, declar'd, *That none deſerv'd it better than* Abdolominus, *who, tho' remotely of kin to the Royal Family, was reduc'd thro' Poverty to cultivate a Garden for a ſmall Stipend in the Suburbs of the City* His *Virtue* and *Probity* were the Caufe of his Poverty, as it happens to many, and as he kept clofe to his daily Labour, he was out of the noife of Arms, which at that time fhook all *Aſia* But on the fudden the two Gentlemen before mentioned enter'd the Garden, with the Royal Apparel, where they found *Abdolominus* pulling up the Weeds and ufelefs Plants When they had faluted him King, one of 'em told him, *he muſt make an exchange of his mean Apparel, for thoſe Royal Robes he beheld in his Hands*, and therefore bid him *wash his Body that was cover'd with Dirt and Filth, and take up a kingly Spirit, and advance his Continency and Moderation, to that high Fortune he was worthy of*, and when he should be seated in the Royal Throne, and had in his Power the Life and Death of his Citizens, not to forget the Condition he was in when the Crown was confer'd upon him, nay, in Truth, for which he was chosen King. This Discourse appear'd to *Abdolominus* like a Dream, and he would now and then ask 'em, *If they were in their Senses to ridicule him after so odd a manner?* But as he was slow in complying, they caus'd him to be wash'd, and having cloth'd him with a purple Garment, interwoven with Gold, and by their Oaths satisfy'd him they were serious, and that he was really pitch'd upon to be *King*, he accompany'd them to the *Palace*. The Rumour of what was done (as it usually happens) soon spread itself over the Town, and some were pleas'd with it, while others were incens'd. The Rich represented to *Alexander*'s Friends *his mean Condition and Poverty*. Wherefore the *King* order'd him to be brought before him, and having view'd him well, he said his Person did not disagree with the account of his Extraction, but *he* desir'd him to inform *him* how he had born his Poverty? To which he reply'd, *Would to God I may be able to bear the weight of the Crown with the same Tranquility of Mind, for these Hands of mine have sufficiently supply'd my Wants, and as I had nothing, so I wanted nothing.* The *King* taking this Answer as a Token of a noble Disposition, not only commanded *Strato*'s *royal Furniture to be deliver'd to him*, but also presented him *with a considerable Part of the Persian Booty*, adding the adjacent Territory to his Jurisdiction. In the mean time *Amyntas* (who we laid before had left *Alexander*, and was fled to

the

the *Persians*) was come to Tripolis with four thousand *Greeks* who had follow'd him, after the last Battle, there having shipp'd off his Soldiers, he sail'd to *Cyprus*, and as every one thought at that Juncture of time that whatever he could get Possession of would be his own of Right, he resolv'd to go to *Egypt*, at this time an Enemy to both Kings Resolving to conform himself to the mutability of the Times, making therefore a Speech to his Soldiers, he gave 'em mighty hopes of succeeding in so great an Attempt, he reminded 'em, *that* Sabaces, *who was Governor of* Egypt, *was kill'd in the Battle, that the* Persian *Forces were without a Leader, and were but few in number, and that the* Ægyptians, *who were always dissatisfy'd with their Governors, would look upon 'em rather to be their Friends than their Enemies*.

Necessity put him upon trying all things, for as he had been disppointed of his first Hopes, he look'd upon the future to be preferable to the present Hereupon the Soldiers unanimously agree to follow him where-ever he should lead them, and he thinking it Prudence not to give 'em time to alter their Minds, brought 'em into the Haven of *Pelusium, pretending he was sent thither before by* Darius Having got Possession of *Pelusium*, he advanc'd to *Memphis* The Rumour of his Arrival being spread up and down, the *Egyptians*, out of their natural Levity, which makes them fitter for Innovations, than for any considerable Performances, came out of their Towns and Villages with a Design to assist him to destroy the *Persian* Garrisons, who, notwithstanding they were alarm'd at the suddenness of the Enterprise, did not cast away all hopes of maintaining their Ground But *Amyntas* having got the better of 'em in a set Battle, drove them into the Town, and having pitch'd his Camp, he led

I 2　　　　　　　　　his

his victorious Army out to pillage and destroy the Country, and as if every thing now lay at his Mercy, he ravag'd whatever belong'd to the Enemy. Wherefore *Mazaces*, notwithstanding he knew his Men were dishearten'd by their late Overthrow, represented to 'em, *that the Enemy was dispers'd up and down, being altogether careless on the Account of their late Victory, and that they might with ease recover what they had lost.*

This Counsel was no less prudent in its Reason, than happy in the Event, for they kill'd 'em every Man, their Leader perishing among the rest. Thus *Amyntas* was punish'd for his Treachery to both Kings, for he prov'd as false to him he went over to, as to him he had deserted. *Darius*'s Lieutenants that had surviv'd the Action at *Issus*, having got together the scatter'd Forces that had fled with 'em, and rais'd what Men they could in *Cappadocia* and *Paphlagonia*, resolv'd to try to recover the Country of *Lydia*. *Antigonus* was Governor there for *Alexander*, who notwithstanding he had sent the greatest part of his Garrisons to strengthen the King's Army, yet despising the *Barbarians*, he drew out his Men, and gave 'em Battle.

Here *Fortune* shew'd herself constant to *Alexander*'s Side, for the *Persians* were routed in three Engagements fought in three several Provinces. About this time the *Macedonian* Fleet sailing from *Greece* overcame *Aristomenes*, whom *Darius* had sent to recover the Coast of the *Hellespont*, and either took or sunk all his Ships. On the other side, *Pharnabazus*, Admiral of the *Persian* Fleet, having forc'd the *Milesians* to pay a considerable Sum of Money, and put a Garrison into *Chius*, sail'd with a hundred Ships to *Andros*, and from thence to *Syphnus*, leaving a Garrison also in those Islands, and exacting a Sum of Money from 'em by

way

Vol 1 Page 197

HERCVLES TYRIVS

COL TYRO METR ACTIA
ERACL
APOLLINIS TYRII MEMORIA

way of Punishment. The great War between the two most powerful Princes of *Europe* and *Asia*, in hopes of an universal Empire, had likewise put *Greece* and *Crete* in *Arms*, for *Agis*, King of the *Lacedemonians*, having got together eight thousand *Greeks*, who were return'd home, having made their Escape from *Cilicia*, march'd against *Antipater*, Governor of *Macedonia*. The *Cretans*, according as they chang'd their Sides, were sometimes garrison'd by *Spartans*, and sometimes by *Macedonians* But these were but trifling Quarrels, and hardly worth Fortune's Concern, who seem'd wholly taken up with that War on which all the rest depended.

CHAP. II.

THE *Macedonians* had already made themselves Masters of all *Syria*, and of all *Phœnicia*, excepting *Tyre*, and the King was encamp'd upon the Continent, from which the Town is separated by a narrow Sea Tyre is the most considerable City of either *Syria* or *Phœnicia*, both for its Largeness as well as Fame, and therefore expected rather to be admitted into *Alexander's* Friendship as an Ally, than to become subject to his Empire On this Account they sent him a Present of a Gold Crown, and a large Quantity of Provisions for his Army, all which the King graciously accepted of as from Friends Then turning to the Ambassadors, *he told 'em he intended to sacrifice to Hercules, who is in great Veneration with the Tyrians, that the Kings of Macedon look'd upon themselves to be descend-*

scended from that God, and that he was moreover advis'd by the Oracle to acquit himself of that Devotion. To this the Ambassadors answer'd, *That there was a Temple dedicated to* Hercules *without the Town, in a Place call'd the* Paletyron, *where the King, if he pleas'd, might discharge that Duty.* This Answer so inflam'd *Alexander*, who could not command his Passion, that he spoke to 'em in this manner, *I perceive that because you live in an Island, you trust so much to the Situation of your City, that you despise my Land Army, but in a little time I'll make you know you are on the Continent, and therefore know, that I'll either be admitted into the Town, or I'll take it by force.*

As they were returning with this Answer, some of the King's Friends endeavour'd to persuade 'em *not to deny the King entrance into their City, since the whole Province of* Syria *and* Phœnicia *had submitted to him.* But they relying on the Strength of the Place, resolv'd to endure the Siege, for the Town was divided from the Continent by a narrow Sea of about four Furlongs in breadth, which is much expos'd to the Southwest Wind, which when it rag'd, beat the Waves so violently against the Shore, that the *Macedonians* could not carry on their Work of Communication between the Continent and the *Island.* Nay, they had much ado to work when the Sea was calm; but when it is disturb'd by this Wind, whatever is cast into it is carry'd away by the violent Motion of the Waves. Nor could there be any Foundation laid so strong, but the Waters would eat their Way through the Joints of the Work, and when the Wind was high, it would carry the Waters above the highest Part. Besides this Difficulty, there was another of no less Consequence, viz. the Walls and Towers of the Town were surrounded with a very deep Sea, so that they could not

plant

Book III. *Quintus Curtius.*

plant any battering Engines againſt 'em, but upon Ships at a great diſtance, and it was impoſſible to apply Ladders to the Walls. Now *Alexander* had no Shipping, and if he had had any, they might eaſily have been kept off by Darts from the Town; beſides, the Waters keeping them in a continual Motion, would have made their Machines ineffectual. Beſides all which, there was an Accident, which, tho' but inconſiderable in it ſelf, yet ſerv'd to encourage the *Tyrians*.

Ambaſſadors were come from the *Carthaginians* to offer their annual Sacrifice to *Hercules*, according to the Cuſtom of the Country, for the *Tyrians* having founded *Carthage*, were in great eſteem with the *Carthaginians*, who reſpected 'em as their Parents. Theſe *Ambaſſadors* exhorted 'em *to undergo the Siege with Courage, and they ſhould in a little time receive Succour from* Carthage, for at that time the *Carthaginians* were very powerful at Sea. Having therefore reſolv'd upon a War, they diſpoſe their Engines on their Walls and Towers, diſtribute Arms to their Youth, and fill their Work-houſes with Artificers, with which the City abounded. In fine, the whole Town was taken up with the Preparations for the War. They provided themſelves with grappling Irons, Crows, and other Inventions for the Defence of Towns; but when the Iron was put into the Forge, as they were blowing the Fire they perceiv'd little Streams of Blood under the Flames, which the *Tyrians* interpeted as an ill Omen to the *Macedonians*, and it happen'd that one of *Alexander's* Soldiers, in the breaking of his Bread, obſerv'd Drops of Blood to riſe out of it. The *King* being ſomewhat alarm'd at this Accident, conſulted *Ariſtander* (who was the moſt skilful of all the Soothſayers) about the meaning of it, who to'd him, *That if the Blood had flown from without, it would have por-*

tended

tended Evil to the Macedonians, *but as it proceeded from the inward Parts, it prognosticated Mischief to the City he was going to besiege.* As *Alexander's* Fleet was at a great distance, and that the long Siege would be detrimental to his other Designs, he sent *Heralds* to them to invite 'em to peaceful Terms; but the *Tyrians*, contrary to the Law of Nations, cast 'em headlong into the Sea. This foul Usage so exasperated the *King*, that he resolv'd upon the Siege, but he was first of all oblig'd to make a Peer, to join the Continent and the Town. Hereupon the Soldiers *were seiz'd with the utmost Despair, seeing the Sea was so very deep, that they look'd upon it to be impossible for 'em, even with the Divine Assistance, to fill it up, where should they find Stones large enough, or Trees tall enough for so prodigious a Work?* since whole Countries would hardly afford enough for the Purpose, the Narrowness of the Strait making the Sea always rough, and the closer it was confin'd, the more it rag'd. However, the *King*, who was not now to learn how to manage the Soldiers Minds, assur'd them, *That* Hercules *had appear'd to him in a Dream, and taking him by the Hand seem'd to conduct him into the City.* At the same time he reminded 'em *of the barbarous Usage to his Heralds, of the Violation of the Law of Nations, and that it was a Shame the Course of their Victories should be stopp'd by a single Town.* There was great Plenty of Stones at hand, in the Ruins of the old Town, and Mount *Libanus* supply'd 'em with Materials for their Boats and Towers. The Work was already swell'd to the Bulk of a Mountain from the bottom of the Sea, but yet it did not reach the Surface of the Water, and the farther it advanc'd into the Sea, the easier whatever was cast therein, was swallow'd up by the deep Abyss. While the *Macedonians* were thus employ'd, the *Tyrians* came out in their Boats, and in a scoffing manner upbraided 'em *with carrying Burdens on their Backs like Beasts, they who were such mighty Warriors.* They also ask'd 'em, *Whether* Alexander *was greater than* Neptune? These Insults serv'd very much to animate the Soldiers. By this time the Work began to shew it self above the Water, and to increase in breadth, drawing nearer to the Town.

When the *Tyrians* beheld the Bulk of the Peer, (which the Sea had hinder'd 'em before from observing how it encreas'd) they came out in little Boats, and row'd round the Work (which was not join'd to the Island) attacking with their Darts those that guarded it. And as they wounded several without a Return, (they being able to advance or retire as they pleas'd) the *Macedonians* were forc'd to interrupt the Work for some time to defend themselves. The *King* therefore caus'd Skins and Sails to be stretch'd out before the Workmen to protect 'em from the Darts, and rais'd two Towers at the Head of the Peer, from whence the *Macedonians* might with ease annoy with their Darts, those of the Enemy that pass'd under in Boats. On the other side the *Tyrians* having landed some of their Soldiers at a considerable distance, so as not to be perceiv'd by the *Macedonians*, fell upon those that were fetching Stones, and cut 'em to Pieces. And on Mount *Libanus* the *Arabian* Peasants attack'd the dispers'd *Macedonians* and kill'd about thirty of 'em, taking also some of 'em Prisoners.

CHAP. III.

THIS made *Alexander* divide his Army, and that he might not be thought to lie idle before a single City, he committed the Siege to *Perdiccas* and *Craterus*, and march'd himself with a flying Camp into *Arabia*. In the mean time the *Tyrians* fitted out a very large Ship, and loaded it to the Sternward with Stones and Gravel, and thereby rais'd the Stem of it very high, and having besmear'd it with a great Quantity of Pitch and Brimstone, they row'd it along, and its large Sails gathering a great deal of Wind, they soon work'd it up to the *Peer*. They that were on Board, having set Fire to the Forecastle, leap'd into little Boats that follow'd for that Purpose. The Ship thus on Fire, quickly communicated its Flames, which before any Help could be brought, had took hold of the Towers and other Works at the Head of the Bank; and they who were in the little Boats, ply'd the Works with burning Torches, and other combustible Materials, proper to feed the Conflagration. The Fire had already gain'd the very Top of the Towers, where some of the *Macedonians* perish'd in the Flames, while others flinging away their Arms, cast themselves into the Sea. But the *Tyrians*, who chose rather to take 'em alive than to kill them, having lam'd their Hands with Sticks and Stones so as altogether to disable 'em, took them into their Boats with Safety. The Works were not only consum'd by the Fire, but the Wind happening to be high that Day, put the Sea into so a great Ferment,

that

that the Waves beating furiously upon the *Peer*, and having loosened the Joints of the Work, the Water forc'd its way through the middle of the *Peer*. When the Stones on which the Earth was cast, were wash'd away, the whole Structure sunk into the Deep, so that *Alexander* at his Return from *Arabia* hardly found any Footsteps left of so vast a Pile. Here, as it is usual in Disappointments, one cast the Fault upon the other; when they might all with more reason have fix'd it on the Tempestuousness of the Sea. The *King* therefore giving Directions for a new Peer, order'd that the Front of it should be carry'd on against the Wind, whereas the side of the old one lay expos'd to it: This was done, that the other Works, lying as it were under the Shelter of the Forepart, might be secur'd thereby. He also augmented the Breadth of it, that the Towers being built in the middle might be less subject to the Enemies Darts. Whole Trees, with their Arms and Branches, were cast into the Sea, upon which they flung great Heaps of Stones; these were cover'd with a new Course of Trees, which they cover'd again with Earth, till by successive lays of Tree, Stones and Earth, the whole Work became one solid Body. The *Tyrians* at the same time omitted nothing that Ingenuity could invent to render the *Macedonians* Labour ineffectual. The greatest Help they received was from their Divers, who entring the Waters out of the Enemies Sight, swam down unperceiv'd to the very Peer, and with Hooks dragg'd after them the Branches that stuck out of the Stones, which drew along with 'em the other Materials into the Deep. The Trunk of their Trees being thus discharg'd of their Load, were easily remov'd; so that the Foundation failing, the whole Superstructure follow'd. While *Alexander* was thus perplex'd in Mind, and deliberating

with

with himself whether he should continue the Siege, or be gone, his Fleet opportunely arriv'd from *Cyprus*, and at the same time *Cleander* with fresh Recruits from *Greece*. The King divided his Fleet, which consisted of one hundred and eighty Ships, into two Squadrons, the one was commanded by *Pyntagoras* King of *Cyprus*, and *Craterus*, the other he commanded himself in the Royal Galley. But altho' the *Tyrians* had a Fleet, yet they did not dare to venture a Sea Fight with *Alexander*, and therefore they plac'd all their Galleys under their Walls. However the King attack'd 'em there, and sunk 'em. The next Day *Alexander* brought his whole Fleet up to the Walls, which he batter'd on all sides with his Engines, but chiefly with those they call *Rams*. The *Tyrians* on their Part were very diligent in repairing the Damage, and began to build a new Wall within the old one, that in case this fell they might still have that for their Defence. But they were now press'd on all sides, for the Peer was advanc'd within the Cast of a Dart, and the Fleet surrounded the Walls, so that they were annoy'd both from the Sea and Land at the same time. Moreover the *Macedonians* had fasten'd their Galleys two and two, Stern to Stern, so that their Sterns were as far distant from each other as the Interval would permit. This Interval between Stern and Stern was made good with Sail-yards and Planks laid across and fasten'd together, and over these, Bridges were laid for the Soldiers to stand upon. In this Order they were tow'd to the City, and the Soldiers, from these Bridges, ply'd the Besieg'd with their Darts, they themselves being out of Danger, by reason the Stems cover'd them. It was Midnight when the King commanded the Fleet to surround the Town in the order we before describ'd, and when the *Tyrians* saw the Ships draw near the City on

all

all sides, their Hearts began to fail 'em. But on the sudden the Sky was overcast with thick Clouds, which presently intercepted the Light that appear'd about that time. Then the Sea by degrees became more horrible, and began to work high, and the Wind still encreasing, the Waves swell'd prodigiously, dashing the Ships one against another. The Violence of the Tempest was such, that the Bands that fasten'd the Galleys were broke, the Scaffolds and Bridges fell with a dreadful Noise, and drew the Soldiers along with 'em into the Deep. And the Ships that were ty'd together, were not to be govern'd in so high a Sea. The Soldiers were a Hindrance to the Seamen, and the Seamen disturb'd the Soldiers in their Duty. And as it frequently happens in such Cases, the Skilful were forc'd to obey the Ignorant. For the Pilots, who at other Times were us'd to command, being threaten'd with Death, obey'd the Orders of others. At length the Sea, as if overcome by the Obstinacy of the Rowers, resign'd the Ships, as to some parting Signal, and they reach'd the Shore, altho' most of 'em much shatter'd. About this time there came thirty Ambassadors from *Carthage*, being rather a Comfort than a Help to the Besieged, for they gave 'em to understand, *that the* Carthaginians *were themselves so engag'd in War, that they did not now fight for Empire, but for Safety.* The *Syracusans* were at this time destroying *Africa* with Fire and Sword, and were encamp'd not far from the Walls of *Carthage*. The *Tyrians* however were not discourag'd, tho' disappointed of so considerable an Expectation, but delivering their Wives and Children to these Ambassadors to be transported to *Carthage*, resolv'd to bear whatever happen'd with the greater Fortitude, since they had the Satisfaction to have secur'd what was most dear to 'em, from sharing in the common Danger. At this very Juncture

Juncture one of the *Citizens* declar'd to the Assembly *That* Apollo, whom the *Tyrians* had a great Veneration for, *had appear'd to him in his Sleep, as if he was going to leave the Town, and that the Peer the* Macedonians *had made, seem'd to him to be chang'd into a Wood.* Hereupon tho' the *Author* was not in great Credit among 'em, yet as they were inclin'd to believe the worst, out of fear, they bound the *Image* with a Golden Chain and fasten'd it to the Altar of *Hercules*, to whom their Town was dedicated, as if they thought by his superiour Power, to retain *Apollo* against his Will. The *Carthaginians* had brought this *Image* from *Syracuse*, and had plac'd it here as being their Original Country, for they were us'd to adorn *Tyre* as well as *Carthage* with the Spoils they took from other Towns: And at this time would fain have persuaded them to renew a Sacrifice, that I cannot believe to be at all acceptable to the Gods, and that the *Tyrians* had laid aside for several Ages, viz *to offer up to* Saturn *a free-born Child*: which Sacrilege (rather than Sacrifice) the *Carthaginians* had receiv'd from their Founders, and are said to have observ'd it till their City was destroy'd. Now had not the Elders (by whose Directions all things were manag'd) oppos'd this barbarous Superstition, it would in all Likelyhood have got the better of Humanity. However their pressing Necessity, which is more efficaciously ingenious than Art, made them not only put in practice the usual Methods of Defence, but inspir'd 'em also with new ones. For, to annoy the Ships that approach'd the Walls, they contriv'd long Rafters, to which they fasten'd Crows, Grappling Irons, Hooks and Scythes, which they discharg'd from their Engines, letting go the Ropes to which they were fasten'd, that they might recover

'em

'em again. These Hooks and Scythes tore to Pieces the Men, and very much damag'd the Ships. They had, besides, another Contrivance, they heated Brass Bucklers as hot as Fire could make 'em, and then fill'd 'em with burning Sand, and boiling Mud, which they pour'd down from the Walls upon the *Macedonians*. None of their Machines were more terrible than this, for if the burning Sand got between the Armour and the Body, as it was impossible to shake it off, it fail'd not to burn whatever it touch'd, so that flinging down their Arms, and tearing every thing off that was to protect their Bodies, they lay expos'd to all manner of Mischief, without being able to do any

CHAP. IV.

BY this time the King was so tir'd with the tediousness of the Siege, that he resolv'd to raise it, and carry his Arms into *Ægypt*. For tho' he had, with incredible Celerity, run over *Asia*, the Walls of one single Town now stop'd his Progress, and hinder'd him from making use of the Opportunity he had, of executing his great Designs. On the other side, he was no less asham'd of going away without carrying his Point, than of being so long about it. Moreover he consider'd his Reputation would suffer (by which he had done more, than by his Arms) if he left *Tyre* as a Witness that he was to be overcome. Therefore, that he might leave no means untry'd, he resolv'd *to make his last Effort with a greater Number of Ships,*
and

and the choicest of his Troops on Board At this time it happen'd that a *Whale* of an unusual Size, (for its Back appear'd above the Water) came and laid it self by the *Peer* side, where having beat the Waves for some time, it rais'd it self so as to be conspicuous to both Parties After this it plung'd again into the Sea near the Head of the Peer, and sometimes shewing it self above the Waves, sometimes hiding itself in the Deep, it shew'd itself for the last time not far from the Walls of the City Both Sides interpreted the Sight of this Monster in favour of their respective Interest The *Macedonians* conjectur'd, *that the Whale pointed to 'em, which way they ought to carry on their Work* And the *Tyrians* concluded, *that* Neptune *had pitch'd upon it, as an Instance of his Right over the usurp'd Sea, and that the new-erected Fabrick would in a little time fall to Ruin* Possessed with this Opinion they fell to feasting, and loaded themselves with Wine And at Sun-rise they mann'd out their Ships which they had adorn'd with Garlands and Flowers, not only presuming the Victory to be certain, but also rejoycing beforehand for it. It happen'd that the *King* had order'd his Fleet to a contrary Part of the Town, and left but thirty of the smallest Rate upon the Shore, two whereof were presently taken by the *Tyrians*, and the rest were in great Danger, till *Alexander* being alarm'd at the Outcry of his Men, came with the Fleet to their Assistance. The first of the *Macedonian* Galleys that came up, was a Galley of five Men to an Oar, which was the swiftest Sailor in the Fleet As soon as the *Tyrians* perceiv'd it, they came against it with two others, one on each side The Cinquereme, plying all its Oars to encounter one of 'em, receiv'd a rude Shock from the Bank of its Adversary, yet grappled with her so as to hold her faft. The other being at liberty, was juft ready to attack her on the contrary fide, when one of *Alexander*'s Galleys came very feafonably to her Relief, and was drove fo violently againft her Enemy, that fhe ftruck the Pilot of the *Tyrian* Galley from his Poft at Stern into the Sea. By this time feveral others of the *Macedonian* Ships were come up, as alfo the *King* in Perfon, which made the *Tyrians* ufe their utmoft Effort to fet their entangled Galley at liberty, which having, tho' with Difficulty, compafs'd, they made to their Haven with all their Fleet. *Alexander* immediately purfu'd them, but could not get into the Haven, by reafon of the Darts with which they ply'd him from the Walls of the City. However he either funk or took moft of their Ships. Then he granted two Days Reft to his Soldiers, after which he advanc'd with all his Ships and Machines, that he might from both attack the Enemy that was already in a great Confternation. The *King*, on this Occafion, plac'd himfelf on the Top of a high Tower, with a great deal of Bravery, but yet greater Danger. For as he was remarkable by his Royal Apparel and the Brightnefs of his Arms, they chiefly aim'd at him. Here he behav'd himfelf with all the Gallantry imaginable, for he kill'd feveral upon the Wall, with his Pike, others in a clofer Engagement, with his Sword and Buckler, he caft headlong into the Sea. For the Tower from which he fought, almoft join'd to the Enemies Walls. The battering Rams had now by their repeated Strokes, beat down great Part of the Fortifications of the Place, the Fleet had enter'd the Fort, and fome of the *Macedonians* had taken Poffeflion of fome of the Towers that the Enemy had deferted, when the *Tyrians*, finking under the Weight of fo many ill Accidents at once, betake themfelves

some

some to the Sanctuary of the Temples, others making fast their Doors, chuse their own way of dying. Some again fell furiously upon the *Macedonians*, resolving not to die unreveng'd. But the greatest Part got up to the Tops of the Houses, and from thence flung Stones, or whatever came next to their Hands, upon the Enemy in the Streets. *Alexander* gave Orders *to spare none but those who had taken Refuge in the Temples, and to set Fire to the Town.* And notwithstanding Proclamation was made accordingly; yet none that could bear Arms, thought fit to seek for Succour from the Gods. The Children of both Sexes, with the young Maidens, fill'd the Temples, and the Men stood at the Entry of their own Houses, ready to fall a Sacrifice to the Soldiers Fury. However, a great many were sav'd by the *Sidonians* that serv'd in *Alexander*'s Army. These having enter'd the Town with the rest of the *Macedonian* Forces, and remembring their Relation with the *Tyrians* (for *Agenor*, as they believ'd, founded both Cities) protected a great many of the Town's People, carrying them on board their Ships, and transported 'em to *Sydon*. There were sav'd, by this means, about fifteen thousand. How much Blood was spilt may be guess'd at from this, that six thousand were found slain within the City Walls. Notwithstanding all this, the *King*'s Anger was not satisfy'd, so that he commanded two thousand of the Enemy that had surviv'd the Soldier's Rage (they being weary with killing) to be crucify'd along the Sea Coast. A sad Spectacle even to the Conquerors themselves! He spar'd the *Ambassadors* of the *Carthaginians*, but declar'd War against 'em, tho' he could not prosecute it immediately, by reason of his other more pressing Affairs. *Tyre* was taken the seventh Month after it was besieg'd, a Town famous to Posterity both for the Antiquity of its Origine, and for its frequent Variety of *Fortune*. It was built by *Agenor*, and held a considerable Time the Sovereignty, not only of the neighbouring Sea, but also of all the Seas where ever its Fleets came. And if we may believe Report, this People was the first that either taught or learn'd Letters. It had planted Colonies almost all over the World, *Carthage* in *Africk*, *Thebes* in *Bœotia*, and *Gades* upon the Ocean. For my part, I am apt to believe, that as the *Tyrians* were Masters at Sea, and often visited Countries unknown to other People, they made choice of such and such Seats for their Youth with which they abounded, or else (for this is also said) that the Island being mightily subject to Earthquakes, the *Inhabitants* (tir'd therewith) were forc'd to settle themselves in other Habitations by dint of Arms. Be it as it will, having undergone many Casualties, and as it were, reviving after being raz'd, by the Help of a long Peace, which makes every thing flourish, it now enjoys a profound Ease under the Protection of the *Roman* Clemency.

CHAP. V.

ABOUT this time, *Alexander* receiv'd Letters from *Darius*, wherein he gives him at last, the Title of *King*, and desir'd ' he would accept of his ' Daughter *Statyra* for Wife, offering him with her, ' all that Tract of Ground that lies between the ' *Hellespont* and the River *Halys*; and that he himself ' would be contented with those Countries that lie
' Eastward

'Eaſtward from thence. That if he found any Dif-
'ficulty to accept of this his Offer, he wiſh'd him
'to reflect, That Fortune ſeldom made any long
'Stay any where, and that the greater Felicity Men
'enjoy'd, the more were they alſo envy'd. That it
'was to be fear'd, leſt by his juvenile Diſpoſition of
'Mind, he ſhould be elated with Vanity, on the Ac-
'count of his Succeſs, after the manner of Birds,
'whoſe natural Lightneſs carry'd 'em up to the Skies.
'That nothing was more difficult, than at his Age to
'be capable of ſo great a Fortune. That as for his
'own part, he ſtill had a great deal left, and ſhould
'not always be ſurpriz'd in Streights. That *Alexan-*
'*der* would find himſelf oblig'd to paſs the *Euphrates*,
'the *Tygre*, the *Araxes*, and the *Hydaſpes*, which
'were like ſo many Bulwarks to his Dominions. That
'in the large Plains he muſt come into, he would be
'aſham'd of his ſmall Number. When would he be
'able to reach *Media*, *Hycarnia*, *Bactra*, and the *In-*
'*dians* that border upon the Ocean? Or the *Sogdians*
'and *Araſchoſians*, who are hardly ſo much as known
'but by their Name, with the other Nations that
'dwell along Mount *Caucaſus*, or the River *Tanais*?
'That were he but barely to travel over theſe vaſt
'Countries without any Oppoſition at all, he would
'find himſelf become old before he could perform the
'Journey. That it was his beſt way not to ſtand
'upon his coming to him, ſince whenever he came, it
'ſhould be to his Ruin.' To which Letter *Alexan-*
der made the following Anſwer by thoſe that
brought it. 'That *Darius* promis'd him what was
'now none of his own. That he offer'd to divide
'that which he had already entirely loſt. That *Lydia*,
'*Ionia*, *Æolia*, and the Coaſt of the *Helleſpont*, were
'actually in his Poſſeſſion by the Law of Arms,
'That

'That it belong'd to the Victorious to prescribe Con-
'ditions, and to the Vanquish'd to receive 'em. If he
'was alone ignorant which of these States he was
'in at present, he might, as soon as he pleas'd, be
'made sensible thereof by another Battle That when
'he pass'd the Sea, he did not propose to himself *Ci-*
'*licia* or *Lydia* (which he look'd upon as an inconsi-
'derable Reward for so great a War) but that *Perse-*
'*polis*, the Capital of his Empire, with *Bactra*, and
'*Ecbatana* and the utmost Bounds of the East, were
'what he design'd to submit to his Power That
'whithersoever he could fly, he could also follow;
'and that having pass'd the Sea, he was not to be
'frighten'd with Rivers.' Thus the *Kings* writ to one
another. In the mean time the *Rhodians* surrender'd
their City and Port to *Alexander* The King conferr'd
the Government of *Cilicia* on *Socrates*, and that of
the Country about *Tyre* to *Philotas* As for *Syria*,
that they call *Cœle*, *Parmenio* had resign'd it to *Andro-*
machus, that he might attend the *King* in the remaining part of the War *Alexander* having order'd *He-*
phæstion to coast along *Phœnicia* with the Fleet, came
with his whole Army to the City of *Gaza* Now
was the Time of celebrating the *Isthmian* Games which
are us'd to be perform'd by the Concourse of all *Greece*
As the *Greeks* are naturally *Time-servers*, it was agreed
in this Assembly, to depute twelve Persons to the
King, to present *him* with a Gold Crown, as an Ac-
knowledgement of his glorious Victories, and of the
great Things *he* had done for the Liberty and Safety
of *Greece* Yet a little before, they were very inquisitive about the Success of the War, their wavering
Minds being ready to strike in with which soever Side
Fortune should favour. However, not only the *King*
was

was employ'd in reducing those Towns that refus'd to submit to his Authority, but his Deputies also (who were great Captains) made several Conquests. *Calas* subdu'd *Paphlagonia*, *Antigonus*, *Lycaonia*, and *Balacrus* having defeated *Idarnes*, *Darius*'s Lieutenant, took *Miletum*, *Amphoterus* and *Hegelochus*, with a Fleet of a hundred and sixty Ships, brought all the Islands between *Achaia* and *Asia*, under *Alexander*'s Obedience. They took Possession also of *Tenedos*, by the voluntary Submission of the Inhabitants. They had a Design to possess themselves of *Chios*, in the same manner. But *Pharnabazus*, *Darius*'s Admiral, having seiz'd those who favour'd the *Macedonian* Faction, put the Government of the Town into the Hands of *Apollonides* and *Athanagoras* (who were in the *Persian* Interest) leaving them a small Garrison for the Defence of it. Notwithstanding this Disappointment, *Alexander*'s Lieutenants continu'd the Siege of the Place, not relying so much on their own Strength, as on the Disposition of the Besieged. Neither were they deceiv'd in their Opinion; for a Dispute arising between *Apollonides*, and the chief Officers that commanded the Garrison, gave the Enemy an Opportunity of breaking into the Town. A Company of *Macedonians* having therefore forc'd one of the Gates, the Inhabitants, pursuant to the Measures before concerted for the Surrender of the Place, join'd themselves to *Amphoterus* and *Hegelochus*, and having put the *Persian* Garrison to the Sword, deliver'd up *Pharnabazus* with *Apollonides* and *Athanagoras* bound, to the *Macedonians*. There were twelve Gallies taken with all their Crew and Marines, besides thirty Ships and Barks belonging to Pyrates, with three thousand *Greeks* that were in the *Persian* Pay. The *Greeks* serv'd to recruit the *Macedonian*

Forces,

Forces, the Pyrates were put to Death, and the captive Powers were diſtributed among the Fleet. It happen'd that *Ariſtonicus* (who had a tyrannical Power in *Methymna*) being ignorant of what had paſa'd at *Chios*, came with ſome Pyrates to the Mouth of the Haven, which was ſecur'd with a Boom, it being then about the firſt Watch, and being aſk'd by the Guard, *Who he was?* He ſaid, *he was* Ariſtonicus, *and came to the Aſſiſtance of* Pharnabazus. The Guard made Anſwer, *That* Pharnabazus *was taking his Reſt, and could not then be ſpoke with; however, as he was a Friend and Ally, he ſhould have Admittance into the Port, and the next Day be introduc'd to* Pharnabazus. *Ariſtonicus* hereupon without Heſitation enter'd the Haven, follow'd by about ten *Pyrates*, but as they were making to the Key, the Guard ſhut up the Haven as before, and having call'd to their Aſſiſtance the whole Corps, they took *Ariſtonicus* and all that were with him Priſoners, without their making the leaſt Reſiſtance. And having put Chains upon them, deliver'd 'em up to *Amphoterus* and *Hegelochus*. From hence the *Macedonians* paſs'd to *Mitylene*, which *Chares* the *Athenian* had lately poſſeſs'd himſelf of, having with him a Garriſon of about two thouſand *Perſians*, but finding himſelf too weak to hold out a Siege, he ſurrender'd the Place upon Condition to retire whither he pleas'd. So he went to *Imbrus*, and the *Macedonians* gave Quarter to the Garriſon.

CHAP.

CHAP. VI.

DARIUS despairing of Peace, which he thought he should have obtained by his Letters and Ambassadors, was now wholly intent on recruiting his Forces, in order to renew the War with Vigor. He therefore summon'd all his Generals to meet at *Babylon*, but he in particular commanded *Bessus*, Governor of the *Bactrians*, to get together as powerful an Army as he could, and to come and join him. These *Bactrians* are the most warlike People of all those Nations, being of a barbarous Disposition, and not at all inclin'd to the *Persian* Luxury. And as they border upon the *Scythians*, who are also a martial People, and accustomed to live by Plunder, they were constantly in Arms. But *Bessus* was suspected to be perfidiously inclin'd, and by his Haughtiness (which made him dissatisfy'd with the second Rank) gave *Darius* great Uneasiness, for as he affected Sovereignty, it was very much fear'd he would play the Traitor, as being the readiest way to attain his End. In the mean time, *Alexander* used all his Endeavours to get Intelligence what Country *Darius* was in, but to no purpose, the *Persians* being very religious Concealers of their *King*'s Secrets. Neither Fear nor Hope can force a Discovery from 'em. The ancient Discipline of their Princes enjoining 'em to Secrecy on Pain of Death. The Intemperance of the Tongue, is with them more severely punish'd than any other Crime. Nor can they imagine him to be capable of great Matters, that finds a Difficulty in being silent, a thing that Nature has made so easie in it self. This was the Cause why *Alexander* (being altogether ignorant of what the Enemy was doing) laid Siege to *Gaza*. *Betis* was its Governor, and was a Man of noted Fidelity to his *King*, and tho' his Garrison was but small, yet he defended the Walls which were of a large Compass. *Alexander* having viewed the Situation of the Place, order'd several Mines to be made, which Work was favour'd by the Lightness of the Ground, for the neighbouring Sea discharg'd great Quantities of Sand upon it, and there were neither Rocks nor Stones to obstruct the Work. The Mines were begun on that side where they could not be perceiv'd by the Besieged, and that they might have no Suspicion of what was doing, the *King* gave Orders to approach the Towers to the Walls. But the Nature of the Ground was no way proper for this Work, for the Sand sinking under the Weight of the Wheels, retarded their Motion, and disconcerted the whole Frame of the Towers, so that the Scaffolds broke, and many of the Soldiers were wounded thereby, besides, there was as much Difficulty to bring the Towers back, as there had been to carry 'em forward. Hereupon *Alexander* gave the Signal for a Retreat, and the next Day he order'd the Town to be surrounded, and as soon as the Sun was up, before his Army advanc'd to the Charge, he offer'd Sacrifice to the *Gods*, after his Country manner, to implore their Assistance. While the *King* was thus employ'd, a Crow happen'd to fly over him, and suddenly let go a Lump of Earth that it held in its Claws, which falling on the *King*'s Head, broke in pieces, and the Crow went and settled on a Tower hard by. The Tower was besmear'd with *Bitumen* and *Sulphur*, which catching hold of the Crow's Wings, so entangl'd its Feathers, that it

Vol. I.   K   struggled

struggled in vain to fly away, and was taken by the Standers-by. The Accident was look'd upon to be important enough to have the Soothsayers consulted about it, for *Alexander* was something inclin'd himself to that kind of Superstition. *Aristander*, who was chiefly credited in this Art, told the King that this *Omen* portended the Ruin of the City, but that he would be in danger of being wounded, and therefore advis'd him, *not to attempt any thing against it that Day*.

Altho' the King was very much concern'd that a single City should, by its Obstinacy, hinder him from passing into *Egypt* with Security, yet he thought it advisable to comply with the Soothsayer's Request, and accordingly gave the Signal for the Retreat. This so encourag'd the Besieged, that sallying out, they attack'd the *Macedonians* in the Rear, thinking that the Enemy's Delay ought to be their Opportunity, but their *Constancy* did not second their *Fury* in the Engagement, for, when they saw the *Macedonians* rally, they presently stopp'd again. By this time the Shouts of those that were fighting reach'd the King, who presently flew to the Assistance of his Men, unmindful of the Danger he had been warn'd of, however, at the intreaty of his Friends, he put on his Armour, which he otherwise rarely wore.

Here a certain *Arabian*, one of *Darius*'s Soldiers, ventur'd upon an Action above his Fortune, and covering his Sword with his Buckler, fell upon his Knees before the King, as if he had deserted to him, whereupon the *King bid him rise, and order'd him to be receiv'd into his Service*, but the Barbarian taking his Sword couragiously into his right Hand, made at the King's Head, who having declin'd the Blow, at the same time cut off the disappointed Hand of the *Barbarian*,

barian, and flatter'd himself that he was now clear'd of the Danger of the Day. However *Fate*, as I take it, is *unavoidable*, for as he was fighting gallantly among the foremost he was wounded with an Arrow, which pass'd through his Armour, and stuck in his Shoulder, from whence *Philip*, his Physician drew it. Now the Blood began to run in a great quantity, and all that stood by were frighten'd, never having known an Arrow penetrate so deep through Armour before. As for *Alexander*, he did not so much as change his Countenance, but bid 'em *stop the bleeding, and tie up the Wound*. Thus he remain'd some time at the Head of the Army, either dissembling or overcoming the Pain, but when the Blood that had been stopp'd by an Application, began to run afresh in a larger Quantity, and the Wound (which by reason of its newness did not at first pain him) upon the cooling of the Blood, began to swell, then he fainted and fell on his Knees. They that were next to him took him up, and carry'd him into his Tent, and *Betis* concluding *him* dead, return'd into the Town in a triumphing manner, but the *King*, impatient of delay, (before his Wounds were cur'd) gave Orders for a Terrass to be rais'd as high as the *City* Walls, which he commanded to be undermin'd. The Besieg'd on their part were not idle, for they had erected a new Fortification of equal height with the old Wall, but that however did not come upon the Level with the *Towers* which were planted on the *Terrass*, so that the inward parts of the Town were expos'd to the Enemies Darts, and to compleat their hard Fate, the Walls were now overthrown by the Mines, and gave the *Macedonians* an opportunity of entering the City at the Breaches. The *King* was at the Head of the foremost, and while he carelesly enter'd the Place, his Leg was hurt with a Stone, notwithstanding struggled in vain to fly away, and was taken by the Standers-by. The Accident was look'd upon to be important enough to have the Soothsayers consulted about it, for *Alexander* was something inclin'd himself to that kind of Superstition. *Aristander*, who was chiefly credited in this Art, told the King that this Omen portended the Ruin of the City, but that he would be in danger of being wounded, and therefore advis'd him, *not to attempt any thing against it that Day*.

Altho' the King was very much concern'd that a single City should, by its Obstinacy, hinder him from passing into *Egypt* with Security, yet he thought it advisable to comply with the Soothsayer's Request, and accordingly gave the Signal for the Retreat. This so encourag'd the Besieged, that sallying out, they attack'd the *Macedonians* in the Rear, thinking that the Enemy's Delay ought to be their Opportunity, but their *Constancy* did not second their *Fury* in the Engagement, for, when they saw the *Macedonians* rally, they presently stopp'd again. By this time the Shouts of those that were fighting reach'd the King, who presently flew to the Assistance of his Men, unmindful of the Danger he had been warn'd of, however, at the intreaty of his Friends, he put on his Armour, which he otherwise rarely wore.

Here a certain *Arabian*, one of *Darius*'s Soldiers, ventur'd upon an Action above his Fortune, and covering his Sword with his Buckler, fell upon his Knees before the King, as if he had deserted to him, whereupon the King *bid him rise, and order'd him to be receiv'd into his Service*, but the *Barbarian* taking his Sword couragiously into his right Hand, made at the King's Head, who having declin'd the Blow, at the same time cut off the disappointed Hand of the Barbarian,

barian, and flatter'd himself that he was now clear'd of the Danger of the Day. However *Fate*, as I take it, is *unavoidable*, for as he was fighting gallantly among the foremost he was wounded with an Arrow, which pass'd through his Armour, and stuck in his Shoulder, from whence *Philip*, his Physician drew it. Now the Blood began to run in a great quantity, and all that stood by were frighten'd, never having known an Arrow penetrate so deep through Armour before. As for *Alexander*, he did not so much as change his Countenance, but bid 'em *stop the bleeding, and tie up the Wound* Thus he remain'd some time at the Head of the Army, either dissembling or overcoming the Pain, but when the Blood that had been stopp'd by an Application, began to run afresh in a larger Quantity, and the Wound (which by reason of its newness did not at first pain him) upon the cooling of the Blood, began to swell, then he fainted and fell on his Knees. They that were next to him took him up, and carry'd him into his Tent, and *Betis* concluding *him* dead, return'd into the Town in a triumphing manner, but the *King*, impatient of delay, (before his Wounds were cur'd) gave Orders for a Terrass to be rais'd as high as the *City* Walls, which he commanded to be undermin'd The Besieg'd on their part were not idle, for they had erected a new Fortification of equal height with the old Wall, but that however did not come upon the Level with the *Towers* which were planted on the *Terrass*, so that the inward parts of the Town were expos'd to the Enemies Darts, and to compleat their hard Fate, the Walls were now overthrown by the Mines, and gave the *Macedonians* an opportunity of entering the City at the Breaches The *King* was at the Head of the foremost, and while he carelesly enter'd the Place, his Leg was hurt with a Stone, notwithstanding

withstanding which, leaning on his Dart, he fought among the first, tho' his old Wound was not yet heal'd, his Resentment was the greater on the account of his having receiv'd two Wounds in this Siege. *Betis* having behav'd himself gallantly, and receiv'd several Wounds, was at last forsaken by his Men, yet this did not hinder him from fighting on, tho' his Arms were grown slippery with his own and his Enemies Blood, but being attack'd on all sides, he was taken alive, and being brought before the *King*, who was overjoy'd that he had him in his Power, insomuch that *he* that us'd to admire Virtue, even in an Enemy, giving way this time to Revenge, told him, *Thou shalt not,* Betis, *dye as thou would'st, but expect to undergo whatever Torments Ingenuity can invent.* At which Threats, *Betis* without making any Reply, gave the *King* not only an undaunted, but an insolent Look, whereupon *Alexander* said, *Do you take notice of his obstinate Silence? Has he either offer'd to kneel down, or made the least Submission? However, I'll overcome his Taciturnity, if by no other means, at least by Groans.* This said, his Anger turn'd to Rage, his *Fortune* having already corrupted his Manners, so that *he* order'd Cords to be run thro' *Betis*'s Heels, and ty'd to the hinder part of a Cart, and in that manner to be dragg'd alive round the City, valuing himself *for having imitated* Achilles *(from whom he descended) in punishing his Enemy.*

In this Action there perish'd about ten thousand *Persians* and *Arabians*, neither was it a bloodless Victory to the *Macedonians.* However, the Siege was not so considerable on the score of the Character of the Town, as for the two Wounds the *King* receiv'd therein. After this the *King* (making the best of his way to *Egypt*) dispatch'd *Amyntas* with ten Galleys to *Macedonia* to raise Recruits; for even his successful

Battles

Vol 1 Page 221

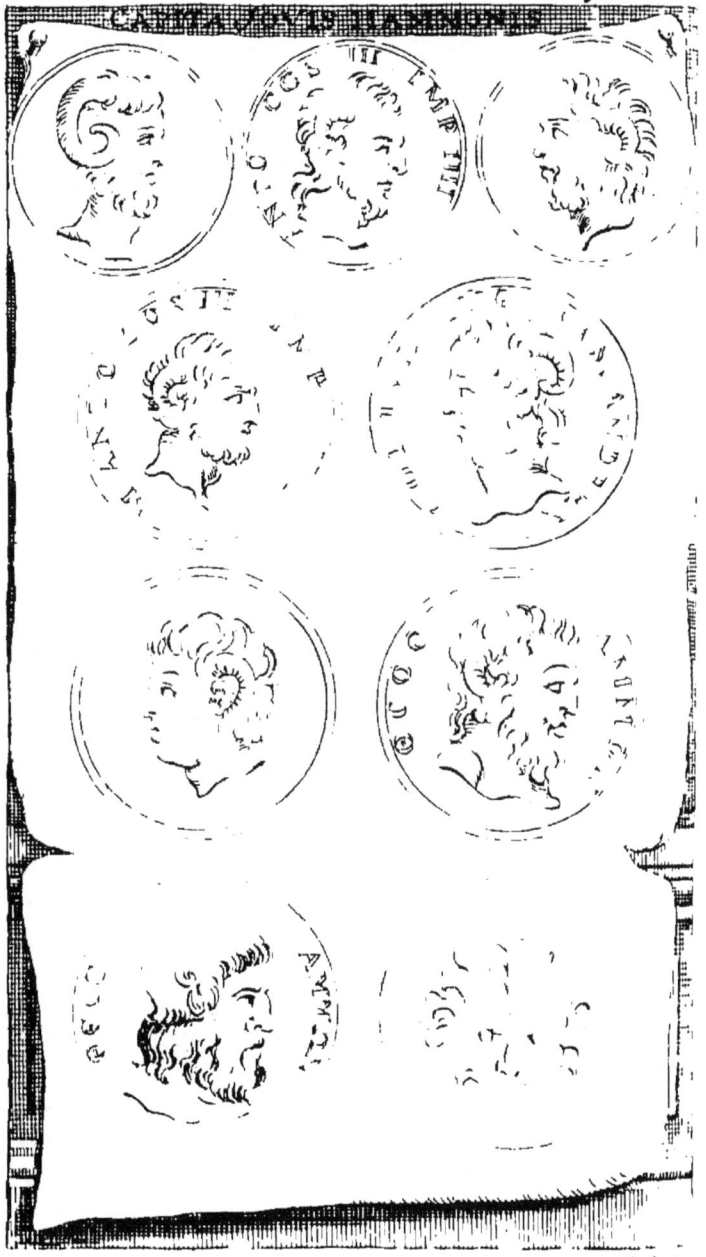

Battles diminish'd his Army, and *he* had not the same Confidence in foreign Soldiers as in those of his own Country.

CHAP. VII.

THE *Egyptians* had for a great while envy'd the *Persian* Grandeur, and look'd upon their Government to be both Avaritious and Insolent, so that at the Rumour of *Alexander*'s coming thither they began to take Courage, for they were so dispos'd to revolt, that they had before joyfully receiv'd *Amyntas* the Deserter, tho' his Power was altogether precarious. They therefore flock'd in great numbers to *Pelusium*, thinking the King would enter that way, and *he* arriv'd in *Egypt* at a place call'd still *Alexander*'s Camp, on the seventh Day after he left *Gaza*. Here he gave Orders to the Foot to repair to *Pelusium* by Land, while he with some chosen Troops was carry'd along the River *Nilus*. The *Persians* being terrify'd at the Revolution, did not dare to wait his coming. He was by this time come within a little way of *Memphis*, where *Mazaces* commanded for *Darius*, but not daring to oppose *Alexander*, he made haste to pass the River, and brought the King eight hundred Talents, and all the royal Furniture. From *Memphis* he continu'd his Course along the same River, and penetrated into the more inward parts of *Egypt*, and having settled the Affairs of the Nation so as to change none of their ancient Customs, he resolv'd to visit the famous Oracle of *Jupiter Hammon*. The way thither was hardly practicable, even to a small Number, without any Incumbrance. There is a scarcity of Water from Heaven as well as Earth, and nothing to be seen but barren Sands, which when thoroughly heated by the Sun, burn the Soles of the Feet. In fine, the Heat is intolerable, but here is not only the excessive Heat of the Sun, and the Drought of the Country to be struggled with, but also with a tenacious kind of Gravel, which lies very deep, and sinking under the Feet makes it very difficult to move. All these Inconveniences were magnify'd by the *Egyptians.* However, *Alexander* was resolv'd to gratify the ardent Desire he had to visit *Jupiter,* whom he either really believ'd to be his Father (not being satisfy'd with his mortal Grandeur) or had a mind the World should think so. He embark'd therefore with those he design'd should accompany him, and sail'd down the River to the Meer call'd *Mareosis.* While he was here, Ambassadors came to him from the *Cyrenenses* with Presents, desiring Peace, and that he would visit their Towns, but the *King* having accepted their Presents, and assur'd 'em of his Friendship, pursu'd his intended Journey. The first and second Days Fatigue seem'd tolerable, for they were not yet come to the vast, naked Solitudes, tho' the Ground here was barren, and as it were dead, but when those unbounded Plains appear'd that are cover'd over with deep Sands, they were at as great a Loss to discover Land as if they had been sailing on the deep. There was not so much as a Tree to be seen, nor the least Token of a cultivated Soil, and they now wanted Water, that which they carry'd with 'em upon Camels being spent, and there was none to be had in those dry Grounds and burning Sands. Besides, the Sun had parch'd up every thing, all was scorch'd and burnt. They were in this distress'd Condition,

when,

when, on the sudden, the Sky was overcast with thick Clouds which intercepted the Sun, whether it were by Accident, or ordain'd as a Present from the Gods to relieve their pressing Calamity, this is certain, it was a seasonable Comfort to them (who were perishing with Heat) even tho' they still wanted Water. But when the Storm broke out into a large and copious Rain, every one laid in his Provision thereof, some of 'em unable any longer to bear their Thirst, receiv'd it with open Mouth as it fell. They had already spent four Days in this vast Solitude, and were not now far off of the Seat of the Oracle, when a great Flock of Crows came towards 'em, and flew gently before their Van, and sometimes settled to give 'em time to come up, and then taking Wing again preceded 'em, shewing them the Way, and as it were discharging the Office of a Guide. At last they reach'd the Place which was consecrated to the God. It seems to surpass Belief, that being situate in so wild a Solitude, it should be encompass'd with Trees that grew so thick as to skreen it on all Sides from the piercing Rays of the Sun, being at the same time water'd with so many gentle Streams as were abundantly sufficient for the Nourishment of these Groves, and to encrease the Miracle, the Air is here so temperate, that it resembles the Spring, and is equally salubrious throughout all the Seasons of the Year. The People that inhabit the Neighbourhood of this Place are, on the East, those that border on the *Ethiopians*, and on the South those that face the *Arabians*, call'd *Trog'odytes*, whose Territory extends itself as far as the Red Sea, to the Westward it has other *Ethiopians*, called *Scenitæ*, to the Northward are the *Nasamones*, who are a People situate near the Flats, and enrich themselves by Piracy, lying in wait upon the Coast, ever ready to make a Prey of those Ships that are stranded, being well acquainted with all the Fords. The Inhabitants of the Wood, who are call'd *Hammonians*, live in Cottages scatter'd up and down, the middle of the Wood serves 'em for a Citadel, being surrounded with a triple Wall Within the first stands the ancient Palace of their *Kings*, in the second they keep their Wives and Children, as also their Concubines, here likewise is the Deity's Oracle, and in the last were the Prince's Guards and the Men at Arms There is another Wood also belonging to *Hammon*, in the middle of which is a Fountain that they call the Water of the Sun. About break of Day this Water is lukewarm, in the middle of the Day, when the heat of the Sun is greatest, the same Water is very cold, towards the Evening it grows warm again, and in the middle of the Night it is scalding hot, and the nearer the Night draws on to Day, its nocturnal Heat decreases, till about break of Day it is lukewarm, as before That which is ador'd for a *God* has not the same Form, under which Artificers use to represent the *Gods*, it very much resembles a *Navel*, being compos'd of an Emerald and other precious Stones. When it is consulted, the *Priests* carry it in a golden Ship, which is set off with a great many silver Cups hanging on each side, and is folow'd by the Matrons and Virgins singing an uncouth sort of a *Hymn*, after their Country manner, by which they imagine *Jupiter is prevail'd upon to render a certain Oracle*

As the *King* advanc'd towards the Oracle, the senior Priest saluted him with the Title of *Son*, assuring him, *That* Jupiter *his Father bestow'd it on him.* To which he reply'd, *That he both accepted it and acknowledg'd it*, for he had now forgot his human Condition Then he ask'd whether his Father did design him the Empire of

the

Vol 1 Page 229

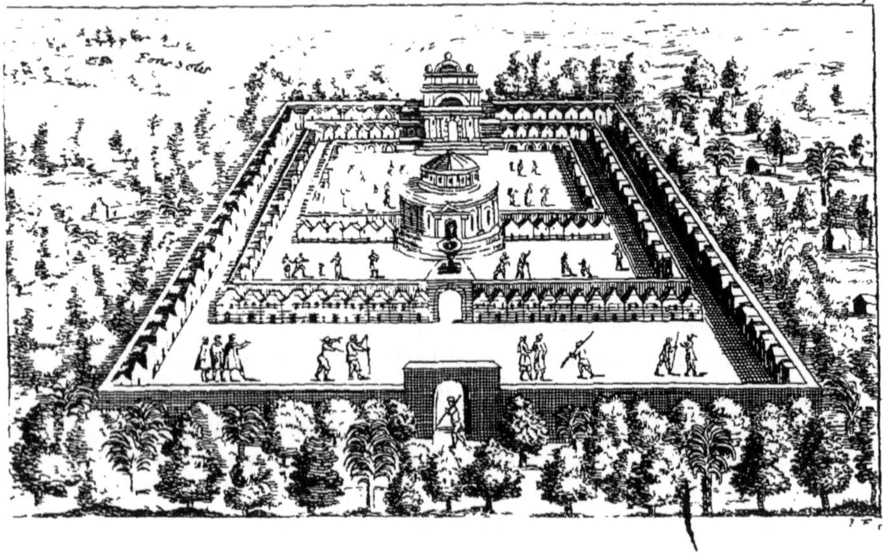

the whole World? And the Prieft, who was equally difpos'd to flatter him, told him, *he should be univerfal Monarch of the whole Earth.* Then he put another Quære, viz *Whether all thofe who were concern'd in his Father's Murther were punifh'd?* To this the Prieft made anfwer, *That it was not in the Power of any mortal to injure his Father, but that all that had a hand in* Philip's *Death had fuffer'd condign Punifhment* He moreover added, *That he fhould continue invincible till he took his Place among the Gods* After this, he offer'd Sacrifice, and made Prefents to the *Priefts* and to the *God*, after which his Friends were likewife permitted *to confult the Oracle*, but they only defir'd to know, *Whether* Jupiter *approv'd of their paying divine Honours to their King?* The Prieft reply'd, *That* Jupiter *was very well pleas'd they fhould pay divine Worfhip to their victorious King* Now whoever would judge fagely of the Sincerity and Credit of the Oracle, might eafily have perceiv'd it was all Impofture by its Anfwers, but when once *Fortune* has prevail'd with Men to commit themfelves entirely to *her*, *fhe* generally makes 'em more greedy of Power than capable of it.

Alexander therefore not only fuffer'd himfelf to be call'd *Jupiter's* Son, but alfo commanded it, and while he thought by this means to caft a greater Splendour on his great Actions, he leffen'd 'em. And notwithftanding the *Macedonians* were accuftom'd to *Kingly* Government, yet as they retain'd ftill the fhadow of a greater Liberty than other Nations, they more obftinately oppos'd his affected Immortality than was expedient either to themfelves or the *King*. But of thefe things we fhall fpeak in their proper Places, and at prefent purfue the reft of his Actions,

K   C H A P,

CHAP. VIII.

Alexander, in his return from *Hammon*, when he came to *Palus Mareotis*, which is not far distant from the Island *Pharos*, having consider'd the Nature of the Place, he design'd at first to build a City in the Island it self, but upon Reflection that the Island was too small for such a purpose, he pitch'd upon that place where *Alexandria* now stands, contracting its Name from its Founder. He took in all that space of Ground that lies between the Meer and the Sea, allotting fourscore Furlongs for the Compass of the Walls, and having appointed proper Persons to supervise the building of the City, he went to *Memphis*.

He was seiz'd with a Desire (no wise to be blam'd indeed, had it been but well tim'd) to visit not only the inward parts of *Egypt*, but also *Æthiopia*. The celebrated Palace of *Memnon* and *Tithonus* was like to draw him (who was naturally greedy of the Knowledge of Antiquity) even beyond the Bounds of the Sun, but the War he had upon his Hands, of which the most difficult part still remain'd, would not allow him time for those idle Journeys, he therefore appointed *Aschylus* the *Rhodian*, and *Peucestes* the *Macedonian*, Governors of *Egypt*, leaving with them four thousand Men for the guard of the Country, and allotted thirty Galleys to *Polemon* to defend the Mouths of the *Nile*, then he constituted *Apollonius* Governor of that part of *Africk* that joins to *Egypt*, and made *Cleomenes* Receiver of all the Tributes arising from *Africa* and *Egypt*, and having commanded the Inhabitants

tants of the Neighbouring Towns to transplant themselves to *Alexandria*, he presently fill'd it with a great Multitude of People. It is said, *That when the King was marking out the Walls of the Town, with a sort of Paste made of Barley Flower, according to the* Macedonian *Custom, the Birds came in Flocks to devour it, and as that was by several interpreted as portending Evil to the City in hand, the Soothsayers on the contrary said it was a lucky Omen, and that it indicated, that the City would be very much resorted to by Strangers, and that she would afford Subsistence to several Countries.*

The *King*, after this, was going down the River *Nile*, and *Hector*, *Parmenio*'s Son (who was in the flower of his Age, and in great Favour with *Alexander*) being eager to follow *him*, enter'd into a little Boat which had more People in it than it could carry, insomuch that it sunk with all those that were on board it. However, *Hector* struggled a long time in the Water, tho' his Cloaths being thoroughly wet, and his Shoes being closely ty'd to his Feet, hinder'd him from swimming, and made a shift at last to gain the Shore half dead, but as soon as he endeavour'd to recover his Breath, which Fear and the Danger had for some time suppress'd, there being no body at hand to assist him (for the rest had sav'd themselves on the other side) he expir'd. The *King* was mightily afflicted at this Accident, and therefore bury'd his Corps after a very magnificent manner.

This Misfortune was aggravated by the Account the *King* receiv'd of the Death of *Andromachus*, his Governor of *Syria*, whom the *Samaritans* had burnt alive. The *King* therefore march'd with the utmost Expedition to revenge his Death, but at his Arrival they deliver'd *him* up the Authors of so barbarous a Crime, al. whom he put to death, and then substituted *Memnon* in his Place. He also put the Tyrants into the hands of the People they had oppress'd, and among those of the *Methymnians*, *Aristonicus* and *Chrysolaus*, whom they first tortur'd in revenge of their Insolence, and then executed, flinging them in contempt over the Walls of the City. Then he gave Audience to the Ambassadors of the *Athenians*, the *Rhodians* and the *Chiotes*, the *Athenians* congratulated him on his Victories, and desired that the *Greek* Captives might be restor'd to their respective Cities. The *Rhodians* and the *Chiotes* complain'd of the Garrisons, and as all their Requests seem'd too just, he gratify'd them. To those of *Mitylene* he restor'd their Securities, in consideration of their Fidelity, and the Money they had advanc'd for the Service of the War, adding a large Tract of Ground to their Territories. He also honour'd the *King* of *Cyprus*, according to the Merit of his Services, who had revolted from *Darius* to *him*, and had supply'd *him* with a Fleet when he besieg'd *Tyre*. He afterwards sent *Amphoterus*, his Admiral, to deliver *Crete* from the Oppression of the *Persians* and *Pyrates*, but he enjoin'd him above all things to clear the Sea from the *Pyrates*, for the two *Kings* being intent upon the War, the Seas were over-run with these Plunderers. Having settled these Matters, *he* dedicated to *Hercules* of *Tyre*, a large Bowl and thirty Cups of Gold, then bending his Thoughts altogether on *Darius*, *he* gave Orders for the Army to march towards the *Euphrates*.

C H A P.

ROTAE CURRUUM FALCATORUM

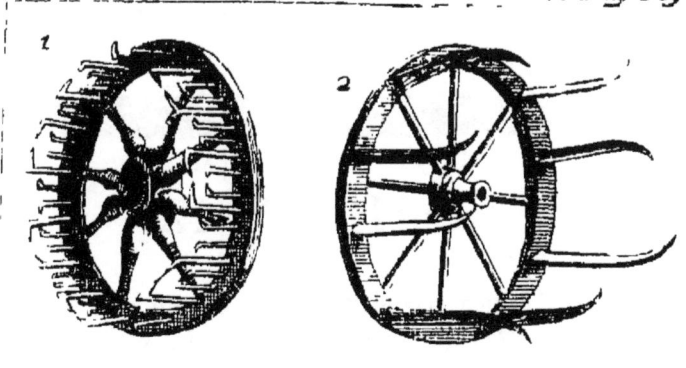

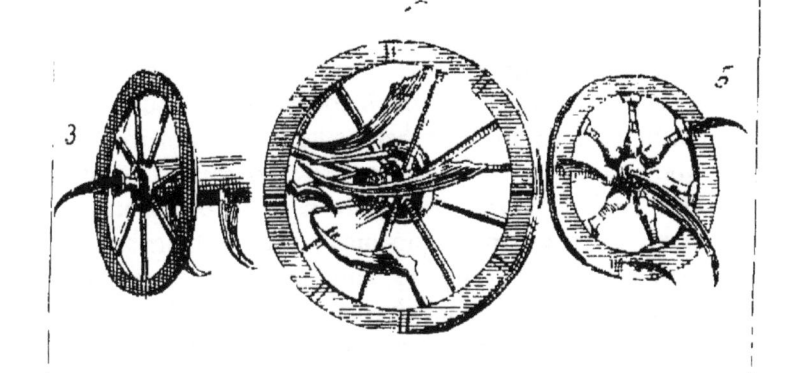

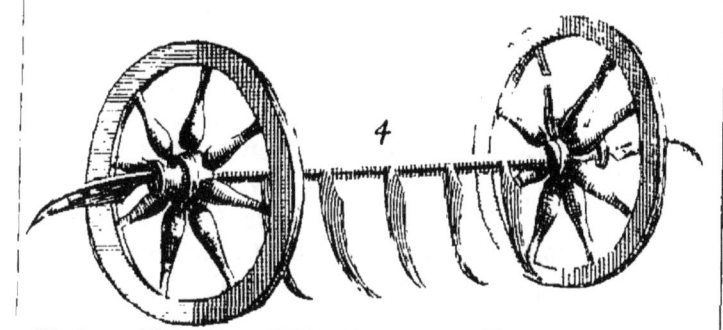

CHAP. IX.

BUT when *Darius* knew for certain that his Enemy was march'd into *Africa*, he was unresolv'd whether he should stay in the Neighbourhood of *Mesopotamia*, or should retire farther into his Dominions; for he concluded he should be better able upon the Place to influence those remote Nations to engage heartily in the War, which the Deputies found great Difficulties to do; but then again being inform'd from good hands, *That* Alexander *was determin'd to follow him with his whole Army into whatsoever Country he went,* as he was not ignorant of the indefatigable Bravery of his Adversary, he sent Orders *to those remote Nations, to send him all the Succour they could to* Babylon. The *Bactrians, Scythians* and *Indians* accordingly repair'd thither with the Troops of the other Nations; his Army being now as numerous again as it was in *Cilicia*, a great many of those that compos'd it wanted Arms, which were getting ready for 'em with the utmost Diligence. The Horses as well as the Riders were provided with Armour of Iron. They who before had only Darts had now Swords and Bucklers given them. And that *his* present Army might be much stronger in Horse than his former was, he distributed a great many Horses to the Foot to be broke.

There were besides two hundred Chariots arm'd with Scythes, which the Nations look upon to be their chief Strength, and very terrible to the Enemy;

at the end of the Pole were fix'd two Pikes arm'd with Iron Spikes, the Spokes of the Wheels were compass'd round with several Darts which pointed forward, and the Fellies were arm'd with Scythes so dispos'd that they cut to pieces whatever stood in their way.

Having thus provided and fitted out his Army, he set forwards from *Babylon*, on his Right he had the *Tigre*, a noble River, and his Left was cover'd with the *Euphrates*. His Army was so numerous, that it fill'd all the Plains of *Mesopotamia*, having therefore pass'd the River *Tigris*, and understanding the Enemy was not far off, he sent before *Satropates* with a thousand chosen Horse, and then detatch'd *Mazæus* with six thousand more, to hinder *Alexander* from passing the *Euphrates*, he was also commanded *to destroy and burn all the Country that would be first expos'd to the Enemy*, for he imagin'd, that not having any other Provisions for his Army than what he got by Pillage, he might be overcome by mere Want, whilst his own was plentifully supply'd with all Necessaries both by Land and by the *Tigre*. *Darius* was by this time come to *Arbela*, which he was destin'd to make glorious by his own memorable Defeat, leaving here the greatest Part of his Baggage and Provisions, he laid a Bridge over the *Lycus*, and pass'd his Army over it in five Days, as he had done before over the *Euphrates*, then advancing about fourscore Furlong farther, he came to another River call'd *Bumado*, where he encamp'd. This Country was very convenient for his numerous Army, being a plain open Ground, and very commodious for the Horse, as being cover'd neither with Bushes nor Shrubs, so that the Eye had an uninterrupted Prospect to discover Things at the remotest distance, and where it seem'd to swell into any thing of an Eminence, he order'd it *to be laid level with the rest*. They that were sent

sent by *Alexander* to take a View of the Enemy's Army, and who made an Estimate of it by the great Tract of Ground it cover'd, could hardly convince him of the Truth of their Report, for he thought it impossible that, after so great a Loss, he should now be stronger than he was at first. However, as *he* despis'd all Danger in general, and particularly that from a Superiority of Number, *he* came in eleven Days to the *Euphrates*, and having laid a Bridge over it, he first pass'd his Horse, and after them the Phalanx *Mazaeus,* who had been sent to oppose his Passage, not daring to make tryal of his Fortune against *him*. Here having granted the Soldiers a few Days, not so much to rest their Bodies as to confirm their Minds, he eagerly pursu'd *Darius*, for he was afraid he might retire to the remotest Parts of his Dominions, and that then *he* should be oblig'd to follow him thro' vast Wilds and Desarts that were destitute of all Necessaries. On the fourth Day therefore he pass'd by *Arbela* and came to the *Tigre.* All the Country beyond the River was yet smoaking; for *Mazaeus* set every thing on fire, as if he had been himself the Enemy. And as the Smoak had caus'd a great Darkness, the King suspecting some Ambuscade, halted for some time, till being inform'd by some Scouts that there was no Danger, he order'd some Horsemen to try the Depth of the Ford of the River. At first it took the Horses up to the Belly, and in the middle it reach'd their Necks.

In all the Eastern Parts there is not any River that runs with so great a Rapidity, many Torrents falling into it, so that it carries even great Stones along with its Stream. From the Swiftness of its Current, it bore the Name of *Tigre*, because an Arrow in the *Persian* Language is call'd *Tigris*. The Foot being divided in-

to

to two Bodies, and encompass'd with the Horse, carry'd their Arms over their Head, and in that order pass'd without much Difficulty, till they came where the River was deepest. The *King* pass'd over among the Foot, and was the first that gain'd the other side, from whence he made Signs to the Soldiers with his Hand, because his Voice could not be heard, where the Ford was shallowest. But they had much to do to keep their Legs, sometimes the slippery Stones deceiving their Steps, and sometimes the Violence of the Water tripping up their Heels. But they that were loaded were hardest put to it, for as they were hinder'd from governing themselves, they were carry'd away by the Rapidity of the Whirlpools. And as every one endeavour'd to recover what he had lost, they struggl'd more among themselves than with the Stream. Besides, the Bundles that floated on the Water bore down a great many of them. Hereupon the *King* cry'd out to 'em, only to take care of their Arms, and that he would make good their other Losses. But they neither harken'd to his Counsel, nor obey'd his Commands, for Fear, besides, their own mutual Clamour made 'em incapable of doing either. At last they got where the Current flows after a gentler manner, and so gain'd the Shoar, without any other Damage than the Loss of a little Lumber.

Here the Army might have been totally destroy'd, had any body dar'd to conquer, but the King's constant good Fortune kept the Enemy at a distance. Thus he pass'd the *Granicus* in the sight of so many Thousand Horse and Foot, that were drawn up on the other side of the River. Thus the Straits of *Cilicia* serv'd him to vanquish so vast a Multitutude of his Enemies. And notwithstanding he might seem bold to

Excess,

Excess, yet he cannot well be censur'd for it, because his continual Success never afforded an Opportunity to conclude him rash.

Mazæus (who, if he had come upon 'em while they were passing the River, might without doubt have destroy'd 'em in that Disorder) never appear'd till they had gain'd the Shoar, and stood to their Arms. He had sent only a thousand Horse before him, which *Alexander* perceiving, he despis'd the insignificant Number, and presently commanded *Ariston*, who was Captain of the *Pæonian* Horse, *to charge 'em briskly*. In this Action the *Pæonians* behav'd themselves gallantly, but particularly *Ariston*, who with his Spear run *Satropates*, the *Persian* Commander, into the Throat, and pursuing him through the midst of the Enemies, threw him off his Horse, and notwithstanding his Resistance, cut off his Head, which he brought, and laid down at the King's Feet, who applauded his Resolution and Bravery.

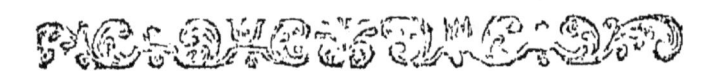

CHAP. X.

THE *King* encamp'd here two Days, and order'd the Army to be ready to march the next, but about the first Watch the Moon suffer'd an Eclipse, and first lost its Planetary Brightness, after which it was overcast with a sanguine Colour, that fully'd all its Light. And as the Soldiers were already solicitous on the Account of the approaching Battle, this Accident struck 'em first with a superstitious Awe, which was succeeded by Fear, insomuch that they complain'd, *That they were dragg'd into the remotest Countries against the Will of the Gods, that the Rivers deny'd them Passage,*

sage, and the Planets refus'd 'em their usual Light. That nothing but vast Wilds and Desarts were to be seen; that the Blood of so many thousand Men must be spilt to gratifie the Vanity of one Man, who not only disown'd his Father Philip, *but let his vain Thoughts climb to Heaven for his Original* The Matter was almost come to a Sedition, when *Alexander,* who was always undaunted, gave Orders *for all the Officers to repair to his Tent*, where he commanded *the Ægyptian Astronomers (*whom he look'd upon to be the best acquainted with the Course of the Heavens and the Planets*) to declare their Opinion concerning the present* Phænomenon. But as they were not ignorant that Time has its constant Revolutions, and that the Moon suffers an Eclipse whenever it gets beneath the Earth, they did not trouble themselves to divulge their Knowledge to the Publick, but only affirm'd, *That the Sun was the* Greeks *Planet, and the Moon the* Persians And that whenever this was eclips'd, *it portended Destruction and Ruin to these Nations* And for Proof hereof, they relate several Instances of the *Persian Kings,* who were warn'd *by the Eclipse of the Moon, that they fought against the Will of the Gods*

There is nothing has so great an Influence over the Minds of the Vulgar, as Superstition, tho' it be otherwise violent, furious, and unconstant, let it but be seiz'd with a vain Religion, and it shall more readily obey the Priests than the Governors.

The Answer of the *Ægyptians* therefore being communicated to the Multitude, reviv'd their drooping Hopes, and animated 'em with fresh Assurance. The *King* thinking it best to make use of their present Disposition, decamp'd at the second Watch, *he* had the *Tigre* on his Right, and on his Left, the *Gordæan* Hills. As he was marching this way, *his* Scouts came to him

about

about break of Day, to let him know *that* Darius *was advancing towards him.* Hereupon he drew up his Army in order of Battle, being himself at the Head, and so continu'd his March. But it prov'd to be only the *Persian* Scouts consisting of about a thousand Men, who made a great Appearance. *Thus when the Truth cannot be discover'd, Fear swells the Account into Falsities.* The *King* understanding the Truth of the Matter, took with him a small Number of Men and pursu'd the Enemy, who presently fled back to their main Body, however he kill'd some, and took others Prisoners, and then dispatch'd a Detachment of Horse to get Intelligence of the Enemy, and to put out the Fires the *Barbarians* had kindled up and down in order to destroy the Villages. For before they took to their Heels, they set Fire to the Roofs of the Houses, and to the Stacks of Corn, so that the Flames being diverted in the upper Parts, had not yet forc'd its way to the lower. The Fires being thus put out, they found great Quantities of Corn, and began also to have Plenty of other Necessaries. This encourag'd the Soldiers to pursue the Enemy, who burnt and laid the Country waste, it being necessary for the *Macedonians* to make what Haste they could after them, to prevent every thing being consum'd. Thus Necessity supply'd the Place of Reason, for *Mazæus,* who before destroy'd every thing at leisure, was at present contented to fly, and left a great deal behind him entire and untouch'd.

Alexander was now inform'd, that *Darius* was come within a hundred and fifty Furlongs of him. Hereupon, having with him Plenty of Provisions, he staid in his Camp four Days. While he remain'd here, some Letters were intercepted that came from *Darius,* whereby the *Greeks* were solicited *to kill or betray the King:* *Alexander* was for some time doubtful *whether he should read*

read 'em to the whole Army or not, becaufe he was pretty well affur'd of the Good-will and Fidelity of the *Greeks* But *Parmenio* put him off of it, by telling *him,* that it was not convenient to communicate fuch things to Soldiers, *fince the King lay expos'd thereby to any one of 'em that would be a Traitor Befides Avarice thought nothing a Crime.* The *King* following this Advice, decamp'd Upon the March one of the captive *Eunuchs,* that attended *Darius's Queen,* brought him word, *that the Queen had fainted, and drew her Breath with Difficulty.* The great Fatigue of the Journey, and Grief of Mind, had fo wrought upon her, that fhe fwooned away between her Mother-in-law and her two Daughters, and fo died, which was immediately notify'd to him by another Meffenger This furprizing Accident fo touch'd the *King,* that he could not have fhewn more Concern, had *he* receiv'd Advice of the Death of *his own Mother* He figh'd, and even wept as *Darius* himfelf would have done, and immediately repair'd to the Tent, where *Darius's* Mother was fitting by the Corps of the deceafed Here the King's Grief renew'd, when he beheld her extended on the Ground. *Darius's* Mother alfo, being by this frefh Evil put in mind of paft Misfortunes, had took the two young Virgins in her Lap, by the way of mutual Comfort, tho' at the fame time fhe ought to have been a real Comfort to them. The young Prince ftood likewife before her, and was by fo much the more to be pity'd, that he was not yet fenfible of the Calamity, though his was the greateft Share Any body would have thought *Alexander* had been lamenting fome of his own Relations; and inftead of giving Comfort, ftood in need of it himfelf *He* abftain'd from eating, and order'd the Funeral to be perform'd after the *Perfian* Manner, and feem'd then to deferve the Reward he has

fince

since had for his Good-nature and Continency. He had never seen her but once, which was the Day she was taken Prisoner, and even then it was *Darius*'s Mother he went to visit. He was so far from receiving any Impression of Lust from her excellent Beauty, that it only serv'd to excite him to Glory and Honour. While Grief fill'd all the Place, one of the *Eunuchs*, nam'd *Tyriotes*, got out at a Back-door, which was less minded than the rest, and fled to the *Persian* Camp, and being taken up by the Guard, was brought before *Darius*, lamenting and tearing his Clothes. As soon as *Darius* saw him in this Condition, he was disturb'd with Variety of Thoughts, and hardly knew what chiefly to fear. 'Thy Looks, *said he*, bespeak some great Mis-
'fortune, but whatever it be, be sure to conceal no-
'thing from me, for by my repeated Calamities, I
'have learn'd to be unhappy, and sometimes even to
'know one's Misery is a Comfort. Say then, dost
'thou bring me (which is what I most suspect, and
'dread to utter) an Account of the Violation of my
'Family's Honour, which to me, and I suppose to
'them, would be more afflicting than the greatest
'Torments?' *To which* Tyriotes *reply'd*, 'Sir, there
'is nothing, I assure you, of what you fear: for what-
'ever Honours are paid by Subjects to Queens, are
'duly paid to yours by the Conqueror, but your Roy-
'al Consort is dead.' At these Words, the whole Camp was fill'd with Cries and Lamentations. And *Darius* no longer doubted, but she had been kill'd for refusing to yield up her Honour, and distracted with Grief, he broke out in these Exclamations, 'What
'Crime have I committed, *Alexander*? which of your
'Relations have I put to Death, that you should pu-
'nish my Cruelty after this manner? You hate me
'without Provocation, but admitting your War to
'be

'be just, ought you for that to wreak your Revenge 'on Women?" Hereupon *Tyriotes* swore by the Tutelar Gods of the Country, *That no ill Usage had been offer'd her, but on the contrary, that* Alexander *express'd no less Grief for her Death, than he himself could do, who was her Husband.* These Words encreas'd his Anxiety, and gave him greater Suspicion that this Tenderness proceeded from the familiar Conversation he had with her; dismissing therefore all that were present, except *Tyriotes* only, he now no longer wept, but sighing said, 'Look thee, *Tyriotes,* thou must not think 'to put me off with Lies, for Torments presently 'shall express the Truth from thee. But I conjure 'thee, by the Gods, not to keep me so long in sus-'pence, if thou hast any Veneration for thy King, 'tell me what I desire to know, and am asham'd to 'utter, did not the youthful Conqueror offer Violence 'to her?' Then *Tyriotes* offer'd *to suffer the Rack, and call'd the Gods to witness, that the Queen had been us'd with all the Respect the strictest Virtue could require.* At last *Darius* being convinc'd of the Truth of what the *Eunuch* said, he cover'd his Head, and wept a long time, and the Tears still flowing from his Eyes, he uncover'd his Face, and holding up his Hands to *Heaven,* he said, *Ye tutelar Gods of my Dominions, my first Request is, that you would vouchsafe to confirm my Kingdom to my self, but if my Ruin be determin'd, I beg no other may be admitted King of* Asia, *than this just Enemy, this merciful Conqueror.*

CHAP.

CHAP. XI.

Notwithstanding *Darius* had twice ask'd for Peace without obtaining it, and thereupon had bent his whole Mind to War, yet, overcome by the Virtue of his Enemy, he made choice of ten of the chiefest of his Relations to make fresh Overtures; whom *Alexander* admitted, having summon'd his Council to attend on that Occasion. Then the eldest of the *Ambassadors* told him, ' That *Darius* did now
' a third time desire Peace of him, not that he was
' compell'd to it by any Force or Necessity, but
' mov'd thereto by his Justice and Continency. That
' such was his generous Behaviour to his Mother, his
' Wife, and his Children, that he should hardly think
' 'em to be Captives, but because they were not with
' himself. You shew a fatherly Care of those that
' are yet living, and honour 'em with the Title of
' Queens, leaving to 'em all the Splendour of their
' former Fortunes. I can read as much Concern in
' your Looks as there was in *Darius*'s when we left
' him, and yet he bewails the Loss of a Wife, and
' you only that of an Enemy. And were it not for
' your pious Care of her Funeral, you would now
' have been at the Head of your Army, drawn up in
' Order of Battel. Now where is the great Wonder,
' if being overcome by so much Bounty and friendly
' Usage, he desires Peace of you? What occasion is
' there for Arms where there is no Hatred? Hereto-
' fore he offer'd you the River *Halys*, that terminates
' *Lydia*, for the Bounds of yo. Empire. Now he
' proffers

'proffers you all the Countries that lie between the
'*Hellespont* and the *Euphrates*, as a Portion with his
'Daughter, which he freely gives you in Marriage.
'He moreover offers to leave with you his Son *Ochus*
'as a Pledge of the Peace, and his Integrity. He
'only requires you will restore to him his Mother and
'Virgin Daughters, for which you shall receive thirty
'thousand Talents of Gold. Were I not already con-
'vinc'd of your Moderation, I would remind you,
'that at this Juncture, it were your Interest not
'only to grant Peace, but readily to accept of it
'Do but look back on the vast Countries you leave
'behind you, and take a view in thought, of what
'still remains to conquer An overgrown unweildy
'Empire is always in Danger, and it is a difficult
'thing to hold fast what you cannot grasp. We see
'those Ships that are of an unweildy Bulk, are not
'easily governed And I cannot tell but *Darius* there-
'fore lost so much, because too much Wealth fur-
'nishes Opportunities for great Losses. There are
'some things much easier to acquire than to keep
'With how much more Ease do our Hands snatch
'things away, than hold 'em afterwards? even the
'Death of *Darius*'s Queen, may make you sensible
'that you have not now so much room left you to
'shew your merciful Temper as before.'

The *Ambassador* having finish'd his Speech, *Alexander* order'd 'em to withdraw, and requir'd those of his Council to speak their Opinions They all remain'd silent for some time, not daring to declare their Sentiments, by Reason they were uncertain how the King himself was disposed At last, *Parmenio* spoke to this effect ' I was of Opinion heretofore, Sir,
' that the Prisoners should have been restor'd to those
' that would have redeem'd 'em at *Damascus*, by
which

Book IV. *Quintus Curtius.*

'which means a considerable Sum of Money might
' have been rais'd, whereas, while you detain 'em,
' they only deprive you of the Service of a great many
' brave Hands, and I cannot but think it now ad-
' viseable to make an Exchange of an old Woman and
' two young Girls (which like a troublesome Luggage,
' only retard your Marches) for thirty thousand Ta-
' lents of Gold. Besides, here is a noble Kingdom to
' be had by Agreement, without so much as running
' the Risk of an uncertain War, none before you
' ever having possess'd all that vast Tract of Land
' that lies between the *Ister* and the *Euphrates*. Turn
' therefore your Thoughts, Sir, upon *Macedonia*, ra-
' ther than on *Bactra* or the *Indies*.' The King was
very much displeas'd with this Speech, and therefore
as soon as he had concluded it, he said, *And I also
would prefer Money to Glory, if I were* Parmenio. *But
as I am* Alexander, *I am secure from Poverty, and I
consider that I am no Merchant, but a King. I don't
pretend to sell any thing, neither will I sell my Reputation. If it be adviseable to restore the Captives, it
is more honourable to deliver 'em up gratis, than for a
Sum of Money.* Then calling in the Ambassadors,
he made 'em this Answer. ' Tell *Darius* (for the Cere-
' mony of Thanks is superfluous between Enemies)
' That the Acts of Clemency and Generosity that I
' have done, were not intended to procure his Friend-
' ship, but were the real Effects of my own good
' Nature. For I don't pretend to shew Hostilities to
' those in Affliction, my Arms are designed for an
' armed Enemy. If he sincerely su'd for Peace, per-
' haps I might deliberate whether I should give it or
' not. But since he has not only sollicited my Sol-
' diers to revolt, but also endeavoured to corrupt my
' Friends with Money to destroy me, I think my

VOL. I. L 'self

'felt oblig'd to pursue him to Destruction, not as a
'just Enemy, but as a Ruffian and a Murtherer. As
'for the Conditions he offers me, they are such, that
'to receive 'em, were to acknowledge him Con-
'queror. He proffers me all behind the *Euphrates*,
'Does he shew his Liberality in that? Where am I
'at this Instant you address to me? Am I not got
'beyond the *Euphrates*? It is plain then, that I am
'already encamp'd beyond the Bounds he offers me
'with his Daughter.

'Drive me then from hence, that I may be sen-
'sible that what you yield to me is your own. He
'shews his Liberality much after the same rate, when
'he offers me his Daughter. Would he not otherwise
'marry her to some of his Servants? It's a mighty
'Favour he does me, to prefer me to *Mazæus*. Go
'therefore and tell your King, that what he has al-
'ready lost, and what he has still to lose, is all to be
'the Reward of War and Victory. That this must
'determine the Bounds of both Empires, and each shall
'be content with what Fortune shall allot him to-
'morrow. If he would be contented with the second
'Rank, and not insist on being upon an Equality with
'me, may be I might grant what he asks; for I did
'not come into *Asia* to receive, but to give. Tell him
'then, that as the Celestial World cannot be govern'd
'by two Suns, so it is inconsistent with the Welfare
'of the Terrestrial one, to be rul'd by two powerful
'Kingdoms. Let him therefore resolve to surrender
'himself to day, or prepare for Battel to-morrow.
'Let him not flatter himself with the Hopes of better
'Fortune than what he has already experienc'd.' To
this the Ambassadors answer'd, 'That since he was
'bent upon War, it was candidly done of him not to
'amuse 'em with the Hopes of a Peace. They there-
'fore

'fore desir'd, they might forthwith repair to their 'Prince, since it was necessary he should likewise pre'pare himself for Battel.' And being accordingly dismiss'd, they acquainted *Darius, That he was on the Point of an Engagement.*

CHAP. XII.

Hereupon *he* immediately dispatch'd *Mazæus* with three thousand Horse, to take Possession of the Passes, and *Alexander* having perform'd the Funeral of *Darius's* Queen, left the heavy Baggage, and whatever could retard his March, within the Camp, appointing a small Guard for its Security, and then advanc'd towards the Enemy He divided his Foot into two Bodies, and posted the Cavalry on the Right and Left of it. The Carriages follow'd in the Rear. Then he sent *Menidas* with a Party of Horse to discover where *Darius* was. But he not daring to advance very far, because *Mazæus* lay in his way, return'd, and told *Alexander* that there was nothing to be heard but the Noise of Men, and the Neighing of Horses. On the other side, *Mazæus* perceiving the *Macedonian* Scouts at a distance, return'd to the Camp, and acquainted *Darius* with the Approach of the Enemy, and as he was desirous of deciding the Matter in the open Plains, he commanded his Soldiers to take to their Arms, and drew them up in order of Battel. In the left Wing were the *Bactrian* Horse, to the Number of a thousand, there were as many *Dahæ*, with four thousand *Arachosians* and *Susians.* These were follow'd by fifty Chariots arm'd with

Scythes. Next unto them was *Beſſus*, with eight thouſand *Bactrian* Horſe, and two thouſand *Maſſagetæ*. Then came the Foot of ſeveral Nations, not mix'd, but in a diſtinct Order, each in their reſpective Corps. Then follow'd *Ariobarſanes* and *Orobates*, who led up the *Perſians*, and had alſo with 'em the *Mardians* and *Sogdians*. Theſe two Generals had their particular Commands, but *Orſines* commanded this Part of the Army in chief. He was deſcended from ſome of the ſeven *Perſians*, and even deriv'd himſelf from *Cyrus*. Theſe were ſucceeded by other Nations hardly known to their Aſſociates. After theſe came *Phradates*, with the *Caſpian* Forces, and fifty Chariots of War. Behind theſe were the *Indians*, and the other Nations that inhabit along the Coaſt of the Red-Sea, rather mere Names than Auxiliaries. This Body was follow'd by fifty other arm'd Chariots, which were join'd by the Foreigners. After theſe came the *Armenians*, diſtinguiſh'd by the Title of *Leſſer*. The *Babylonians* follow'd theſe, and both were clos'd by the *Belitæ*, and thoſe who inhabit the *Coſſean* Hills. After theſe march'd the *Gortuans*, *Æubæans* originally, and had formerly follow'd the *Medians*, but were now degenerated, and wholly ignorant of the Cuſtoms of their Country. The *Phrygians* and *Cathonians*, and then the *Parthians* who formerly came out of *Scythia*, brought up the Rear. This was the Order of the Left Wing. The Right was form'd by the Troops of the greater *Armenia*, the *Cadusians*, *Cappadocians*, *Syrians*, and *Medians*; theſe had likewiſe with 'em fifty arm'd Chariots. The Total of the Army amounted to forty five thouſand Horſe, and two hundred thouſand Foot. Being drawn up after this manner, they advanc'd ten Furlongs, and then were commanded

manded to halt, and expect the Enemy under their Arms

At this very Juncture a sudden Fear, of which no Cause could be given, seiz'd *Alexander*'s Army, every one was amaz'd, and a secret Dread spread it self over all their Hearts. The Brightness from the Clouds (it being Summer-time) at a distance appear'd to them like so many flaming Fires round about 'em, which they took for those of *Darius*'s Camp, so that they were afraid they had inconsiderately advanc'd amongst the Enemies Guards. Had but *Mazæus* fallen upon 'em, while they were still possess'd with this Fear, he might have given 'em a great Blow. But he remain'd idle on the Eminence he had taken Possession of, very well pleas'd that he was not attack'd himself.

Alexander being inform'd of the Fright his Army was in, *order'd the Signal to be given for a Halt*, and then commanded 'em *to lay down their Arms, and rest their Bodies*, giving them to understand, *That there was no Cause at all for their Fear, the Enemy being yet at a good distance*. At last they recover'd their Spirits and resum'd their Arms. However *Alexander* thought it the best way to remain in that very Place where he then was, and fortify his Camp.

The next Day *Mazæus*, who had posted himself (as we said) on an Eminence from whence he could discover the *Macedonians* Camp, whether it were because he had no other Orders than barely to take a View of the Enemy, repair'd to *Darius*. Hereupon the *Macedonians* presently took Possession of his Post, for it was safer than the Plain, and they could from thence take a Prospect of the *Persian* Army. For notwithstanding the moist Hills sent up such a Mist as hinder'd 'em from taking a distinct View of their several Divisions and their Order of Battle, yet it did not hinder them from a general Survey. The Multitude overspread the Plains like an Inundation, and the Noise of so many thousands, even at that distance, fill'd their Ears.

The *King* began now to waver in his Mind, and tho' it was too late, would sometimes weigh his own Resolution, and sometimes *Parmenio*'s Advice, for he was advanc'd so far, that he could not retire with any manner of Safety, without he were victorious. He was alarm'd at the vast Multitude of his Enemies, in comparison of his own small Number. But then again he recall'd to mind the many great Actions he had atchiev'd with that little Army, and the many Nations he had conquer'd with it. So that Hope having got the better of Fear, and concluding that Delays were dangerous, since thereby Despair might gain Ground on the Minds of his Men, he dissembl'd his Thoughts, and commanded *the mercenary* Pæonian *Horse to advance*. And having divided his *Phalanx*, as we said before, into two Bodies, he plac'd his Cavalry on each Wing. By this time the Mist was clear'd up, so that *Darius*'s Army was plainly to be seen. And the *Macedonians*, whether out of Alacrity, or being tir'd with the Tediousness of any longer Delay, gave a great Shout, after the manner of Armies before they engage, and the *Persians* return'd the same, filling the neighbouring Woods and Vallies with a dreadful Sound. And notwithstanding the *Macedonians* could hardly be hinder'd from rushing furiously on the Enemy, yet *Alexander* thought it still more adviseable to fortify his Camp on the Hill, and accordingly order'd a Trench to be cast up round it, and the Work being speedily perform'd, he repair'd to his Tent, from whence he could behold the Enemy's whole Army.

CHAP

CHAP. XIII.

HERE a perfect Image of the ensuing Danger, presented itself before his Eyes, the Horses, as well as Men, glitter'd in Armor, and the Care the Generals took to ride through the Ranks of their respective Divisions, made him sensible that the Enemy was preparing with all possible Diligence for the approaching Battel, besides several things, which tho' of little Moment themselves, such as the Noise of the Multitude, the Neighing of the Horses, the Brightness of their Arms, disturb'd his Mind that was full of Solicitude for the future Event

Therefore whether he was yet unresolv'd, or by the way of Tryal, to know how they stood affected, he call'd a Council, and ask'd 'em what they thought most adviseable in the present Juncture Parmenio (who was the most experienc'd of all the Generals in the Art of War) *was rather for surprising the Enemy than for an open Battel* He said, *they might easily be vanquish'd, in the dead time of the Night For as they consisted of Nations so different in their Custom and Speech, how would they be able in the Confusion of the Night, ever to rally if set upon in their Sleep, and terrify'd with the unforeseen Danger? Whereas in the Day-time, the frightful Aspects of the* Scythians *and the* Bactrians, *with their rough Visages and long Hair, and the monstrous Size of their vast Bodies, might strike a Dread in the Soldiers, who are more liable to receive Impressions from Trifles, than from Realities, moreover, their small Number would be in Danger of being sur-*

rounded

rounded by so great a Multitude: for they had not now the Straits of *Cilicia* and narrow Passes to fight in, but the Plains and open Fields. They were almost all of *Parmenio*'s Opinion, and *Polypercon* did not scruple to declare, *That the Victory depended on the Execution of it*. The *King* therefore looking on *Polypercon* (for as he had lately been severer with *Parmenio* than he wish'd, he could not find in his Heart to reprove him again) said, *This subtile Wisdom you advise me to, belongs to Thieves and Robbers*, for their chief Aim is to deceive. But I shall not always suffer either Darius's Absence, or the Straitness of the Place, or a Surprize in the Night, to rob me of my Glory. I am determin'd to attack him openly, and had rather have occasion to blame my Fortune, than be asham'd of my Victory. Besides, I am very well assur'd, that the Persians keep strict Guards and stand to their Arms, so that it were impossible to fall upon 'em at unawares. Wherefore prepare your selves for Battel.

Having thus encourag'd 'em, he dismiss'd 'em to refresh themselves. Now *Darius* imagining the Enemy would have done as *Parmenio* propos'd, had order'd, *That the Horses should stand ready bridl'd all the Night, and a great Part of the Army to be under their Arms, and the Watches to be strictlier kept than usually*. His whole Camp was illuminated with Fires, and he himself with his Generals and Relations rid about the Divisions that were upon Duty. Then invoking *the Sun that they call* Mithres, *and the sacred and eternal Fire, to inspire his Army with a Courage worthy their ancient Glory, and the Acts of their Predecessors*, and declar'd, that if it was possible for the Mind of Man to guess at Tokens of the Divine Assistance, it was plain, that the Gods were on their side. It was they who struck the Macedonians lately with a sudden Fear, they
being

being still in great Confusion, as appear'd by their running about and flinging down their Arms. That the time was now at hand, that the Tutelar Gods of Persia had pitch'd upon to punish those mad men, and that their General was no wiser than the rest. For after the manner of wild Beasts, he look'd so greedily upon his Prey, as like them, to fall into the Snares which were set before it.

The *Macedonians* were in the same Solicitude, and pass'd that Night in as much fear as if the Battel had been to be then fought. *Alexander* himself was more terrify'd than ever he had been before, and call'd for *Aristander* to offer up Vows and Prayers. He therefore being cloath'd in white, and carrying sacred Herbs in his Hand, with his Head cover'd, pray'd with the King who implor'd the Protection of *Jupiter*, *Minerva*, and *Victory*. Afterward having offer'd Sacrifice, according to their *Rites*, he return'd to his Tent to take his Rest the remainder of the Night. But he could neither sleep nor compose the Disturbance of his Mind. One while he resolv'd to charge the *Persians* Right Wing first, sometimes he thought it best to attack their main Body, and then again he doubted whether it might not be more adviseable to fall upon their Left Wing. At last his Body being tir'd with the Anxiety of his Mind, he fell into a profound Sleep. As soon as it was light, the Officers repair'd to his Tent to receive Orders, and were much surpriz'd at the unusual Silence they found there. For he us'd to send for 'em, and sometimes reprimand their Laziness, they therefore wonder'd, that being on the very brink of Danger, he was not yet stirring, some were of Opinion he did not rest, but shrunk out of Fear. A the same time none of the Guards dar'd to enter the Tent, and yet the Time of Action drew nigh, and the

L 5 Soldiers

Soldiers did not dare to take to their Arms, or form their Ranks, without their General's Orders. *Parmenio* therefore having waited a considerable time, commanded 'em to refresh themselves, and there being a Necessity now for the drawing up of the Army, he went into the Tent, and not being able to wake the *King* by calling upon him, he touch'd him with his Hand, and told him, *it was broad Day, and the Enemy was advancing towards them in order of Battel; while your Soldiers, for want of Orders, are still without their Arms. What is become, Sir, of your wonted Vigor of Mind? You us'd to prevent the most early* To this *Alexander* reply'd, *Do you think it was possible for me to compose my self to Rest, till I had calm'd the Anxiety of my Thoughts?* This said, he commanded him to give the Signal for Battel But as *Parmenio* persisted in his Admiration *how he could sleep so securely*, he told him, *there was no reason to wonder at it, for while* Darius *was burning the Country, destroying the Towns and Villages, and spoiling the Provisions, it was impossible for him to be easie, but now that he prepares to give me Battel, What should I fear? He has now granted me all I desire However I shall satisfie you farther hereafter as to this Matter, in the mean time every one of you repair to your respective Commands, and I'll be with you presently, and then I'll tell you what you are to do*

He very rarely hearken'd to the Admonitions of his Friends when Danger was at Hand; however, now having put on his Armour, he came to the Army The Soldiers had never seen him so chearful before, and they conjectur'd from his undaunted Countenance, that the Day was their own

The *King* first of all, order'd 'em to level the Works, and then drew up the Army after this manner In the Right Wing were those Horse which they call *Agema*,

Agema, commanded by *Clitus*, to whom he join'd *Philotas*'s Troops, and the Cavalry of several other Commanders, the last Regiment was that of *Meleager*, which was next to the *Phalanx*. After the *Phalanx*, were the *Argyraspides*, these were commanded by *Nicanor*, *Parmenio*'s Son. *Coenos* with his Troops, were a Body of Reserve, after him were *Orestes* and *Lynceftes*, and next to these *Polypercon*, who commanded the Foreigners. *Amyntas* had the chief Command of this Division. *Philogus* led the *Balacri*, who were lately took into the Alliance. This was the Disposition of the Right Wing. In the Left was *Craterus* with the *Peloponnesian* Horse, and with him were also the *Achians*, *Locrensians*, and *Malæans*. These were clos'd by the *Thessalian* Horse, commanded by *Philip*. The Foot were cover'd by the Horse. This was the Order of the Left Wing. Now, that he might not be surrounded by the Multitude, he had posted a strong Body of Reserve in the Rear, and had on the Wings, Troops in readiness to relieve in such a Case; not fronting as the rest of the Army did, but on the Flanks, that in case the Enemy endeavour'd to surround them, they might be ready to engage them. Here were posted the *Agrianians*, commanded by *Attalus*, as also the *Cretan* Archers. The Ranks in the Rear, were to front outwardly, that the Army might be secure every way. Here were the *Illyrians*, with the Mercenaries and the Light arm'd *Thracians*. In fine he had so dispos'd his Army, that it fronted every way, and was ready to engage on all Sides, if attempted to be encompass'd. Thus the Front was not better secur'd than the Flanks, nor the Flanks better provided for than the Rear.

He order'd 'em, *That in case the* Barbarians *let loose their arm'd Chariots with Shouts among 'em, to open to the Right and Left, and let them silently pass by,* being well assur'd they would do no Mischief if they were not oppos'd in their Passage. *But if they sent them upon 'em without shouting, that then they should terrifie them with their Conclamations, and stick the affrighted Horses with their Darts.* They that commanded the Wings, were order'd *to extend 'em as much as they could, without leaving the Center too thin, that they might not by too close an Order be in danger of being surrounded.* The Biggage and the Prisoners (amongst whom were *Darius*'s Mother and Children) were plac'd on a rising Ground not far from the Army, with a moderate Guard. The Left was commanded by *Parmenio*, as it us'd to be, and the *King* himself commanded the Right. The Armies were not come within the Cast of their Darts, when *Bion* a Deserter came riding on full speed to the *King,* and acquainted him, that *Darius* had planted Iron Caltrops all over that Ground *where he expected the* Macedonian *Horse, and by a certain Sign,* shew'd him the Place, that his Men might avoid it. *Alexander* having order'd the Deserter to be secur'd, call'd together his Generals, and imparted the Information to 'em, requiring them *to decline that Place, and to acquaint their Men with the Danger.* However, it was impossible for the whole Army to hear this, the Noise of both Armies taking away the Use of the Ears, so that *Alexander* riding about, spoke to the Captains and those that were next him, in the following manner.

CHAP·

CHAP. XIV.

'YOU that have march'd through so many Coun-
' tries in hopes of the Victory, for which you
' are going to fight, have now but this single Danger
' left to encounter with. Then he *reminded 'em* of
' the River *Granicus*, and the *Cicilian* Mountains, that
' *Syria* and *Egypt* had been conquer'd by 'em, with
' only passing through the same, which were so many
' Encouragements and Pledges of their future Glory.
' That the *Persians* were Fugitives, rally'd together in
' their Flight, and would only fight now, because
' they could not fly any farther. That this was the
' third Day they had lain under their Arms, trembling
' and almost dead with Fear, without daring to make
' the least Motion. That there could not be a greater
' Demonstration of their Despair, than their burning
' their Towns and Country, by that very Procedure
' acknowledging all to be the Enemies that they
' could not destroy. That the empty Names of un-
' known Nations, ought not in the least to terrify
' 'em, for it was of no moment to the War, who
' they call'd *Scythians* or *Caducians*. It being plain from
' their being unknown, that they are insignificant Peo-
' ple, since it is impossible brave Men should lie buried
' in Obscurity and Oblivion, whereas Cowards, when
' forc'd from their lurking Retreats, bring into the
' field nothing but a barbarous Title. As for the *Mace-*
' *donians*, they have so signaliz'd their Virtue, that
' there is not the least Corner of the Earth that is ig-
' norant of their Glory. Do but behold the uncouth
' Ap-

'Appearance of the *Barbarians*, how forrily they are
' arm'd! fome of 'em have only a Dart, others a Sling
' to caft Stones, while very few of 'em have proper
' Arms Therefore, notwithftanding the Enemy be
' fuperior in number of Men, yet you have the Ad-
' vantage of Soldiers Moreover, he did not require
' 'em to exert their Bravery, unlefs he encourag'd 'em
' by his Example. He *aſſur'd* 'em, he would fight in
' in Perfon before the Colours, and that he fhould
' efteem the Wounds he there receiv'd, as fo many Or-
' naments to his Body That they knew very well
' themfelves, that all partook of the Booty, except
' himfelf. That he made no other Ufe of the Rewards
' of his Victories, than to adorn and honour them with
' them This was what he thought fit to fay to the
' gallant and brave. But if there were any amongft
' them of a different Difpofition, he muft acquaint
' them, that they were now advanc'd fo far, that
' it was impoffible to fly That having behind them
' fuch vaft Countries, fo many Rivers and Moun-
' tains to oppofe them, there was no Paffage open to
' their own Homes, but what they fhould make them-
' felves Sword in hand

Thus he animated the Captains, thus *he* encourag'd the Soldiers who were near him.

Darius was on the left Wing of his Army, having with him a ftrong Guard of chofen Horfe and Foot, and defpis'd the fmall number of the Enemy. judging, that by their extending their Wings to the utmoft, their main Body muft needs ftand very thin Being therefore feated aloft in his Chariot, he addrefs'd him- felf both by Looks and Gefture, to the Troops that were about him on the Right and Left; telling them,
, That we who were a little while fince, Lords of
, all the Countries between the Ocean and the *Helle*
' *ſpont,*

'spent, are now reduc'd to fight, not for Glory, but
'for Safety; nay, for what we even prefer to our
'Safety, our Liberty. This Day will either restore, or
'put an end to the largest Empire the World has seen.
'At the River *Granicus* we engag'd the Enemy with
'an inconsiderable Part of our Forces when we were
'overcome in *Cilicia*, we had *Syria* to repair to, and
'the *Tigris* and *Euphrates* were as Bulwarks to our
'Dominions Now we are got where there is no
'room left for Flight, every thing behind our Backs
'being exhausted by the Continuance of the War.
'The Towns are dispeopled, and there are not hands
'to cultivate the Earth Our Wives and Children also
'follow the Army, and will certainly fall a Prey to
'the Enemy, if we are backward in exposing our
'Lives for those dear Pledges. As for what depended
'on me, I have taken care to have such an Army
'as the largest Plains are hardly able to contain I have
'furnish'd it with Horses and Arms, and have taken
'care to supply it with Provisions, and have chosen
'such a place to fight in, where all our Forces may
'be display'd. The rest depends on your selves, do
'but dare to conquer and the Work is done Renown
'and Fame are but weak Arms against brave Men,
'therefore do not regard 'em in the Enemy For it
'is his Rashness you have hitherto fear'd, and mi-
'staken for Courage, which when its first Fury is
'spent, becomes languid and dull, like those Animals
'that have lost their Stings These spacious Fields
'discover the small Number of the Enemy, which
'the *Cilician* Mountains hid. You see how thin their
'Ranks are, how their Wings are stretch'd out, their
'Center is in a manner vacant, as for the Rear, they
'seem by their facing outwards to be ready to run
'away, they may be trod to death by the Horses,
'tho'

' tho' I were barely to send my arm'd Chariots among
' 'em. If we gain this Battle it puts an end to the
' War, for they have no Place to escape to; they are
' inclos'd between the *Tigris* and the *Euphrates*. What
' before was advantageous to them, is now become
' a Nuisance. Our Army is light and ready on all
' Occasions, theirs is loaded with Booty. They are,
' as it were, entangled in our Spoils, so that we may
' kill 'em with ease. The same things shall be both
' the Cause of our Victory and its Reward. If any of
' you are startled at the Renown of the Nation, think
' with your selves, that only their Arms are there, and
' not their Persons, for a great deal of Blood has been
' spilt on both sides, and in a small number the Loss
' is soonest felt. As for *Alexander*, how great soever
' he may appear to the Cowardly and Fearful, he is
' still but one Individual, and, in my Opinion, both
' rash and foolish. Now nothing can be lasting that
' is not supported by Reason, and though he
' seems to be successful, yet at long run he'll pay for
' his Temerity. Besides, the Turns and Revolutions of
' Things are of short Duration, there is no such thing
' as an unmix'd Felicity. Perhaps it is the Will of the
' Gods, that the *Persian* Empire (which by a Series of
' Success for these two hundred and thirty Years, has
' rais'd itself to the highest pitch of Grandeur) should
' receive this violent Shock without being overthrown,
' to put us in mind of human Frailty, of which we
' are too forgetful in Prosperity. A little while ago
' we our selves carry'd the War into *Greece*, and now
' we are forc'd to drive it from our own Country.
' Thus we are tost by the mutability of Fortune, for
' one Nation is not capable of the Empire we both af-
' fect, but admitting we were destitute of Hopes, yet
' Necessity ought to animate us, our Case is so de-
                                            ' plorable.

Book IV. *Quintus Curtius.*

'plorable My Mother, Daughters, and Son *Ochus*
'(who was born with a Right to succeed in the Em-
'pire) together with several Princes descended from
'Royal Blood, and your Generals, who were like so
'many Kings, all wear his Chains; nay, I my self
'am more than half a Captive, unless you exert your
'selves Free my Bowels from their Bondage, restore
'to me those dear Pledges, (for which I am willing
'my self to die) my Mother and Children, for I have
'lost my Wife in that Prison. Think with your
'selves how they all reach out their Hands to you,
'implore the Assistance of the Gods, beg your Help,
'Pity and Fidelity, to deliver 'em from Servitude,
'Fetters, and a precarious way of living Can you
'believe they are easie under those they would hardly
'vouchsafe to command? But I perceive the Enemy
'approaches, and the nearer the Danger draws, the
'less am I satisfy'd with what I have said I conjure
'you then by the Tutelar Gods of our Country, by
'the eternal Fire that is carry'd before us on Altars,
'by the Splendor of the Sun that rises within the Li-
'mits of my Empire, by the everlasting Memory of
'*Cyrus*, who transfer'd the Empire from the *Medes*
'and *Lydians* to the *Persians*, to free our Name and
'Nation from the utmost Disgrace Fall on chear-
'fully, and full of Hopes, that you may transmit to
'Posterity the Glory you have receiv'd from your Pre-
'decessors You carry in your right Hands your Li-
'berty, Relief, and all our future Hopes Whoever de-
'spises Death is least liable to it, the fearful only fall a
'Prey to it. I ride in a Chariot, not only to comply
'with the Custom of my Country, but also that I
'may be the better seen by all, and I am not against
'your imitating of me, according as I give you an
'Example either of Fortitude or Cowardice.'

CHAP.

CHAP. XV.

IN the mean time *Alexander*, that he might avoid the Place of Ambuscade, discover'd by the Deserter, fetch'd a Compass, and that he might encounter with *Darius*, who led the Left Wing, caus'd his Army to march in an oblique Line. *Darius* also on his side advanc'd towards him, and commanded *Bessus to charge* Alexander's *Left Wing with the* Messagetan *Horse in the Flank* He had before him the arm'd Chariots, which upon the Signal given, broke in furiously amongst the Enemy, and were driven with a loose Rein, that by the suddenness of the Surprize they might do the greater Execution, some were destroy'd by the Pikes that stuck out at the end of the Poles, and others were cut to pieces by the Scythes plac'd on each side

The *Macedonians* did not give way gradually, but taking to their Heels, confounded their Ranks, and *Mazæus* perceiving their Disorder, that he might strike the greater Fear into 'em, sent a thousand Horse to plunder their Baggage, thinking that the Captives that were guarded with it, would, at the Approach of their Friends, break loose and make their escape *Parmenio*, who was in the Left Wing, was not insensible of what was doing, he therefore immediately dispatch'd *Polydamus* to the *King*, to acquaint *him* with the Danger, *and know his Pleasure upon this Occasion* The *King* having heard *Polydamus*, made this Answer, *Tell* Parmenio, *that if we get the Day, we shall not only recover our own, but also be Masters of all the Enemy has, and*

there-

Book IV. *Quintus Curtius.*

therefore let him not weaken the Army on that Account, but continue fighting Manfully, and after mine, and my Father Philip's *Example, despise the loss of the Baggage.*

In the mean time the *Barbarians* were pillaging the Camp, and having kill'd a great many of those that guarded it, the Prisoners broke their Chains, and arming themselves with what came next to their Hands, they join'd the Horse, and fell also upon the *Macedonians*, who were now in a doubtful Condition. Some of the Prisoners ran for joy to *Sisigambis*, and told her *Darius* had got the Victory, that a mighty Slaughter had been made of the Enemies, who were at last stripp'd of all their Baggage and Booty, for they concluded the *Persians* had every where the same Fortune, and were now as Conquerors running about for Plunder. And notwithstanding they would fain have prevail'd with *Sisigambis* to moderate her Grief, yet she remain'd in the same State as before, without speaking one Word, or changing her Countenance, but sate as if she were immoveable, (and seem'd to be afraid by too early a Joy to provoke Fortune) insomuch that the Standers by could not make any Judgment of her Inclinations.

While these things were doing, *Amyntas*, one of *Alexander*'s Colonels of Horse, came to the Assistance of those that guarded the Baggage, whether of his own Motion, or by the *King*'s Orders, is uncertain; but he was soon oblig'd to retire to *Alexander*, not being able to sustain the Shock of the *Cadusians* and *Scythians*, having been rather a Witness of the loss of the Baggage than a Rescuer. *Alexander* upon this was so transported with Grief, that he knew not what to resolve upon, he began to fear, and not without cause, lest the Concern for the loss of their Booty might draw the Soldiers from the Fight, he therefore sent *Aretes*
with

with the Pikemen call'd *Sariſtophori*, againſt the *Scythians*. By this time the Chariots having put the firſt Ranks into Confuſion, were drove againſt the *Phalanx*, the *Macedonians* were ſo far from being diſhearten'd at this, that they open'd to the Right and Left, according to their former Inſtructions, and made a Lane for 'em to paſs through; and ſtanding in cloſe Order like a Bulwark, ſtuck the Horſes with their Pikes as they went at random, and then ſurrounding the Chariots, brought headlong down thoſe that defended 'em. Here was ſo great a Slaughter made of Horſes and their Drivers, that it quite fill'd and choak'd up that Space, the Drivers could now no longer guide the affrighted Cattle, and the Horſes, by their kicking and flinging, had not only broke their Traces, but alſo overturn'd the Chariots, and being wounded, dragged after them the Men that were ſlain, neither being able to ſtand ſtill for their Fright, nor to advance, being faint with the loſs of Blood. However, a few of theſe Chariots pierc'd clear through to the Rear, and mangled the Bodies of thoſe they fell amongſt, after a moſt deplorable manner, the Ground was ſtrew'd with their diſſected Limbs, and as they were heated, and their Wounds freſh, they were not ſenſible of much Pain, ſo that notwithſtanding their maim'd and weak Condition, they did not let their Arms drop, till by exceſſive bleeding they fell down dead. In the mean time, *Aretes* having kill'd the Captain of the *Scythians* that were pillaging the Baggage, preſs'd hard upon 'em, but the *Bactrians* coming ſeaſonably to their Aſſiſtance, turn'd the Fortune of the Fight again. A great many *Macedonians* were trampled under foot in the very firſt Charge, the reſt fled back to *Alexander*, hereupon the *Perſians* gave ſuch a Shout as Victors are us'd to give,

and

and rush'd furiously on the Enemy, as if their Defeat had been univerfal

Alexander therefore check'd those that were frighten'd, and encourag'd 'em, and renew'd himself the Fight, that began to grow languid. Thus having inspir'd 'em with fresh Vigour, he commanded 'em to charge the Enemy The *Persians* right Wing was very much weaken'd by the Detachment of *Bactrians*, which were sent to seize the Baggage , *Alexander* therefore attack'd their loose Ranks, and made a great Slaughter of the Enemy, which being perceiv'd by the *Persians* left Wing, and thinking they had it in their Power to furround *Alexander*, they fell upon his Rear Here the *King* had been in great Danger, as being in the middle of his Enemies, if the *Agrian* Cavalry had not clapt Spurs to their Horfes, and charg'd the *Barbarians* that furrounded him, and by that means forc'd 'em to face about to defend themfelves

The Troops were hard put to it on both fides, for *Alexander* had the Enemy both before and behind , and thofe who attack'd his Rear were themfelves very much prefs'd by the *Agrian* Forces The *Bactrians* alfo, who were now return'd from pillaging the Baggage, could not recover their Poft, and feveral Battalions feparated from the reft, fought with the next of the Enemies that came in their way The two *Kings*, who were now near one another, encourag'd their refpective Troops , a greater Number of *Persians* were flain, the Number of the wounded was almoft equal *Darius* was in a Chariot, and *Alexander* on Horfeback , they were both guarded by felect Soldiers that had not the leaft thought of themfelves, for if their *King* fell, they neither would, nor could be fafe, and they look'd upon it as a noble Thing to die in the Prefence of their Sovereign , and thofe were expos'd to the greateft Danger,

Danger, who exerted themselves most for the Preservation of the *King*, whom they guarded, for every one coveted the Honour of killing the Prince of the adverse Party. Now whether it was an Illusion of the Eyes, or a Reality, they who were about *Alexander* thought they saw an *Eagle* hovering over the *King*'s Head, no wise terrify'd either by the Noise of the Arms, or the Groans of the dying Men, and appear'd a long time about *Alexander*'s Horse, rather suspended in Air than flying. It is certain, *Aristander* having put on his white Garment, and carrying a Lawrel in his Hand, shew'd this Sight to the Soldiers, who were attentive to the Fight, *as an infallible Token of the Victory*. They were then animated with fresh Courage and Assurance, who before were drooping, and their Alacrity encreas'd when *Darius*'s Charioteer was slain, neither did the *Persians* or *Macedonians* doubt but the *King* was kill'd. Hereupon *Darius*'s Relations and Attendants disturb'd the whole Army (which till then fought with almost equal Advantage) with mournful Howlings, and barbarous Cries and Lamentations. This caus'd those on the Left to take to their Heels, and desert the Chariot, which those on the Right receiv'd immediately into the middle of their Division. It is said, *Darius* having drawn his Sword, was unresolv'd, whether he ought not to avoid a shameful Flight by an honourable Death. But perceiving, as he sate aloft in his Chariot, that some Part of his Army still maintain'd the Fight, he was asham'd to leave 'em destitute of a Head. While *he* remain'd thus between Hope and Despair, the *Persians* gave way by little and little, and broke their Order. *Alexander* mounting a fresh Horse (for he had already tir'd several) continu'd sticking those that resisted him in the Face, and those that fled from him in the Back. By this time it was

no

no longer a Fight, but a perfect Maſſacre, and *Darius* himſelf turn'd his Chariot to make the beſt of his Way. The Victors purſu'd the routed, but the Clouds of Duſt that roſe up to the very Skies, intercepted their Sight, ſo that they wander'd like Men in the Dark, rallying now and then at the Sound of a known Voice, as at a Signal. It is true, the Noiſe of the Reins with which they ſtruck the Horſes that drew *Darius*'s Chariot, were ſometimes heard by 'em, which was all the Footſteps they had to purſue him by.

CHAP. XVI.

BUT in the *Macedonians* Left Wing, which was commanded by *Parmenio*, as we ſaid before, the Succeſs of both Parties was very different. For *Mazæus* with all his Cavalry charg'd furiouſly the *Macedonian* Horſe, and preſs'd hard upon 'em, and as he was much ſuperior in Number, began to ſurround the Foot. When *Parmenio* diſpatch'd Meſſengers to the King to let him know the Danger they were in on that Side, and that unleſs they were ſpeedily ſuccour'd, they ſhould of neceſſity be forc'd to fly. *Alexander* had purſu'd the Enemy a conſiderable way when this melancholy News was brought him; hereupon he ſtop'd both Horſe and Foot, and in a Rage cry'd out, *That the Victory was ſnatch'd out of his Hands, and that* Darius *was more fortunate in his Flight, than he in his Purſuit* In the mean time the Account of the King's Defeat had reach'd *Mazæus*, who thereupon (notwithſtanding he was much the ſtronger) did not preſs now ſo violently

Danger, who exerted themselves most for the Preservation of the *King*, whom they guarded, for every one coveted the Honour of killing the Prince of the adverse Party. Now whether it was an Illusion of the Eyes, or a Reality, they who were about *Alexander* thought they saw an *Eagle* hovering over the *King*'s Head, no wise terrify'd either by the Noise of the Arms, or the Groans of the dying Men, and appear'd a long time about *Alexander*'s Horse, rather suspended in Air than flying. It is certain, *Aristander* having put on his white Garment, and carrying a Lawrel in his Hand, shew'd this Sight to the Soldiers, who were attentive to the Fight, *as an infallible Token of the Victory.* They were then animated with fresh Courage and Assurance, who before were drooping, and their Alacrity encreas'd when *Darius*'s Charioteer was slain, neither did the *Persians* or *Macedonians* doubt but the *King* was kill'd. Hereupon *Darius*'s Relations and Attendants disturb'd the whole Army (which till then fought with almost equal Advantage) with mournful Howlings, and barbarous Cries and Lamentations. This caus'd those on the Left to take to their Heels, and desert the Chariot, which those on the Right receiv'd immediately into the middle of their Division. It is said, *Darius* having drawn his Sword, was unresolv'd, whether he ought not to avoid a shameful Flight by an honourable Death. But perceiving, as he sate aloft in his Chariot, that some Part of his Army still maintain'd the Fight, he was asham'd to leave 'em destitute of a Head. While *he* remain'd thus between Hope and Despair, the *Persians* gave way by little and little, and broke their Order. *Alexander* mounting a fresh Horse (for he had already tir'd several) continu'd sticking those that resisted him in the Face, and those that fled from him in the Back. By this time it was no longer a Fight, but a perfect Massacre, and *Darius* himself turn'd his Chariot to make the best of his Way. The Victors pursu'd the routed, but the Clouds of Dust that rose up to the very Skies, intercepted their Sight, so that they wander'd like Men in the Dark, rallying now and then at the Sound of a known Voice, as at a Signal. It is true, the Noise of the Reins with which they struck the Horses that drew *Darius*'s Chariot, were sometimes heard by 'em, which was all the Footsteps they had to pursue him by.

CHAP. XVI.

BUT in the *Macedonians* Left Wing, which was commanded by *Parmenio*, as we said before, the Success of both Parties was very different For *Mazæus* with all his Cavalry charg'd furiously the *Macedonian* Horse, and press'd hard upon 'em, and as he was much superior in Number, began to surround the Foot When *Parmenio* dispatch'd Messengers to the *King to let him know the Danger they were in on that Side, and that unless they were speedily succour'd, they should of necessity be forc'd to fly* Alexander had pursu'd the Enemy a considerable way when this melancholy News was brought him, hereupon he stop'd both Horse and Foot, and in a Rage cry'd out, *That the Victory was snatch'd out of his Hands, and that* Darius *was more fortunate in his Flight, than he in his Pursuit* In the mean time the Account of the *King's* Defeat had reach'd *Mazæus*, who thereupon (notwithstanding he was much the stronger) did not press now so violently

lently on the *Macedonians*: *Parmenio* was altogether ignorant why the Fight flacken'd, however, he laid hold of the Opportunity like an experienc'd General, and having call'd to him the *Thessalian* Horse, he said to 'em, *Do you not see how those who a little while ago bore so furiously down upon us, being suddenly terrify'd, grow slow in their Attacks? For certain it is our King's Fortune that also gives us the Victory. The Field is cover'd with slaughter'd* Persians, *why are you idle? Are you not a Match for 'em, even now that you see them ready to fly?*

What he said seem'd so probable, that they resum'd fresh Courage, and clapping Spurs to their Horses, charg'd the Enemy vigorously, who now no longer gave way by little and little, but retreated so fast, that nothing was wanting to make it a perfect Flight, but that they did not as yet turn their Backs. However, as *Parmenio* was still ignorant how it far'd with the *King*, he kept his Men back, by this Means *Mazæus* had time given him to fly, he therefore repass'd the *Tigre*, not the nearest way, but fetching a great Compass, and for that Reason with the greater Safety, and came to *Babylon* with the broken Remains of the routed Army. *Darius* made towards the River *Lycus*, with a few that accompany'd him in his Flight, and having pass'd the same, was wavering whether he ought not to cause the Bridge to be broke, for he was inform'd the Enemy would soon be there. But then again, he consider'd the many thousands of his Men that were not yet come to the River, and would, if the Bridge were broke, certainly fall a Prey to the Enemy. He therefore left it standing, and declar'd as he went away, *That he had much rather leave a Passage to them that pursu'd him, than deprive those of it that fled after him.* And having travell'd over a vast Tract of Ground, *he* reach'd *Arbela* about Midnight. Who can imagine or comprehend, even in Thought, the various sporting Turns of Fortune here, the Havock that was made of both Officers and Soldiers, the Flight of the Vanquish'd, the private Slaughters and universal Massacres? Fortune seems in this single Day to have heap'd together the Occurrence of a whole Age. Some took the shortest Way, while others fled through the Woods, and sav'd themselves by private Ways unknown to the Pursuers. There was a confus'd Mixture of Horse and Foot without Leaders, of the arm'd with the unarm'd, and of the sound with the infirm and wounded.

But at last Fear getting the better of Compassion, those that could not keep pace with the rest in the Flight, were left behind bewailing their mutual Calamities, the fatigu'd and wounded were parch'd up with Thirst, to relieve which, they flung themselves prostrate on the Banks of every Stream, and swallow'd the Water with insatiable Greediness, which being muddy, presently swell'd their Intrails, and their Limbs being relax'd and numm'd therewith, the Enemy overtook 'em, and rous'd 'em up with fresh Wounds. Some finding the neighbouring Brooks taken up by others, straggled farther that they might drain every Place of what Water they could find, there was not so out of the way, or dry a Puddle, that could escape the Drought of the thirsty Searchers. The Villages near the Road resounded with the Cries and Lamentations of the old People of both Sexes, who, after their barbarous manner, still call'd upon *Darius* as their King.

Alexander having check'd his Pursuit, (as we said before) was come to the River *Lycus*, where he found the Bridge loaded with a Multitude of the flying Enemy, a great many whereof, finding they were closely pursu'd, cast themselves into the River, and being encumber'd with their Arms, and tir'd with the Action and their Flight, were swallow'd up by its rapid Stream. In a little time, not only the Bridge could not contain the Fugitives, but even the River it self was crowded with 'em, by their indiscreet casting themselves upon one another, *for when once Fear had seiz'd their Minds, they valu'd nothing, but what caus'd that Fear.*

Alexander being entreated by his Followers, *not to suffer the Enemy to escape with Impunity,* alledg'd for Excuse of this Permission, *That their Weapons were blunted, their Arms tir'd, and their Bodies spent with so long a Chase, besides all which, Night was coming on* But in reality, he was in pain for his Left Wing, (which he thought was still engag'd) and so was resolv'd to return to its Assistance He had hardly fac'd about, when Messengers came to him from *Parmenio* with the agreeable News, that his Part of the Army was also Victorious *He* was never in greater Danger during the whole Day, than upon his return to the Camp There was but a small Number with him, and they were not in Order, but careless, transported with the Victory, for they concluded all the Enemy's Army was either fled, or slain However, contrary to their Expectation, all on the sudden there appear'd a Body of *Persian* Horse, which at first halted, but having discover'd the inconsiderable Number of the *Macedonians,* they charg'd 'em vigorously The *King* rid at the Head of his Men, rather dissembling, than despising the Danger But here again, *he* was attended by his usual Prosperity, for the *Persian* Commander coming against him with more Fury than Discretion, the *King* run him through with his Spear, and afterwards dealt the like Usage to several others who came in his way

His

His Friends likewise fell upon the Enemy, who was now in Disorder. On the other side, the *Persians* did not die unreveng'd, for the whole Armies did not engage more eagerly than these tumultuary Troops. At last, it being duskish, they thought it more advisable to fly, than to continue the Fight, and therefore made their Escape in different Troops.

The *King* having clear'd himself of this imminent Danger, brought his Men safe to the Camp. There fell of the *Persians* this Day, according to what Account the Victors could take, Forty Thousand, and of the *Macedonians*, less than Three Hundred. This Victory was owing more to the King's Bravery, than Fortune. Here it was his Courage, and not the Advantage of Ground, that conquer'd. He had drawn up his Army most skilfully, and fought himself most gallantly. He shew'd the highest Wisdom in despising the Loss of the Baggage and Booty, since all depended on the Issue of the Battel, and notwithstanding the Event was yet undetermin'd, he even then behav'd himself like a Conqueror. Then having struck a Terror into the Enemy, he afterwards routed them; and which is to be wonder'd at in so violent a Temper, *he* pursu'd them with more Prudence than Eagerness. For had he continu'd his Pursuit, while one Part of his Army was still engag'd, he had either run the Risque of being overcome through his own Fault, or had been indebted to another for the *Victory*, or had he been dishearten'd at the sudden Appearance of the Body of Horse that fell upon him as he return'd to his Camp, he must either, though a *Conqueror*, have shamefully fled, or perish'd miserably.

Neither ought his Officers to be defrauded of their due Praise, for the Wounds they receiv'd were so many Tokens of their Bravery. *Hephæstion* was run through the Arm with a Spear, *Perdiccas, Cænus,* and *Menidas* were almost kill'd with Arrows. And if we will make a true Judgment of *Macedonians,* at that time we must own, *That the King was worthy of such Subjects, and they of so great a King.*

Quintus Curtius.

BOOK V.

CHAP. I.

WERE I now to relate what was transacted in the same Space of time, either in *Greece*, *Illyrium*, or *Thrace*, by *Alexander*'s Conduct or Appointment, according to their ordinal Occurrence, I should be forc'd to interrupt the Series of the Affairs of *Asia*, which I think more proper to represent entirely, with the same Connexion and Order in my Work, as they hold in respect to the Time of their Performance, down to the Flight and Death of *Darius*. I shall therefore begin with those things that happen'd after the Fight of *Arbela*, where *Darius* arriv'd about Midnight, as did also great part of his Friends and Soldiers, whom Fortune had guided thither in their Flight. *Darius* having therefore call'd them together, told 'em, *That he did not doubt but A-*

lexander *would repair to those Cities and Countries that were most celebrated for Riches and Plenty of all things. That he and his Soldiers had now no other Thoughts but of enriching themselves with the noble Spoils that lay expos'd to 'em. That this would be of great use to himself in his present Circumstances, since he should thereby have time with an unincumber'd Body of Men, to retire to the Deserts. And as the remote Parts of his Dominions were still untouch'd, he might easily there raise fresh Forces to prosecute the War withal. Let 'em there rifle my Treasures which they have so long thirsted after, these will but make them the easier Prey to me for the future, for I have found by Experience that rich Furniture, and a great Train of Concubines and Eunuchs, are only so many Impediments and Clogs, which when Alexander shall draw after him, he'll be inferiour to those he has overcome*

This Speech appear'd to all that heard it full of Despair, for they plainly saw thereby, that he yielded up the wealthy City of *Babylon,* and that the Conqueror would also take Possession of *Susa,* and the other Ornaments of the Kingdom, which were the Cause of the War But *he* continu'd to represent to 'em, *That in Adversity fine Speeches were of no use, but only those that were suitable to the present Exigency of Affairs That the War was to be made with Iron, and not with Gold With Men, not with City Houses And that all things follow'd those that were arm'd That his Predecessors had after this manner recover'd their primitive Grandeur, though they had been unfortunate at first* Therefore whether *he* by this Speech gave 'em fresh Courage, or that they respected his Sovereignty more than they approv'd his Counsel, *he* enter'd the Borders of *Media* A little while after *Arbela,* which was full of the Royal Furniture and Treasure, was surrender'd to *Alexander.* Here were found four thousand Talents, besides

besides which, the Wealth of the whole Army was lodg'd here.

The *King* soon decamp'd from hence, being forc'd thereto by the Sickness that began to infect his Army, occasion'd by the Stench of the dead Bodies that almost cover'd all the Field.

In his March he had on his Left the plain Country of *Arabia*, so much celebrated for its odoriferous Products. The Lands that lye between the *Tigris* and the *Euphrates* are said to be so fruitful and rich that the Inhabitants are forc'd to check the Cattle in their Pasturage, for fear they should kill themselves by Surfeits. The Cause of this Fertility proceeds from these two Rivers, which communicate their Waters throughout the whole Territory by the hidden Veins in the Earth. Both these Rivers have their Source in the Mountains of *Armenia*, and afterwards dividing themselves, continue their different Courses. Their greatest Distance about the Mountains of *Armenia* is, by those who have measur'd it, reported to be two thousand five hundred Furlongs. These Rivers, when they begin to cut their way through the Lands of *Media* and *Gordia*, by degrees draw nearer to one another; and the farther they run, the narrower is the Interval between them. They are nearest each other in those Plains which are by the Inhabitants call'd *Mesopotamia*, which lies between 'em; from whence they continue their Course through the *Babylonian* Borders, and at last empty themselves into the *Red Sea*.

Alexander in four days came to the City call'd *Memnis*. Here there is a Cave which has in it a Fountain that emits a vast Quantity of bituminous Matter, so that it is probable enough, the Walls of *Babylon*, which are a prodigious Work, are cemented with that Matter.

As *Alexander* was continuing his March towards *Babylon*, *Mazæus* (who had fled thither from the Battel) came with his Children that were at the Age of Maturity, and surrender'd himself and the Town to the King His Submission was very acceptable to the King, by reason the Siege of so strong a Place must of necessity have been tedious Beside this, his Quality and Bravery were very considerable, and he had but lately distinguish'd himself in the last great Action, and whose Example wou'd be a great Inducement to others to imitate him. The King therefore receiv'd him and his Children very graciously, however he form'd his Army which he led in Person into a Square, commanded 'em to enter the Town in that Order, as if they had been going to an Engagement The Walls were fill'd with *Babylonians* who flock'd thither, eager to behold their new *Sovereign*, but the greatest part went out to meet him Among these were *Bagophanes* Governor of the Castle, and Keeper of the King's Treasure, who was unwilling to be outdone in Zeal by *Mazæus* The Road was strew'd all over with Flowers and Garlands, and adorn'd on each Side with Silver Altars, which were fill'd, not only with Frankincense, but all manner of Perfumes He was follow'd by the Presents he design'd the King, viz. Droves of Cattle and Horses, with Lyons and Leopards in strong Cages for that Purpose. These were follow'd by the *Magi* singing Hymns after the manner of the Country After these came the *Chaldeans*, and not only the *Babylonian* Prophets, but also the Musicians with their respective Instruments These are us'd to sing the Prince's Praise, and the *Chaldeans* are addicted to the Consideration of the Motions of the Planets, and declare the Vicissitudes of the Seasons. These were clos'd by the *Babylonian* Cavalry, whose rich Cloathing and Furniture, for them-

selves

selves and their Horses, denoted Luxury rather than Magnificence. The *King* commanded the Multitude of Town's People to follow in the Rear of his Foot, and being encompass'd by his Guards, enter'd the City in a Chariot, and then repair'd to the *Palace*. The next Day *he* took a View of *Darius*'s Furniture, and all his Treasure. The Beauty and Antiquity of the Place attracted not only *Alexander*'s Eyes, but likewise those of all that beheld it. *Semiramis* founded it, or, as a great many affirm, *Belus*, whose Palace is still to be seen. The Walls are made of Brick, and cemented with Bitumen, and are thirty two Foot in breadth, so that two Chariots that meet, might safely pass by each other. They were one hundred Cubits in height, and the Towers that were at certain Distances, were ten Foot higher than the Walls. The Compass of the whole Work took up three hundred sixty eight Furlongs. It is said that each Furlong was finish'd in a single Day. The Buildings are not contiguous to the Walls, but at the Distance of an Acre from them. Nay the City is not wholly taken up with Houses, but only ninety Furlongs thereof, nor do all the Houses join to one another, as I suppose, because it was judg'd safer to have 'em scatter'd up and down in several Places. The rest is sow'd and plough'd, that in case of a Siege the Inhabitants may be supply'd with Corn within themselves. The *Euphrates* runs through the City, and is kept on both sides by very strong Banks, which are themselves a prodigious Work. But these have behind 'em large and deep Caves, to receive the rapid Streams, which otherwise, when they rise above the Banks, would be apt to bear down the Houses, if it were not for these subterraneous Receptacles. These Caves are also lin'd with Brick, and cemented with Bitumen. The two

M 5   Parts

Parts of the Town have a Communication with each other by a Stone-Bridge, built over the River, which too is rank'd amongst the Wonders of the East. For the *Euphrates* carries with it a very deep Mud, which makes it very difficult to clear its Channel so perfectly as to find a firm Foundation. Moreover the great Heaps of Sand that gather about the Pillars that support the Bridge stop the Course of the Water, which being by that Confinement check'd, beats more furiously against it than it would do if it had a free Passage. The Castle is twenty Furlongs in circumference, the Towers are thirty Foot deep within the Ground, and eighty Foot in height above it. On the Top of the Castle are the Pensile Gardens, so much celebrated by the *Greek* Poets; they are of equal height with the Walls of the Town, and are mighty pleasant both on the account of their shady Groves, and the Tallness of the Trees that grow there. This bulky Work is supported by Pillars, over which there runs a Pavement of square Stone, able to bear the Earth which is laid upon it to a great depth, and the Water with which it is irrigated. This Pile carries Trees of so large a dimension, that their Boles are eight Cubits about, and fifty Foot in height, and altogether as fruitful as if they grew in their natural Soil. Now notwithstanding time preys by little and little, not only on artificial Works, but even upon Nature herself, yet this huge Pile which is pester'd with the Roots of so many Trees, and loaded with the weight of so large a Grove, remains still entire. It is supported by twenty large Walls, distant eleven Foot from one another, so that they who behold these Groves at a distance would take 'em to be so many Woods growing upon their Mountains. It is reported that a *King* of *Syria* reigning in *Babylon*, contriv'd this mighty work to gratify his

Queen,

Queen, who being wonderfully delighted with Woods and Forests in the open Fields, perſuaded her Husband to imitate the Beauties of Nature in this Work.

The *King* reſided longer here than he had done any where; nor could there be any Place more deſtructive of *military Diſcipline*. Nothing can be more corrupt than the Manners of this City, nor better provided with all the Requiſites to ſtir up and promote all ſorts of Debauchery and Lewdneſs; for Parents and Husbands ſuffer their Children and Wives to proſtitute themſelves to their Gueſts, if they are but paid for the Crime. The *Kings* and *Noblemen* of *Perſia* take great Delight in licentious Entertainments: And the *Babylonians* are very much addicted to Wine, and the Conſequences of Drunkenneſs. The Women in the Beginning of their Feaſts are modeſtly clad, then after ſome time, they lay aſide their upper Garment, and violate their Modeſty by degrees; at laſt (without Offence be it ſpoken) they fling away even their lower Apparel. Nor is this the infamous Practice of the *Courtizans* only, but likewiſe of the *Matrons* and their Daughters, who look upon this vile Proſtitution of their Bodies as an Act of Complaiſance. It is reaſonable to think that that victorious Army, which had conquer'd *Aſia*, having wallow'd thirty four Days in all kind of Lewdneſs and Debauchery, would have found itſelf much weaken'd, for any following Engagements, if an *Enemy* had preſented it ſelf. But that the Damage might be leſs ſenſible, it was from time to time as it were renew'd with freſh Recruits. For *Amyntas* the Son of *Andromenes*, brought from *Antipater* ſix thouſand *Macedonian* Foot, and five hundred Horſe of the ſame Nation, and with theſe ſix hundred *Thracian* Horſe, and three thouſand five hundred of that Country's Foot. There came alſo from *Peloponneſus* four thousand mercenary Foot, and three hundred and eighty Horse. The said *Amyntas* likewise brought him fifty young Gentlemen of the Nobility of *Macedonia*, to serve as Guards of his Person. Their Office is to serve the *King* at Table, and attend him with Horses when he goes upon Action, to accompany him a hunting, and do Duty by turns at his Chamber-Door. It is here they learn the first Rudiments of War, and lay as it were the Foundation of their future Preferment to be Generals in the Army, or Governors of Provinces.

The *King* having appointed *Agathon* Governor of the Castle of *Babylon*, assigning him seven hundred *Macedonians* and three hundred *Mercenaries* for that Purpose, left the Government of the *Territory* and *City* to *Menetes* and *Apollodorus*, allotting them a Garrison of two thousand Foot and one thousand Talents, commanding both *to make new Levites to recruit the Army*. He gave to *Mazæas*, who came over to him, the Superintendency of *Babylon*, and order'd *Bagophanes*, who had surrender'd the Castle to him, to follow him. He gave the Government of *Armenia* to *Mithrenes*, who had yielded up *Sardis*. Out of the Money found in *Babylon* he order'd every *Macedonian* Trooper six hundred *Denarii*, and five hundred to every foreign Trooper, and to every Foot Soldier **two hundred**.

CHAP. II.

ALexander having settled things after this manner, march'd into the Country, call'd *Satrapene*. The Soil whereof being fruitful, and affording

Plenty of all kinds of Provisions, *he* stay'd here the longer. And that Idleness might not impair the Courage of his Soldiers, he appointed Judges, and propos'd Prizes to those that should distinguish themselves in military Exercises. Those Eight that should be judg'd the bravest, were each to be made Colonels of a thousand Men, and were call'd *Chiliarchæ*. This was the first Institution of Regiments of this Number, for they before consisted but of five hundred, and did not use to be the Reward of Bravery. A great Number of Soldiers flock'd hither to behold the noble Spectacle, and at the same time were so many Judges of the Behaviour of each Contender, and also of the Justice of the Sentence of the Judges themselves, since it was impossible to conceal whether the Honour was bestow'd on the account of Merit, or out of Favour. The first Prize was adjudg'd to *Adarchias* the Elder, who had been chiefly instrumental in renewing the Fight at *Halicarnassus*, where the young Soldiers gave Ground. The next was given to *Antigenes*. *Philotas Angeus* had the third, and *Amyntas* obtain'd the fourth. After these *Antigonus* was thought worthy, and next to him *Lyncestes Amyntas*. The seventh Place was awarded to *Theodotus*, and the last to *Hellanicus*.

He also made several useful Alterations in military Discipline, from what had been practis'd by his Predecessors. For whereas before, the Horse were divided into Corps, according to their respective Nations, *he* took away this Distinction, and appointed 'em Colonels of his own chusing, without having any regard to their Nations.

It was usual upon a Decampment, to give the Signal by Sound of Trumpet, but as very often that was not sufficiently heard, being drown'd by the Noise of the Soldiers in their Hurry. *He* therefore order'd that a

long

long Pole for the future should be set over his Tent, from whence the Signal might be observ'd by all, which was Fire in the Night, and Smoak in the Day.

As the *King* was on his March to *Sufa*, *Abulites*, who was Governor of that Province, sent his Son to meet him on the Road, and assure him he was ready to surrender the Town. It is uncertain, whether he did this of his own Accord, or by *Darius*'s Order, thereby to amuse *Alexander* with the Booty. However, the *King* receiv'd the Youth very graciously, and was conducted by him to the River *Choaspes*, whose Waters are reported to be very sweet and soft. Here *Abulites* met the *King* with Presents of Regal Magnificence. Amongst other things there were *Dromadaries* of an extraordinary Swiftness, twelve *Elephants* brought from *India* by *Darius*'s Order, but were not now a Terror to the *Macedonians*, as they were intended, but a Help. Fortune having transferr'd the Riches of the Vanquish'd to the Victor. Having enter'd the Town, he took out of the Treasury a prodigious Sum, *viz.* fifty thousand Talents of Silver, not coin'd, but in the Wedge and Bar. Several *Kings* had been a long time heaping up these vast Treasures, as they thought, for their Children, and Posterity, but one single Hour put them all into the Hands of a foreign Prince.

He then seated himself in the Regal Throne, which, being much too high for his Stature, his Feet could not reach the Ground, one of his Pages therefore brought a Table and set it under his Feet. Hereupon one of *Darius*'s Eunuchs wept, which the *King* observing, enquir'd into the Cause of his Grief. Then the Eunuch told him, *that* Darius *was us'd to eat upon that Table, and that he could not behold, without shedding Tears, the Table, which was consecrated to his Master's Use, apply'd in a manner so insulting and contemptuous.* At these

Words, the King was seiz'd with a modest Shame, for having violated the Houshold Gods, and commanded it to be taken away. But *Philotas* intreated him by no means to do so, but on the contrary to take it as a good Omen, that that Table, off of which his Enemy us'd to eat, was now become his Footstool.

Alexander designing now to pass into *Persia*, gave the Government of *Susa* to *Archelaus*, leaving him a Garrison of three thousand Men; *Xenophilus* had the Charge of the Castle, having with him for Garrison the superannuated *Macedonians*. The Care of the Treasury was committed to *Callicrates*, and the Lieutenancy of the County of *Susa* was restor'd to *Abulites*. *Darius*'s Mother and Children were likewise left here.

The *King* receiv'd about this time several Garments, and a great Quantity of Purple from *Macedonia*, which was sent him as a Present, with the Workers of them; he order'd 'em immediately, *to be carry'd to* Sisygambis: For he shew'd her all manner of Respect, and even paid her the Duty of a Son. He charg'd the Messengers at the same time to tell her, *that if the Clothes pleas'd her, she should let her Grand-Children learn to work 'em, and make Presents of 'em*. At these Words she fell a weeping, and thereby sufficiently declar'd how unacceptable the Present was to her; for there is nothing the *Persian* Ladies have more in contempt, than even to let their Hands touch Wool. They who carry'd the Presents acquainted *him*, that Sisygambis *seem'd afflicted*. The *King* hereupon thought himself oblig'd to go and comfort her, and excuse himself for his Oversight, which accordingly he did, and told her, *Mother, the Cloaths I now have on, were not only a Present from my Sisters, but also their Work. Our different Customs led me into my Error. I desire therefore you would not misinterpret my Ignorance. I hope I have hitherto carefully*
enough

enough observ'd those of your Customs that come to my Knowledge. When I understood it was not the Practice of Persia, for Sons to sit in their Mothers Presence without their Leave first obtain'd, every time I came to visit you, I kept standing, till you signify'd to me I might sit. And whenever you offer'd to fall down in honour of me, I never would suffer it. In fine, as a Token of the perfect Veneration I have for you, I give you always that Title which is only due to my dear Mother Olympias.

CHAP. III.

THE *King* having reliev'd her Uneasiness after this manner, came in four Encampments to a River, call'd by the Inhabitants *Pasitigris* It has its rise in the Mountains of the *Uxians*, and continues its Course in a furious manner among the Rocks for the Space of fifty Furlongs between its grovy Banks; after which it runs through the Plains in a smoother Channel, and is navigable, and having pass'd through a fruitful Soil, for the Space of six hundred Furlongs with a gentle Stream, it empties it self into the *Persian* Sea

Alexander having pass'd this River with nine thousand Foot, the *Agrians*, mercenary *Greeks*, and three thousand *Thracians*, came into the Country of the *Uxians*, it borders upon the Territory of *Susa*, and extends it self as far as the Frontiers of *Persia*, leaving but a narrow Passage between it and the *Susians* Madates had the Government of this Country, who was no Time-server, but was resolv'd to run all Hazards for the sake of his Allegiance. However, those that were acquainted with the Roads, inform'd *Alexander*, That there

Vol 1 Page 280.

OLYMPIAS

enough observ'd those of your Customs that come to my Knowledge. When I understood it was not the Practice of Persia, for Sons to sit in their Mothers Presence without their Leave first obtain'd, every time I came to visit you, I kept standing, till you signify'd to me I might sit. And whenever you offer'd to fall down in honour of me, I never would suffer it. In fine, as a Token of the perfect Veneration I have for you, I give you always that Title which is only due to my dear Mother Olympias.

CHAP. III.

THE *King* having reliev'd her Uneasiness after this manner, came in four Encampments to a River, call'd by the Inhabitants *Pasitigris*. It has its rise in the Mountains of the *Uxians*, and continues its Course in a furious manner among the Rocks for the Space of fifty Furlongs between its grovy Banks; after which it runs through the Plains in a smoother Channel, and is navigable, and having pass'd through a fruitful Soil, for the Space of six hundred Furlongs with a gentle Stream, it empties it self into the *Persian* Sea.

Alexander having pass'd this River with nine thousand Foot, the *Agrians*, mercenary *Greeks*, and three thousand *Thracians*, came into the Country of the *Uxians*, it borders upon the Territory of *Susa*, and extends it self as far as the Frontiers of *Persia*, leaving but a narrow Passage between it and the *Susians*. *Madates* had the Government of this Country, who was no Time-server, but was resolv'd to run all Hazards for the sake of his Allegiance. However, those that were acquainted with the Roads, inform'd *Alexander*, *That there*

Vol 1 Page 280

OLYMPIAS

there was a bye-way through the Mountains, that led to the back side of the City, and therefore if he sent a few light-arm'd Men that Way, they might make themselves Masters of a higher Ground, than that of the Enemies.

The *King* liking the Advice, pitch'd upon those that gave it to serve as Guides to his Men, and order'd *Tauron*, with fifteen hundred Mercenaries, and about a thousand *Agrians* to execute it, and set out after the Sun was down. As for himself, *he* decamp'd at the third Watch, and about break of Day had pass'd the Straits, and having cut down Timber to make Hurdles, and other necessary Engines, to cover those that should advance the Towers, began the Siege of the Place; here was nothing to be seen but craggy Rocks and Precipices, the Soldiers were therefore repuls'd, as not having the Enemy only to encounter with, but also the Difficulties of the Place, notwithstanding which they advanc'd, for the *King* was among the first, and would sometimes ask 'em, *if having reduc'd so many strong Towns, they were not asham'd to be baffled in the Siege of a small insignificant Castle?* The *King* was now attack'd at a distance, and not being to be prevail'd upon to withdraw, the Soldiers form'd a Tortoise with their Bucklers, to protect him from the Arrows, Darts, and Stones that were levell'd at him from the Walls. At length *Tauron* appear'd with his Detachment above the Castle, at whose sight the Enemy's Courage began to flag, and the *Macedonians* fought with more Vigour. The Townsmen were now attack'd both before and behind, and nothing could stop the Fury of the Enemy, some few were for dying resolutely, but more were inclin'd to fly, and a great Number retir'd into the Castle. From hence they deputed thirty Ambassadors to implore his Mercy, but they receiv'd for Answer, *That there was no room for Pardon.* Being therefore seiz'd with

with the dread of future Torments, they dispatch'd Deputies to *Sisygambis*, *Darius*'s Mother, by a private way unknown to the Enemy, to intreat her *to use her Interest with the King in their Behalf*, for they were not ignorant that he lov'd and honour'd her as a Parent. They were the more encourag'd to this, because *Madates* had marry'd her Sister's Daughter, and was nearly related to *Darius*. *Sisygambis* refus'd to comply with their Request for a long time, telling them, 'That it did not suit with her present Circum-
'stances to turn Intercessor for others, and that she
'had reason to fear tiring the Clemency of the Con-
'queror; besides that, she oftner reflected on her be-
'ing at present a Captive, than of her having been a
'Queen.' However, at last being overcome by their Importunity, *she* writ a Letter to *Alexander*, wherein
'she begg'd his Pardon for the Liberty she took to in-
'tercede for the Besieged, for whom she implor'd his
'Mercy, and hop'd he would at least forgive her,
'for soliciting his Indulgence in the Behalf of a Fri
'and Relation, who was now no longer an Enemy,
'but an humble Suppliant for his Life.'

Here now is a remarkable Instance of the *King*'s Moderation and Goodness at this time, for *he* not only, at her Request, pardon'd *Madates*, but granted to all their Liberty, as well to those that were Captives, as those who surrender'd themselves, confirming their Immunities. *He* likewise left the Place untouch'd, and permitted 'em to cultivate their Lands Tax free. *She* could not have obtain'd more of *Darius*, though her Son, had *he* been Conqueror. *He* afterwards united the *Uxian* Nation to the Government of *Susa*, then having divided his Army with *Parmenio*, he commanded him to march through the flat Country, while he with the light-arm'd Forces, took his Way along

the

the Mountains, which run in a perpetual Ridge into *Perſia*.

Having ravag'd all this Country, *he* arriv'd the third Day on the Borders of *Perſia*, and on the fifth *he* enter'd the Straits which they call *Pylæ Suſidæ Ariobarzanes*, with twenty five thouſand Foot, had taken Poſſeſſion of theſe Rocks, which were on all ſides ſteep and craggy, on the tops whereof the *Barbarians* kept themſelves, being there out of the Caſt of the Darts. Here they remain'd quiet on purpoſe, and ſeem'd to be afraid till the Army was advanc'd within the narroweſt Part of the Straits, but when they perceiv'd 'em to continue their March, as it were in contempt of 'em, they rowl'd down Stones of a prodigious Bigneſs upon 'em, which rebounding often from the lower Rocks, fell with the greater Force, and not only cruſh'd ſingle Perſons, but even whole Companies. They likewiſe ply'd their Slings and Bows from all Parts, even this did not ſeem a Hardſhip to theſe brave Men, but only that they were forc'd to periſh unreveng'd, like Beaſts taken in a Pitfall. Upon this, their Anger turning into Rage, they caught hold of the Rocks, and helping one another up, did all they could to get to the Enemy, but the Parts they laid hold on giving way to the Strength of ſo many Hands, fell upon thoſe that looſen'd them. In theſe ſad Circumſtances they could neither ſtand ſtill nor go forward, nor protect themſelves with their Bucklers, by reaſon of the great Size of the Stones the *Barbarians* puſh'd upon 'em. The *King* was not only griev'd, but aſham'd *he* had ſo raſhly brought his Army into theſe Straits. Till this Day *he* had been invincible, having never attempted any thing in vain. *He* had enter'd the Straits of *Cilicia* without Damage, and had open'd himſelf a new Way by Sea into

into *Pamphilia*, but here that Happiness which had always attended him, seem'd to be at a stand, and there was no other Remedy but to return the same Way he came. Having therefore given the Signal for a Retreat, he commanded the Soldiers to march in close order, and to join their Bucklers over their Heads, and so retire out of the Straits, after they had advanc'd thirty Furlongs within them.

CHAP. IV.

THE *King*, at his Return from the Straits, having pitch'd his Camp in a plain open Ground, not only held a Council on the present Juncture of Affairs, but also was so superstitious, as to consult the Priests concerning what was most advisable to be done. But what, in such a Case, could *Aristander* (who was then in greatest Esteem) pretend to foretel? Laying aside therefore the unseasonable Sacrifices, *he* gave Orders to bring to him such Men as were well acquainted with the Country; these Men told him of a Way through *Media*, which was safe and open, but the *King* was asham'd to leave his Soldiers unbury'd, for there was no Custom more religiously observed amongst the *Macedonians*, than that of burying their Dead. He therefore commanded *the Prisoners he had lately taken to be brought before him*, among these, there was one who was skill'd in both the *Greek* and *Persian* Languages; this Man told him, *It was in vain for him to think of leading his Army into* Persia, *over the tops of the Mountains, that the narrow Ways lay all among Woods, and were hardly passable to single Persons,*

all

all the Countrey being cover'd with Woods, which were in a manner united by the intermixture of their Branches. For *Persia* on one side is hemm'd in by a continual ridge of Mountains that extend themselves sixteen hundred Furlongs in length, and one hundred and seventy in breadth, beginning at Mount *Caucasus*, and reaching as far as the Red Sea, which serves for another Fence where the Mountains fail. At the foot of the Hills is a spacious Plain very fertil, and thick set with Towns and Villages. The River *Araxes* runs thro' these Plains into the *Medus*, carrying along with it the Rivers of several Torrents. The *Medus*, which is a less River than that it receives, empties itself into the Sea to the southward. No River can contribute more to the Production of Grass than this, for whatever Land it waters, it clothes it with Flowers and Herbage. Its Banks are also cover'd on both sides with Plane Trees and Poplars, so that to those who behold it at a distance, the Woods upon the Banks seem to be contiguous to those upon the Mountains, because the shaded River glides along in a low Channel, and the little Hills that border upon it are well cloth'd with Wood, this fruitful Water penetrating through the Earth to the Roots of the Trees.

There is not any Countrey in all *Asia* more healthful than this, the Air is temperate, and on one side the long ridge of Mountains, with their shady Groves alleviate the excessive Heat of the Sun, and on the other the adjoining Sea cherishes the Ground with its moderate Warmth.

The Prisoner having given this Account, the *King* ask'd him, *whether he had what he said by the Relation of others, or by his own Inspection?* He made Answer, that *he had been a Shepherd, and knew all those byways perfectly well, and that he had been twice taken*

Prisoner, once by the Persians *in* Lycia, *and now by himself.* This Answer put the King in mind of the Oracle that had told *him, a* Lycian *should be his Guide into* Persia, having therefore made him large Promises, suitable to the present Necessity, and the Prisoner's Condition, *he* order'd him *to be arm'd after the* Macedonian *manner, and in the Name of Fortune to lead the way, which* (*notwithstanding its seeming Impracticableness*) *he did not doubt to pass thro' with a small number, unless he imagin'd that* Alexander *could not do that for the sake of Glory and Honour, that he had done on the account of his Flock.* Hereupon the Prisoner persisted to urge *the difficulty of the Undertaking, especially for Men in Arms* To which the King reply'd, *Take my Word for it, none of them that are to follow will refuse to go wherever you lead 'em.* Then having committed the Guard of the Camp to *Craterus,* with the Foot he commanded, and the Forces under *Maleager,* and a thousand Horse Archers, *he* order'd him *to observe the same Form of Encampment, and to keep a great many Fires, that the Barbarians might by that think the King was there in Person, but if he found* Ariobarzanes *got Intelligence of his March thro' the winding narrow ways, and thereupon made Detachments to oppose his Passage, that then* Craterus *should use his utmost Efforts to terrify him, and oblige him to keep his Troops together to oppose the present Danger, but if he* (the King) *deceiv'd the Enemy, and gain'd the Wood, that then, upon the Alarm among the Enemies endeavouring to pursue the King, he should boldly enter the Straits they had been repuls'd in the Day before, since he might be sure they were undefended, and the Enemy turn'd upon himself.*

At the third Watch, he broke up in great Silence, without so much as the Signal from the Trumpet, and follow'd his Guide towards the narrow Way. Every
light-

light-arm'd Soldier had Orders *to carry with him three Days Provision.* But besides the Steepness of the Rocks, and the Slipperyness of the Stone that often deceiv'd their Feet, the driven Snow very much incommoded them, for it sometimes swallow'd them up as if they had fallen into Pits, and when they were help'd up by their Companions, they rather drew them after 'em, than got them out. Moreover the Night, and unknown Country, besides the Uncertainty whether the Guide was faithful or not, very much encreas'd their Fear. *For if he deceiv'd the Guards, and made his Escape, they were liable to be taken like wild Beasts. So that the King's and their Safety, depended on the Fidelity and Life of one Man.* At length they gain'd the top of the Mountain. The Way to *Ariobarzanes* lay on the Right-hand. Here *he* detach'd *Philotas* and *Cænus*, as also *Amyntas* and *Polypercon*, with a Body of the lightest-arm'd, with Instructions, *that by reason there was Horse intermix'd with the Foot, they should march leisurely through that Part of the Country where the Soil was fruitful and afforded Plenty of Forage.* He also appointed some of the Prisoners for their *Guides.* As for *himself*, taking with him *his* Guards, and those Troops call'd the *Agema*, he march'd with a great deal of Difficulty through a By-path, remote from the Enemies Out-guard. It was now the middle of the Day, and his Men being tired, it was necessary to give them some Rest, for they had still as far to go, as they were already come, though it was not so steep and craggy.

Having therefore refresh'd his Men both with Food and Sleep, at the second Watch he continu'd his March, without any great Difficulty. However, by reason of the Declivity of the Mountains towards the Plain, there was a great Gulph (occasion'd by the meeting of several

ral Torrents that had wore away the Earth) which stopt their further Progress. Besides, the Branches of the Trees were so entangled one within the other, and join'd so close, that it oppos'd their Passage like a thick Hedge. This cast 'em into the utmost Despair, and they had much ado to retain their Tears. The Darkness of the Night also increas'd their Terror, for if any Stars appear'd, they were intercepted by the close Contexture of the Boughs. The very Use of their Ears was also taken away, for the Wind was high and blew so violently among the Trees, that the Noise of the interfering Branches was still greater. At last the long-expected Light lessen'd the Terrors which the Night had enhanc'd, for by fetching a small Compass, they declin'd the Gulph, and now every one began to be a Guide to himself. Having therefore gain'd the top of a Hill, from whence they could discover the Enemy's Out-guards, they resolutely shew'd themselves at the back of the Enemy, who mistrusted no such thing. Those few who dar'd engage, were kill'd, and the Groans of those that were dying, together with the dismal Appearance of those that fled to their main Body, struck such a Terror amongst 'em, that they took to their Heels without so much as trying their Fortune.

The Noise having reach'd *Craterus*'s Camp, he presently advanc'd to take Possession of those Streights where they had been baffled the Day before. At the same time, *Philotas* with *Polypercon*, *Amyntas*, and *Cænus*, who had been order'd to march another way, was a fresh Surprize to the *Barbarians*, who were now surrounded on all Sides by the *Macedonians*, notwithstanding which, they behav'd themselves gallantly, which makes me believe, that Necessity emboldens the most cowardly, and that oftentimes Despair is the

Cause

Cause of Hope: for naked as they were, they clos'd in with those that were arm'd, and by the Bulk of their Bodies, brought 'em down to the Ground, and then stuck several of 'em with their own Weapons. However, *Ariobarzanes* with forty Horse, and about five thousand Foot, broke thro' the *Macedonian* Army (a great many falling on both sides) and endeavour'd to possess himself of *Persepolis* the chief City of the Country. But being deny'd Entrance by the Garrison, and the Enemy pursuing him closely, he renew'd the fight, and was slain with all his Men. By this time *Craterus* marching with the utmost Expedition, also join'd the King.

CHAP. V.

THE *King* fortify'd his Camp in the same Place where he had defeated the Enemy. For notwithstanding he had gain'd a compleat Victory, yet the large and deep Ditches in many Places retarded his March, and so *he* thought it more adviseable to proceed leisurely, not suspecting so much any Attempt from the *Barbarians*, as the Treachery of the Ground.

In his March *he* receiv'd Letters from *Tiridates* (Keeper of the Royal Treasure) wherein he notify'd to *him, That upon Advice of his Approach, the Inhabitants would have rifled the Treasury, wherefore he desir'd him to hasten his March, and come and take Possession of it. That the Way was safe, although the River* Araxes *run a-cross*. I cannot applaud any Military Virtue of *Alexander's* so much as his Expedition in all Actions. Leaving therefore his Foot behind, *he* march'd all

all Night with his Cavalry, notwithstanding their late Fatigues, and arriv'd by Break of Day at the *Araxes*. There were several Villages in the Neighbourhood, which having pillag'd and demolish'd, he made a Bridge of the Materials. The King was not far from the Town, when so sad a Spectacle presented it self to his Eyes, as can hardly be parallell'd in History. It consisted of four thousand *Greek* Captives, whom the *Persians* had mangled after a miserable manner. For some had their Feet cut off, others their Hands and Ears, and all their Bodies were burnt with barbarous Characters, and thus reserv'd for the cruel Diversion of their inhuman Enemies; who now finding themselves under foreign Subjection, did not oppose their Desire to go out and meet *Alexander*. They resembled some strange Figures more than Men, being only distinguishable as such by their Voice. They drew more Tears from their Spectators, than they shed themselves; for in so great a Variety of Calamities, notwithstanding they were all Sufferers, yet their Punishment was so diversify'd, that it was a difficult matter to determine which of 'em was most miserable. But when they cry'd out, *that at last* Jupiter *the Revenger of* Greece *had open'd his Eyes*, all the Beholders were so mov'd with Compassion, that they thought their Sufferings their own. *Alexander* having dry'd his Eyes (for he could not forbear weeping at so sad an Object) bid 'em *have a good Heart*, and assur'd 'em, *They should see their native Country, and their Wives again*, and then encamp'd at two Furlongs distance from the Town.

These *Greeks*, in the mean time, withdrew themselves to deliberate concerning what they should desire the *King* to do for 'em. Some were for asking *a Settlement in* Asia, others *were for returning home*, when *Euthymon* the *Cymaon* spoke to 'em after the following manner

manner · 'They who a little while ago were asham'd
'to come out of their dark Dungeons to implore Re-
'lief, are now for exposing their hideous Sufferings to
'all *Greece*, as if it were an agreeable Spectacle, when
'at the same time, it is hard to determine, whether
'we our selves are more asham'd or griev'd at our
'Misfortunes. Those bear their Afflictions best, who
'hide them. There is no Country so suitable to the
'Wretched, as Solitude, and an absolute Oblivion of
'their former State For they who rely much on
'the Compassion of their Friends, are ignorant that
'Tears are soon dry'd up. No Body can love sincerely
'those they loath, for as Calamity is full of Com-
'plaints, Prosperity is disdainful. Every one considers
'his own Circumstances, when he deliberates concern-
'ing those of others, and were we not equally mi-
'serable, we had long ago loath'd each other. Is it a
'Wonder, that the Happy delight in one another?
'Let us therefore, I beseech you, (since we may be
'said to be long since dead) seek for a Place where we
'may bury the Remains of our mangled Carcases,
'and conceal our Deformities in a foreign Country.
'We should be very agreeable Objects to those Wives
'we marry'd in our Youth ! Can you imagine our
'Children (who are now in the Flower of their Age
'and Prosperity) will own us ? Or will our Brothers
'be better-natur'd to the Refuse of Jayls? Besides, how
'many is there amongst us who can travel so far ? It
'is a likely matter, that at this distance from *Europe*,
'banish'd to the remotest Parts of the East, loaded
'with Years and Infirmities, having lost the greatest
'of our selves, we should be able to undergo those
'Fatigues that have tir'd even the victorious Army.
'Then what will become of our present Wives (that
'Chance and Necessity forc'd us to take, as the only

N 2   Comfort

'Comfort in our Misery) and small Children? Shall
'we drag them along with us, or leave 'em behind us?
'If we take 'em with us, no body will own us. Shall
'we then leave these present Comforts, when it is al-
'together uncertain, whether we shall live to see those
'we go to? Let us therefore resolve to hide our selves
'among those who began to know us in our State of
'Misery.' This was *Euthymon's* Sentiment. But *The-*
tetus the *Athenian* oppos'd thus. 'There is no Per-
'son of any religious Principles, who values his Friends
'by the outward Figure of his Circumstances, especi-
'ally when it is the Inhumanity of an Enemy, and
'not Nature, that is the Cause of their Calamity. He
'deserves all kind of Evil, who is asham'd of acci-
'dental Misfortunes. He can have no other Motive
'to think so hardly of the rest of Mankind, and to
'despair of Pity, but because he would refuse it to a-
'nother. The Gods now offer'd 'em what they could
'never have hop'd for, *viz.* the Blessing of returning
'to their native Country, their Wives and Children,
'and whatever Men value Life for, or despise Death
'to preserve. Why do we not then break out of this
'Prison? Our native Air is quite different from this,
'the Light it self seems another thing. The *Greeks*
'Manners, Religion, and Language are in request with
'the *Barbarians*, and shall we, whose Birthright they
'are, voluntarily forsake 'em? when at the same time
'our greatest Misery is to be depriv'd of these Bles-
'sings. As for my Part, I am resolv'd to return home
'to my native Country, and to lay hold of the King's
'extraordinary Bounty. If any amongst us are so fond
'of those Wives and Children that Servitude has forc'd
'upon 'em, they may continue here; however, they
'ought to be no hindrance to those to whom nothing
'is dearer than their native Country.'

Some

Some few were of this Opinion, the rest were overcome by a long *Habit*, which is stronger than *Nature*, they agreed therefore *to desire the King to assign 'em some Place for their Habitation*, and chose a Hundred out of their Body, to prefer their Petition. *Alexander* thinking they would ask, what *he himself* intended for 'em, told 'em, *He had order'd every one of them a Horse, and a Thousand Denary, and that when they should come to Greece, he would so provide for 'em, that (except the Calamities they had experienc'd in their Captivity) none should be happier than they* At these Words, they fell a weeping, and being dejected, could neither look up, nor speak, which made the *King* enquire into the Cause of their Sadness. Then *Euthymon* made an Answer suitable to what he had said to his Companions. Hereupon the *King*, mov'd with their Misfortune and Resolution, order'd *Three Thousand Denary* to be distributed to every one of 'em, besides Ten Suits of Cloaths, with Cattle, Sheep, and such a Quantity of Corn, as was sufficient to cultivate the Land that was assign'd them.

CHAP. VI.

THE next Day, having call'd together all his Generals, he represented to 'em, *That no City had been more mischievous to the* Greeks, *than this Seat of the ancient Kings of* Persia From hence came all those vast Armies From hence Darius *first*, and then Xerxes, *made their impious Wars upon* Europe *It was therefore necessary to raze it, to appease the* Manes *of their Ancestors* The Inhabitants had abandon'd it, and were fled some one way, and some another; so that the *King* led the *Phalanx* into it, without farther delay. He had before this made himself Master of many Towns of Regal Wealth and Magnificence, some by Force, and some by Composition; but the Riches of this exceeded all the rest. Hither the *Persians* had brought all their Substance; Gold and Silver here lay in Heaps. Of Cloaths there was a prodigious Quantity. The Furniture of the Houses seem'd not only design'd for Use, but for Luxury and Ostentation. This gave occasion to the Conquerors to fight among themselves, each taking for an Enemy, his Companion that had got the richest Spoils; and as they could not carry off all they found, they were now no longer employ'd in taking, but in picking and chusing. They tore the Royal Garments, every one being willing to have his Share of 'em. With Axes they cut in pieces Vessels of exquisite Art. In fine, nothing was left untouch'd, nor carry'd away entire; the Images of Gold and Silver were broke in pieces, according as every one could lay hold of them. *Avarice* did not only rage here, but *Cruelty* likewise; for being loaded with Gold and Silver, they would not be troubled to guard their Prisoners, but inhumanly kill'd 'em, and now barbarously murder'd those they had at first shewn Mercy to in hopes of Gain. This occasion'd a great many to prevent the Enemy, by a voluntary Death; so that putting on their richest Apparel, they cast themselves headlong from the Walls, with their Wives and Children. Some set Fire to their Houses, (which the Enemy design'd to do) and perish'd, with their Families, in the Flames. At last the *King* gave Orders, *not to injure the Persons of the Women, nor meddle with their Apparel.*

The immense Treasures taken here exceeded all belief. But we must either doubt of all the rest, or believe,

lieve, that in the Exchequer of this Place was found a hundred and twenty thousand Talents, which the King designing for the Use of the War, caus'd *Horses and Camels to be brought from* Sufa *to* Babylon, *to carry it off for that purpose*. This Sum was afterward increas'd, by taking *Perfagada*, wherein were found six thousand Talents. *Cyrus* had built this City, and *Gobares*, who was Governor thereof, surrender'd it to *Alexander*.

The King made *Nicarthides* Governor of the Castle of *Perfepolis*, leaving with him a Garrison of three thousand *Macedonians*. He also continu'd *Tyridates* (who had deliver'd up the Treasure) in the same Honours he had enjoy'd under *Darius*.

Alexander left here the greatest Part of his Army, with the Baggage, under the Command of *Parmenio* and *Craterus*, and taking with him a thousand Horse, and part of the light-arm'd Foot, penetrated farther into the Country of *Persia*, under the *Pleiades*, about the beginning of Winter. On his Way, *he* was very much incommoded with Storms of Rain, and Tempests that seem'd intolerable, notwithstanding which, *he* pursu'd *his* intended Progress. *He* was now got into a Country cover'd over with Snow and Ice. The sad View of the Place, and the impassable Wastes and Solitudes, struck the tir'd Soldier with Horror, who now began to think he was got to the End of the World. They beheld with Astonishment the frightful Solitudes, which had not the least Signs of human Culture; they therefore requir'd him to return, *before the very Light and Heavens fail'd 'em*. The King forbore chastising 'em in the Amazement they were in, but leaping from his Horse, march'd on foot before 'em thro' the Snow and Ice. They were asham'd not to follow him, therefore first his Friends, then the Captains, and at last the Soldiers march'd after him.

The *King* was the first that with a Pickaxe broke the Ice, and made himself a Passage, then the rest imitated his Example. At length having made their way through Woods almost impassable, they began to discover here and there some Tokens that the Place was inhabited, as also Flocks of Sheep wandering up and down. The Inhabitants live in Cottages, and thought themselves sufficiently secur'd by the Impracticableness of the Country. At the sight of the Enemy, they presently kill'd those who could not follow them, and fled to the remotest Mountains, which were cover'd with Snow; but after some Conferences with the Prisoners, their Fright abated, and they surrender'd themselves to the *King*, who was no way severe to them.

Alexander having ravag'd the Country of *Persia*, and reduc'd several Towns under his Obedience, came at last into the Country of the *Mardians*, who are a warlike Nation, and very different from the rest of the *Persians* in their manner of living. They dig themselves Caves in the Mountains, where they dwell with their Wives and Children, feeding on their Flocks, or wild Beasts. The Women are not of a softer Nature than the Men, they have bushy Hair, and their Garments hardly reach their Knees. They bind their Forehead with a Sling, which serves them both for Ornament and Weapon. However, the same Torrent of *Fortune* bore down this Nation, as it had done the rest, so that on the thirtieth Day after he departed from *Persepolis*, he return'd thither again.

Then he made Presents to his Friends, and to the rest according to their respective Merit, distributing amongst 'em almost all that had been taken in the Town.

CHAP.

CHAP. VII.

BUT the excellent Endowments of his Mind, that noble Disposition whereby he surpass'd all the *Kings* his Predecessors, that manly Constancy in surmounting Dangers, that unparallell'd Celerity in undertaking and executing the greatest Designs, his inviolable Faith to those who submitted to him, and his wonderful Clemency towards his Prisoners, were all sully'd by his excessive Love of Wine. For notwithstanding his Enemy and Rival for the Empire, was at this time making the greatest Preparations to renew the War, and the late conquer'd Nations were yet uneasie under his new Government, yet *he* would spend the Day-time in revelling and feasting, to which Entertainments the Women were also admitted, not such whom it was a Crime to violate, but such as were common, and whose Conversation was a Disgrace to a Man in Arms. One of these, whose Name was *Thais*, being heated with Wine, told *him, he could not do any thing that would more oblige all the* Greeks, *than if he burnt the Palace of the Kings of* Persia. *That they expected this by way of Reprisal for those Towns of theirs the* Barbarians *had destroy'd.* This drunken Harlot had no sooner spoke her Opinion in a Matter of so great a Consequence, but presently some of the Company (who were also loaded with Wine) applauded the Proposal, and the *King* not only heard it with Patience, but eager to put it in Execution, said, *Why do we not revenge* Greece ? *Why do we delay setting Fire to the Town ?* They were all heated with Wine, and in that drunken Condition immediately rise to burn that City they had spared in their Anger. The *King* shew'd 'em the Example, and was the first that set Fire to the Palace, after which his Guests, Servants, and Concubines did the same. There being a great deal of Cedar in this noble Structure, it presently took Fire, and communicated the Flames. The Army which was encamp'd not far from the Town, no sooner perceiv'd the Conflagration, but, imagining it to be casual, they ran to help to quench it. But being come to the Entrance of the Palace, and seeing the *King* himself carrying fresh Flambeaux to increase the Fire, they flung down the Water they had brought, and fed the Flames with dry Materials.

This was the End of the noblest City of the East, from whence so many Nations receiv'd their Laws, which had been the Birth-place of so many *Kings*, formerly the chief Terror of *Greece*, had fitted out a Fleet of a thousand Sail of Ships, and sent out Armies, that, like an Inundation, almost cover'd all *Europe*, had laid Bridges over the Sea, and hollow'd Mountains to make the Sea a Passage, and in so long a time as has elaps'd since its Destruction, never was rebuilt. For the *Macedonian Kings* made choice of other Towns for their Residence, which are now in the Possession of the *Parthians*. The Ruin of this City was so compleat, that were it not for the River *Araxes*, we should hardly know where it stood. This River run at no great Distance from the Walls of this Town, which (as the neighbouring Inhabitants rather conjecture than certainly know) was situate about twenty Furlongs from it.

The *Macedonians* were asham'd so famous a City should be destroy'd by their *King* in a drunken Humour. They therefore made a serious Matter of it, and persuaded themselves, *it was expedient it should be consum'd this way*. But as for *Alexander*, as soon as Rest had re-

stor'd

fter'd him to himſelf, it is certain *he* repented of what *he* had done, and *he* ſaid, *the* Perſians *would have made more ample Satisfaction to* Greece, *had they been neceſſitated to behold him ſitting in* Xerxes*'s Throne in his Royal City.*

The next Day *he* order'd thirty Talents to be given to the *Lycian*, who had been his Guide into *Perſia*. From hence *he* paſs'd into the Country of *Media*, where he was met by new Recruits from *Cilicia*. They conſiſted of five thouſand Foot, and one thouſand Horſe, both the one and the other were under the Command of *Plato* the *Athenian*. Having receiv'd this Reinforcement, *he* reſolv'd to purſue *Darius*.

CHAP. VIII.

THIS *Prince* was by this time got to *Ecbatana*, which is the Capital of *Media*. The *Parthians* are now in Poſſeſſion of this Town. it is the Royal Seat during the Summer. *Darius* intended from hence to go into *Bactra*, but fearing to be prevented by *Alexander*'s Celerity, he alter'd his Mind and ſhaped his Courſe another way. *Alexander* was fifteen hundred Furlongs Diſtance from him, but now *he* thought no Diſtance remote enough, againſt *his* Expedition. *He* therefore rather prepar'd himſelf to fight, than to fly. *He* was follow'd by thirty thouſand Foot, amongſt whom were four thouſand *Greeks* of an invincible Fidelity to the laſt towards the *King*. He had alſo four thouſand Slingers and Archers, beſides three thouſand three hundred Horſe which conſiſted chiefly of *Bactrians*. They were commanded by *Beſſus*, who was Governor

of the City as well as Country of *Bactriana*. *Darius* with these Forces march'd at some Distance from the High-way, commanding those who guarded the Baggage to go before. Then having call'd a Council, *he* spoke to this Effect 'If Fortune had link'd me with
' Cowards, who preferr'd any kind of Life to an ho-
' nourable Death, I would rather chuse to hold my
' Tongue, than waste my Breath in Speeches to no
' Purpose, but I have had greater Experience than I
' could wish, both of your Courage and Fidelity, so
' that I ought rather to endeavour to shew my self
' worthy of such Friends, than in the least doubt of
' your being like your selves Out of so many thou-
' sand that were under my Command, you only have
' faithfully adher'd to me, tho' twice conquer'd, and
' twice forc'd to fly Your Fidelity and Constancy
' make me believe I am still a *King* It is true, the
' Traitors and Deserters at present reign in my Towns,
' but it is not because they are thought worthy of
' that high Station, but only to try by their Rewards,
' to shake your Loyalty Notwithstanding which you
' have chose rather to share my Fortune than that of
' the Conqueror, and thereby shew'd your selves wor-
' thy to be recompenc'd by the Gods, if it should not
' be in my Power. There can be no Posterity so deaf,
' no Fame so ungrateful, as not with due Praises to
' extol you to the Skies. Therefore notwithstanding I
' had some thoughts of flying, contrary, Heav'n
' knows, to my own Disposition, yet relying on
' your Bravery, I am willing to meet the Enemy For
' how long must I be an Exile in my own Kingdom?
' How long must I in my own Dominions fly before
' a Foreigner and strange King, when I have it in my
' own Power to try the Fortune of War once more,
' and either recover what I have lost, or at least die

' an honourable Death ? Unless it should be thought
' better to lie at the Conqueror's Mercy, and after the
' Example of *Mazeus* and *Mithrenes* receive perhaps
' the precarious Sovereignty of a single Nation. But
' I hope the Gods will never suffer any Body to take
' the Diadem from my Head, or bestow it on me;
' neither will I, while alive, resign my Empire, my
' Kingdom and Life shall end together. If you are
' thus dispos'd, if this be a fix'd Resolution among
' you, none of you need to doubt of his Liberty;
' none of you shall be subject to the disdainful Haugh-
' tiness of the *Macedonians* Your Right-hands shall
' either revenge your Sufferings, or put an End to
' 'em I am my self an Instance of the Mutability of
' Fortune, and I have Reason to hope for her gentler
' Revolutions But if the Gods have no Regard to
' just and religious Wars, it will still be in the Power
' of the Brave to die honourably I therefore conjure
' you by the glorious Actions of our Ancestors, who
' have held the Government of all the Eastern King-
' doms with so much Praise, by those great Men, to
' whom the *Macedonians* formerly paid Tribute, by
' the vast Fleets that have been sent into *Greece*, by
' the Trophies of so many Kings. I once more beg
' and beseech you to arm your selves with a Courage
' worthy your noble Extraction and Nation, and that
' you will bear with the same Constancy you have
' hitherto shewn, whatever Fortune shall for the fu-
' ture alot you As for my own part, I am resolv'd to
' signalize my self for ever, either by a glorious Vi-
' ctory, or a brave Engagement.

CHAP.

CHAP. IX.

WHILE *Darius* was saying these things, the Appearance of the present Danger was so frightful to them, that the Minds and Hearts of them all were seiz'd with Horror, none of 'em knew either what to think or say. At last *Artabazus*, the oldest of his Friends, and who, as we said before, had formerly resided with *Philip*, declar'd himself to this purpose. *We are ready, Sir, to follow you into the Field in our richest Apparel and brightest Armour, with this Disposition, That we neither despair of Victory, nor fear our Fate.* The rest seem'd to be of the same Mind.

But *Nabarzanes*, who had enter'd into an abominable, and before that time, unheard-of Conspiracy, to seize the *King*, by the Help of those Troops they each commanded, with this Design, that if *Alexander* pursu'd them, to deliver him alive into *his* Hands, and thereby ingratiate themselves with *him*, since *he* could not but be mightily pleas'd to have *his* Enemy in *his* Power, but if they found they could make their Escapes, then to kill *Darius*, and seizing the Kingdom, renew the War again. As they had for some time been hatching this Treason, *Nabarzanes* laid hold of this Occasion to pave the Way to his wicked Purpose, and said, *I am sensible, Sir, that what I am going to say, will not at first be grateful to you. But we see Physicians cure desperate Diseases with rough Medicines, and the Masters of Ships, when they fear a Shipwreck, fling a great Part of their Goods over board to save the rest. However, I do not offer to persuade you to sustain any Loss. But on* the contrary, by salutary Measures to preserve both your self and Kingdom. The Gods seem to be against us in the War we make, and Fortune is obstinate in her Persecution of the Persians. We must therefore begin a-new, with better Omens. Resign your Empire and the Management of Affairs for a while to another, who shall be no longer King than till the Enemy withdraws from Asia; and then the Conqueror shall restore the sacred Depositum into your hands again. Reason seems to promise this would not be long a doing. Bactra is yet entire; the Indians and the Sagæ are still at your Devotion. There are so many Nations, so many Armies, so many thousands of Horse and Foot to renew the War with, that there is still more left to carry it on, than has been lost. Why should we then, after the manner of Brutes, run headlong to Destruction? It is the Business of brave Men to despise Death rather than hate Life. Cowards are sometimes by continual Hardships, brought to have a mean Opinion of themselves, and Despair, whereas true Courage leaves nothing untry'd. Death therefore is the last Remedy, which then to embrace chearfully, is sufficient. Let us then repair to Bactra, which will be a safe Retreat, and let Bessus who is Governor of that Country, be constituted King for a Time, and when the present Troubles shall be happily settl'd, he shall restore to you, as to his lawful Sovereign, the Empire which he only receiv'd in Trust.

It is no wonder Darius was transported at this Discourse, altho' he was yet ignorant of the impious Designs it was intended to promote. Thou vile Slave, said he, hast thou found a proper Time to disclose thy Parricide? And having drawn his Sword, he seem'd dispos'd to kill him, but Bessus and the Bactrians, with dejected Looks interpos'd, tho' they intended at the same time, to have bound him if he had persisted.

In the mean time *Nabarzanes* made his Escape, and *Bessus* follow'd him, and they both immediately drew off their Troops from the rest of the Army, in order to take private Measures. After their Departure, *Artabazus* made a Speech suitable to the present Juncture of Affairs, and endeavoured to appease *Darius*'s Anger. He entreated him *to bear patiently the Folly or Error of those who were devoted to his Service, and to consider, that* Alexander *was approaching, who would be found a heavy Burthen, tho' they were all ready and united: What would* he *then be, if any of those who had follow'd him in his flight, should be alienated from his Interest?* Darius was in this persuaded by him, and notwithstanding he design'd to have decamp'd, yet in the present Confusion of Affairs, he resolv'd to continue in the same Place. But being oppress'd with Grief and Despair, he shut himself up in his Tent. The Army being now under no one's particular Command, were variously dispos'd, and they did not now, as heretofore, deliberate in common, which *Patron*, who was Captain of the *Greeks* perceiving, he order'd his Men *to take to their Arms, and to be ready on all Occasions.* The *Persians* had withdrawn themselves, and *Bessus* was with the *Bactrians*, and labour'd to bring the *Persians* over to him. He represented to them the Wealth of *Bactriana*, which was still untouch'd, and at the same time reminded 'em of the Risks they would unavoidably run, if they stay'd where they were. But the *Persians* were all of one Mind, and said, *it was a Crime to desert the King.*

While these things were doing, *Artabazus* discharg'd the Duty of a General. He went about the *Persians* Tents, exhorting them sometimes apart, and sometimes all together, and did not leave them till he was pretty well assur'd of their Obedience. Then returning

turning to *Darius*, he with much Difficulty at last prevail'd with him *to eat, and demean himself like a King.*

CHAP. X.

BUT *Bessus* and *Nabarzanes* were bent upon the Execution of their execrable Design, being inflam'd with an impotent Desire of reigning. At the same time it was impossible for 'em to compass that Authority while *Darius* was living, for amongst these People the *Majesty* of *King* is held in the greatest Veneration. At the very Name, they assemble together from all Parts, and constantly pay *him* the same Adoration in Adversity, which he us'd to receive from them in his Prosperity. The Countries these impious Wretches were Governors of, serv'd to swell their ambitious Minds, for it was as large in extent, and as powerful in Men and Arms, as any of those Nations whatever, making almost the third Part of *Asia*. The Number of young Men was sufficient to make good the vast Armies *Darius* had lost. This made them not only despise *Darius*, but even *Alexander* himself, and imagine, that if they could but make themselves Masters of those Countries, they might be able to restore the *Persian* Empire.

After a long Consultation, they resolv'd to seize the *King* by the *Bactrian* Soldiers, who were intirely at their Devotion, and then send a Messenger to *Alexander* to let *him* know they were ready *to deliver him into his Hands alive.* If (which was what they fear'd) he should detest their Treason, then they design'd to kill

Darius, and repair with their Forces to *Bactra*. But it was impossible for them to seize *Darius* openly, there being so many thousand *Persians* ready to assist him; besides which, they were also afraid of the Fidelity of the *Greeks*. They therefore resolv'd to compass by Stratagem what they could not effect by Force, and counterfeit a Repentance of their Fault in withdrawing themselves from the Army, and likewise to excuse their Consternation to the *King*.

In the mean time, they dispatch'd Emissaries to solicite the *Persians* to a Revolt, and try to shake their Constancy, by Hopes on the one side, and Fear on the other. They insinuated to 'em, *That they expos'd themselves to manifest Ruin, and inevitable Destruction That* Bactriana *was ready to receive them, and bestow on them Presents and Riches as much as even their Desires could conceive.*

While these Things were in Agitation, *Artabazus* came to them, either by the *King*'s Order, or of his own Motion, and assur'd them, *Darius*'s *Anger was appeas'd, and that he was ready to shew 'em the same Favour as before* Hereupon they wept, and excus'd their Fault, and begg'd of *Artabazus to intercede in their behalf, and implore the King's Mercy*. The Night being pass'd after this manner, *Nabarzanes* repair'd to the Entry of the King's Tent with the *Bactrian* Soldiers, covering his secret Treachery, with a specious Pretext of a solemn Duty

Darius having given the Signal to march, seated himself in his Chariot, according to Custom, and *Nabarzanes* with the other *Parricides* flung themselves upon the Ground, and hypocritically worshipp'd *him* they design'd suddenly to have in their Custody as a Prisoner, shedding at the same time Tears, the usual Marks of Repentance, *so false is the Heart of Man, and so practis'd in Dissimulation.* Darius

Darius, who was himself naturally sincere, and of a mild Disposition, was mov'd by their Prayers and submissive Behaviour, and not only believ'd what they said, but even wept himself. But this it self had no Influence over the Hearts of these Wretches, to make 'em repent of their villainous Designs, tho' their Eyes were Witnesses how worthy a Person they deceiv'd, both as a Man, and as a *King*. As for his part, not dreaming of the Danger that was at hand, he made all the haste he could to escape falling into the Hands of *Alexander*, whom he only dreaded.

CHAP. XI.

*P*ATRON who commanded the *Greeks*, commanded his Men *to put on their Armour, which us'd to be carry'd with the Baggage, and to be ready on all Occasions, to execute his Orders.* He follow'd the *King*'s Chariot, watching for an Opportunity to speak to *him*, for he had penetrated into *Bessus* his Design, which *Bessus* mistrusting, would not depart from the Chariot, but follow'd it close, rather like one who guarded *Darius* as a Prisoner, than as an Attendant of the *King*. *Patron* therefore having waited a considerable Time, often suppressing what his Tongue was just going to utter, (as hesitating betwixt Fidelity and Fear) kept his Eyes fixt on the *King*, who at last *(*perceiving *x*) sent *Bubaces* one of his *Eunuchs to him*, to inquire, *if he had any thing to say to him. Patron* made answer *yes, but without a Witness.* Being hereupon commanded *to draw near*, without any Interpreter, *for* Darius understood *Greek* very well, He told the *King; Sir, of fifty thousand* Greeks *that we were*

were in your Service, there is now but a small Number of us left, who have accompany'd you in all your Variety of Fortune; and are the same towards you in your present Condition, as we were in your most prosperous State. Whatever Place you shall repair to, we shall consider as our own Homes and native Country. Your Prosperity and Adversity, have link'd us to you. I therefore beg and beseech you by this our invincible Fidelity, to pitch your Tent amongst us, and suffer us to be the Guards of your sacred Person. We have lost Greece, and have no Bactriana to repair to. All our Hope is in your self, and I wish we had no Reason to distrust others. It is needless to say more. As I am a Foreigner and Stranger, I should not ask to have the Guard of your Royal Person, if I thought it could be safe with any other.

Notwithstanding *Bessus* was ignorant of the *Greek* Tongue, yet his guilty Conscience made him believe *Patron* had discover'd him; but he was put out of his Pain by one that understood the *Greek* Language, and had heard what was said. *Darius* no way frighted, as could be perceiv'd by his Countenance, ask'd him *the Cause of his Advice*. Whereupon, thinking it dangerous to delay it any longer, he reply'd, *Sir*, Bessus *and* Nabarzanes *have conspir'd against you, your Fortune and Life are in the utmost Peril. This Day will be either yours, or the Parricides last.* Had the King heeded this Information, *Patron* had had the Glory of preserving his Life. Now let them turn this to a Jest that will, who hold that human Affairs are guided by a blind Chance, for my part I believe they depend upon an eternal Decree, and on a Chain of hidden Causes, and that every one performs his Race under the Direction of an immutable Law, which has long since determin'd its Period. *Darius*'s Answer was, *That although the Fidelity of the* Greek *Soldiers was sufficiently known to him,*

yet

yet he was resolv'd never to withdraw himself from his native Subjects That it was more vexatious to him to distrust than to be deceiv'd. That he would rather suffer whatever Fortune had decreed, than seek for Safety among Strangers, and that he had already liv'd too long, if his own Soldiers plotted his Destruction. Patron therefore desparing of the King's Welfare, return'd to his Post, ready to run any Hazard for his Preservation.

CHAP. XII.

BESSUS had in a manner resolv'd upon killing the King forthwith, but apprehending he should not ingratiate himself with *Alexander*, unless he deliver'd him up alive, he defer'd his intended Villany to the next Night. In the mean time he came to *Darius*, and *gave him thanks that he had so prudently declin'd the Treachery of a perfidious Man, who began already to have an Eye on* Alexander's *Riches, for most certainly he designed to have made him a Present of the King's Head, but it was no wonder that a mercenary Man made a Traffick of every thing, since he had neither Pledge nor Home, and was in a manner banish'd out of the World; a false Friend and a doubtful Enemy, and always ready to serve those who bid most* After this he began *to justify himself, and call'd the Tutelar Gods of the Country to witness his Innocence and Fidelity* Darius by his Countenance seem'd to believe him, tho' he no way doubted of the *Greeks* Information, but in the present Juncture it was equally dangerous to distrust his Subjects, or to be betray'd by them. There were thirty thousand of 'em whose Inclination to Villany

was

was to be suspected, and there were but four thousand *Greeks* under *Patron,* to whom if he should commit the Care of his Person, distrusting his own Subjects, he saw they would make that the Excuse of their Parricide, and therefore he chose rather to perish undeservedly, than to give 'em a pretext for their Crime. However, *he made answer to Bessus, That Alexander's Justice was not less known to him than his Valour. That they were deceiv'd who expected from him a Reward for their Treason, since there could not be a more rigid Chastiser of Infidelity.* The Night drawing on, the *Persians,* according to Custom, laid by their Arms, and went to the next Village to supply themselves with Necessaries, but the *Bactrians,* by *Bessus*'s Order, stood to their Arms. In the mean time, *Darius* sent to *Artabazus* to come to him, and having related what *Patron* had told him, *Artabazus* was for his passing immediately into the *Greeks* Camp, assuring him that the *Persians* would not fail to join him as soon as they understood his Danger, but being doom'd to his Lot, *he* was no longer capable of wholesome Advice, so that embracing *Artabazus* for the last time (who was the only Comfort he had in his present Circumstances) they both wept bitterly, and the *King* was forc'd at last to order him to be taken from him, he being unwilling to leave him. *Darius* cover'd *his* Head that *he* might not see him depart in so much Affliction, and then flung himself upon the Ground. At the same time his Guards, whose Duty it was to defend the *King*'s Person at their own Perils, fled from their Post, not thinking themselves a Match for the Conspirators whom they expected every Minute The *King* was now in a manner left alone, there remaining with him only a few *Eunuchs,* who did not know where to go. In this solitary Condition *he* ruminated on seve-

ral

ral things, till tir'd with that Lonesomness which he had had recourse to, to ease *his* Mind, *he* order'd *Bubaces* to be call'd to *him*, who being come, *he* said, *Get you gone likewise, and take care of your selves, you have, according to your Duty, adher'd firmly to your Prince's Interest to the very last. For my part, I'll here expect my Doom. Perhaps you may wonder I do not with my own Hand end my Days. But I had rather perish through another's Crime, than by my own.*

At these Words the Eunuch not only fill'd the Tent, but the whole Camp, with mournful Cries and Lamentations, then several others enter'd also, and tearing their Cloaths bewail'd the deplorable Condition of their *King*. At last these Howlings reach'd the *Persians* Quarters, who seiz'd with Terror, did neither dare to take to their Arms for fear of the *Bactrians*, nor keep themselves quiet, lest they should be thought shamefully to desert their Sovereign.

A various dissonant Clamour run through the Camp, which was now without a Head or Director, they who belong'd to *Nabarzanes* and *Bessus*, grounding upon these doleful Lamentations, told 'em, *The King had laid violent Hands upon himself* They therefore flew to the Tent with those who were to be the Executioners of their abominable Villany, and understanding at their Arrival there that the *King* was living, these Wretches order'd *him* to be seiz'd and bound

Thus *he* who a little while ago was carried in a magnificent Chariot, and honour'd by *his* Subjects as if *he* had been a *God*, was now (without the Concurrence of foreign Power) made a Prisoner by his own Slaves, and put into a sorry Cart, cover'd over with Skins. The *King's* Money and Furniture is rifled and plunder'd, as if it had been done by the Laws of War,

and

and having after this manner loaded themselves with Booty, the Wages of the vilest Impiety, they fled.

Artabazus, with those under his Command, and the *Greek* Troops, march'd towards *Parthia*, thinking themselves to be safer any where than in the Society of *Parricides*; as for the *Persians*, (*Bessus* having made 'em vast Promises, but chiefly because they had no body else to follow) they join'd the *Bactrians*. However, that it might not be said they did not honour their *King*, they bestow'd golden Fetters upon *Darius*, *Fortune seeming industrious to find out new ways to insult this Prince* Now that he might not be known by his Apparel, they cover'd the Cart, as we said before, with sordid Skins, and caus'd it to be drawn by Strangers, that he might not be discover'd to any that should enquire after him, the Guards following at a distance.

CHAP. XIII.

*A*Lexander being inform'd *Darius* was broke up from *Ecbatana*, leaving the Road that led to *Media*, resolv'd to follow *him* with the utmost diligence While *he* was at *Tabas*, which is a Town situate in the extreme Parts of the *Paratacene*, Deserters acquaint him, that *Darius* was making all the haste *he* could to get into the *Bactriana* Afterwards he was more certainly inform'd by *Bagysthenes* the *Babylonian*, *That the King was not as yet in Chains, but was in the greatest Danger, either of losing his Life or being made a Prisoner*

The *King* having therefore call'd a Council, told 'em, ‘ We have still to execute a matter of the greatest
‘ Con-

'Consequence, but the Labour will be very short;
'for *Darius* is not far from hence, either de-
'serted or slain by his own Men. Our Victory de-
'pends on our making our selves Master of his Per-
'son, and this mighty thing is to be compass'd by
'Expedition' To which they all reply'd, 'That they
'were ready to follow him where-ever he pleased, and
'desir'd him neither to spare their Labour or their
'Lives' Hereupon *he* led the Army with such Expedition that it resembled more a Race than a March,
he did not so much as let them rest in the Night. After this manner he march'd five hundred Furlongs, and
was now come to the place where *Bessus* had seiz'd
Darius. Here *Melon*, *Darius*'s Interpreter, is taken Prisoner, for being sick, *he* had not been able to follow
the Army, so that finding himself surpriz'd by *Alexander*'s Expedition, he feign'd himself a Deserter. By
this Man he was inform'd of every thing, but it was
now requisite to give his Army rest, *he* therefore made
choice of six thousand Horse, to whom *he* added three
hundred of those they call *Dimachæ*, these were heavy-
arm'd Horse, but if Occasion and the Place requir'd it,
they serv'd also on foot.

While *Alexander* was thus employ'd, *Orsillos* and
Mythracenes, who detested *Bessus*'s Parricide, surrender'd
themselves to *him, and acquainted him, that the* Persians *were five hundred Furlongs off, but they would shew
him a nearer Way* The *King* receiv'd them graciously,
and in the beginning of the Night taking them for
his Guides, he set forwards with the light Horse, commanding the *Phalanx* to follow as fast as they could.
He march'd in a square Body, and so moderated his
Speed as not to leave any of *his* Men behind *him*;
they had already march'd three hundred Furlongs, when
Brocubelus, Mazaus's Son, (who had been heretofore

Governor of *Syria*, but was now also come over to *Alexander*) inform'd *him, That* Bessus *was but two hundred Furlongs off, and that his Army (which mistrusted nothing) observed no manner of Order in their March, that they seem'd to make towards* Hircania, *and if he hasten'd his March, he might come suddenly upon 'em as they were disperc'd up and down* He told him also, That Darius *was still alive*

This Account made him still more eager to overtake him, so that clapping Spurs to their Horses they made all the haste they could After some time they came within the noise of the Enemy, but the Clouds of Dust intercepted the sight of 'em, he therefore now abated his speed, to give the Dust time to settle again upon the Ground. In a little time they were discover'd by the *Barbarians*, whose flying Army they likewise perceiv'd, and, in all Probability, would have had the worst of it, if *Bessus* had been as resolute to fight as he had shewn himself to commit the Parricide, for the *Barbarians* were much superior in Number and Strength, besides, they were fresh, whereas *Alexander*'s Army was fatigu'd But the very Name of *Alexander*, and his Fame, which are of great Moment in War, made 'em take to their Heels. *Bessus*, and the rest of his Associates, came now to *Darius*, and desir'd *him to get on Horseback, and make his Escape from the Enemy*, but he refus'd it, and told 'em, *That the avenging Gods were at hand* And invoking *Alexander*'s Justice, said, *He would not follow any longer Parricides* This so inflam'd their Anger, that they cast their Darts at *him*, and having given *him* several Wounds, they left *him*, they also wounded the Horses that drew *him*, that they might not be able to go any farther, killing likewise the two Servants that attended on the King

After the Commission of this Villany, they took different Courses in their Flight. *Nabarzanes* made towards *Hircania*, and *Bessus* towards *Bactriana*, being accompany'd with only a small number of Horsemen. The *Barbarians* being forsaken by their Leaders, dispers'd themselves here and there, according as they were directed by Fear or Hope, about five hundred Horse had got together, and seem'd unresolv'd, whether they should defend themselves, or fly.

Alexander understanding the Enemy's Consternation, detach'd *Nicanor* with part of his Cavalry to stop the Enemy's Flight, and follow'd himself with the Remainder. About three thousand of those who made Resistance were kill'd, and the rest were driven like Sheep or Cattle, without any farther Mischief, the King having given Orders *to abstain from shedding any more Blood*. None of the Prisoners could give any Account of *Darius*, every one examin'd strictly whatever he could lay his hands on, and yet they could not make any Discovery of him.

Alexander made such violent haste that he had hardly three thousand Horse with him, but several Bodies of the Fugitives fell into the hands of those that follow'd *him*. It is almost incredible, that there should be more Prisoners than there were Men to take 'em; Fear had so robb'd 'em of all manner of Sense, that they could not so much as reflect either on the inconsiderable number of the Enemy, or their own Multitude.

In the mean time, the Cattle that drew *Darius* having no body to govern them, were got out of the Highway, and having wander'd about four Furlongs stopp'd in a certain Valley, being faint both by their Wounds and the Heat. There was a Spring not far off, which some of the Country had shew'd to *Poly-*

stratus a *Macedonian*, who almoſt periſhing with Thirſt. While he was here drinking Water out of his Helmet, he obſerv'd the Darts that ſtuck in the Bodies of the wounded Cattle, and wondring they were not rather taken away than kill'd, he perceiving at the ſame time the Voice of a Man half dead, out of a natural Curioſity could not help reaching into the Waggon to diſcover what might be hid there, and ſo removing the Skins which cover'd it, he found *Darius* there, wounded in ſeveral parts of his Body. *Darius* underſtood ſomething of the *Greek* Language, and upon this Occaſion ſaid, *That at leaſt it was a Comfort to him in his preſent Calamity, that he had the Opportunity of ſpeaking to one that underſtood him*, and ſo ſhould not utter his dying Words in vain, he order'd him therefore to tell *Alexander*, *That tho' he had never deſerv'd any thing at his hands, yet it was his Lot to die very much indebted to him for his good Offices. That he gave him a great many Thanks for the Civilities he had ſhewn his Mother, Wife and Children, to whom he had not only granted Life, but maintain'd alſo according to their former Rank and Dignity, whereas he was depriv'd of all theſe Bleſſings by his own Kinſmen and Friends, to whom he had given both Life and Kingdoms. That he therefore out of Gratitude begg'd of the Gods, that they would bleſs his Arms, and make him Conqueror of the whole World. That he hop'd he would not neglect revenging the baſe Uſage he had receiv'd from Traytors, not only on his private Account, but for Example ſake, and the good of all Kings, ſince it would be no leſs Glorious to him than Beneficial.* He was now faint, and call'd for ſome Water, which being brought to him by *Polyſtratus*, he drank, and then ſaid to him, *Whoever thou art, it adds to all my other Misfortunes, that I have not wherewith to acknowledge this great kindneſs, but Alexander will do it for me, and*

the

the Gods will reward him for his extraordinary Humanity and Clemency towards my Family, thou shalt give him therefore my Hand, as the only Pledge I have of the Sincerity of my Wishes.

Having utter'd these Words, and taken *Polyſtratus* by the Hand, *he* expir'd. When *Alexander* was inform'd of it, *he* came to the Place, and reflecting how unworthy that Death was of his high Rank, he wept, and taking off his Cloak spread it over the dead Body, afterwards *he* caus'd it to be dress'd in royal Apparel, and sent it to *Syſigambis*, to be bury'd after the manner of the *Kings* of *Perſia*, among the Royal Tombs of his Anceſtors.

QUINTUS CURTIUS.

BOOK VI.

CHAP. I.

WHILE these Things were transacting in *Asia*, there happen'd some Disturbance in *Greece* and *Macedonia*. *Agis*, the Son of *Archidamus*, who was slain as he assisted the *Tarentins*, on the same Day that *Philip* overcame the *Athenians* near *Chæronea*. This Prince, out of an Emulation to *Alexander*'s Courage and Virtue, solicited his Citizens *not to suffer* Greece *to be any longer oppress'd by the* Macedonians, *for if a Remedy were not apply'd in time, they would not fail to be enslav'd after the same manner*, it was necessary therefore, he said, *to exert themselves while the* Persians *were still able to make some Resistance, that if they staid till they were quite reduc'd, it would be to no purpose then to assert their ancient Freedom against so mighty a Power*. The *Lacedemonians* being stir'd up by this Speech,

Speech, only waited for a favourable Opportunity to begin the War, and being encourag'd by *Memnon*'s Success, they began to join their Counsels to his, and notwithstanding *he* was taken off in the beginning of his prosperous Career, they still pursu'd their Measures with the same Vigour. *Agis* went to *Pharnabazus* and *Autophradates*, and obtain'd from them thirty Talents and ten Galleys, which *he* sent to his Brother *Agesilaus*, to enable him to pass into *Creet*, whose Inhabitants were divided in their Affections to the *Lacedemonians* and *Macedonians*. Ambassadors were also sent to *Darius* to solicit for a larger Sum of Money, and a greater Number of Ships, and altho' the *Persians* had been lately defeated near *Issus*, it was so far from being a hindrance to their obtaining their Demands, that it made them more readily comply therewith; for as *Alexander* was intent on his Pursuit after *Darius*, who led him still farther into the Country, a great Number of the hir'd Troops, after this Battle, fled into *Greece*, so that *Agis*, by the means of the *Persian* Money, took eight thousand of 'em into his Service, and by their Assistance retook the greatest part of the *Cretan* Towns. But when *Memnon*, whom *Alexander* had sent into *Thrace*, had stir'd up the *Barbarians* to revolt, and *Antipater* was march'd with an Army from *Macedonia* to compose those Troubles. The *Lacedemonians* laying hold of that Opportunity, brought almost all *Peloponnesus* (except a few Towns) over to their Interest, and having raised an Army of twenty thousand Foot, and two thousand Horse, gave the Command of it to *Agis*. *Antipater* being inform'd hereof, settled the Affairs of *Thrace* as well as he could, return'd to *Greece* with all possible Diligence, and there gather'd what Forces he could from the Friends and *Cities* that were in Alliance with *Alexander*, so that in a little time he found himself at

O 4   the

the Head of forty thousand effective Men. There came to him also a strong Body from *Peloponnesus* but as he had some distrust of 'em, he dissembled his Suspicion, and thank'd 'em *for shewing themselves so ready to defend* Alexander's *Dignity against the* Lacedemonians, *and assur'd them, he would not fail to acquaint the King therewith, who in time would also thank them himself, but at the present he did not want any farther Reinforcement, that therefore they might return home, having sufficiently discharged the Obligations of their Alliance*

Then he dispatch'd Expresses to *Alexander*, to acquaint him with the Commotions in *Greece*, who overtook him at *Bactra* In the mean time *Antipater* obtain'd a compleat Victory in *Arcadia*, *Agis* being kill'd in the Battle

However, *Alexander* (being inform'd before of these Disturbances in *Greece*) had taken all the proper Measures against 'em, which the distance of Place could allow, for he had order'd *Amphoterus* to sail to *Peloponnesus* with the *Cyprian* and *Phœnician* Ships, and had also directed *Menetes* to convoy three thousand Talents to the Sea-side, that he might be near at hand to supply *Antipater* with what Money he should know he wanted. He knew very well of what Moment the Issue of these Troubles might prove to all his other Affairs, and yet when *he was* inform'd of the *Victory obtain'd by* Antipater, comparing that Action with his own Atchievements, *he* in derision call'd it *the Battle of the Mice*, yet in the beginning of this War, the *Lacedemonians* were not unsuccessful, for encountering with *Antipater*'s Forces near *Corrhagus*, a Castle in *Macedonia*, they had the Advantage, the report of which Success drew over to their Party, those whose Minds were in suspence, till they saw which way Fortune would incline There was but one Town among the

Eleans

Elæans and *Achæans*, viz. *Pellene*, that did not enter into their Alliance. In *Arcadia*, *Megalopolis* also remain'd faithful to the *Macedonians*, out of respect to *Philip*'s Memory, from whom they had received Favours, but at the same time it was closely besieg'd, and could not have held out long, had not *Antipater* come seasonably to its Relief, who having pitch'd his Camp not far from that of the Enemy's, and finding himself, upon a Comparison of his and their Strength, not only superiour to them in Number of Men, but also in all military Provisions, he resolv'd to come to an Engagement as soon as ever he could. On the other side, the *Lacedemonians* did not decline coming to an Engagement, so that a Battle was fought that very much afflicted the *Spartan Affairs*; for, confiding in the straitness of the Place where they fought, (which render'd the Enemy's Advantage in Number almost of no use to them) they behav'd themselves gallantly for a while, nor did the *Macedonians* shew less Vigour in their Resistance, which occasion'd a great deal of Blood to be spilt on both Sides, but *Antipater* sending seasonably fresh Succours to that Part of his Army that labour'd most, the *Lacedemonians* were oblig'd at last to give Ground. *Agis* no sooner perceiv'd this, but with the Royal Regiment (which was compos'd of the stoutest Men) *he* flung himself where the Fight was sharpest, and killing those who were most forward to resist, he drove a great Part of the Enemies before him. They who were before victorious, now began to fly, till they drew their too eager Pursuers into the open Plain; a great many were kill'd in the Flight, but the *Macedonians* had no sooner gain'd a Ground where they could rally, and recover their Order, but they renew'd the Fight, which was for a while continu'd with equal Bravery on both Sides. Of all the *Lacedemonians*, the

King diftinguifh'd himfelf moft, he was not only remarkable by his Arms and Perfon, but alfo by his Greatnefs of Soul, in which alone *he* was invincible: *He* was attack'd on all Sides, both at a diftance and near at hand, yet he maintain'd the Fight a confiderable time, receiving fome of the Darts in his Buckler, and declining others by his extraordinary Agility, till being at laft run through both his Thighs with a Spear, and having loft a great Quantity of Blood, his Strength fail'd him. Then his Attendants took him upon his Buckler, and carry'd him in hafte to the Camp, tho' the violent Motion was very painful to him by reafon of his Wounds. The *Lacedemonians* did not for this leave off Fighting, but as foon as ever the Ground was more favourable to them than the Enemy, they clos'd their Ranks, and gallantly receiv'd their furious Charges. It is believ'd there never was a more defperate Fight than this, wherein were engag'd the Armies of the two moft warlike Nations in the World, and for a confiderable time with equal Advantage. The *Lacedemonians* reflected on their former Glory, and the *Macedonians* were animated by their prefent Grandeur, thofe fought for Liberty, and thefe for Sovereignty. The *Lacedemonians* wanted a Head, and the *Macedonians* were ftraiten'd for room. The various Changes and Accidents of this Day were fuch as fometimes encreas'd the Hope, and fometimes the Fear of both Parties, as if Fortune had on purpofe equally difpens'd her Favours to thefe brave Men. But the ftraitnefs of the Place where the Fight was ftill obftinate, and the Victory wavering, would not permit the whole Forces to engage, fo that there were more Spectators than Combatants, and thofe on each fide who were out of the caft of the Darts, encourag'd their Companions by their Acclamations. However, the *Lacedemonians* began now to faint, and could hardly hold

hold their Arms, that were flippery with Blood and Sweat, so that the Enemy still pressing upon 'em, they at first gave way, and were at last put to an open Flight The Conqueror pursu'd the scatter'd Forces, and having pass'd over all the Ground the *Lacedemonian* Army at first took up, was in pursuit of *Agis* himself. But *he* no sooner beheld his Men flying, and the Enemy drawing near *him*, than *he* commanded those who carry'd *him* to set *him* down, and then try'd whether his Limbs were able to second his Resolution, but finding they were not, he plac'd himself on his Knees, and having put on his Helmet, and cover'd *his* Body with *his* Buckler, he with *his* Right Hand shak'd *his* Spear, and challeng'd any of the Enemies to come and take away *his* Spoils Not one of 'em dar'd to come near *him*, but a great many cast their Darts at him afar off, which he return'd again upon the Enemy, till at last one of 'em lodg'd it self in his naked Breast The same was no sooner pull'd out of his Wound, but he grew faint, and gently lean'd his Head on his Buckler, and soon after resigning his Spirit with his Blood, he fell dead upon his Arms.

There were slain of the *Lacedemonians* five thousand three hundred and sixty, and of the *Macedonians* three hundred, but there hardly returned to the Camp a single Person that was not wounded. This Victory did not only quell the *Spartans* and their Confederates, but disappointed all those who depended on their Success. *Antipater* was not unsensible that the Hearts of those that congratulated his Victory did not agree with their outward Appearance, but as he desir'd to put an end to the War, it was necessary for him to be deceiv'd; and notwithstanding he was pleas'd with his Success, yet he was afraid of *Envy*, because what he had done exceeded his Station, for tho' *Alexander* was very desirous

to

to have his Enemies overcame, yet *he* could not easily brook that *Antipater* should be the Conqueror, for he look'd upon that Honour that was granted to another, to be a Derogation to his own. This was the reason why *Antipater* (who knew his Disposition perfectly) did not dare to conclude any thing upon the Victory, but had recourse to the Council of *Greece*, to determine what was fit to be done. The *Lacedemonians* desir'd nothing more of it, than that they might be allow'd to send Ambassadors to the *King*, which being granted, he readily pardon'd 'em all, except the Authors of the Rebellion. The *Megalopolitans*, whose City was besieg'd after the Defection, were order'd to pay to the *Achæans* and *Ætolians* one hundred and twenty Talents. Thus ended this War, which being kindled on the sudden, was nevertheless finish'd before *Alexander* defeated *Darius* at *Arbela*.

CHAP. II.

Alexander, whose *Genius* was better qualify'd for the Toils of War, than for Ease and Quiet, no sooner found himself deliver'd from Military Cares, but he presently gave himself up to all manner of Voluptuousness, and he that had shewn himself invincible to the Arms of the *Persians*, was easily subdu'd by Vice. He delighted in unseasonable Entertainments, and would pass whole Nights in Drinking and Revelling, having with *him* Crowds of Prostitutes, in a word, *he* struck in o all the foreign Manners, as if he thought them preferable to those of his own Country, and by that Procedure

cedure offended both the Eyes and Minds of his own People to such a degree, as to be look'd upon by the major Part of 'em as an Enemy, for *he* in a manner forc'd the *Macedonians* (who were tenacious of their own frugal Discipline, and were accustom'd to relieve the Wants of Nature with a cheap Diet, and such as was easily procur'd) to indulge the foreign Vices of the conquer'd Nations This occasion'd several Conspiracies against him, the Soldiers mutiny'd, and in the height of their Grief would speak their Minds freely; hence proceeded his groundless Suspicions, his indiscreet Fears, and other Evils of the like nature, which we shall hereafter give an Account of

As *Alexander* therefore pass'd the Nights as well as Days in unseasonable Feasting, he reliev'd the Satiety of these Entertainments with Plays and Musick, and was not contented with such Performers as he had from *Greece*, but order'd also the Women that were Prisoners *to sing after their manner*, whose uncouth and barbarous Songs were altogether disagreeable to the *Macedonians*, who were Strangers to it Among these Women he observ'd one to be more dejected than the rest, and seem'd modestly to resist those who would introduce her for that Purpose, she was a perfect Beauty, and her becoming Modesty made her Charms still more conspicuous Her cast down Eyes, and the Care she took to hide her Face as much as she could, gave the *King* some reason to suspect she was of too high Rank to be expos'd at those ludicrous Entertainments, he therefore ask'd her, *Who she was?* She answer'd, *She was Grand-Daughter to* Ochus, *who not long ago had been King of* Persia, *and whose Son was her Father, and that she was married to* Hiftaspes, *who was himself a Relation of* Darius, *and had had the command of a considerable Army* The *King* retain'd yet some small Remains

mains of *his* former Virtues, respecting therefore in *her* Adversity, *her* Royal Extraction, and so celebrated a Name as was that of *Ochus*, *he* not only commanded *her* to be set at liberty, but also to be restor'd to all *her* Possessions, and gave Orders to have her Husband found out, that he might restore her to him.

The next Day after, *he gave Orders to Hephastion to cause all the Captives to be brought before him*, and having examin'd into every one's Extraction, he separated those that were nobly descended from the rest. These were ten in Number, amongst whom was *Oxathres*, *Darius*'s Brother, who was not less deserving for his natural Endowments, than for his eminent Rank. The last Booty amounted to twenty six thousand Talents, of which Sum twelve thousand were distributed among the Soldiers by the way of *Donative*; and the like Sum was embezell'd by those who had the Care thereof.

At this time there was a Nobleman of *Persia*, whose Name was *Oxydates*, still detain'd in Prison, and was destin'd by *Darius* to suffer capital Punishment, *Alexander* not only set him at liberty, but also conferr'd upon him the Satrapship of *Media*. As for *Darius*'s Brother, he receiv'd him into the Band of his Friends, and preserv'd to him all the Honour due to his illustrious Birth.

From hence he march'd into *Parthiene*, which was then a contemptible Nation, but at this time is the most considerable of all those that lie behind the *Euphrates* and the *Tigris*, and extends it self as far as the Red-Sea. The *Scythians* made themselves Masters of this champian, fruitful Country, and are troublesome enough to their Neighbours, they have Territories likewise in *Europe* and *Asia*, those who inhabit above to *Bosphorus* belong to *Asia*, and those that are in *Europe*, enjoy the Countries that lie on the Left of *Thrace*, as far as

the

the *Boryſthenes,* and from thence to the *Tanais,* another River. The *Tanais* runs between *Europe* and *Aſia,* and it is no way doubted, but the *Scythians,* from whence the *Parthians* deſcend, came not from the *Boſphorus,* but out of *Europe.*

There was at this time a famous City call'd *Hecatomphylos,* which had been built by the *Greeks.* Here the *King* remain'd ſome time, being ſupply'd with Proviſions from all Parts. While he encamp'd in this Place, a ſudden Rumour aroſe, without any other Ground or Author than the wanton Idleneſs of the Army, that the King *being contented with what he had done, deſign'd to return forthwith to* Macedonia. The Soldiers hereupon run to their Tents, like mad Men, and pack'd up their Baggage; one would have thought the Signal had already been given to decamp.

The Camp was now all in Confuſion, ſome running up and down to ſeek their Comrades, and others loading the Waggons, ſo that it came at laſt to the *King's* Ears. This Rumour was ſtrengthned by thoſe *Greeks* whom *Alexander* had diſmiſs'd, with Orders to return to their own Homes, having given ſix thouſand *Denarij* to each Trooper, and from hence the reſt of the Army concluded that the War was at an End.

Alexander, who had reſolv'd within himſelf to paſs into *India,* and the remoteſt Parts of the Eaſt, was no leſs alarm'd hereat, than the Conſequence of the thing requir'd; he therefore order'd all the General Officers to repair to his Tent, and there with Tears in his Eyes, complain'd to them, *That he was ſtop'd in the middle of his glorious Career, and compell'd to return home more like one that was conquer'd, than a Conqueror, and this not thro' the Cowardice of his Army, but the Envy of the Gods, who had on the ſudden infus'd into the Minds of the brave Men that compos'd it, a longing Deſire to ſee their*

own

own Country, whither in a little time he intended to lead 'em himself, loaded with Honour and Glory. Hereupon every one of them offer'd afresh their Service to *him*, and begg'd to be employ'd in the most difficult Undertakings, assuring *him, He need not doubt of the Soldiers ready Obedience, if he would but make them a proper Speech, suitable to the present Occasion; since they were never known to depart from him in the least, dispirited or dejected, whenever he thought fit to diffuse amongst 'em his own Alacrity, and some Portion of the Vigour of his great and noble Mind.* He therefore promis'd *to do as they desir'd,* and order'd them *to go and prepare their Ears for his Purpose*, and having maturely consider'd with *himself* all that was requisite on this Occasion, *he* order'd the Army *to be drawn out*, and then made the following Speech to 'em.

CHAP. III.

'IT is not to be wonder'd at, Soldiers, that when you
' look back on the many great Things we have
' done, a Desire of Rest, and a Satiety of Glory should
' steal upon you. For, passing over the *Illyrians*, the
' *Triballi, Bœotia, Thrace, Sparta,* the *Achæans,* and *Pe-*
' *loponnesians*, all whom I have subdu'd, either in Per-
' son, or by my Appointment and Directions, we en-
' ter'd upon a War at the *Hellespont*, and deliver'd the
' *Ionians* and *Æolia* from the cruel Servitude of the *Bar-*
' *barians*, and have made our selves Masters of *Caria,*
' *Lydia, Cappadocia, Phrygia, Paphlagonia, Pamphilia, Pi-*
' *sidia, Cilicia, Syria, Phœnicia, Armenia, Persia, Media,*
' and *Parthiene*. I have conquer'd more Provinces,
' than

' than others have taken Towns, and I cannot tell,
' but in this Recital, the great Number may have made
' me still forget some. If therefore I were certain,
' these Countries we have over-run in so short a time,
' would remain firm to us, I would then, even against
' your Wills, Soldiers, be for returning to my houshold
' Gods, to my Mother, and Sisters, and the rest of my
' Citizens, that I might there chiefly enjoy with you,
' the Praise and Glory we have acquir'd, where we
' can have a full Fruition of the Rewards of our Vi-
' ctories, in the joyful Conversation of our Children,
' Wives, and Parents, in a profound Peace and secure
' Rest, and an undisturb'd Possession of the Fruits of
' our Bravery But as our Empire is yet new, and
' (if we will speak the Truth) even precarious; since
' the *Barbarians* bear our Yoke at present but with a
' stiff Neck, it is Time, Soldiers, that must tame their
' Minds, and soften their savage Temper. Do we not
' see, that the very Fruits of the Earth require their
' proper Seasons to ripen in? So great an Influence has
' Time even over those Things that are void of Sense.
' Can you imagine then, that so many Nations, enur'd
' to the Empire and Name of another, disagreeing
' with us in Religion and Manners, as well as Lan-
' guage, can be perfectly subdu'd the Day they are
' overcome? No, Soldiers, it is your Arms that re-
' strain 'em, and not their Wills And tho' your Pre-
' sence keeps them in awe, when once you are absent,
' they'll declare themselves your Enemies. We have
' to do with wild Beasts, which, when taken and shut
' up, are tam'd by length of Time, a thing not to be
' hop'd for otherwise, from their own fierce Natures
' I am talking all this while as if we had wholly sub-
' du'd all *Darius*'s Dominions, but that's a Mistake,
' for *Nabarzanes* possesses *Hyrcania*, and *Bessus* has not
' only

'only seiz'd *Bactriana*, but also threatens us Besides
'the *Sogdians*, the *Dahæ*, the *Massagetæ*, the *Sacæ*, and
'the *Indians*, are yet unconquer'd. All these, as soon
'as our Backs are turn'd, will pursue us, for they may
'be said to be of the same Nation, not Strangers and
'Foreigners. And it is observable, that all Nations
'more willingly obey their own Sovereigns, tho' their
'Government be never so harsh We must therefore,
'Soldiers, either resign what we have with so much
'Pains acquir'd, or subdue the rest For as Physicians
'leave nothing in the Bodies of their Patients that can
'endanger a Relapse, so must we lop off whatever can
'annoy or resist our Empire A small Spark neglect-
'ed, has often been the cause of great Conflagrations.
'Nothing can safely be despis'd in an Enemy Whom-
'soever you contemn, becomes more couragious by
'your Negligence *Darius* himself did not come to
'the *Persian* Empire, by Right of Hereditary Successi-
'on, but got into *Cyrus*'s Throne, through the Inte-
'rest of *Bagoas* the Eunuch, that you may not think
'it so difficult a Task for *Bessus* to take Possession of
'a vacant Kingdom But, Soldiers, we have certainly
'committed a great Crime, if we conquer *Darius* to
'no other purpose, but to deliver up his Dominions to
'one of his Servants, who, with the utmost Auda-
'ciousness, kept his Sovereign in Chains, at the
'time he stood most in need of Assistance, and to
'whom we that had conquer'd him, had certainly
'shewn Mercy, and at last barbarously murther'd him,
'to rob us of the Glory of preserving him. Will you,
'after all this, suffer such a Wretch to reign? whom
'I long to see nail'd to a Cross, and by that ignomini-
'ous Death, make ample Satisfaction to all Kings and
'Nations, for his execrable Treachery. But if, upon
'our return home, you should immediately hear that

'this

' this Villain was burning the *Greek* Towns, and lay-
' ing waste the *Hellespont*; how sensibly you'd be
' griev'd, that *Bessus* should run away with the Re-
' ward of your Victories! How quickly would you
' arm! What Haste would you then make to recover
' your own! But is it not much better to suppress him
' at once, while he is still full of Apprehension, and
' hardly knows what to do? We have but four Days
' March to come at him, we who have made our Way
' thro' so many deep Snows, pass'd so many Rivers,
' and climb'd over so many Mountains We shall meet
' with no Sea to stop our March, neither shall have the
' Straits of *Cilicia*, to obstruct our Passage, all the Way
' is plain and open We may be said to stand at the very
' Door of Victory We have only a few Fugitives and
' Ruffians to reduce It will be a glorious Work, and
' deserve to be transmitted to Posterity amongst your
' most memorable Achievements, that you were so far
' from suffering your Hatred to *Darius*, who was your
' Enemy, to continue after his Death, that you even took
' Satisfaction of his Parricides, not suffering any wicked
' Person to escape unpunished. This once done, how
' much more willingly will the *Persians* obey us, when
' they come to understand that you undertake pious
' Wars, and that it is *Bessus*'s Crime, and not his Name,
' you are offended at?'

CHAP. IV.

THIS Speech was receiv'd by the Soldiers with all possible Chearfulness, and they desir'd him to lead them where-ever he thought fit The *King* therefore laid hold of their present Disposition, and passing thro'

Parthiene,

Parthiene, he came the third Day to the Borders of *Hircania,* where he left *Craterus* with the Forces he commanded, and those that were under *Amyntas;* adding thereto six hundred Horse, and as many Archers, with Orders to secure *Parthiene* from the Incursions of the *Barbarians.* He gave to *Erigyius* the Care of the Baggage, appointing him a small Body for that purpose, and commanded him to march along the plain Country, while he himself with the *Phalanx* and Cavalry, having march'd a hundred and fifty Furlongs, incamp'd in a Valley, at the Entrance into *Hyrcania.* Here there is a Wood, the Trees whereof are very tall, and stand thick, so that it is very shady, and the Soil of the Valley is very fat, being plentifully water'd by the Streams that descend from the Rocks. At the Foot of these Hills the River *Ziobertis* rises, which for the Space of three Furlongs runs entire in one Channel, and afterwards is divided by a Rock, and so pursues two different Courses, between which it dispenses all its Waters. At some distance it unites again, and runs in a rapid Stream like a Torrent, and by reason of the Rocks through which it passes, becomes more violent, and then precipitates it self under Ground, pursuing its subterranean Course for the Space of three hundred Furlongs, and then rises again as from a new Spring, and cuts it self a new Channel much larger than its first, it being thirteen Furlongs in Breadth. After which, contracting it self again, it runs between straiter Banks, and at last falls into another River call'd *Rhidagus.* The Inhabitants affirm, that whatever is cast into the Cave nearest its Source, and where it first hides it self under Ground, comes out at the other Mouth, where the River opens it self, when it appears again. *Alexander* therefore caus'd two Bulls to be cast into it where the Waters enter the Earth, whose Bodies were afterwards

seen, where the River breaks out again, by those who were sent to examine into that Matter. In this Place *Alexander* had rested his Army four Days, when he received Letters from *Nabarzanes* (who had conspir'd with *Bessus* against *Darius*) to this effect 'That he
' had never been *Darius*'s Enemy. That on the contra-
' ry, he had always advis'd him to what he thought
' most conducing to his Advantage and Interest, for
' which faithful Counsel he had like to have been kill'd
' by him. That *Darius* entertain'd some Thoughts of
' committing the Guard of his Person to Foreigners,
' which was not only against all Law and Reason, but
' a great Reflection on his own Subjects Fidelity, which
' they had preserv'd inviolate to their Kings, for the
' space of two hundred and thirty Years. That finding
' himself in so doubtful and dangerous a Condition, he
' had took that Counsel which the present Necessity of
' his Circumstances had suggested to him. That *Da-*
' *rius* having kill'd *Bagoas*, had satisfy'd his People
' with no other Excuse, than that he had kill'd him
' who was plotting and contriving his Death. There
' is nothing so dear to wretched Mortals as Life, out
' of Love to which, he had been driven to the last
' *Extremities*, but however, he had been forc'd there-
' to by irresistible Necessity, it being far from his own
' Inclination and Choice. That in general Calamities,
' every one is apt to consult his own Interest and
' Welfare. However, if he thought fit to command
' him to come to him, he would readily obey him with-
' out the least Apprehension or Fear; for he could not
' suppose that so great a King would violate his Pro-
' mise, it not being usual for the Gods to deceive one
' another. That if he did not think him worthy the
' Honour of his Royal Word, there were Places enow
' where he could be safe, and that all Countries were
' alike to a brave Man.   Hereupon

Hereupon *Alexander* made no Difficulty to give him his Royal Security (after the manner the *Persians* are us'd to receive the same) *that if he came, he should not be injur'd.* Notwithstanding which, he march'd his Army in Order of Battel, sending Scouts before *him,* to discover the Places *he* was to pass through The light-arm'd Troops compos'd the Van, then follow'd the *Phalanx,* and the Baggage came in the Rear of that. As they were a warlike Nation, and the Situation of the Country was such as render'd it of difficult Access, the *King* thought it proper to be the more circumspect and wary in his March For the Valley extends it self as far as the *Caspian* Sea, and seems to stretch it self out in two Arms, the middle whereof strikes into a Hollow, so that it resembles the Horns of the Moon, before that Planet fills up its Orb On the Left are the *Cercetæ,* the *Mosyni,* and *Chalybes,* and on the other side are the *Leucosyri,* and the Plains of the *Amazons,* it has those to the Northward, and these to the Westward. The *Caspian* Sea-Water not being so brackish as that of others, feeds Serpents of a prodigious Bigness, and Fish of a quite different Colour from those of other Seas. Some call it the *Caspian,* and others the *Hyrcanian* Sea. Some say, that the *Palus Mæotis* falls into it, and bring that for an Argument why this Sea's Waters are sweeter than those of others When the North Wind blows, it swells the Sea, and forces it violently on the Shore, carrying its Waves a great way into the Country, where it stagnates for some time, till the Heavens changing their Aspect, these Waters return to the Sea again with the same Impetuousness they first broke their Bounds, and so restore the Land to its own Nature. Some have been of Opinion, that these Waters do not come from the *Caspian* Sea, but do fall

from

from *India* into *Hyrcania*, whose lofty Situation (as we said before) by degrees sinks into this perpetual Vale. From whence the *King* march'd twenty Furlongs by a Way almost impassable, having a Wood hanging in a manner over it, besides which Difficulties, the Torrents and Standing Waters obstructed his Passage, but as no Enemy appear'd, *he* made a shift to get through it. And at last marching farther on, *he* came into a better Country, which besides other Provisions with which it abounded, there was great Plenty of Apples, and the Soil was very proper for Vines. There is also a kind of Tree that is very common here, and very much resembles an Oak, whose Leaves are in the Night laden with Honey, but unless the Inhabitants gather it before the Sun rises, the least Heat thereof consumes it.

The *King* having march'd thirty Furlongs farther, was met by *Phrataphernes*, who surrender'd himself to him, and all those who had fled with him, after *Darius*'s Death. *Alexander* receiv'd him graciously, and afterwards arriv'd at a Town call'd *Arvas*. Here *Craterus* and *Erigyus* join'd him, bringing along with them *Phradates*, who had the Government of the *Tapurians*. The *King*'s taking him also into his Protection, was an Example to a great many others, to trust themselves to his Clemency. He afterwards appointed *Menapis* Governor of *Hyrcania*, who had in *Ochus*'s Reign, taken Refuge with King *Philip*. He likewise restor'd to *Phradates* the Government of the *Tapurian* Nation.

CHAP.

CHAP. V.

Alexander was now come to the utmost Bounds of *Hyrcania*, when *Artabazus* (who, as we before took notice, had always firmly adher'd to *Darius*) came to him with *Darius*'s Relations, his own Children, and a Body of *Greek* Soldiers. The *King* immediately offer'd him his Right-hand, for he had been formerly entertain'd by *Philip*, when in *Ochus*'s Reign, he had been forc'd to fly from his Country. But the chief Cause of his receiving him so kindly, was his firm Adherence to his Prince's Interest to the last. Finding himself therefore so graciously receiv'd, he address'd himself to the *King* in these Words. *Long may you reign in perpetual Felicity. As for my own part, I am sufficiently happy on all other Accounts: I have but one Grievance, and that is, that my advanc'd Age will not permit me to enjoy your Goodness long.* He was in the ninety fifth Year of his Age, and was accompany'd by his nine Sons which he had all of one Woman. These he also presented to the *King*, and wish'd *they might live so long, as they might be serviceable to his* Majesty.

Alexander for the most part walk'd on foot, but then *he* order'd *Horses to be brought for himself and Artabazus*, lest if he walk'd himself on Foot, the old Man should be asham'd to ride. Afterwards having pitch'd his Camp, he order'd *the* Greeks who came along with *Artabazus, to be brought before him*. But they made answer, *that unless he took the* Lacedemonians *also into his Protection, they would deliberate amongst themselves*

themselves what Measures they should take They were Ambassadors from the *Lacedemonians* to *Darius*, who being overcome, they join'd those *Greeks* that were in the *Persian* Service. But *Alexander* without giving them any Promise or Security, commanded them *to come immediately and submit to what he should alot them.* They demurr'd upon the Matter some time, being of different Opinions, however, at last they promis'd to come. But *Democrates* the *Athenian*, being conscious to himself, that he had always oppos'd as much as he could the *Macedonians* Prosperity, despairing of Pardon, run himself through with his Sword, the rest according to their Agreement surrender'd themselves to *Alexander*. They were fifteen hundred Soldiers of them, besides fourscore and ten, who had been sent *Ambassadors* to *Darius*. The greatest part of the Soldiers were distributed among the Troops by way of Recruit, and the rest were sent home. As for the *Lacedemonians*, he commanded them *to be kept in Custody*. The *Mardians* are a Nation bordering upon *Hyrcania*, a hardy People, and accustomed to live by thieving. They alone neither sent *Ambassadors* to *Alexander*, nor gave the least Token to imagine, they would obey his Orders. This rais'd his Indignation, that a single Nation should hinder him from being thought invincible. Leaving therefore his Baggage under a sufficient Guard, he advanc'd towards them with his best Troops. He had march'd all the Night, and by Break of Day the Enemy appear'd in sight. But it was rather a tumultuous Alarm than a Fight, for the *Barbarians* were soon driven from the Eminences they possess'd, and put to Flight, and the neighbouring Villages being deserted by the Inhabitants, were plunder'd by the *Macedonians*. But the Army could not penetrate into the more inward Parts of the Country, without being much

Vol. I P harrass'd

harrass'd and fatigu'd. The Tops of the Hills are encompass'd with high Woods, and impassable Rocks, and the *Barbarians* had secur'd by a new kind of Fortification, what was plain and open. The Trees are set thick on purpose, then they with their Hands bend the tender Branches downwards, and having twisted them together, they set them in the Ground again, where taking Root, they put out fresh Branches, which they do not suffer to grow according to the Appointment of Nature, but they so intermix them, that when they are cloath'd with Leaves, they in a manner hide the Ground. Thus the Way was perplex'd with one continu'd Hedge, by the means of these interwoven Boughs, which like so many Snares caught hold of those that pass'd thro' 'em. In this Case there was no Remedy but cutting down the Wood. But this again was a very laborious Task, for the Boles of the Trees were full of Knots, which made them very hard to cut, and the implicated Boughs, like so many suspended Circles, by their tender Pliantness gave way, and baulk'd the Force of the Stroke: On the other side the Inhabitants are so habituated to run like wild Beasts among these Coverts, that on this Occasion they enter'd the Wood, and gall'd the Enemy with their Darts. *Alexander* was therefore oblig'd (after the manner of Hunters) first to find out their Haunts, by which means he destroy'd a great many of them, and at last order'd his Army *to surround the Woods, and if they found any Entrance, to break through the same.* But as they were altogether ignorant of the Country, they wander'd up and down like Men lost, and some of 'em were taken by the Enemy, and with them the *King's* Horse *Bucephalus*, which he did not value after the rate of other Cattle, for he would suffer no Body but *Alexander* to mount him, and whenever

ver he had a Mind to get upon him, he would kneel down and receive him on his Back, as if he was sensible who it was he carry'd. The *King* therefore being transported with Anger and Grief, even beyond what was decent, order'd his Horse to be sought after, and gave the *Barbarians* to understand by an *Interpreter, that if they did not restore him, not one of them should escape alive.* This Declaration so terrify'd them, that they not only restor'd the Horse, but made him also other Presents. However, this did not appease the *King*'s Anger, so that *he commanded the Woods to be cut down, and caus'd Earth to be brought to fill up the hollow Part of the intricate Covert.* The Work was pretty well advanc'd, when the *Barbarians* despairing of their being able to defend the Country, surrender'd themselves to the *King*, who receiving Hostages from them, appointed *Phradates* to be their Governor, and on the fifth Day return'd from thence to his Camp, where having confer'd on *Artabazus* double the Honour *Darius* had bestow'd on him, he sent him home.

Then he continu'd his March to the City of *Hyrcania*, where he was no sooner arriv'd than *Nabarzanes* yielded himself to the *King* upon his Parole, making him at the same time very noble Presents; among the rest was *Bagoas*, an Eunuch, who was in the flower of his Youth, and had been familiarly us'd by *Darius* formerly, and was now by *Alexander*; it was chiefly at this Eunuch's intreaty that *he* pardon'd *Nabarzanes*.

The Nation of the *Amazons* (as we said before) borders upon *Hyrcania*, and inhabits the Plains of *Themiseyra*, along the River *Thermodoon Thalestris* was the Name of their Queen, who had in her Subjection all the Country that lies between Mount *Caucasus*, and the River *Phasis*. This *Queen* was come out of her

Dominions, inflam'd with a desire to see *Alexander*; and being advanc'd pretty near the Place where *he* was, *she* sent Messengers before to acquaint *him, that the Queen was coming to have the satisfaction of seeing and conversing with him* Having obtain'd admittance, *she* commanded the rest of *her* Followers to stay behind, and taking with *her* three hundred of *her* Female Militants, *she* advanc'd As soon as *she* came within sight of the *King*, *she* leap'd from *her* Horse, holding two Javelins in *her* right Hand. The *Amazons* Apparel does not cover all their Bodies, for their left Side is naked down to the Stomach, nor do the Skirts of their Garments (which they tie up in a knot) reach below their Knees. They preserve their left Breast intire that they may be able to suckle their Female Off spring, and they cut off and sear their Right, that they may draw their Bows, and likewise cast their Darts with the greater ease *Thalestris* look'd at the *King* with an undaunted Countenance, and narrowly view'd his Person, which did not come up to the Fame of his great Exploits, for the *Barbarians* have a great Veneration for a majestical Presence, esteeming them only capable of performing great Actions, whom *Nature* has favour'd with an extraordinary Personage Being ask'd by the *King*, *Whether she had any thing to desire of him?* She did not boggle to tell *him*, *That her Errand was to have Children by him, she being worthy to bring him Heirs to his Dominions, as for the Female Sex, she would retain that herself, and restore the Male to the Father.* Hereupon *Alexander* ask'd her, *If she would accompany him in his Wars?* To which she excus'd herself, *with her having left no Body to take care of her Kingdom* Her Passion being greater than the *King*'s, oblig'd him to stay here a little while, so that he entertain'd her thirteen Days to gratifie *her* Desire,

Desire, after which *she* return'd to her Kingdom, and the *King* march'd into *Parthiene*.

CHAP. VI.

HERE *he* gave a Loose to all his Passions, and laying aside *his* Continency and Moderation (which are eminent Virtues in an exalted Fortune) deliver'd himself up to Voluptuousness and Pride. *He* now look'd upon the Manners, Dress, and wholsome Discipline of the *Kings* of *Macedon*, as things beneath his Grandeur, and therefore emulated the *Persian* Pomp, which seem'd to vie with the Majesty of the Gods themselves. *He* began to suffer the Conquered of so many Nations to prostrate themselves on the Ground, and worship him, and hop'd by degrees to enure 'em to servile Offices, and make them like Slaves He wore about his Head a purple Diadem, intermix'd with white, and took the *Persian* Habit, without fearing the Omen of passing out of the Dress and distinguishing Tokens of the Conqueror, into those of the Conquer'd, nay, he would say himself, that *he* wore the *Persian* Spoils, but the misfortune was, that *he* at the same time imbib'd their Manners, for the outward Magnificence of Apparel was follow'd by an inward Insolence of Mind And notwithstanding *he* still seal'd those Letters *he* sent into *Europe* with his usual Seal, yet he affix'd that of *Darius* to all those he sent into *Asia*, it appearing plain from thence, that one Mind was not capable of the Fortune of both. *He* oblig'd also *his* Friends, *his* Captains and chief Officers of *his* Army to dress after the *Persian* manner, and tho'

P 3 within

within themselves they despis'd the same, yet they did not dare to refuse complying, for fear of incurring his displeasure. The same Number of Concubines that *Darius* had, (*viz.* three hundred and sixty) fill'd the Royal Palace, and these were attended by Crowds of *Eunuchs*, who were themselves accustom'd to supply the place of Women. The old Soldiers who had serv'd under *Philip*, publickly detested this Luxury, and foreign Excesses, as being altogether strangers to such Voluptuousness, insomuch that it was the general talk throughout the Camp, ‘ That more was lost by ‘ the Victory than gain'd by the War, since they might ‘ properly be said to be conquer'd themselves, when ‘ they were thus enslav'd to foreign Customs and Man- ‘ ners, and, in fine, all the Reward they were like ‘ to receive for their long Absence from their native ‘ Country, was to return home in captive Habits. ‘ That it was high time for 'em to be asham'd of ‘ themselves, when they saw their King affect to re- ‘ semble rather the Conquer'd than the Conquerors, ‘ and of King of *Macedonia* become one of *Darius*'s ‘ Satraps.

As *Alexander* was not ignorant that his Behaviour displeas'd his chiefest and best Friends, as well as his Army in general, he endeavour'd to recover their Affection by *his* Liberality and Bounty, but the Rewards of Servitude are always disagreeable to free and noble Souls, that therefore the Discontent might not break out into Sedition, he thought it adviseable to put an end to these Effects of Idleness by the Toils of Wars.

Bessus had now assum'd the Royal Robes, and order'd *himself* to be call'd *Artaxerxes*, and was gathering together the *Scythians*, and the other Inhabitants along the *Tanais*. *Satibarzanes* was the Person that gave *him* this Account, whom *he* had taken into *his* Protection,
confirming

confirming to him the Government he held before But finding *his* Army heavy laden with rich Spoils, and other Materials of Luxury, which was a great hindrance to their Expedition in their Movements, *He first ordered his own Baggage to be brought into the middle of the Plain, and then that of all the rest of the Army, excepting only what was absolutely necessary* The Plain into which the laden Carriages were brought, was very spacious and large Every one now impatiently expected what would be his next command, when *he* order'd *the Cattle to be taken away*, and then setting fire to *his* own Baggage, *he commanded the rest to do the like to theirs* It was a great Mortification to set fire themselves to those things they had so often rescu'd from the Flames the Enemy had kindled to destroy 'em, yet no Body dar'd to lament the loss of the reward of his Blood, seeing the *King's* Furniture underwent the same Fate This done, *Alexander* made a short Speech to 'em which alleviated their Grief, and they were now pleas'd to find themselves more fit for the Service of the War, and more ready upon all Occasions, rejoicing, *That by the loss of their Baggage, they had preserv'd their Discipline* They therefore began their March towards *Bactriana*, but *Nicanor*, *Parmenio*'s Son, being snatch'd away by sudden Death, was a great Affliction to the whole Army The *King* was more griev'd thereat than any Body, and would fain have stopt there some time, that he might be present at the Funeral himself, but the scarcity of Provisions oblig'd him to hasten his March, leaving therefore *Philotas* with two thousand six hundred Men to perform the funeral Rites to his Brother, *he* with the rest of the Army advanc'd towards *Bessus* As *he* was upon *his* March, he receiv'd Advice from the Neighbouring *Satraps*, that *Bessus* was advancing towards him with an Army in a hostile manner, and that *Satibarzanes*, whom *he* had lately confirm'd in his Government over the *Arians*, was also revolted from *him*.

Hereupon, notwithstanding *he* was intent upon *Bessus*, yet judging it more advisable to suppress *Satibarzanes* first, *he* took with *him* the light-arm'd Foot, and the Cavalry, and marching with the utmost diligence all the Night, *he* came unexpectedly upon him. *Satibarzanes* being inform'd of *his* Arrival, took along with him two thousand Horse (for a greater Number could not be got together in the Hurry and Confusion he was in) and fled to *Bactriana*, the rest of his Party sav'd themselves in the neighbouring Mountains. There was a Rock which towards the West was very steep, but to the Eastward was of a more easie and gentle Descent, being cover'd with Wood, and having a Fountain from whence the Water ran in great abundance, it was two and thirty Furlongs in Circumference, the top of it was a green Plain. Here they plac'd the useless Multitude, while they employ'd themselves in casting Stocks of Trees and great Stones upon the Enemy. They were about thirteen thousand Men in Arms.

Alexander having left *Craterus* to continue the Siege of the Rock, made all the haste *he* could to overtake *Satibarzanes*, but understanding he had gain'd too much Ground of *him*, *he* return'd to the Siege of those who had posted themselves on the Mountains. At *his* Arrival *he* commanded the Army *to clear that part of the Way to the Rock, which was any wise practicable*, but when this was done, impassable Rocks and Precipices presented themselves afresh, so that their Labour seem'd to be lost, where Nature it self oppos'd the Undertaking. However, as his Mind was fram'd to struggle with the greatest Difficulties, finding it was

impossible

impossible to advance, and dangerous to retire back; he apply'd his Thoughts to all manner of Contrivances, and he no sooner rejected one, but his Mind suggested him another. As he was still labouring to find out an Expedient for his Purpose, Nature supply'd the deficiency of Reason The Wind was Westward, and blew very fresh, and the Soldiers had cut down a great deal of Wood, thereby to open themselves a Passage thro' the Rocks, and the vehement heat of the Sun had dry'd the Wood *Alexander* therefore caus'd a great Pile to be made that the Fire might not want Fuel to nourish it, at last so many Trees were heap'd upon one another that they equall'd in height the top of the Mountain, then he order'd this huge Pile to be set on Fire on all sides The Wind carry'd the Flame into the Enemies Faces, and the Smoke, like a black Cloud, darken'd the very Skies, the Woods rung with the crackling caus'd by the Flames, which were now no longer confin'd to the Soldiers Pile, but communicated themselves to the next growing Trees The *Barbarians*, to avoid the greatest of Torments, endeavour'd to make their Escape thro' any part of the Wood that was not yet on fire, but where the Flame yet granted them a Passage the Enemy was ready to receive them, so that there was a horrible kind of variety in their manner of perishing, some cast themselves into the middle of the Flames, and some flung themselves headlong from the Rocks, while others expos'd themselves to the fury of the Soldiers, a few that were half consum'd with Fire, were taken Prisoners.

From hence *Alexander* return'd to *Craterus*, who was at present besieging *Artacaena*, he had prepar'd every thing for the King's Arrival, and waited only for his coming, to resign to him (as decency requir'd) the Honour of taking the Town *Alexander* therefore order'd der'd the Towers to be advanc'd to the Walls of the Place, at the sight whereof the *Barbarians* were seiz'd with such a Consternation, that extending their Hands upon the Walls in a suppliant manner, they intreated *him to turn his Anger upon* Satibarzanes, *the Author of the Defection, and grant them his Pardon, who laid themselves at his Mercy.* Hereupon the King not only pardon'd them, but rais'd the Siege, and restor'd to the Inhabitants all that belong'd to 'em. Upon *his* leaving this Place, *he* was met by a fresh supply of Recruits: *Zoilus* brought with him out of *Greece* five hundred Horse, and *Antipater* had sent three thousand more from *Illyrium*, *Philip* had likewise with him one hundred and thirty *Thessalian* Troopers, there came also from *Lydia* two thousand six hundred Foot and three hundred Horse of the same Nation. Being reinforc'd with these Troops he advanc'd into the Country of the *Drangæ*, who are a warlike Nation, and were at this time under the Government of *Barzaentes*, who was concern'd with *Bessus* in the Treason against *Darius*. This Traitor, to avoid the Punishment due to his Crime, was fled to *India*.

CHAP. VII.

HERE the *King* had encamp'd during nine Days, and altho' *he* was a Prince of undaunted Resolution, and had shewn *himself* invincible, yet *he* had like to have been taken off by domestick Treason

Dymnus was a Man who had none of the greatest Interest at Court, and entertain'd at this time an unwarrantable Passion for a discarded *Eunuch* call'd *Nichomachus,*

machus, being intirely subdu'd thereby, thinking he ingross'd him to himself, coming therefore to the Youth at a certain time like one astonish'd (as might be perceiv'd by his Countenance) he took him privately into a Temple, and told him, *He had Secrets of the greatest Importance to impart to him*, and as the *Eunuch* was very attentive to what he said, *Dymnus* conjur'd him *by their mutual Love, and the Pledges they had given each other thereof, to give him the Sanction of a solemn Oath, that he would never reveal what he should impart to him*. *Nichomachus* thinking he would communicate nothing to him after so religious a manner that could be Perjury to him to disclose, *swore by the Gods there present, that he would not* Upon this Assurance *Dymnus* told him, *There was a Conspiracy against the King which would be put in Execution in three Days, and that he himself was concern'd therein, with several other brave Men of the first Rank.* The young Man had no sooner heard this than he let him understand, *He had not given his Faith to conceal so black a Treason, and that no Religion could bind him to Secresie in a Crime of that nature* Hereupon *Dymnus* was in a manner distracted between Love and Fear, and taking the Eunuch by the Hand, with Tears in his Eyes, first intreated him *to be concerned in the Enterprize, or if he could not do that, at least that he would not betray him, of whose Affection, among other Instances, he had this strong Proof that he entrusted him with his Life*

The Youth persisting in an obstinate abhorrence of the Design, *Dymnus* threaten'd to kill him, telling him, *The Conspirators would begin their glorious Undertaking with his Death*, sometimes he call'd him *effeminate Coward*, and sometimes *Betrayer of his Friend*. Then he try'd to move him by large Promises, even
that

that of a Kingdom, but finding him no way to be prevail'd upon, he drew his Sword, and put it sometimes to the Eunuch's Throat, and sometimes to his own, so that at last, what with Threats, and what with Intreaty, he brought him *to promise not only to keep the Secret, but also to be concern'd in the Execution thereof* Notwithstanding which, his Mind adher'd firmly to its first Resolution, shewing himself thereby worthy to have been Virtuous and Chaste However, he feign'd himself *so enslav'd by his Love for* Dymnus, *that he could refuse him nothing*, and then desir'd to know, *Who were his Partners in this Undertaking*, for he said, *it was of the greatest Importance with whom he embark'd in a Design of this nature*

Dymnus, who was infatuated with his Passion and Crime, return'd him Thanks, and at the same time congratulated him, *That being himself a brave Youth, he did not scruple to associate himself with* Demetrius, *one of the King's Guards,* Peucolans *and* Nicanor, *he added to these* Aphæbetus, Loceus, Dioxenus *and* Amyntas Nichomachus, after this (being dismiss'd by him) immediately repair'd to his Brother Cebalinus, and imparted to him what he had heard. It was agreed between 'em, *that the Informer should remain in the Tent, for fear if he should be seen in the King's Apartment, not being us'd to have admittance there, the Conspirators should conclude they were betray'd* Ceballinus himself waited without the Porch (not being allow'd a nearer access,) expecting the coming in or out of some of those who were familiar with the King, to introduce him to his Majesty It happen'd that Philotas, Parmenio's Son, upon some unknown Account, remain'd last with the King, Cebalinus therefore (at his coming out) with all the outward marks of Grief and Disturbance, communicated to him what his

Bro-

Book VI. *Quintus Curtius.* 249

Brother had told him, and begg'd of him *to acquaint the King therewith as soon as possible* Philotas commending his Fidelity, immediately went back to the *King*, and having discours'd with him on several other things, did not so much as mention what *Cebalinus* had inform'd him of At Night as *Philotas* was coming out of the Palace, the young Man, who waited for him in the Porch, ask'd him, *Whether he had acquitted himself of his Promise, in reference to what he had intrusted him with* Philotas excus'd himself to him, and told him, that the *King* was so taken up with other Affairs that he had not had an opportunity to do it. *Cebalinus* therefore attended again the next Day, and as *Philotas* was going to the *King*, he put him in mind of what he had told him the Day before, and *Philotas* promis'd him afresh *to take care of it*, however, he did not then neither acquaint the *King* therewith *Cebalinus* hereupon began to distrust him, and thinking it to no purpose to trouble him any farther, he addres'd himself to *Metron* Master of the *King*'s Armory, and imparted to him what he had told *Philotas* *Metron* immediately hid *Cebalinus* in the Armory, and repair'd to the *King* (who was then bathing himself) and *inform'd him of what he had heard.* The *King* presently sent Guards to seize *Dymnus*, and then came into the Armory, whom as soon as *Cebalinus* saw, transported with Joy he told him, *He was glad he had found a means to save him from the wicked Designs of his Enemies* Alexander having duly inquir'd into the whole matter, ask'd *Cebalinus, How long it was since* Nichomachus *had given him this Information?* To which he answer'd, *That it was now the Third Day* Alexander concluding, that he could not conceal it so long without being guilty himself, commanded him to be secur'd, but *Cebalinus* declaring loudly, *That the Moment he heard of* it, he had acquainted Philotas therewith, of which his Majesty might be satisfy'd if he ask'd Philotas himself. The King farther inquir'd, Whether he had press'd Philotas to impart it to him? which Cebalinus affirming to have done, Alexander lifting his Hand to Heaven, with Tears in his Eyes complain'd highly of the Ingratitude of the Person whom he had honour'd with the first place in his Friendship.

In the mean time Dymnus, who was not ignorant on what Account he was sent for by the King, wounded himself grievously with his Sword, but being hinder'd by the Guards from killing himself outright, they brought him to the Palace, where the King fixing his Eyes upon him, said to him, What great Mischief have I done to thee, Dymnus, that Philotas should seem to thee worthier of the Kingdom of Macedon than my self? Dymnus's Speech now fail'd him, so that giving a great Groan, and turning his Face from the King, he fell down dead.

The King afterwards sent for Philotas, who being come, he said to him, ' That Cebalinus, who would
' deserve the worst of Punishments if he should have
' conceal'd two Days together the Knowledge of a
' Conspiracy against my Life, casts the blame upon
' Philotas, to whom, he says, he immediately gave an
' Account thereof. The easie access you have to my
' Person makes your Guilt the greater, if you wink'd
' at it, and I must own, it would have better become
' Cebalinus than you to have been so negligent in a
' matter of that Consequence. You have a favourable
' Judge, if you can with Justice deny what you ought
' not to have committed.' To this Philotas, without the least sign of Fear, as far as could be perceiv'd by his Countenance, reply'd, ' That it was true Ce-
' balinus had acquainted him with the regardless In-
' formation

'formation of a ſorry *Catamite*, which the Incon-
'ſiderableneſs of the Author made him think not
'worthy of Credit, ſince he thought he ſhould by
'ſuch a Diſcovery only expoſe himſelf to the Laughter
'of the more judicious. However ſince *Dymnus*
'had kill'd himſelf, how groundleſs ſoever the Ac-
'count might be, he own'd it ought not to have
'been conceal'd, then embracing the King, he begg'd
'of him to have a greater Regard to his paſt Life,
'than to a Fault which conſiſted only in Silence, and
'not in any Matter of Fact.' I cannot determine
whether the *King* really credited what he ſaid, or
only ſuppreſs'd his Anger, but it is certain *he* gave
him *his* Right Hand, as a Pledge of *his* being recon-
cil'd to him, and told him, ' He look'd upon him ra-
'ther to have deſpis'd the Information than con-
'ceal'd it

CHAP. VIII.

THIS did not however hinder the *King* from calling a Council of his Friends, to which *Philotas*
was not ſummon'd, and *Nichomachus* was brought before 'em. Here he related all that he had told the *King*.
Craterus was of the Number of thoſe the *King* had the
greateſt Eſteem for, and on that account, ſomewhat
jealous of *Philotas*'s Intereſt. Moreover, he was not
inſenſible, that *Philotas* had often tir'd the *King*'s Ears
with extravagant exaggerations of his Behaviour and
Service, who tho' he did not on that ſcore ſuſpect
him to be evilly diſpos'd, yet *he* thought him a little
too

too arrogant *Craterus* therefore thinking he could not have a more favourable Opportunity to suppress his Rival, covering his Hatred with the specious Appearance of Zeal and Piety, said, 'Would to God, Sir, 'you had deliberated with us at first, concerning this 'Affair, we had then endeavour'd to persuade you (if 'you were resolv'd to pardon *Philotas*) to have let him 'remain'd in Ignorance, how much he was indebted 'to you, rather than (having brought him in Fear of 'his Life) force him to make deeper Reflections on 'his own Danger, than on your Goodness For he 'may always have it in his Power to conspire against 'you, though you may not always be able to par-'don him. Do not therefore imagine, that he who 'dar'd to undertake so foul a Crime, can be alter'd in 'his Disposition by a Pardon He knows very well, 'that they who by unpardonable Faults have exhausted 'your Mercy, have no room left to hope for it any more. 'And admitting he may be alter'd by Repentance, or 'overcome by your Clemency, yet I am sure his 'Father *Parmenio*, who has the Command of so great 'an Army, and is in so confirm'd a Credit with the 'Soldiers, in fine, who in point of Authority with 'them, is little inferior to your self, will not be very 'well pleas'd to stand indebted to you for the Life of 'his Son There are some Kindnesses which we hate, 'a Man is always asham'd to confess he has deserv'd 'Death He would therefore rather have the World 'think you have done him an Injury, than given him 'his Life From whence I infer, that you will be 'forc'd to contend with them for your Safety There 'are still Enemies enow to encounter with, secure 'therefore your Person against domestick Treasons. 'These once remov'd, I fear no foreign Evil' This was *Craterus*'s Sentiment. The rest were also of O-
pinion,

pinion, *he would never have stifled a Discovery of that Moment, unless he were either Principal in the Conspiracy, or an Accomplice* 'For, *said they*, who that had the
'least spark of Piety or good Disposition, (though
'we were not of the Band of your Friends, as he
'was, but of the Dregs of the People) having heard
'what he had been told, would not have presently
'run to the King and acquainted him therewith? But
'he who was *Parmenio*'s Son, General of the Horse, and
'privy to the King's most secret Affairs, could not so
'much as imitate *Cebalinus*'s Example, who the Mo-
'ment he was inform'd by his Brother of the Dan-
'ger, came and declar'd the same to him, nay, he
'was so far from detecting the Mischief himself, that
'he pretended the King was not at leisure, for fear
'the Informer should address himself to somebody
'else, and so the Villany might come to light *Ni-
'chomachus*, notwithstanding his Oath to the Gods,
'made all the haste he could to discharge his Con-
'science, but *Philotas* having pass'd the best part of
'the day in Merriment with the King, could not find
'in his Heart to add, to his other long and per-
'haps superfluous Discourses, a few Words of the
'greatest Moment and Importance to the King's Safe-
'ty. But admit, *say they*, that he did not give Credit
'to the Report, on the Account of the Youth of the
'Informers, What then made him keep 'em in Sus-
'pense for two Days, as if he had believ'd it? Certain-
'ly he ought to have dismiss'd *Cebalinus*, if he slighted
'his Information. Every Man in his own private Pe-
'ril, may rely upon his Bravery and Courage, but
'where the King's Safety is in Danger, we ought
'there to be credulous, and not despise even false Dis-
'coveries' They all therefore agreed, he ought to
be compell'd to declare his Confederates. The *King*
having

having commanded them not to divulge the Matter, dismiss'd them. And that *he* might not give the least Suspicion of his new Measures, he gave publick notice, that the Army should decamp the next Day. He also invited *Philotas* to his last Supper, and vouchsaf'd not only to eat, but also to converse familiarly with him *he* had already condemned.

At the second Watch, *Hephastion, Craterus, Coenus* and *Erigyius,* of the Band of his Friends, and *Perdiccas* and *Leonatus* his Esquires, attended by a few others, enter'd the Palace without Lights, and presently gave Orders to the Guards, to be arm'd all the time they were upon Duty. Soldiers were now planted at all the Avenues, and some Horse were order'd to guard the Roads, that nobody might escape to *Parmenio,* who was then Governor of *Media,* and had the Command of a great Army. *Attarras* at this time enter'd the Palace with three hundred arm'd Men, unto whom were appointed ten of those that had the Guard of the King's Person, who were every one follow'd by ten of those call'd Men at Arms. These were sent to seize the other Conspirators, and *Attarras* going with three hundred Men to take *Philotas,* made choice of fifty of the most resolute amongst 'em, and broke open his Door, having plac'd the rest round the House, to prevent his making his Escape. But *Philotas* was in a profound Sleep, either from the Consciousness of his Innocency, or from some Fatigue, so that *Attarras* seiz'd him in that Condition. Being now awak'd, as they were putting him in Chains, he cry'd out, *The Bitterness of my Enemies Malice, O King, has overcome thy Goodness.* Having utter'd these Words, they cover'd his Head, and brought him to the *Palace.* The next Day the King commanded the *Macedonians* to appear at the *Palace* with their Arms; they amounted to about

six

six thousand Men, besides a Crowd of Rabble and Camp Followers. The Men at Arms conceal'd *Philotas* amongst their Body, that he might not be seen publickly, till the *King* had spoke to the Soldiers, it being an ancient Custom with the *Macedonians*, for the Army to judge of capital Crimes in time of War, and the People in time of Peace, so that the *King*'s Power signified nothing unless *he* first persuaded them of his Opinion. *Dymnus* his Body was first brought before 'em, the major part being ignorant what was his Crime, or how he came to be kill'd.

CHAP. IX.

THIS being done, the *King* came out to the Army, carrying in his Countenance all the Tokens of an afflicted Mind, the general Sadness of all his Friends at the same time, gave them no small Expectation of the Event. The *King* remain'd some time with his Eyes fix'd on the Ground, as if he was astonish'd and dismay'd. At last recovering his Spirits, he express'd *himself* thus ‘ I had like, Soldiers, to have been
‘ snatch'd from you by the wicked Contrivance of a
‘ few Persons. It is by the Providence and Mercy of
‘ the Gods, that I am now alive. Your venerable
‘ Aspect inflames my Anger still the more, against the
‘ execrable Parricides, for the greatest, nay, the only
‘ Advantage I propose to my self from Life, is, that I
‘ am able to return Thanks to so many gallant Men,
‘ who

'who have deserv'd well of me.' Here he was interrupted by the Soldiers Lamentations, and every Body's Eyes were now fill'd with Tears. Then continuing his Speech, he said, 'If what I have already told you, 'raises such Emotions in you, how much greater shall 'I excite, when I shew you the Authors of this hor- 'rible Design? I tremble at the mentioning of 'em, 'and as if it were still possible to save 'em, I am un- 'willing to declare their Names. However, I must over- 'come my former Friendship for them, and let you 'know who these impious Wretches are. For which 'way can I conceal so abominable a Crime? Know 'then, Soldiers, that *Parmenio* in his advanc'd Age, 'loaded with my Father's and my Favours, and the 'most ancient of all my Friends, is the chief Leader 'in this detestable Enterprize, and *Philotas* has been his 'Instrument to corrupt *Peucolaus*, *Demetrius*, and *Dymnus* (whose Body lies there before you) and se- 'veral others equally mad, to be Partners with him 'in taking away my Life.' At these Words the whole Camp was in an Uproar, complaining with the utmost Indignation against the detestable Plot, after the manner of Soldiers when they are either mov'd by Affection or Anger. Then *Nichomachus*, *Metron*, and *Cebalinus* were produc'd, and each declar'd to the Army their respective Informations. But not one of them in his Evidence, charg'd *Philotas* to have any hand in the Conspiracy, so that the Anger of the Assembly being appeas'd, they remain'd silent after the Informers Declaration. But the *King* immediately ask'd 'em, 'What his Design could be, who could suppress 'an Information of this nature? That it was not 'ill-grounded, appear'd sufficiently from *Dymnus*'s kil- 'ling himself. And *Cebalinus*, as uncertain as he was 'of

'of the Truth of the Matter, did not refuse being
'tortur'd, to verify he had receiv'd such an Account
'from his Brother, and *Metron* did not delay one
'Moment to discharge himself of the Trust repos'd in
'him, insomuch that he broke into the Place where
'I was bathing. *Philotas* was the only Person a-
'mongst 'em all that fear'd nothing, nor believ'd any
'thing. What a Hero is this! Had he been touch'd
'with the Danger of his Sovereign, would he have
'heard it unmov'd, without the least Token of Con-
'cern? Would he not have lent an attentive Ear to
'an Accusation of that Importance? The Matter is
'this, his Crime lay lurking under his Silence, and the
'greedy Hopes of a Kingdom, drove him headlong
'on the worst of Villanies. His Father commands in
'*Media*, and he himself is in that powerful Station
'with me, that relying on his Interest with my Offi-
'cers, he aspir'd to greater things than he was ca-
'pable of. I suppose my having no Issue, made him
'despise me. But *Philotas* is mistaken, for you your
'selves are my Children, Parents, and Relations. While
'you are safe, I cannot be destitute of either.' After
this, he read to 'em an intercepted Letter of *Parmenio*'s to his Sons *Nicanor* and *Philotas*, which certainly did not contain in express Terms any criminal
Matter. For the substance of it was this. *First take
Care of your selves, and then of those under you. By
these means we shall compass our Desires.* Here the King
took notice, ' That he writ after this obscure manner,
' that if it came safe to his Sons, it might be under-
' stood by their Accomplices, and in case it was in-
' tercepted, it might deceive the ignorant. But it may
' be objected, that *Dymnus* in his Discovery of the
' Conspirators, made no mention of *Philotas*. Yet this

' it

'it self, is not so much an Argument of his Inno-
'cency, as of his Power; for it shews he was so much
'fear'd even by those he might have betray'd, that at
'the same time they confess themselves guilty, they
'don't so much as dare to name him. However, *Phi-*
'*lotas*'s Life sufficiently detects him. For when *Amyn-*
'*tas* my Kinsman conspir'd against me in *Macedonia*,
'he was not only privy to it, but also a Confederate.
'Moreover, he marry'd his Sister to *Attalus*, than
'whom I have not had a greater Enemy. And when
'I writ to him, out of Familiarity and Friendship,
'to acquaint him with the Report of the Oracle of
'*Jupiter Hammon*, he made no scruple to return me
'this Answer, *That he rejoic'd I was receiv'd into the*
'*number of the Gods, yet he could not but pity those who*
'*were to live under a Prince that exceeded the Condition*
'*of Man* These are plain Indications, that his Mind
'has been long since alienated from me, and that he
'envy'd my Glory. Notwithstanding all these Pro-
'vocations, Soldiers, I have endeavour'd to put a good
'Construction upon 'em as long as I could For I
'thought it was rending some part of my Bowels
'from me, to discard those I had heap'd so many Fa-
'vours upon But the Case is alter'd, it is no longer
'Words we have to resent The Temerity of the
'Tongue has proceeded to the Execution of the
'Sword, which, if you dare believe me, *Philotas* has
'been sharpening against me. If he has been guilty
'of these things, whither shall I fly, Soldiers? Whom
'shall I intrust with my Life? I made him General
'of my Cavalry, which is the chiefest part of my Ar-
'my, and plac'd him at the Head of the noblest Youth
'in *Europe* I committed to his Custody my Safety,
'Hopes and Victories. Besides all which, I have ad-
'vanc'd

'vanc'd his Father to the same Pitch of Grandeur al-
'most to which you have rais'd my self: I have made
'him Governor of *Media*, than which there is not a
'richer Country, and have intrusted him with the
'Command of so many considerable Cities, so many
'thousands of our Associates. From whence I ex-
'pected upon Occasion, my chiefest Support, Sol-
'diers, I have found the greatest Danger. How much
'happier had I been, had I fall'n in Battle a Prey to
'my Enemies, rather than the Victim of a Citizen!
'But I have escap'd those Dangers which I only
'fear'd, and have fall'n into those I did not in the
'least suspect. You have frequently exhorted me,
'Soldiers, to take care of my Safety. It lies in your
'Power now to secure it, whatever you advise me
'to I'll do. It is your selves, and your Arms, I
'have recourse to for my Protection, I would not be
'safe against your Wills, and if you desire I should, I
'cannot be so unless you vindicate my Cause.

Hereupon he order'd *Philotas* to be brought forth; he had his Hands ty'd behind him, and his Head cover'd with an old Veil. It was easily perceivable they were mov'd at so lamentable a Disguise, tho' heretofore they us'd to behold him with Envy. They had seen him the Day before, General of the Horse, they knew he had supp'd with the *King*, and now on the sudden, they saw him not only accus'd, but condemn'd and bound. They also reflected on the hard Fortune of *Parmenio*, who was not only a great Captain, but an illustrious Citizen, and had not only the Misfortune to lose two of his Sons lately, *viz.* *Hector* and *Nicanor*, but now stood accus'd in his Absence, with the only Son he had left.

Amyntas

Amyntas therefore perceiving the Multitude inclin'd to Pity, endeavour'd to exasperate 'em again, telling them, *They were all betray'd to the* Barbarians; *that none of 'em would return to their Wives, their Country, or their Friends: That they should be like the Body without a Head, without Life or Name, a mere Sport in a strange Country, to their Enemies.* This Speech was not so acceptable to the *King,* as *Amyntas* expected, because, by putting them in mind of their Wives and Country, it cool'd their Courage to After-Expeditions. Then *Cænus,* notwithstanding he had marry'd *Philotas*'s Sister, inveigh'd against him more than any Body, and declar'd him to be *the Parricide of his King, Country, and of the whole Army,* and taking up a Stone that lay at his Feet, was going to fling it at his Head, desiring thereby, as some thought, to secure him from future Torments; but the *King* laying hold of his Hand, hinder'd him, telling him, *he ought to have the Liberty to plead, without which he would not suffer him to be judg'd.* *Philotas* being accordingly order'd to speak for himself, was so stupify'd, either from the Guilt of his Conscience, or the Greatness of the Danger he was in, that he could neither lift up his Eyes, nor so much as utter the least Syllable, but burst out into Tears, and fainting away, fell into the Arms of him that held him. Afterwards having recover'd his Spirits and Speech, he wip'd away his Tears, and seem'd to prepare himself to speak. Then the King turning to him, said, *The* Macedonians *are to be your Judges. I desire to know, whether you design to speak to 'em in your Country Language or not.* To which *Philotas* reply'd, *There are a great many others here besides the* Macedonians, *who I believe will understand me better, if I use the same Tongue you your self spoke in, for no other Reason, as I suppose, than that you might be understood by the greater Number.* The *King* then

then bid 'em take notice, *how he even hated his Country's Tongue, which no Body disdain'd but himself. But let him use what Language he pleases, so you do but remember that he equally abhors our Manners and our Speech.* Which said, *he* withdrew.

CHAP. X.

THEN *Philotas* began. ' It is an easie matter for
' the Innocent to find Words, but it is very hard
' for a Man in Distress to be moderate therein So that
' between the Innocence of my Conscience, and the
' Severity of my Fortune, I am at a stand how to suit
' my Discourse both to my Mind and Circumstances
' He that is my properest and best Judge, has with-
' drawn himself, why he would not hear what I had
' to say, I cannot imagine, since after he had heard
' both Parties, he had it still in his Power as well to
' condemn as absolve me, whereas if he does not hear
' what I say in my Defence, I cannot hope to be dis-
' charg'd by him in his Absence, who condemn'd me
' while present But notwithstanding the Defence of a
' Man in Chains, is not only superfluous, but also odi-
' ous, since it does not so much inform, as seem to
' reprove his Judge: Yet in what manner soever I am
' oblig'd to speak, I shall not desert my own Cause,
' neither shall I give any Body leave to say, that I con-
' demn'd my self What my Crime is I cannot tell,
' not one of the Conspirators so much as names me
' *Nichomichus* has given no Information against me,
' and *Cebalinus* could not know more than he had been
' told All which notwithstanding, the King believes

'me to be the Contriver and chief Manager of the
'Confpiracy. Is it likely *Dymnus* would pafs over
'him, whofe Directions he follow'd? More efpecially
'when being ask'd, who the Confederates were, I
'ought (tho' falfely) to have been nam'd, for the greater
'Encouragement of him who feem'd to be afraid. For
'having difcover'd the Plot, it cannot be thought he
'omitted my Name, that he might fpare an Accom-
'plice For when he confefs'd the Matter to *Nichoma-*
'*chus,* who he thought would not divulge Secrets re-
'lating to himfelf, he nam'd all the reft, without ma-
'king the leaft mention of me Pray, Brother Soldiers,
'if *Cebalinus* had not addrefs'd himfelf to me, and had
'had no Mind I fhould know any thing of the Mat-
'ter, fhould I to-day be making my Defence, with-
'out having been fo much as nam'd by any of the In-
'formers? It is a very likely matter, that he that does
'not conceal himfelf, fhould fpare me! Calamity is
'fpightful, and moft commonly he that fuffers for
'his own Guilt, is well enough pleas'd that others
'fhould fhare the fame Fate. Shall fo many guilty
'Perfons, when put upon the Rack, refufe to tell
'the Truth? It is obferv'd, that no Body fpares him
'that is to die, and for my part, I believe he that is
'to die, fpares no Body I muft therefore come to
'my true Crime, and the only thing I can be charg'd
'with Why did you then conceal the Treafon? Why
'did you hear it without any Concern? Of what Force
'foever this may be, you pardon'd it, *Alexander,* up-
'on my Confeffion, where-ever you are, and having
'given me your Right Hand, as a Pledge of your Re-
'conciliation, I was one of them that fupp'd with you
'that Night If you believ'd what I faid, I am clear'd,
'if you pardon'd me, I am difcharg'd. Stand at leaft
'to your own Judgment. What Crime have I com-
                                                 ' mitted

' mitted since last Night, that I left your Table? What
' new Crime have you been inform'd of, to make you
' alter your Mind? I was in a profound Sleep, not
' dreaming of my Misfortunes, when my Enemies, by
' their binding of me, wak'd me. How came it to
' pass, pray, that a Parricide and a Traitor slept so
' quietly? For a guilty Conscience will not suffer its
' wicked Owners to be at rest. The Furies distract
' their Minds, not only while they are contriving the
' Parricide, but even after they have put it in Executi-
' on. My Security was grounded, first upon my In-
' nocency, and next on your Right Hand. I was not
' afraid other Peoples Cruelty should have more Power
' with you, than your own Clemency. However, that
' you may have no Reason to repent you believ'd me,
' do but reflect that the Information was brought to
' me by a Youth, who could bring no Witness, nor
' Security of the Truth of what he said, and yet would
' have fill'd the Palace with Apprehensions had he been
' heard. Unhappy Man that I am! I thought my
' Ears had been impos'd upon by a trifling Quarrel be-
' tween the Lover and his *Catamite*; and I distrusted
' the Truth of the Information, because he did not
' give it in himself, but sent it by his Brother. Besides,
' I could not tell but he might disown having sent *Ce-*
' *balinus* on any such Account, and then I should have
' been suspected to have contriv'd it on purpose to
' bring several of the King's Friends into Trouble. Thus
' altho' I have offended no Body, I have found Ene-
' mies that wish my Ruin, rather than my Safety.
' How much Ill-will should I have procur'd my self,
' had I provok'd so many innocent Persons? But *Dym-*
' *nus* kill'd himself, it is true, however I could not
' divine that he would do so. From hence 'tis plain,
' that the only thing that gives Credit to the Informa-
' tion,

'tion, was what I could not any way be mov'd with,
'when *Cebalinus* communicated it to me. Again, had I
'been concern'd with *Dymnus* in the abominable Trea-
'son, I ought not to have diffembled the Matter for
'two Days, when I knew we were betray'd. It had
'been the eafieft thing in the World to have difpatch'd
'*Cebalinus* out of the way. Befides, after the Difco-
'very of the Plot, I enter'd into the King's Chamber
'alone, and with my Sword by my Side, What then
'could be my Motive, not to put it in Execution?
'Did not I dare to go about it without *Dymnus*? At
'this rate, he muft be the chief Confpirator, and *Phi-
'lotas*, who afpir'd to the Kingdom of *Macedonia*, de-
'pended on him. Now pray tell me your felves, which
'of you have I endeavour'd to bring over to my Inte-
'reft? What Leader or Commander have I chiefly
'courted? It has been objected to me, that I defpis'd
'my native Language, and the Manners of the *Mace-
'donians*. This, I cannot but own, would have been
'a ready way to have obtain'd the Crown I am faid
'to have thirfted after. You are all fenfible, that our
'own Language is almoft out of ufe, by the long
'Converfation we have had with Foreigners, and the
'Conquerors, as well as the Vanquifh'd, have been o-
'blig'd to learn a new Expreffion. Thefe Charges do
'not affect me any more, than *Amyntas*'s treafonable
'Practices againft the King, with whom I do not dif-
'own to have had a Friendfhip, but I cannot think
'my felf guilty on that Account, unlefs it be a Crime
'for us to love the King's Brother. But if, on the con-
'trary, we were oblig'd to refpect a Man in that high
'Station, pray tell me how I am guilty, fince I could
'not divine it was flagitious? Muft the innocent
'Friends of the Guilty be involv'd in their Ruin? If
'that be reafonable, why have I liv'd fo long? If it
'be

' be unreasonable, why must I now at last suffer for it?
' Oh! but I writ in my Letter, that I pity'd those
' who were to live under him, who believ'd him-
' self *Jupiter*'s Son. It is true, and you your selves
' forc'd me not to conceal my Thoughts. I do not
' deny that I writ thus to the King, but I did not write
' so to any Body else of the King, I therefore did not
' seek to create him Ill-will, but, on the contrary, I
' had a tender Care for him. I thought it was more
' worthy *Alexander* to be satisfy'd within himself of
' his divine Extraction, than to boast of it publickly
' And because the Oracle is infallible, I'll willingly rely
' on the Testimony of the God Let me be a Priso-
' ner till *Hammon* is consulted about the secret and my-
' sterious Crime Certainly he that has acknowledg'd
' our King for his Son, will not suffer any that have
' conspir'd against his Offspring to remain undetected,
' but if you look upon Torments to be more certain
' in this Case than the Oracle, I do not even refuse
' that Testimony of my Innocency. It is usual for
' those who are accus'd of capital Crimes, to exhibit
' their Parents or next Relations as Pledges for them,
' but I have lost my two Brothers lately, and I cannot
' at this distance produce my Father, neither dare I
' name him, since he is equally accus'd with me, for
' it seems it is not enough for him to be depriv'd of
' so many Children as he had, and to have but one left
' to comfort him in his old Age, unless that be also
' taken from him, and he himself perish with him in
' the same Pile. Must you then, my dear Father, not
' only die for me, but also with me? I am the unhap-
' py Wretch that take away your Life, and put a Pe-
' riod to your old Age! Why did you beget me in the
' Displeasure of the Gods? I cannot determine whether
' my Youth be more miserable, or your gray Hairs:

'I am snatch'd away in the Bloom of my Years, and
'the Executioner must put an end to your Days, whom
'the Course of Nature would have taken out of the
'way, had Fortune had but a little Patience. The
'mention I make of my Father, puts me in mind how
'cautious I ought to have been in communicating *Ce-*
'*balinus*'s Information, for *Parmenio* being advis'd,
'that *Philip* was brib'd to poison the King, writ a Let-
'ter on purpose to dissuade him from taking the Me-
'dicine he prepar'd for him, was there any Credit
'given to my Father in this Case? Had his Letters
'any Authority with the King? Nay, how many
'times have I my self been ridicul'd for my Credu-
'lity, when I have imparted what I heard? Now if
'we must be odious when we inform, and suspected
'when we conceal, because we don't give Credit to
'the Discovery, what must we do?' Here one of
the Standers-by cry'd out by the way of answer, *Not
plot against those who have deserv'd well of us.* To
which *Philotas* reply'd, *Thou say'st well, whoever thou
art. If it therefore appears that I have conspir'd, I
don't refuse to suffer, and so shall conclude my Defence,
since I find my last Words disagreeable to you.* This said,
they who had him in Custody took him away.

CHAP. XI.

THERE was amongst the Captains one named
Belon, a very brave but unpolish'd Man, he had
been a long time in Arms, and from a private Centinel,
had rais'd himself to the Post he was then in. This
brutishly audacious Officer perceiving the Assembly
stood

stood mute, represented to it, 'That they had frequent-
'ly been thrust out of their Quarters, to make room
'for the very Scum of *Philotas*'s Servants, that the
'Streets were full of his Waggons laden with Gold and
'Silver, and that he would not so much as suffer any
'of his Fellow-Soldiers to be lodg'd near his Quarters,
'but kept them at a distance for fear of being di-
'sturb'd in his Rest, not allowing them even to whi-
'sper, much less make any Noise, that they had been
'always the Subject of his Ridicule, and were some-
'times call'd by him *Phrygians*, sometimes *Paphlago-
'nians*, and that he was so haughty, as to hear his
'own Country-men by an Interpreter. What can be
'his Reason to have *Hammon* consulted, he that did
'not scruple to tax the Oracle with lying, when it
'acknowledg'd *Alexander* for *Jupiter*'s Son, for he
'had great Reason to fear the King should contract Ill-
'will by what the Gods themselves bestow'd upon
'him He did not consult the Oracle, when he con-
'spir'd against the Life of his Sovereign and Friend,
'but he would now have it consulted, that in the
'mean time his Father, who commands in *Media*,
'might be solicited, and with the Money he has in his
'Custody procure other Desperadoes to associate them-
'selves with him in his Villany. That it was their
'Business to send to the Oracle, not to be inform'd of
'what the King had told them himself, but to give
'Thanks to the Gods, and offer up their Vows for
'their Sovereign's Preservation

This incens'd the whole Assembly, and the Guards
cry'd out, that it belong'd to them to take Satisfaction
of the Parricide, and that they ought to tear him in
pieces *Philotas*, who was afraid of greater Torments,
was well enough pleas'd with this saying The *King*
returning

returning now to the Assembly, adjourn'd the Council to the next Day, either that *Philotas* might be tormented in Prison, or that he might in the mean time get better Information of the Conspiracy; and notwithstanding the Night drew on, he summon'd his Friends to come to him, the rest of 'em were for having *Philotas* ston'd to Death, according to the *Macedonian* Custom, but *Hapheſtion*, *Craterus* and *Cœnus* were of opinion, *That the Truth ought to be forc'd from him by Tortures*, and then those who had been of another Sentiment came over to their Advice. The Council being therefore dismiss'd, *Hephæſtion*, *Craterus* and *Cœnus* got up in order to have *Philotas* tortur'd, and the *King* calling *Craterus*, had some private Discourse with him, the Substance whereof was never known, and then retir'd into his Closet, and there remain'd alone a considerable part of the Night, expecting the Event of the Tortures. The Executioners brought now before *Philotas* all the Instruments of Cruelty, and he of his own accord ask'd 'em, *Why they delay'd killing the King's Enemy and Murtherer, who confess'd the Fact? What occasion is there for Torments? I own I contriv'd the Mischief, and would have executed it.* Then *Craterus* requir'd he should make the same Confession upon the Rack. While they laid hold of him, and were stripping him and binding his Eyes, he to no purpose call'd upon the Gods of the Country, and the Laws of Nations. They made him pass thro' the severest Torments, as if he had been actually condemn'd, and out of their Zeal for the *King*'s safety, most miserably tore his Body. And notwithstanding they made use both of Fire and Scourges, rather by the way of Punishment than Examination, he was so far from crying out, that he did not so much as yield a Groan, but when his Body swell'd with

with Ulcers, and the Scourges cut to the Bones, not being any longer able to contain himself, he promis'd them *if they would leave off tormenting him, he would discover to them what they desir'd to know* · But he requir'd they should swear by the *King*'s safety, that they would torture him no more, and that the Executioners should be sent away; both which being granted him, he ask'd *Craterus, what he would have him tell him?* *Craterus* was very much incens'd hereat, thinking he mock'd him, and call'd back the Executioners. *Then* Philotas *desir'd a little time to recover his Spirits, and promis'd to tell 'em all that he knew* In the mean time the chief Officers of the Cavalry, and they who were nearly related to *Parmenio* (hearing that *Philotas* was put upon the Rack, and dreading the *Macedonian* Laws, which ordain, that the nearest Relations of those that conspire against the King, shall dye with them) some kill'd themselves, and others fled to the Mountains and Desarts, the whole Camp was in a Consternation, which the *King* being inform'd of, he caus'd Proclamation to be made, *That he remitted the Law relating to the Kindred of Traytors* Philotas in the mean time made the following Confession, that he might not be any more tormented, but whether what he said was true or false is hard to determine.

' You are not ignorant, *said he*, how familiar my
' Father was with *Hegelochus*, I mean that *Hegelochus*
' that was kill'd in Battel, he was the cause of all
' our Misfortunes; for when the King order'd himself
' to be saluted *Jupiter*'s Son, this Man took it so
' heinously, that he said, Shall we acknowledge him
' for King, who is asham'd to own *Philip* for his Fa-
' ther? We are undone if we suffer this, for he not
' only despises Men but the Gods themselves, who de-
' sires to be thought a God, We have lost *Alexander*,

'we have lost our King; he is fallen into that insuf-
' ferable Pride, that makes him odious, both to the
' Gods, to whom he equals himself, and to Mankind
' that he despises. Have we spilt our Blood to make
' him a God, who now disdains us? Believe me, if
' we will but shew our selves Men, we may be also
' adopted by the Gods. Who reveng'd the Death of
' *Alexander*, great Grandfather of our *Alexander*, or
' that of *Archelaus*, or *Perdiccas*? Nay, has not he
' himself pardon'd those that kill'd *Philip*? This is
' what *Hegelochus* said at Supper, and the next Day,
' early in the Morning, my Father sent for me, he
' was melancholy, and saw that I was also sad, for
' what we had heard made us very uneasie, that
' therefore we might know whether what he said was
' the effect of Wine or Premeditation, we sent for him,
' and being come, he of his own Motion repeated what
' he had said before, and added, that if we dar'd to
' be Leaders in the Enterprize, he claim'd the next
' Place to us, if we did not approve of it, he would
' faithfully keep our Counsel. *Parmenio* did not think
' it proper, while *Darius* was alive, since the Enemy
' would reap the Advantage of *Alexander*'s Death,
' and not we, but *Darius* being dead, *Asia* and all
' the East would fall as a Reward to those that should
' kill the King. The Advice was approv'd, and Faith
' mutually promis'd between the Parties. As for what
' relates to *Dymnus*, I know nothing of it; and after
' this Confession, what will it avail me that I am
' altogether innocent of this last Plot?' Then they
tormented him afresh, and struck him themselves in
the Face and Eyes with their Darts, and at last extorted from him a Confession of that Crime likewise.
As they requir'd him to give an orderly Account of
the whole Contrivance: He answer'd, ' That as it
' seem'd

'seem'd probable that the King would remain a con-
'siderable time in *Bactriana*, he was afraid his Father,
'who was seventy Years of Age, and at the head of
'a great Army, and had the Custody of a vast Trea-
'sure, might dye in the mean time, and then being
'deprived of such Supports, it would be to no purpose
'for him to kill the King, he therefore design'd to
'hasten the Execution while the reward of it was
'still in his own Hands.' This he said was the whole
History of the Matter, *and if they did not believe his
Father to be the Author of it, he was ready to undergo
the Tortures again, tho' he was too weak to bear 'em.*
Hereupon they conferr'd together, and having concluded they had made sufficient Enquiry, they return'd
to the *King*.

The next Day the *King* order'd his Confession to be
read to the Assembly, and because *Philotas* was not
able to go, he caus'd him to be brought before it.
Here he again own'd it all to be true. They proceeded next to the Examination of *Demetrius*, who was
accus'd to be one of the Confederates in the last Conspiracy, but he made great Protestations, and with an
undaunted Mind and Countenance deny'd, *that he had
ever intended any thing against the King, and for his
greater Justification he desir'd to be tortur'd.* Then *Philotas* casting his Eyes about, spy'd a certain Person
nam'd *Calis*, not far from him, *and bid him come
nearer.* But *Calis* in the utmost Confusion refus'd to do
it, so that *Philotas* said to him, *Will you suffer* Demetrius *to lie, and cause me to be tortur'd again?* At these
Words *Calis* became speechless, and turn'd as pale as
if he had no Blood left in his Body. The *Macedonians*
now began to suspect *Philotas* maliciously accus'd those
that were innocent, because neither *Nichomachus*, nor
Philotas in his Tortures, had nam'd the Youth. However,

ver, when he found himself surrounded by the *King's* Officers, he confess'd that both *he* and *Demetrius* were guilty. Hereupon all those who were nam'd by *Nichomachus*, were according to the *Macedonian* Laws (upon a Signal given) ston'd to Death.

It is certain the *King* here run a great Risk, both as to his Safety, and his Life; for *Parmenio* and *Philotas* were so powerful and so well belov'd, that unless it appear'd plain they were guilty, they could never have been condemn'd, without the Indignation of the whole Army. For while *Philotas* deny'd the Fact, he was look'd upon to be very cruelly handled; but after his Confession, there was not any of his Friends that pity'd him.

The End of the First Volume.